BEST MUSIC WRITING
2010

PREVIOUS EDITIONS OF
BEST MUSIC WRITING:

BEST MUSIC WRITING

2010

Ann Powers, *Guest Editor*

Daphne Carr, *Series Editor*

DA CAPO PRESS
A MEMBER OF THE PERSEUS BOOKS GROUP

Set in 10 point Warnock Pro by the Perseus Books Group

Cataloging-in-Publication data for this book is available from the Library of Congress.

First Da Capo Press edition 2010
ISBN: 978-0-306-81925-4

Published by Da Capo Press
A Member of the Perseus Books Group
www.dacapopress.com

Da Capo Press books are available at special discounts for bulk purchases in the U.S. by corporations, institutions, and other organizations. For more information, please contact the Special Markets Department at the Perseus Books Group, 2300 Chestnut Street, Suite 200, Philadelphia, PA 19103, or call (800) 810-4145, ext. 5000, or e-mail special.markets@perseusbooks.com.

10 9 8 7 6 5 4 3 2 1

CONTENTS

Introduction
by Ann Powers

Here's a conversation I have at least once a week.

"What do you do?" says the nice acquaintance—a mom I've met at a bowling party, maybe, or one of my husband's colleagues at the university where he teaches, encountered in the wine line at some professional to-do.

"I'm a music writer," I say.

"Oh, that must be fun," my interlocutor replies. Blank stare. "So . . . what does that mean?"

After we determine that, yes, I've met Prince, and certainly I've lost some hearing going to so many concerts, the conversation usually dries up. Beyond mentioning their favorite artists, if they have any, and asking me what I'm listening to lately (answer: everything, that's my job), most people just don't have a lot to say about music. On a daily basis, it's background for them, even if it's also sometimes meant the world.

Don't tell me this is because I'm in my forties, past the age of loving music to distraction. It's not only true of the parental set I know from squiring around my six-year-old. I've had the same discussion with fourteen-year-olds, college kids, even the boho professionals who work in related fields like arts programming or librarianship. These friends respect my labor in the pop trenches and are curious about my world; most would never invoke the cliché about writing/music/dancing/architecture that justifies anti-intellectualism and reinforces an outdated high-low cultural divide. Most admire what I do, in the abstract.

They just can't see their own way into my song-soaked, rhythm-crazy view of the world.

Which is funny, because many of them live there, too. I constantly witness people engaging in the same practice that occupies so much of my life, simply without committing their acts to text. Real-life examples: when Rebecca talks to her son Walter about what makes that new Avett Brothers record so much better than the last one, that's thinking hard about music. So are Pauline's breakdown of how the drums inspire the martial moves in her capoeira class, Greg's argument, with DVD examples, of what makes a great Bollywood soundtrack, and Kathy's morning-after report of the U2 concert at the Rose Bowl.

Not to mention all the arguments: about what Obama should have on his iPod, whether garage rock is different than punk rock, if Cher should be forgiven for introducing Auto-Tune to the world, which Al Green album is the best, why rap is in decline (or is it?). And the personal stuff. There's a lifetime inside a simple statement like, "My kid loves the Ramones!" Music writing solidifies these passionate exchanges about the sounds that help us define and express our feelings, feel our bodies, and keep moving through life.

Music itself is a call that demands response. It organizes desire, sorrow, and joy into a form both primal—the ear is the first sense organ to begin working when we are in the womb—and intensely communal; in every known culture, some form of music has been a constant in everyday life. Making music or listening to it is part of how we grow; sharing music is what helps us create community. You don't have to be a musician, or even a major music geek, to exist within that realm. Musical expertise, the star-fan division of labor so prevalent in the classic rock era is, after all, a relatively new concept. "A couple of generations ago, before television, many families would sit around and play music together for entertainment," wrote scientist and musician Daniel J. Levitin in his 2006 bestseller *This Is Your Brain on Music: The Science of an Obsession.* "Nowadays there is a great emphasis on technique and skill, and whether a musician is 'good enough' to play for others. Music making has become a somewhat reserved activity in our culture, and the rest of us listen." Until recently, the same was generally true about music writing. The lucky (or foolish, given the pay scale) few published their thoughts, and the rest of us read. Yet most everyone is all ears and in tune, responding to each other by channeling the power of the music we hear, and love or hate.

Broadband-enabled interactivity had already endangered Levitin's postulation by the time his book was published, though the vestigial allure of virtuosity remained powerful on "American Idol" and in competitive shredding games like "Rock Band." It's hardly news that Consciousness 2.0 is dissolving the century-old division between amateur and professional in the music sphere. In his recent article "The New Parlor Piano: Home Recording and the Return of the Amateur," the historian Karl Hagstrom Miller notes that in 2007 the money spent on musical instruments nearly matched income going to prerecorded music. "Acquiring the skills for creative musical expression is more popular than it has been for almost a century," he writes. "Making music is in. Becoming famous: wildly overrated."

The same is true of music writing, which rarely brought fame anyway, or even a decent living. These days, music writing is in, maybe more than it's ever been. But declaring yourself a music writer (FOR REALS, as the kids in Cali and on the Internet say) is wildly overrated. There's no money in it—a reality of nearly every career choice aside from nursing in these times of economic collapse and restructuring, but particularly true in both journalism and the music industry, two fields hit extra hard by the web's flattening effect on information flow. There's also precious little authority of the old kind. Expert pronouncements and writerly pirouetting no longer pay any kind of rent.

You know the lament: as bloggers replace critics, and Tweeters replace bloggers, respected media organs shut down, the very sentence structures that once made thought elegant give way to cheap acronyms, and chaos ensues. This environment, the argument goes, is highly threatening to sustained thought. Forget having your life changed by a great music book, the way mine was by Greil Marcus's *Mystery Train* in 1985. We can't even trust anyone to tell us whether the new Justin Timberlake album deserves five stars.

But I think despair is boring. It lands the worrier in the time-travel trap of longing for the past while fearing the future. It obscures the present. The present is unstable, but that's what makes music writing—and all cultural writing, in fact—so exciting a practice these days. We have to dump our expectations and try to use our voices and our minds in different ways.

Greil Marcus, the guest editor of last year's *Best Music Writing* volume, wrote about the "sense of contingency and urgency" that motivated many of the pieces he chose for the book. Guess what? A year later, the mood hasn't changed. There's plenty of panic among writers; everybody's organizing panels on "The Death of the Critic" (I did it myself, at the University of Southern California in 2008) and applying to grad school, the default move of the suddenly unemployable brainiac. The elegy for writing has become a literary subgenre in and of itself. I've included one here—Christopher Weingarten's speech at the Twitter-oriented 140 Characters conference, a jeremiad that's also a powerful kick in the pants.

As with all transitional times, though (and the Buddhist in me quotes William James: *life is in the transitions as much as in the terms connected*), the emerging reality shares space with what's proven effective in the past. This volume is chock-full of music writing from all over the stylistic spectrum; the selection is an argument that all of these approaches serve their purpose, and relate to each other, and should survive.

The two pieces most often recommended to me by outside lobbyists are classics of their kind. Jason Fine's profile of Merle Haggard, from *Rolling Stone* magazine, demonstrates what comes of the old-fashioned culture reporter's skills: patience, good listening, and legwork. Greg Tate's *Village Voice* cover essay about Michael Jackson epitomizes the kind of historically river-deep, intellectually mountain-high cultural criticism that a veteran can execute because he has spent a lifetime exploring his subject. Both were published in hallowed old-media institutions; I'm glad *Rolling Stone* had the resources to support Jason's extended hang with Merle, and that the *Voice* still occasionally gives Tate, a titan of our field, a chance to meditate on a subject at length.

But then the other selection inspired by Michael Jackson's legacy— and my favorite from the avalanche of great writing that came after the King of Pop's death, which I hope will make for its own volume one day—came to me not from a bastion of dead-tree journalism, but within my e-mail box. Jason King's exhaustive, emotionally rich overview of

Jackson's music and celebrity was just something the NYU professor, musician, and producer had to write in the wake of the loss. It's as strong as anything published in a newspaper or magazine of record.

The same is true of a country-focused piece that a conservative thinker might contrast with Fine's: Robert Christgau's essay on Brad Paisley, which appears on the website for the big-box bookseller Barnes & Noble. There was a time when something published on a retail outlet website would have immediately been disqualified as catalog fodder, not real music writing. The Dean of American Rock Critics, who was rudely displaced from his *Village Voice* job a few years ago due to "budget cuts," proves that such distinctions no longer hold. Major thinkers take their minds and ears along wherever they go.

One of the fundamental lessons of the blues—"You gotta move," as the old song says, itself slipping from the fingers of the Rev. Gary Davis to Mississippi Fred McDowell to the Rolling Stones—is increasingly relevant to music people in the disaster-prone twenty-first century. Popular music writing initially flourished in carefully cultivated crash pads like *Rolling Stone* and *Creem* ("America's Only Rock 'n' Roll Magazine," back in the 1970s), then was dispersed into the mainstream media. The semi-professionalization of the field—few legitimate jobs, many ways to make a scanty living if you also participated in the black market by selling promo records—created a strange hybrid identity for music writers. We are snobs obsessed with expertise, prone to bashing others on the head with Top 10 lists; yet we are also outcasts, stuck in the back pages of respectable publications, and denied the legitimizing gestures of the media and academic establishments (a pop critic has never won the Pulitzer; popular music studies is a growing field, but still a bastard one at most universities). There's also the problem all writers on the arts face: an arm's length away from those who "really create," we wonder if our own creativity counts.

The psychic challenge of occupying two discordant identities—the expert and the illegitimate child—has challenged many music writers. It's resulted in an irritating stereotype, too: the nerdy snob, brilliant but pathologically awkward, as portrayed by Phillip Seymour Hoffman in homage to Lester Bangs in *Almost Famous*. This character, almost always the kind of white man whose machismo was thwarted by a lack of athletic ability and who isn't much of a dancer either, is a bane in two ways: it makes those who actually resemble him feel bad, and it prevents others—women, queer men, people of color—from seeing themselves in the role. (It's notable that Cameron Crowe, the director of *Almost Famous* and one of my first inspirations as a writer, possessed enough social graces to both make it in Hollywood and marry one of rock's queen bees, Nancy Wilson of Heart.)

I hope the diversity in this book sheds a final corrective light on the truism that a music writer can be only one kind of person. The institutional racism and heterosexism that afflicts every aspect of our culture still affects music writing, lending more opportunity to a privileged few. Yet one of the best things about the slow collapse of mainstream media hierarchies is that other points of view have gained force as the bricks move and fall. On the "queer word art" blog *Bully Pulpit*, Tavia Nyong'o offers a take on Adam Lambert that's more frankly sexual than anything I could have written in my job at the *Los Angeles Times*, and cuts to the groin of the "Idol" star's appeal. Nikki Darling's fearless inquiry into the sexuality and gender play in hard (pun intended) rock was killed by *The Believer* and published by the author herself on her blog. It made me think about W. Axl Rose in ways I'd never done before, and I've spent years thinking about that dude.

It might seem like I'm setting up a split between great but conservative old-media music writing and great and more daring stuff floating around the Internet. Let me knock that down right now. Another of my favorite pieces from last year was from the same publication that declined to publish Nikki Darling's Rose essay: Michelle Tea's incredibly well-executed tour diary about accompanying Beth Ditto, the paradigm-shifting frontwoman for the Gossip, through the hotel room and runway receptions of Paris Fashion Week. I chose to open the book with this piece because, to me, it has everything: personal investment and cultural analysis, a timeless passion about music and an awareness of trends, a strong personal voice and plenty of room for others to speak.

I will offer you a metaphor through which you might experience the book. It's a trope adopted by most of the editors of this series, I've noticed, because, being insecure music-writer types, few of us feel wholly comfortable embracing the simple idea of a "best" list: Imagine its covers as the walls of a club, or a basement rec room, or wherever you might gather with people to listen to music and talk about it.

Tea's article starts the conversation. There in the corner, veteran R&B chronicler Lola Oguinnaike discusses the rookie status of hip hop star Drake with Mark Swed, my colleague and the classical critic at the *Los Angeles Times*, who offers his own notes on L.A. Philharmonic newbie Gustavo Dudamel as a comparison. Chicago writer and activist Jessica Hopper carries on a private conversation with Seattle musician and Renaissance Man Sean Nelson about how loving one kind of rock or another affects your views of sex, friendship, even God. Josh Kun offers a beer to Hua Hsu and points out that his investigation of Mexican regional music traveling via cellphones relates to Hsu's essay about the end of white America. Erika Villani and Maura Johnston chat about Kanye West and Jay Z—and get into some serious talk about what it's like to be a woman making a mark on the male-dominated comments boards of music blogs.

Hey, it's getting loud in here.

What's most fun to me about this fantasy is that it presents music writers as social beings, thinkers who don't just hunker down in their rooms with their headphones on, but who thrive on interaction with each other and with the myriad characters who create and sustain music culture worldwide. That privacy does prove necessary for some efforts, like Chris Estey's beautiful and gut-wrenching memoir told through the grooves of a Phil Ochs album, or Philip S. Bryant's poetic reminiscence of the way the experience of listening to jazz records defined his father's closest friendship. But for the most part, the private part of music writing is inseparable from the communal activities of mutual education, establishing taste hierarchies, spreading news, and sharing opinions.

Sometimes this involves taking on received wisdom, as Nitsuh Abebe does in his warm, sharp analysis of the mainstreaming of "indie." Or it's about exploring why classics become that way, as the team from XXL magazine does so well for Nas's *Illmatic* album. Or it means connecting history to the present, as Alex Ross does so beautifully in his discussion of the seventieth anniversary of Marian Anderson's concert on the steps of the Lincoln Memorial, which celebrates the soprano while confronting the enduring racial divide in the classical world.

The social work of the music writer can involve uncovering lost stories, like that of "America's first rock star," Eva Tanguay, whom independent scholar Jody Rosen brings to life; or throwing light on hidden scenes, like the Iowa noise music underground David Morris exposes. It might mean taking on the news—two pieces here take on the messy horror of the Chris Brown–Rihanna domestic violence case. It may reflect deep listening, as in Sasha Frere-Jones's analysis of music by The-Dream, or looking in new ways, as Mary Gaitskill does when faced with a video by Lady Gaga.

The communities through which music writers develop and thrive are not strictly imaginary. Readers who've followed my work will uncover many real-life connections between myself and various contributors. I work with some now, have worked with many others in the past, and have had long conversations over cocktails or Chinese noodles with still others. The gang that's risen up around the Pop Conference, the annual gathering of scholars, journalists, musicians, and music lovers held at Seattle's Experience Music Project (it moves to UCLA in 2010) and organized by my husband, Eric Weisbard, is also heavily represented. Call it conflict of interest if you must. The Pop Conference has provided a formal space for music writing during a tumultuous time, and in doing so has supported and produced some of the best work of the decade. I'm glad to feature a slice of it.

There are pieces in this anthology by people with whom I've quarreled, and others by ones I've never met. I've omitted good work by great friends and mentors and younger writers I might call protégés (if I didn't find that term embarrassingly self-congratulatory). This volume will never be complete to me, because it's just one view of the chatter and answer song that music inspires. Still, I'm proud of it. It feels alive.

When I began writing about music in high school, I did it because I felt like an outsider in my hometown scene, where I so wanted to find my place. It took years for me to not feel awkward in a room full of musicians, partly because as a woman I was nearly always outnumbered, and partly because many musos have a deep suspicion of the verbal, which left talkative me feeling like a giant intrusive chump. Over the years, I found virtuosos who are also great conversationalists. I got over my fear of packs of dudes, and got far along enough in my career that now my reputation sometimes precedes me like a friendly yenta. Nobody—not even my perennially insecure self—can deny that I found a way inside the pop world. I thank the elders who nurtured me, the peers who challenged me and cheered me on, and the youngers who've gifted me with respect and renewed inspiration.

Yet in my heart, I still feel like an outsider—an inside-outsider, I guess, at home in the floating world of pop fanatics and grateful for the constant connection music brings, but always aware of the borders of my own body and the limits of my own point of view. Music has given me a way to cross those existential boundaries, to better understand the joy and hope that comes from human connection, to hear myself and become one with strangers through other people's riffs and beats and sighs and screams.

Music writing allows me to respond to this ego-rearranging force in a way that helps me understand what happened, and keeps happening, between music and me. What happened when I heard "The Miseducation of Lauryn Hill" on a scratchy dubbed cassette in my kitchen in Brooklyn, or saw Paul McCartney sing "Yesterday" at an Amoeba Records in-store in Hollywood, after three decades of loving the song. What happened the first time I heard Nick Drake whisper and P.J. Harvey scream. What happens on a festival field with 60,000 people, and in a dive bar with 75. What will happen right now, when I pick up my MP3 player and take it for a walk, and tomorrow, when I hear the new noise that will spin me around in a direction I didn't know I could go.

Know what I'm talking about? You've been there. You've thought about music this way, felt it, talked it over. You may never put it down on paper or in the data flow. But you're music writing, too.

The Gossip Takes Paris
Michelle Tea

*In Europe, Beth Ditto is a music and fashion icon, so fa-
mous she cannot ride the tube. In her native land, she's just
another feminist punker from Arkansas.*

*DISCUSSED: Accidentally Brain-Damaged Cats, Super-
model BFFs, The Dark Family Landscapes of Joyce Carol
Oates, The Cure, The Designer Swag Rich-Poor Paradox,
Too Punk to Prom, Perkins Pickles, Galoshes for Fat Girls,
Knits v. Crochets, The Novels of Jacqueline Susann, Furred
Motorcycle Helmets, The Best SNL Appearance since Nir-
vana, Miss Piggy.*

DAY ONE

Sisterhood Ass Tattoos

It is early March in Paris and I'm at the Westin, crashing in a room
paid for by the Italian luxury brand Fendi, best known for its clever
purses. Given it's Fashion Week, the streets outside my hotel are packed
with women so beautiful and so insanely tall they look like aliens, carrying portfolios and cradling cell phones and moving as if by sonar.

My room was meant for one Tara Perkins, a girl with two different
names for two different lives. Under the alias Annie Oakley she created
and manages the Sex Workers' Art Show Tour, a traveling cabaret
featuring performances by people whose art is informed by their time
working in the sex industry. As Tara Perkins, she's manager for the
Gossip, an indie-punk band with overtly queer/feminist lyrics who,

1

though they've been little known in their native US, are huge overseas, in large part because of their charismatic, outspoken, fat, femme lead singer, Beth Ditto.

Beth is short and her body is a stack of curves upon curves. Her hair changes so swiftly you could mistake it all for wigs, from a black bouffant to short, choppy, and orange to the jet-black asymmetrical bob she wears to Fashion Week. Also of note, Beth is a lesbian, and is super outspoken about it. Same goes for feminist. Same goes for her emergence from a legacy of backwoods Arkansas poverty that few people escape.

But even in Portland, Oregon—where Beth lives in a ramshackle house with her best friend and her pet, a brain-damaged, blind cat that was accidentally killed while getting spayed, then revived in present, imperfect condition—people have little idea how insanely famous Beth and the Gossip have become in Europe. Unless they are total music nerds with a subscription to London's *New Musical Express*, they likely don't know that the influential magazine voted Beth Ditto the number one coolest person in the world in 2006 (the first time in the history of the magazine that a female had been so dubbed). The following year Beth was naked on the *NME* cover, covered in giant lipsticked lip-prints. By 2007, the London paparazzi began behaving badly, flinging themselves in front of Beth's cars, clambering up the sides of buildings Spider-Man-style. She turned up on Jonathan Ross, Britain's David Letterman, telling stories about her pothead cousin shooting backyard squirrels to satisfy his stoner munchies. She began penning an advice column, "What Would Beth Ditto Do?," for the *Guardian*. She accepted an offer to design a line of clothes for Evans, the plus-size women's clothing chain owned by Topshop's parent company.

By the time Fashion Week 2009 rolls around, Beth is naked on the cover of *Love*, a new magazine created by British fashion avatar Katie Grand. A larger-than-life blowup of the photo—featuring Beth with messy, flame-colored hair, topless, holding a ruffled fuchsia bolero jacket against her crotch—is plastered onto the side of a building in London, and it is official: Beth Ditto can no longer safely ride the Tube.

Even Karl Lagerfeld is obsessed with her, he who infamously declared the existence of fat French people more alarming than the scourge of anorexia (and this during that fashion season where starving models were dropping like flies, one on his very own runway). Currently designing not only his eponymous collection but also for Chanel and Fendi, Lagerfeld invited the Gossip to headline the Fendi party scheduled to close out a Fashion Week in a time when rich people are feeling poor and the notion of luxury is being scaled back from, oh, five-thousand-dollar dresses to, um, four-thousand-dollar dresses. Who better to end the party than a girl who grew up in a part of Arkansas with no MTV, no telephones, no indoor plumbing, and no money?

As Beth's fame overseas has grown, many of her most loving fans have been fashion people. Though many would think of the term *fashion people* and conjure rail-thin, snotty, sickeningly wealthy women and their male counterparts, in reality a lot of fashion people are ex-nerds, small-town gays who dressed eccentrically and got made fun of for being flamboyant and fruity. In other words, most fashion people aren't so different from Beth. Beth's inroads to the fashion world have included playing at the opening of Alexander McQueen's Los Angeles boutique in a custom hand-spangled McQueen catsuit; hanging out with the McCartney sisters, designer Stella and photographer Mary, in the UK; repeatedly visiting the Vivienne Westwood press office to receive steep discounts on voluminous dresses and a rainbow assortment of jelly shoes. She's had outfits made for her by Charles Anastase (a silk-cotton dress printed with animals devouring each other), Louis Vuitton (a red lamé skirt), and Gareth Pugh (a totally shredded black dress). And she's cultivated a BFF-ship with Kate Moss, a model who, you might think, would be on Beth's shit-list for popularizing the strung-out-skinny look. But then you would be underestimating the seriousness of the SISTERHOOD tattoo inked across Beth's ass. Beth and Kate became friends after the *NME* pitted them against one another in the "Sexiest Woman in Rock" category at their awards show. Beth made a snarky comment about *NME* standing for New Model Express, and pointed out that sleeping with musicians doesn't make you one. (Kate Moss won.) The media went apeshit at the thought of the fat punk and the skinny model having a hatefest, but Beth's beef was with the magazine, not with Kate, who showed up at a Gossip show in Los Angeles shortly thereafter. The two spent the rest of the night hanging out in a hotel bathroom singing Rolling Stones songs.

Queer Theory

So the reason I'm staying in Tara's room at the Westin is because Tara will be staying in Beth's room. Beth is actually afraid of the dark, and needs her manager to sleep with her. I can imagine less-fun job duties than reporting for nightly slumber parties with Beth.

As I wait for Beth and Tara to arrive from London Fashion Week, I rendezvous with some queer Parisian acquaintances who regard my posh hotel room and my participation in Paris Fashion Week with a complicated horror. They have a queer punk activist's hatred of capitalism; one boy feels like a freakish dirtbag in the lush environment of the Westin, with its Versailles-inspired mirrored halls, its wooden elevators and *trompe l'oeil* wallpaper, its ornate chandeliers modestly wrapped in dusky screens. But the girls—the girls are femmes, and I watch them wobble between criticism of the madly consumerist culture of Fashion Week and a longing to sink into the unbridled excess of it. I understand, sisters. For a long time I hated beauty for the way people used it as a measuring stick to beat people, especially women. But I came to believe in a vast idea of beauty, one that included me and all my beautiful weirdo friends. As for more conventional beauty, I didn't have to hate it just because people let it make them stupid. My attitude moved from the conceptual to the concrete: Take a beautiful dress. Say it's a Rodarte dress, made by these sort of creepy, goth-ish sisters who live with their parents in Pasadena. Their dresses messed them up while wearing them on a jaunt through the space-time continuum. They are torn tulle and stiff corsets and lots of lace and flowers and fluffy bullshit stuck all over the place. Parts make you wonder if these sisters, the Mulleavy sisters—see, even their names make you think of the dark family landscape of a Joyce Carol Oates novel—are employing some sort of spider-beast to do their weaving. The dresses cost upward of ten thousand dollars at Barneys. At one time in my psychological development, this would have made me hate the dresses, hate the designers, hate those poseur Mulleavy sisters, hate anyone and everyone who could afford them, hate capitalism, hate the world, hate the universe and whatever string of incomprehensible events led to the big bang. Now I think—when I go into Barneys to visit these dresses (the way I have gone into the SPCA to visit with various animals I can't adopt), to just pet their glorious fabrics and marvel at the endless detailing and giggle at the whimsical appliqués—I think: It isn't the dress's fault that it's so expensive. I love it like a living thing, and visit at this department store. I don't love a painting on a museum wall any less for my not being able to own it, do I? This is the relationship I have cultivated with this level of fashion. And all of this is to say that I understand the struggle my queer punk friends are having around me, a person they like, taking such joy in these symbols of everything bourgeoise they are trying to smash by—well, I'm not sure *how* they are trying to smash bourgeoise culture, exactly, but certainly the first step is not supporting it, so no, they will not go to the Stella McCartney party with me later that week, but they do hope I have a good time.

DAY TWO

Those Tolerant Europeans

Beth and Tara just moved into their hotel room and it looks like they've been living in it for a week. There is shit everywhere, clothes bursting from flung-open suitcases. Beth blares the Modern Lovers on her iPod. "You like them? I knew you'd like them! I'm playing them for you!" On their mantle sits a dramatic headpiece by Noel Stewart, a grand white plastic bow affixed to a headband that, when worn, looks like it is taking flight from your head. The pair went shopping in London, hitting designers' press offices, where high-end clothing is given away or offered at a steep discount to celebrities. "If people think you're rich they give you things," Beth says. "If they think you're poor, they don't give you anything."

Beth and Tara are trying to figure out if it's OK to go to breakfast in their pajamas. "It's Europe, they're very tolerant," Tara quips. Tara is wearing a pink SSION T-shirt and sweats. Beth throws a long, stripey sweater that looks sort of Rick Owens-y over her seafoam-green pajamas and decides to take breakfast in her socks. "Deal with it, world!" she says, and keeps saying it. One thing about Tara and Beth is that they are hilarious, and the form their hilarity takes is a constant banter that is generally absurd and self-deprecating with occasional streaks of meanness.

Beth slides through the mirrored hallway in her socked feet. A word about Beth's face: It is beautiful and strange in an otherworldly way. She is pale the way maidens in fairy tales are pale, and she has gotten rid of her eyebrows, which makes you want to keep staring and staring at her face, wondering what the fuck *is* it about that face of hers. Having no eyebrows makes a person look like an alien or a drag queen or a doll, and Beth looks a little like all of these things. Then there are her eyes, which are a spooky, fragile shade of blue. She is gorgeous the way models are known to be gorgeous; that is, pretty with a shot of something weird you can't put your finger on.

Talk turns to proms. Beth *loved* her proms. She went to both her junior and senior proms, and her aunt made both her dresses. "I was so dressed up! I love getting dressed up," she sighs. "Both my proms were in the school cafeteria." Tara says she got caught sneaking her boyfriend into her house a week before her junior prom, was forbidden from going by her pissed-off parents, and was forced to return her dress. By the time senior year rolled around, she was too punk to try again. "I wish I was too punk," Beth says sadly.

After breakfast, the wearing of socks throughout the Westin continues. "We're adults!" Beth hoots, waggling her feet. "We're punk!" She references her friend the Portland zinester Nicole J. Georges, who holds *punk* as a trapdoor that lets you escape any breach of good conduct or manners. "We're punk!" Beth explains to strangers as we board the elevator and return to our rooms for a nap before the Nina Ricci show that night.

The Nina Ricci Show That Night

"That's Anna Wintour right in front of us," Tara whispers to me in the hugely dark hangar where the Nina Ricci show is unfurling itself before our eyes. Our seats couldn't be shittier, aren't seats at all, because we were made late by our desire to have our hair and makeup done by Beth, who threatens regularly and seriously to throw this rock-and-roll life away and pursue beauty school. I'm wearing a full face of makeup, including powder that settles into my wrinkles and makes me look ten years older. But my hair has been smoothed out with a flat iron, smoothed and given a little *flip* right at the end, and it looks fucking awesome.

Fashion shows only last about fifteen minutes, and Nina Ricci's had already started when we showed up at the gates, Beth set upon by totally adorable-looking fashion kids, queer boys with great style and no connections, who love Nina Ricci designer Olivier Theyskens, and who also love Beth. "You're Beth Ditto?!" one boy in heavy glasses and bright clothes asks/proclaims. Beth gets sort of nervous and sweet, sort of guilty, because the boy wants to come in with us and she can't bring him and she just doesn't like saying no to people like that, leaving a gaggle of cool kids on the other side of the gate. But it's not a Gossip show—Beth herself is lucky to be getting in.

"I've got survivor's guilt," she says. "I've got punk guilt." I shrug the kid's predicament off easily. "Whatever," I said, "you've done your time outside the show, everyone does." Beth shakes her head. "I actually haven't. I've been really charmed."

All the shows we'll see this week are previewing clothes for the Fall–Winter 2009–10 season. The clothes we see at Nina Ricci are insane. *Aeon Flux*–y, sci-fi, comic-book goth, skintight bodices and slinky floor-length skirts with fat, crazy ruffles at the crotch. The impossibly tall models are made impossibly taller by virtue of their fetish-height, heelless platform shoes. That's right, heelless. Google it. They seem to be on stilts, walking with an awkward, creepy gait, wearing tiny, molded hats that dip over their faces. With the vision-obscuring hats and those chunky hooves on their feet, I don't understand how they don't wipe out, but they don't. They're so beautiful it's sickening. Dresses have black trains as ethereal as shadows; they stick ever so slightly to the ground, resisting motion. Then, the lights go out. The electronica shifts to drums, sad and angry and tribal, familiar. It's the Cure, *Pornography*. Oh my god, Olivier Theyskens is so cool! I get goose bumps and my eyes well up with tears as the models are sent back in an endless stream. Oh my god, I'm crying at a fashion show. I love *Pornography*, Robert Smith's jumbled mumbles like he's talking backward. The lights return and the models are sent back in a river of rich sparkle and spindly, architectural wonder. Olivier Theyskens comes out for his bow but I can barely see him, just the lights shining off his glossy hair as he turns and ducks backstage. It's his final collection for Nina Ricci; the owners had been trying to fire him for a while.

In the cab back to the Westin, Tara simultaneously tries to buy Beth a house in Portland and begin a lawsuit against the College of William and Mary. Tara bought her own house in Portland from a tour bus while traveling with the Gossip on the *True Colors* tour. "Nothing can ever happen in a normal way," she says ruefully.

Tara then starts communicating with Sony, which is releasing the Gossip's next album in the US. The Rick Rubin–produced record is due out on June 22, and is, as of yesterday, officially done. "Well, what's it called?" I ask, excited. I should tell you, the Gossip are my favorite band. Because Beth has come out of the same DIY, queer, punk, West Coast scene that I'm from, it's easy to forget, while sitting in a cab with her, the awe she inspires in me. Especially when she performs. You can't really say you know the Gossip—their music or even what they are about—until you've seen them live. Seeing Beth Ditto sing must be the same sensation sought by tornado chasers who risk their lives to get close to that powerful cloud. Her presence is mighty and her voice is mightier, seems to be something she is pulling up from the earth through the soles of her feet, all while emitting a fierce, energetic force field. She runs hot, can break a sweat sitting still, so onstage she is known to strip to her underwear.

"I can't tell you what the record is called," Beth demurs. "I just can't yet. Superstition won't let me." (In April, the title is leaked; it's *Music for Men*.) The cab cruises along the Seine, past a giant mural bearing depictions of various occupations children can aspire to when they grow up. "How about a mural of twenty things my friends' brothers can be?" Beth suggests. "Drug dealer!" She looks at Tara. "Pickle prince!" Tara's brother is starting a pickle business, called Perkins Pickles. Beth entertains herself creating jingles for Perkins Pickles:

> *If you're jerkin'*
> *For the workins'*
> *Pick the perfect pickle, Perkins!*
> *Salty sweet, bread and butter*
> *Trust me, girls, there is no other,*
> *Don't believe me? Ask his mother!*
> *Perkins Pickles!*

Actually, Beth entertains herself and others writing jingles for life, all day, everyday. Her thoughts come to her in melody, so often whole thought processes are sung in little harmonies. Or a rewritten tune will get stuck in her mouth and sung again and again, such as *Bonjour, mes amis* to the tune of "Come On Eileen," or "Come and wear my Dior" to the opening of the *Three's Company* theme song.

"I need to get money for Tara Perkins and money for the Gossip," Tara says when we get out of the cab, and we walk together to an ATM. The neighborhood is, I think, Palais Royale, and it is super posh.

"I want to design a pair of galoshes for fat girls," Beth says, and details her vision for a pair of galoshes that won't get stuck on a big girl's calf—funnel shaped, with a series of ties that cinch the rubber to the leg. They sound awesome, and now that Beth is partnering with the plus-size emporium Evans, when she has little ideas like this she can actually make them happen. Which is crazy. Beth wore a pair of fat-un-friendly galoshes at Glastonbury, a British music festival on farmland prone to flooding. They became stuck to her body, and getting them off turned into a carnival involving Kate Moss's bodyguard pouring essential oil down her legs while Kate Moss's boyfriend, Jamie Hince from the Kills, tried to keep her laughing. "And I was not wearing underwear," she recalls.

DAY THREE

Getting Over The Hating On

Usually Japanese shows start ten to fifteen minutes late, so since we're not concerned about missing Issey Miyake, I'm sitting still for another Beth Ditto makeover. Again with the powder that seeks and illuminates lines I didn't know my face had, but my eyes look awesome—swoopy black and dramatic—and my straightened hair continues to render me unrecognizable to myself, a delight. I'm wearing a black satin high-waisted skirt. It's by Vivienne Westwood, which means it's got this crazy black satin shark fin that juts bizarrely out to one side. Beth is sporting a sequined zip-up jacket by Marc by Marc Jacobs. It's very *Desperately Seeking Susan*, and Beth decides it will be her trademark look for the week. Beth and Tara and I talk about growing up broke. It is so truly bizarre that we are here, all three of us together, that the lives we improbably built from art and activism have led us to this moment at a posh hotel at Paris Fashion Week. Tara, who ran away from a nonfunctioning home in Detroit and got a job at Subway; Beth, whose former bandmate Kathy saved up money slinging corn dogs at the A&W in Olympia, Washington, and bought Beth a ticket out of Arkansas; me, who hauled myself to San Francisco with hooker money and a hippie hand drum. Getting a political consciousness about class and poverty usually means you spend a good chunk of your life hating on people with money and moneyed culture, and so it is with this background that the three of us sit beneath the chandelier in this hotel room thinking about the edge of unease that mars the ability to really *fling* yourself into the present moment, always with the shadow of whomever you left behind at your back—an alcoholic mom, a mom working a fast-food job, a mom who just lost her house.

"I remember when I moved to San Francisco, I saw Dorothy Allison read for the first time," I start. "Oooh I love Dorothy Allison," Beth says in a reverential tone. Tara loves Dorothy Allison, too. You have to be a moron *not* to love Dorothy Allison, but for poor girls who pick up *Bastard Out of Carolina* in their twenties, Dorothy Allison is a sort of guru. "She was talking about being poor," I continued, "and how she didn't *want* to be poor, how it wasn't romantic, how only people who were never poor think it's romantic to be poor." It was life-changing to hear someone I idolized state that she didn't want to be poor, and state it so strongly; in my addled brain, the best solution to the poverty problem I'd come up with was that *everyone* should be poor, and whoever desired something more was the enemy. But Dorothy Allison was the opposite of the enemy, and so a splinter was sunk into my bravado, and even now, when I am in situations that trigger those class wounds— sitting in a five-star hotel in a designer skirt on my way to a fashion show—I think, Well, Dorothy Allison doesn't want to be poor, I don't have to want to be poor, either.

"It's an important phase," Beth says about that bravado, the loyalty to poverty and pride in having nothing. "You empower yourself, and get rid of all that shame from your childhood." Truly. But then what empowers you to break out of poverty, and to rid yourself of the shame of succeeding?

Empathy For Sean Penn

Issey Miyake does not make me cry. There is a beautiful winter coat that looks decorated by one of those Spirograph toys from the '70s, loops and loops. There are dresses that look pieced together from a jagged, subtle patchwork. There are black leggings with iridescent stripes, colorful gowns that look like chiffon squares piled into a person-size column. The models walking across the light-up floor at the Carrousel du Louvre are more diverse than the white-and-blond bonanza at Nina Ricci last night; those models were so uniform that Tara Perkins gasped aloud when they were sent out en masse—she thought it was the same three models coming out again and again. Issey Miyake has a black model, an Asian model, a foxy androgynous model with a pompadour and a big nose. He has real martial-arts artists coming out between sets, women with athletic bodies punching the air and making gut-ripping growls. At the end, the designer himself bounds onto the stage and sweetly strikes a pose alongside them, nearly getting punched in the face by a choreographed fist. After the show, Beth, who had front seats, is mobbed by photographers asking her what she thought of the show. "I loved that none of the shoes were heels," she says about the flats—gray, with neon yellow or fuchsia soles—sent out with everything from pants to gowns. Beth lives her life in Vivienne Westwood for Melissa jelly flats. I stand off to the side with Tara, who hovers hawklike on Beth's periphery, always, waiting for a situation to be managed. This is her job. I mention the andro model, a dreamy tinge to my voice, and she wrinkles her face like I passed gas. "It looked like birds had picked away her flesh, leaving bones for them to nest in."

At the Vivienne Westwood show I have my first experience of the paparazzi. They come charging toward us, a dense cloud of men in black holding giant strobing machines to their faces, hollering in chaotic rounds, "Beth Beth Beth Beth Here Here Here Here Look Here Look Here Look Here Beth Beth Beth!" This provokes in my body a panicky sensation of being attacked, and I instantly understand why Sean Penn and others haul off and punch these camera-wielding maniacs. It is a miracle more paparazzi don't get punched. How do celebrities live like this, hounded by a bunch of maddeningly loud, overbearing, downright scary men chasing you and yelling at you, without losing their minds?

Beth looks sort of scared. Maybe her response to the fear is to act super-duper *nice*, 'cause that's what she does, she acts really nice, really sweet, gives everyone a photo if she can. It is Tara's job to play bad cop to Beth's good cop, barking "No" and "Let's go," dragging Beth away by force when she needs to. "Sorry!" Beth yells kindly back at the wall of men.

"Believe me, Beth would not let me do any of that if it's not what she wanted," Tara says. "You know her. She does exactly what she wants to." So Beth plays the acquiescent celebrity, regretfully waving good-bye when her hard-assed manager yanks her away. This works for smaller crowds, but the crew is intense at the Place Vendôme outside Vivienne Westwood. With the aid of Frederic the gentle stylist—he of the limpid blue eyes and smoothly shaved head and the witty designer scarves—we form a pod around Beth and smuggle her into the show. It reminds me of clustering around a woman and walking her through a gang of Christians protesting a women's health clinic—a similarity made more intense by the presence of anti-fur protesters holding full-color posters of skinned dead animals. Paparazzi and fur protesters are present at all the shows, but not as severely as at Vivienne Westwood. The designer's new spokesmodel is Pamela Anderson, and she is scheduled to walk the runway; it's almost certainly her celebrity status that drew the extra cameras, and her PETA activism that spurred the protesters.

The room the show is to happen in looks either massively under construction or deeply deteriorating, it's hard to say which. For sure it seems like pigeons are about to fly out from all the chalky holes in the ceiling. Beth is seated in the front row, conducting a steady run of interviews. One journalist after another ambles up with a microphone or a camera or recorder. She's wearing a vibrant red Westwood dress that fits her amazingly well; her jagged black bob, quite short, looks great against her white skin and complements the dress's bold color. She looks rad, per usual.

Tara sits beside Beth while Frederic and I huddle behind them. Beth asks me to take a picture of her ass with my cell phone to make sure her butt crack isn't visible in photos. Eventually, the show begins. There are lots of what I peg as knits, but which Beth later suggests are *crochets*. Of course! This is high fashion! With their deliberate fuck-head hairdos of musses and tangles, the models look like they've just rolled themselves up in giant balls of yarn and slunk onto the catwalk. Some models look like they are crying. I start tripping out on this. Are the models crying? People get so crazy when they don't eat food and I'm sure these girls just aren't eating well. But they're not, it turns out, crying. I think they just worked multiple shows and their eyes are irritated from so much eye makeup. Back to the clothes. The sweaters are complicated. There are those tulle skirts with the backside blown straight up, as if hit by a big gust of wind. Are those crocheted chaps? Amazing! There is Pamela Anderson, again and again and again, all blond hair and a giant, California smile. I truly do not understand why she is the spokesmodel. She is a distraction from the clothes and to the organic flow of the catwalk. It makes me think that perhaps Ms. Westwood, who is getting on in the years, has gone a bit daffy.

We get to go backstage, which in this case is downstairs, a room that reveals the whole building to be a former bank by the presence of a giant steel vault in the center. Beth gets whisked away by some stylists, but not before detailing her three favorite things: (*1*) getting dressed every day, (*2*) Googling *mystery*, (*3*) dressing her friends.

Tara is alarmed that Beth has vanished. The space feels like a grammar-school cafeteria, with the fold-out tables holding stacks of plastic cups. Ducking behind a beam at the back of the room, I find a mousy lady with humble vibes. "I make Vivienne's hats," she says in a British tweet. This is Prudence, creator of Prudence Millinery. "After the shows I always hide from Andre." Andre is Andreas Kronthaler, Vivienne's ruggedly handsome, much younger husband. "We had an argument Saturday." Prudence continues baring her soul to me, even though I am a stranger who is writing everything she says in a notebook. Heedless, on she goes. "I just can't handle the stress." She dips her tiny face around the beam. "Is he coming? Oh, no." "The hats were so great!" I console poor Prudence. "Vivienne said, 'Make them look fucked.'" "They did," I assure her. "They did look fucked. They looked like someone ran them over with a horse-drawn cart, then left them with a drunkard for mending." "Oh, good," she says earnestly, but her face still looks drawn and nervous.

Tara pops her blizzard of hair around the bend. "Did they go that way?" She motions to the front of the room, where Vivienne Westwood stands, ringed by lights and cameras, regal in her long, carroty hair and some sort of quilty-looking cape. Beth is there, waiting to meet the queen of punk. More than any single individual, Vivienne Westwood has most influenced the way I look, starting back when I was thirteen, fourteen, fifteen years old, all the way up to now. I follow Tara over to where Beth hovers on the outskirts of the media, breathlessly observing her idol. "Her skin is so beautiful," Beth says, and it's true. Pale like she's never seen the sun, her age etched into it like a design. Eyebrows veer off the sides of her temples, drawn on. But it's really the time on her face that strikes you, and strikes you as beautiful. "Aging is punk," I realize, and say it aloud. "Aging *is* punk," Beth agrees. "So is cellulite." When it's Beth's turn to meet the Dame, she engages her on the subject of Leonard Peltier, the American Indian Movement activist accused of killing a couple of FBI agents in the '70s. He has been imprisoned ever since. Vivienne Westwood has lobbied heavily for his release and uses her media attention whenever possible to spotlight his struggle. After Vivienne confusingly suggests Leonard Peltier could maybe get his own ass out of prison if he just, like, *said* he did it—Really? Is she really saying that? Am I totally hearing things wrong?—Vivienne then admits that she does not know who Beth is, but is impressed at how informed she is about the plight of Leonard Peltier. "I'm a lesbian," Beth says. "We know about these things."

DAY FOUR

For The Love Of Swag And Kanye

"Is wearing a designer to their show like wearing a band's concert shirt to their concert?" Tara asks nervously. "I don't know," I say. "Is it bad to wear a band's concert shirt to their concert?" Today's first show is Jeremy Scott. Asked during an interview whom he would most like to dress, the designer said Dolly Parton and Beth Ditto, and a friendship was born. Jeremy Scott's club-kid clothing is stretchy and fun, and Tara and Beth both have pieces made from fabric screened with images of anthropomorphic hot dogs and pretzels and puffs of cotton candy. Tara removes a snug red and white Jeremy Scott sweater after Beth says, "I don't like it. I'm gonna be honest."

"It seems a little ski-lodge-y for a fashion show," Tara concurs. Beth is wearing a skin-tight Jeremy Scott dress, black and covered with images of people wearing 3-D glasses. It's very '80s new wave, the way '80s new wave played with '50s kitsch. It's '50s kitsch via '80s new wave reinterpreted by someone making hip-hop-influenced club clothes in 2009.

What I see when I walk into the Jeremy Scott show makes me suck in my breath with excitement. Each front-row seat is topped with a Jeremy Scott for Longchamp tote. They are folded into neat little squares— red canvas covered with the designer's curling black telephone design, and brown leather handles. All I wanted from Fashion Week, really, was to get a free bag and see Kanye West. Here was a free bag. But I did not have front seats, I had standing room. So did Tara. Only Beth had a front seat. The two seats next to hers were open. The bags were just sitting there. Just sitting there! The media hoopla that surrounds Beth keeps people away. The lights dimmed. I threw my ass on a Longchamp bag and Tara sat down next to me. "Gimme," I said, and took her bag and smooshed it next to mine, beneath my ass. I opened my Moleskine to take notes. I drew a little picture of a crying stick figure punching another stick figure in the face. THIS IS WHAT WILL HAPPEN IF SOMEONE TRIES TO TAKE OUR BAGS FROM US I wrote at the top of the page, and flashed it at Tara.

The show was pretty awesome. Toni Basil's "Mickey" came over the speakers, and a bunch of models came out wearing clothes inspired by Mickey Mouse. At the end of the show, Jeremy Scott ran out in gym pants and a mullet, and we joined the crush of people trying to get backstage. Right as I am almost through the door, I look to my right. Kanye West. Right there, one person away from me, also getting crushed on his way to the door. He's wearing white Wayfarers and a pink and white sweater, probably Jeremy Scott. His lady friend, Amber Rose, is wearing wraparound Chanel sunglasses with a gold and leather braided chain affixed to the bridge and draped down the back of her neck. Plus a sage green patent-leather Jeremy Scott motorcycle jacket. She is lunatic-hot. I hug the stolen Longchamp bags to my chest happily. I have seen Kanye West *and* scored a bag. Yes!

Backstage we shuffle Beth past Fischerspooner toward the designer, who is getting his photo taken with Kanye. Off to the side, a separate clutch of photographers snap pictures of Amber Rose, who pouts and poses and generally makes love to all the cameras. Beth is invited into

Jeremy's media circle for a round of photos with him and Kanye. "Your *Saturday Night Live* performance was the best one since Nirvana," she tells the rapper, and his face lights up with joy. Kanye West has good vibes. "Did you hear that?" Kanye calls back to Amber Rose. "She said my *SNL* performance was the best one since Nirvana!"

I Have A Favorite Model

Next up is Loewe, which is pronounced *Low-vay—thank you*, Beth and Tara, for catching that—and is held in a hall that is like a caricature of French luxury, with marble busts and marble floors and a string quartet and everyone seated at little café tables with waiters bearing trays of crustless sandwiches and bitter espressos and slender goblets of champagne. We are late, and they scramble to seat us. I wind up very close to where the models will soon be walking. "It would be so funny if Michelle fell out of her seat and onto the runway," Beth says. "I would seriously shit my pants." The models come out wearing leather everything. Leather dresses, leather shirts, leather pants, leather leggings, and of course leather bags and leather shoes. Once again we are seated across from Anna Wintour and her sidekick, *Vogue's* creative director, Grace Coddington, who, like Vivienne Westwood, has unruly red hair, appears to be letting herself age, and seems all the more punk and awesome for it. At a nearby table is *Harper's Bazaar* editor Glenda Bailey. The model Raquel Zimmermann comes down the runway and I get excited. "That's my favorite model!" I hiss at Tara, surprising myself. I have a favorite model? I noticed her in Fendi ads because she sort of resembled my friend Sharon, and then I projected all the good feelings I have about Sharon onto this model, and *voilà*, I have a favorite model. But there *is* something cool about her. She seems strong, and tough, and like she's laughing at everything on the inside. Not in a mean way, just in the way you'd hope a model would be laughing at everything on the inside, because she's smart and sees how fucking absurd everything is but still can't argue with the beauty of an exquisitely cut leather dress. Beth loved the leather dress, too, and tells the designer, the young, humble, handsome-in-a-nerdy-way Stuart Vevers, when we meet him backstage. "That would probably fit me," she says about it. "That's how I judge things."

DAY FIVE

"A Fashionable Darth Vader"

Maybe you already knew that the '90s were back, but in case you didn't, Beth says the models were all wearing Doc Martens on the Gaultier runway last night. She loved it. "He wants me to walk in his show next time," she said. Gaultier sent the plus-size model Velvet D'Amour down the runway in 2006, not as a real move to integrate people of different shapes into his shows but to use her to comment on Spain's announcement to start regulating body size on runways in hopes of stopping models from dying of anorexia.

Conversation takes a random turn, as it will. Beth and Tara discuss their shared hatred of the extremely muscular Black Flag singer and spoken-word performer Henry Rollins. "He can eat a dick in hell," Beth says. "I want to have a public spar with him. Any asshole who reads a jihad book on a flight to Australia right after 9/11—there's just twenty-five things wrong with that. For one, what if you were a person of color reading that book? He is just filled with rage." She pauses. "I do want him to pick me up, though."

"He's like a shell-shocked Vietnam vet who never went to war," says Tara.

"He's like Andrew Dice Clay but political," Beth agrees. "He's like a shell-shocked Andrew Dice Clay who never went to war."

Up in the hotel room we all prepare for Karl Lagerfeld. Beth is wearing a simple, gorgeous cobalt blue Lanvin dress she found at Nordstrom in Los Angeles for three hundred dollars, with a pair of Karl Lagerfeld for Repetto sandals topped with Karl Lagerfeld for Repetto perforated patent-leather cuffs snapped around her ankles. What are these cuffs? They're like, like—*ankle collars, maybe?* Frederic Baldo suggests as he deftly snaps one above her sandal. They flare out like the ruffles on a frilly pair of ankle socks but not so babyish. They're like spats for femmes. I want a pair badly. Frederic attaches one to Beth's other ankle. "The gentle hands of Frederic!" Beth coos. Tara sticks her head out of the shower. "You have a *New York Times* interview!"

"Hey, I made up a joke," Beth says. One effect of Beth's insomnia is jokes. They come to her when she can't sleep, or when she finds herself suddenly awake in the middle of the night. "What do D&D-playing goth couples fight about the most? The thermoLeStat! Get it?" This joke was inspired by Beth always being hot and Tara always being cold and their subsequent bickering over the thermostat.

We walk to the Lagerfeld show, which should be no big whoop as it is just across the street in the Tuileries, but there are heels on Beth's Karl Lagerfeld for Repetto sandals, and Beth cannot walk in heels. She steadies herself on Frederic—who, we are all shocked—shocked!—to learn—is not being paid to dote on Beth. Not paid to get us all into the shows, to carry the jacket Beth is too hot to wear, to snap ankle collars around her ankles and to gently, as is his manner, teach us to better our French. Frederic shrugs bashfully. "I just do it for fun."

Inside the Tuileries, Beth's precarious balance is further compromised by the gravelly, uneven ground. She threatens to pull the shoes off and just walk barefoot through the garden, which reminds Tara of the time they did that show in Australia and Beth walked shoeless through glass and mud and had to have it all picked out of her feet afterward. "It was worth it," Tara sighs wistfully. "It was an amazing show." And I am reminded that, like me, Tara is a fan of the Gossip, a big fan of this person who is her friend and now, oddly, both her employer and charge. "How do you know Beth?" I ask her. "Just from Olympia," she says. "Me and my ex-girlfriend Will would follow her around and look at her butt. True story."

Walking up to the throng of people waiting in gray drizzle to enter the tent housing the Lagerfeld show, we move through a group of paparazzi and end up with our photos on *New York Times* online. We stream toward the warehouse, the photographers trailing to the side, screaming for Beth. She flashes them her armpit and we enter the tent.

The tent is dark. We can feel the ceilings somewhere above our heads; before us stands the hulking backside of a wall of risers, and beneath our feet a plasticky carpet is oddly squishy. "This feels like one of those Christian haunted houses," Beth says, stepping gingerly in her Repettos, half-expecting an undead actor with exaggerated Kaposi's sarcoma lesions to pop out of the darkness. Instead we are startled by "the biggest media in Germany," who pokes a fuzzy mic in Beth's face and asks how it feels to be at Paris Fashion Week. "I feel crazy," she says. "It feels surreal. I feel really lucky."

The German asks if Paris is the capital of fashion. Then he asks if Beth thinks fashion is important. "I think fashion is really important," she says. "I don't think it's the *most* important." We shake the German and deposit Beth in her seat in the front. Tara and I have seats a few rows up, and Frederic is cheerfully in standing room. Before I leave, Beth begs for a slice of paper from my Moleskine, to origami into a fan. She is sweating in her sleeveless Lanvin, waving her hand in front of her perfectly made-up face, trying to preserve her work. Beth is currently favoring dramatic black eye-makeup with lips the same color as the skin of her face. The affect is startling and avant-garde and very sophisticated. I tear her a piece of paper and she folds it into a wimpy accordion. "I'm going to give this to Karl Lagerfeld," she jokes. "Since he lost weight it will be the perfect size."

The lights come down. An electronic band, Metronome, composed of three men, walks slowly down the runway, playing a song, in Lagerfeld suits, looking disheveled. It sets a nice mood, but I am impatient for the models. And then they come. The colors are black and gray, with ropey silver detailing, and the cuts are severe, clean, militaristic. The models' hair—uniformly blond—is crimped and brushed into wide, thick manes. Unless they are wearing furred motorcycle helmets, as lots of them are. They are crazy and bulbous on the models' heads, taking luxury to new, fuck-you levels. Some have fur scarves dipping down the back of the helmet onto the neck, like a babushka tied around a grandmotherly head of curlers, only it's fur and it's tied around a motorcycle helmet. The helmets, I realize, have little pockets on the outside for you to slip your iPod into, and there are headphones built inside. It's a total environment, these helmets. Some are not furred but extravagantly jeweled. A cavity-sweet Stooges cover accompanies the models down the runway. "This is like the Pussycat Dolls doing 'Search and Destroy,'" Tara comments. We whisper about how wiggy Anna Wintour's bob looks. She and Grace Coddington are again seated across the runway from us.

When Lagerfeld sends the models out at the end of the show, it makes me breathe funny, and I feel the sting of the same tears provoked at Nina Ricci. There is something so overwhelming, so insane and gorgeous and fascist about this army of too-tall, too-pretty, too-identical women marching out together wearing fur helmets and giant shoes. I flash on the work of Vanessa Beecroft, whose assemblages of live girls, naked, a whole bunch of them together, reference fashion runways, and I instantly understand what she is trying to evoke. It's really, really powerful. I'm sort of scared of these women, and I want to be among them, too, and maybe I would also like to gobble them up, like a terrible ogre devouring a child. They turn and leave. We get a peek at Karl, and the show is done. So much work for fifteen minutes, and in the case of the Karl Lagerfeld line, the clothes aren't even for sale. I guess if you're a crazy-rich fashion lady you can have him couture you something, but mainly what we all just witnessed functions as a very elaborate, very expensive performance piece.

Beth and Karl meet backstage, and it's fairly anticlimactic, though seeing Karl Lagerfeld in the flesh is special. He has found one outfit and he has stuck with it—the snowy ponytail, man makeup on his aging face, his short collar starched up his throat, those motorcycle gloves on his fingers, and always the sunglasses, giving him the aura of a fashionable Darth Vader. I take a picture with my cell phone of Lagerfeld resting his arm on Beth's shoulder, dipping into her ear to speak to her in the backstage cacophony. Behind me the boys from Metronome lean against a wall, drinking champagne and smoking cigarettes, looking over it.

DAY SIX

Otherwise Known As Stella McCartney's Dad

We are in a car on our way to the Stella McCartney show. Frederic and I sit in the narrow jump seats that fold like Murphy beds from the back of the front seats. It feels like we are being trundled through Paris in a carriage. "We're running roughshod," Tara says. "This one time, I had gotten a job that paid, I think, twelve dollars an hour, and me and my friends were talking about how, wow, that's so much money, what are we going to do, buy a cart of sweetmeats and run roughshod over the countryside? Because that's what they do in *The Brothers Karamazov*, and it's the downfall of the family."

In a couple more days Tara, Beth, and the rest of the Gossip will train it over to London to take the photos that will be used to promote the forthcoming album. "I don't know who the stylist is, and that makes me nervous," Beth says. Originally, the band's look was to be in the hands of *Love* editor Katie Grand, but she seems to be backing out. "What makes a bad stylist?" I ask. "Um, someone who brings all black, or all Torrid," Tara says, referencing the Hot Topic for fat girls mall chain. "People who want me to dress burlesque," Beth adds. Magazines are always wanting to dress Beth burlesque, in feathers and corsets and other looks that died out around the turn of the present century, or else they want her to be naked. Beth's onstage strippage has more in common with Iggy Pop's frolic in broken glass than a burlesque act. It's sexy, but it's punk, and functional, 'cause she's overheating. This public near-nudity may be the reason why stylists keep wanting her sexed up and naked, but some of it has to be laziness on the part of stylists unused to dressing fat girls. Putting a girl of Beth's size boldly nude on the cover also has both a radical freshness *and* a more cynical shock appeal, and both surely sell magazines, but at this point Beth has been nude on the cover of the now-defunct lesbian sex mag *On Our Backs, NME,* and *Love.* Our carriage sits idly in the street while some people unload a truck in front of us. "These people are wild as fuck," Tara observes. "Block the street for an hour? You'd get beaten if you did that in New York."

At Stella McCartney I sit directly behind the designer's dad, and take pictures with my cell phone of him hugging Pink. I snap a few more of Kanye and Amber Rose, watching him stroke the back of her neck with his finger. The famously leather-and-fur-free designer sends out some innovative winter coats that look like they've been woven from clean dryer lint. I love them.

Backstage at Stella McCartney is like a daycare, with people holding babies or else trying to roll them in strollers through the crowds of photographers. There's Twiggy. There's the iconic Italian fashion maven Anna Piaggi, looking like Quentin Crisp in drag, a shrunken leather Stephen Jones Union Jack top hat pinned to her head and Baby Jane makeup coloring her face. There is Nan Goldin—Nan Goldin!—whom I try, unsuccessfully, to befriend. An Italian journalist breaks us up with predictable questions: Nan, what did you think of the show? "Yes," she replies.

Back at the hotel, a crisis. Last night a French rat dashed across Beth and Tara's newly upgraded room, taking refuge beneath the sink. The hotel workers tried to convince Tara that what she'd seen was just an adorable mouse, not a rat at all. Tara, who sort of didn't care all that much, feigned outrage. "It was like a pageant," she says. "The pageantry of my indignation." "That should be the title of your memoir," I say. The worker pried the bottom off the sink, revealing a dish full of rat poison.

The next crisis is that we have all been invited to lunch with the McCartneys—Stella, Mary, Paul, etc.—but the French style magazine *Libération Next* has rented a suite and has been assembling a wardrobe of designer items, and Beth is due there fifteen minutes ago for a photo shoot. "We can't do it," Tara says. "Yes, we can," Beth insists. "No, we can't," Tara maintains. "Yes, we can," says Beth. "We just got an invitation to have lunch *with the McCartneys.*" She says it stressed and slow, in case Tara is confused about what is actually happening. "That's crazy." Tara shakes her wonderful hair. "They're all here." She means the stylist, the photographer—Roxanne Lowit, who has shot Andy Warhol and Klaus Nomi, among others—the hair stylist, the makeup artist, plus bigwigs from Sony, all of them waiting for Beth's arrival. "That would be really bad," Tara says. "That would be ridiculous."

"Long story short, if I want to go, I'll go," says Beth. "Period. Do y'all want to go to lunch with a Beatle?"

"I don't really care about the Beatles," Tara admits.

"Are you drunk?" Beth demands, and turns wistful. "My mother loves the Beatles."

We sit together in the room, waiting for a phone call letting us know if we can be excused from the photo shoot to lunch with a Beatle. In the meantime we watch the SSION video for "Bullshit," in which twenty-five pounds of mashed potatoes were colored with brown tempura paint and made to look like a pile of excrement that the band falls into. The video ends, no phone call comes, perhaps *Libération Next* will not even deign to dignify such an outrageous question with a response. We leave the rat-infested hotel room for the *Libération Next* megasuite down the hall.

The *Libération Next* suite has the smoky, delicious smell of a hot iron on really expensive fabrics. A cute stylist boy works the wrinkles out of a pink-and-white-striped Sonia Rykiel smock. Beth is seated behind the hotel room's desk, which has become a makeup table, and the makeup artist, a British ex-goth with a long, bleached ponytail, gets to work darkening Beth's lids. Roxanne Lowit compliments Beth's ethereal eyes. "Thank you," she says, almost uneasily. "I always feel like they're weird." Beth is exhausted. "It would be amazing if you could just paint my eyes on, and my lips, and I could just fall asleep and y'all could take my picture."

I get kicked out of the suite before the shoot begins, because loomers make Beth nervous when she's getting her photo taken. Despite the amazing, brightly colored Sonia Rykiels, despite the complicated striped and hooded Castelbajac that looks like a wearable beach umbrella, despite a couple of sharply androgynous YSL suits, the *Libération Next* people style Beth half-naked in a corset and feather boa and arrange her cheesecake-style on a Fendi fur bedspread.

DAY SEVEN

Muppet Inspiration

Beth is super excited about Jean-Charles de Castelbajac, whose theme for Fall '09 is the Muppets. Beth has long cited Miss Piggy as a personal hero—fat, femme, glamorous, bossy—and has worked the puppet into her own designs for Evans: a radical and cheeky move, putting a pig on a T-shirt being marketed to fat girls, and totally Beth's style. The larger Castelbajac theme is comics, and the stage backdrop is the heavily pixelated mouth of a woman—red-lipped, Brenda Starr–y, Roy Lichtenstein–esque. In front of the darkly opened mouth is music equipment, soon to be taken up by Le Corps Mince de Françoise, an all-girl synth band that sounds like a harsher Ladytron.

Castelbajac's clothes make Jeremy Scott's look conservative. There is a clear plastic trench coat stuffed with blond hair. Black gloves with silver zippers up every finger. A tiny Kermit the Frog top hat. An entire suit cut from Muppet-covered fabric. A hot-pink fake-fur hand muff stitched with the face of Muppet drummer Animal. Dresses with hairy tops printed with the faces of Andy Warhol, Clint Eastwood, Michael Jackson. At the end of the show the models toss fake dollar bills printed with Barack Obama's face and the order BE POP! scrawled across them in fake lipstick. Backstage, the designer beams. His collection was a mad success.

DAY EIGHT

The Gossip Arrives

Tara and Beth moved out of their rat-infested room and into the one left behind by *Libération Next* after the shoot. One giant sitting room with a circle of pillow-thick sofas and armchairs. A giant bedroom simply wrecked with fashion, with boxy shopping bags sent over from Hermès and Dior and Issey Miyake. Two bathrooms, an outdoor patio as big as my room, and free Internet for Tara. The night of the Fendi party, this is where we gather.

The rest of the Gossip have arrived. This would be Hannah Blilie, an impish hairdo who replaced original drummer Kathy Mendonca. Kathy split to go to midwifery school just before the band broke overseas. Beth is fiercely protective of Kathy, her first girl-crush ever, and gets pissed if anyone mentions the Gossip and their newfound success in front of her.

Hannah was playing drums for the punk band Shoplifting before becoming an actual member of the Gossip. She is amiable and quiet with full sleeves of tattoos up her forearms. The other actual member is Nathan Howdeshell, who plays guitar and, on the new CD, keyboards. Nathan's talk is fast and constant, suffused with insane enthusiasm for his subjects, declaring most everything "A-maaay-zing!" or "Hi-LARE-i-ous." The Knife song "Heartbeats" is "the most heartbreaking song ever!" In addition to playing for the Gossip Nathan is (*1*) starting a record label, vinyl only, called Painekiller, after his alias, Brace Paine; (*2*) curating art shows, recently with Deitch Projects at Art Basel Miami Beach; (*3*) creating art, like the three-hour video installation *Girls Gone Oscar Wilde*, in which fair maidens "resist work, bare their ankles, and read poetry in slow motion"—this still in the conceptual stage—and (*4*) making a porn with his girlfriend, whose name is Olivia and who is also a drummer and who has black hair and big red glasses on her face and is sporting a fur she nabbed earlier at the Fendi press room and is, like Nathan, a fast talker. I do not think the couple is planning to actually be in the porn, but I could be wrong. Rounding out the Gossip, on bass, is touring member Chris Sutton of Dub Narcotic Sound System, a tall, intensely good-natured Aquarius sporting a fine Fendi fisherman's cap also lifted from the press office earlier. It is extra cute that Chris is currently playing with the Gossip, because while they were put-upon punk teens in Arkansas, Nathan helped bring Dub Narcotic Sound System to town, and Beth interviewed Chris for a zine she never did. "I'm still aspiring to do a zine," she quips, ducking beneath a chandelier wall sconce to check her makeup on the mirrored wall. Also present: hair stylist Lyndell Mansfield, who looks exactly the way I fantasized everyone looked in New York or London in the '80s—bleached, curly hair, thick black Siouxsie makeup, loads of silver jewelry, tight white jeans with wide holes down the side strung with chains. Her boyfriend is Tommy, a cherubic poet with a dangly crucifix earring who looks like a young Marc Bolan. Who else? My French friend Deb Degouts, a musician who is such a fan of the Gossip she is unable to speak in their presence, only chain-smoke; Karen Goldie Sauvé, an Amazonian party planner managing tonight's soiree. Karen is so tall, her belted fluffy blue Fendi dress comes up short on her tanned and rather powerful legs. Maybe she looks like a drag queen and maybe she looks like a character from a Jackie Susann novel. She is informing Beth of the choreography of the post-show photography. How they will not take a million pictures with Kate Moss and Karl Lagerfeld before the show, out of respect for her performance. They will take a million pictures afterward, backstage.

There are eight pieces of fabric dangling from the mantle and the back of an armchair. They gleam darkly, completely spangled. It's Beth's Lagerfeld-designed stage outfit, and it's actually genius. Karl must have watched Gossip footage and noted that show after show, Beth takes off her clothes, because he made her a wonderful Russian nesting doll of an outfit. Beneath each garment removed lies another scrap of glittered couture, and another. Sequined underwear, shorts, a skirt, a corset, a top. A garment that is like a hula skirt, only instead of grass there are long strips of fur. Beth can't quite figure out what to do with it. She looks sleek and bejeweled in her custom gear, her hair a precise mess of jet spikes. Lyndell reclines on a sofa, having just swallowed a Xanax bummed off Alexander McQueen's best friend. "Do they have Xanax in our country?" asks Tommy, meaning Britain. They do. "If you say you haven't been coping well lately, they'll give it to you," Lyndell offers helpfully.

The Fendi party is at a club on Rivoli. The VIP Club, no joke. There is a round of photos as the group enters the club, and another round in front of a wall papered with Fendi's Lagerfeld-designed double-*F* logo. The club is madness; we catch only a glimpse of its craze as we're led past a glass-walled, truly VIP balcony where King Lagerfeld holds court, up a shabby staircase, and down a decrepit hallway into a cramped and stuffy room that appears to be under construction. It is empty but for some chairs, a bare clothing rack, and a table loaded with bottles of Coke, cans of French energy drinks, and plastic trays of creepy-looking supermarket sushi. "Really?" Tara lifts the edge of a tray and lets it fall with disgust. Hannah goofs with it. "Want some? Looks good!" Soon Kate Moss will arrive, in a silver lamé Fendi gown that doesn't seem to fit her properly, a Fendi fox-fur chubby covering her shoulders. She'll be with her boyfriend, Jamie from the Kills, who was recently hanging out with Nathan at strip joints in Portland, much to Kate's consternation. "What, all the girls are feminist!" Nathan defends himself. Soon men wearing leather kilts will come bearing great glass bowls laden with ice and champagne. Karl Lagerfeld himself will arrive, with a gang of stupidly handsome Italian male models. Karen Goldie is orchestrating everything nervously, drinking nervous glasses of champagne and smoking nervous cigarettes, even though "my boyfriend doesn't know I smoke." When it is time we're all led back through the dumpy labyrinth to a little hallway where we linger, the whole group of us, waiting for a Fleetwood Mac song to end so the band can take the stage. Beth has decided to wear the wild fur skirt on her head, like a headdress. "It's like Cher drag," Nathan says. Fleetwood Mac ends and in a rush the band is funneled through a crowd and onto the stage. The rest of us, the stylists and girl-friends and managers and supermodels and hangers-on, we dash behind them, up to the front of the stage, and watch Beth strut easily to the mic, grab it, and declare, "I'm very, very rich!" as she flings her fur headpiece into the audience. Lyndell catches it and tucks it away. Beth has decided this is the last time she'll wear fur; the skirt gets re-gifted to Hannah's femme girlfriend, Brandy, who recently spent a Halloween dressed as Donatella Versace.

I don't even see Beth's skirt come off, but before the first song is over—"A love song for the homosexuals!"—it's been kicked off the edge of the stage, and Karl, above us on his balcony, seizes up for a moment. Somehow a fedora has gotten onto Beth's head. The backdrop is a giant Fendi logo superimposed with the Gossip's logo, which is just the word *Gossip* in an impatient scrawl. All around us, the walls, giant LED screens, are flashing with the words FENDI © BETH, AND FENDI © GOSSIP. Even though I have been here all week, knowing that every moment was leading to this, watching Beth accosted by photographers and flattered by designers, I still cannot get over how this little band that I have known for so long, this indie queer feminist punk band, is the absolute star of the Fendi show. The reality is staggering. In many ways it shouldn't be a surprise—less-talented, less-interesting, less-charismatic artists get famous all the time. They just tend not to be so outspokenly queer, so flamboyantly fat, so poor in their roots, so disconnected from the music industry, with no secret dad producer or mom publicist. The Gossip got to this lit-up stage in Paris through the force of their own dogged dedication to their DIY garage-rock band. It makes my eyes fill with fucking tears, real tears this time, not those pretty-provoked goose bumps. Watching Nathan dance around, kicking his feet out in his white jazz shoes, my vision goes blurry. Nathan was the punk kid who got fagbashed all the time in Arkansas for looking like a weirdo. Beth was the fat girl who got taunted and fucked with by packs of loser boys, and here they are, and here I am, weirdly, writing about them, beside my good friend Tara, who is, weirdly, managing them, and I turn to her and shout, "I'm crying!" over the soulful gusts of Beth's voice, and Tara nods and yells, "Me too!," her eyes glassy.

On the stairs that lead up to the stage sits Kate Moss, wiggling around besides the twelve-year-old heir to the Fendi empire, who is at her first rock show and wearing platform shoes and leather leggings. Moments earlier, when a friend of Kate's tried to push past me in the tight space, Kate lifted her hands, placed them on my thighs, and gave me a shove. I wobbled in my platform boots but did not fall, my hip propped on Lyndell. I looked at Kate Moss with an expression I hoped had read: Really, Kate Moss? I took note of the incident in my Moleskine.

Now I watch her pump her fist in the air, looking at Beth with pure adoration, and she seems like a benevolent fairy. The room is being transformed with the magical power of the Gossip's utter realness and authenticity, with the heartbreaking power of Beth's voice. There is no room for bad vibes, not even toward rude supermodels.

Michael Jackson
The Man in Our Mirror

Greg Tate

Black America's eulogies for the
King of Pop also let us resurrect his best self.

What Black American culture—musical and otherwise—lacks for now isn't talent or ambition, but the unmistakable presence of some kind of spiritual genius: the sense that something other than or even more than human is speaking through whatever fragile mortal vessel is burdened with repping for the divine, the magical, the supernatural, the ancestral. You can still feel it when you go hear Sonny Rollins, Ornette Coleman, Aretha Franklin, or Cecil Taylor, or when you read Toni Morrison—living Orishas who carry on a tradition whose true genius lies in making forms and notions as abstract, complex, and philosophical as soul, jazz, or the blues so deeply and universally felt. But such transcendence is rare now, given how desperate, soul-crushing, and immobilizing modern American life has become for the poorest strata of our folk, and how dissolute, dispersed, and distanced from that resource-poor, but culturally rich, heavyweight strata the rest of us are becoming. And, like Morrison cautioned a few years ago, where the culture is going now, not even the music may be enough to save us.

The yin and yang of it is simple: You don't get the insatiable hunger (or the Black acculturation) that made James Brown, Jimi Hendrix, and Michael Jackson run, not walk, out the 'hood without there being a 'hood—the Olympic obstacle-course incubator of much musical

Black genius as we know it. As George Clinton likes to say, "Without the humps, there's no getting over." (Next stop: hip-hop—and maybe the last stop, too, though who knows, maybe the next humbling god of the kulcha will be a starchitect or a superstring theorist, the Michael Jackson of D-branes, black P-branes, and dark-energy engineering.) Black Americans are inherently and even literally "damaged goods," a people whose central struggle has been overcoming the non-person status we got stamped and stomped into us during slavery and post-Reconstruction and resonates even now, if you happen to be Black and poor enough. (As M-1 of dead prez wondered out loud, "What are we going to do to get all this poverty off of us?") As a people, we have become past-masters of devising strategies for erasing the erasure. Dreaming up what's still the most sublime visual representation of this process is what makes Jean-Michel Basquiat's work not just ingenious, but righteous and profound. His dreaming up the most self-flagellating erasure of self to stymie the erasure is what makes Michael Jackson's story so numbing, so macabre, so absurdly Stephen King.

The scariest thing about the Motown legacy, as my father likes to argue, is that you could have gone into any Black American community at the time and found raw talents equal to any of the label's polished fruit: the Temptations, Marvin Gaye, Diana Ross, Stevie Wonder, Smokey Robinson, or Holland-Dozier-Holland—all my love for the mighty D and its denizens notwithstanding. Berry Gordy just industrialized the process, the same as Harvard or the CIA has always done for the brightest prospective servants of the Evil Empire. The wisdom of Berry's intervention is borne out by the fact that since Motown left Detroit, the city's production of extraordinary musical talent can be measured in droplets: the Clark Sisters, Geri Allen, Jeff Mills, Derrick May, Kenny Garrett, J Dilla. But Michael himself is our best proof that Motown didn't have a lock on the young, Black, and gifted pool, as he and his siblings were born in Gary, Indiana: a town otherwise only notable for electing our good brother Richard Hatcher to a 20-year mayoral term and for hosting the historic 1972 National Black Political Convention, a gathering where our most politically educated folk (the Black Panther Party excepted) chose to shun Shirley Chisholm's presidential run. Unlike Motown, no one could ever accuse my Black radical tradition of blithely practicing unity for the community. Or of possessing the vision and infrastructure required to pull a cat like Michael up from the abysmal basement of America and groom him for world domination.

Motown saved Michael from Gary, Indiana: no small feat. Michael and his family remain among the few Negroes of note to escape from the now century-old city, which today has a Black American population of 84 percent. These numbers would mean nothing if we were talking about a small Caribbean nation, but they tend to represent a sign of the apocalypse where urban America is concerned. The Gary of 2009 is considered the 17th most dangerous city in America, which may be an improvement. The real question of the hour is, How many other Black American men born in Gary in 1958 lived to see their 24th birthday in 1982, the year *Thriller* broke the world open louder than a cobalt bomb and remade Black American success in Michael's before-and-after image? Where Black modernity is concerned, Michael is the real missing link: the "bridge of sighs" between the Way We Were and What We've Become in what Nelson George has astutely dubbed the "Post-Soul Era"—the only race-coded "post" neologism grounded in actual history and not puffery. Michael's post-Motown life and career are a testament to all the cultural greatness that Motown and the chitlin circuit wrought, but also all the acute identity crises those entities helped set in motion in the same funky breath.

From Compton to Harlem, we've witnessed grown men broke-down crying in the 'hood over Michael; some of my most hard-bitten, 24/7 militant Black friends, male and female alike, copped to bawling their eyes out for days after they got the news. It's not hard to understand why: For just about anybody born in Black America after 1958—and this includes kids I'm hearing about who are as young as nine years old right now—Michael came to own a good chunk of our best childhood and adolescent memories. The absolute irony of all the jokes and speculation about Michael trying to turn into a European woman is that after James Brown, his music (and his dancing) represents the epitome—one of the mightiest peaks—of what we call Black Music. Fortunately for us, that suspect skin-lightening disease, bleaching away his Black-nuss via physical or psychological means, had no effect on the field-holler screams palpable in his voice, or the electromagnetism fueling his elegant and preternatural sense of rhythm, flexibility, and fluid motion. With just his vocal gifts and his body alone as vehicles,

Michael came to rank as one of the great storytellers and soothsayers of the last 100 years.

Furthermore, unlike almost everyone in the Apollo Theater pantheon save George Clinton, Michael now seems as important to us as an image-maker—an illusionist and a fantasist at that—as he was a musician/entertainer. And until Hype Williams came on the music-video scene in the mid '90s, no one else insisted that the visuals supporting r&b and hip-hop be as memorable, eye-popping, and seductive as the music itself. Nor did anyone else spare no expense to ensure that they were. But Michael's phantasmal, shape-shifting videos, upon reflection, were also, strangely enough, his way of socially and politically engaging the worlds of other real Blackfolk from places like South Central L.A., Bahia, East Africa, the prison system, Ancient Egypt. He did this sometimes in pursuit of mere spectacle ("Black and White"), sometimes as critical observer ("The Way You Make Me Feel"), sometimes as a cultural nationalist romantic ("Remember the Time"), even occasionally as a harsh American political commentator ("They Don't Care About Us"). Looking at those clips again, as millions of us have done over this past weekend, is to realize how prophetic Michael was in dropping mad cash to leave behind a visual record of his work that was as state-of-the-art as his musical legacy. As if he knew that one day our musical history would be more valued for what can be seen as for what can be heard.

(Having said that, my official all-time-favorite Michael clip is the one of him on *Oprah* viciously beatboxing [his 808 kick sound could straight castrate even Rahzel's!] and freestyling a new jam into creation—instantaneously connecting Michael in a syncopating heartbeat to those spiritual tributaries that Langston Hughes described, the ones "ancient as the world and older than the flow of human blood in human veins." Bottom line: Anyone whose racial-litmus-test challenge to Michael came with a rhythm-and-blues battle royale event would have gotten their ass royally waxed.)

George Clinton thought the reason Michael constantly chipped away at his appearance was less about racial self-loathing than about the number-one problem superstars have, which is figuring out what to do when people get sick of looking at your face. His orgies of rhino- and other plasty's were no more than an attempt to stay ahead of a fickle public's fickleness. In the '90s, at least until Eminem showed up, hip-hop would seem to have proven that major Black pop success in America didn't require a whitening up, maybe much to Michael's chagrin. Critical sidebar: I have always wanted to believe that Michael was actually one of the most secretly angry Black race-men on the planet. I thought that if he had been cast as the Iraqi nativist who beat the shit out of Marky Mark in Ridley and Russell's *Three Kings* while screaming, "What is the problem with Michael Jackson? Your sick fucking country makes the Black man hate his self," Wahlberg would have left the set that day looking like the Great Pumpkin. I have also come to wonder if a mid-life-crisis Michael was, in fact, capable and culpable of having staged his own pedophilic race-war revival of that bitterly angry role? Especially during those Jesus Juice–swilling sleepovers at his Neverland Plantation, again and again and again? I honestly hope to never discover that this was indeed the truth.

Whatever Michael's alienation and distance from the Black America he came from—from the streets, in particular—he remained a devoted student of popular Black music, dance, and street style, giving to and taking from it in unparalleled ways. He let neither ears nor eyes nor footwork stray too far out of touch from the action, sonically, sartorially, or choreographically. But whatever he appropriated also came back transmogrified into something even more inspiring and ennobled than before. Like the best artists everywhere, he begged, borrowed, and stole from (and/or collaborated with) anybody he thought would make his own expression more visceral, modern, and exciting, from Spielberg to Akon to, yes, OK, smartass, cosmetic surgeons. In any event, once he went solo, Michael was, above all else, committed to his genius being felt as powerfully as whatever else in mass culture he caught masses of people feeling at the time. I suppose there is some divine symmetry to be found in Michael checking out when Barack Obama, the new King of Pop, is just settling in: Just count me among those who feel that, in Michael Jackson terms, the young orator from Hawaii is only up to about the Destiny tour.

Of course, Michael's careerism had a steep downside, tripped onto a slippery slope, when he decided that his public and private life could be merged, orchestrated, and manipulated for publicity and mass con-sumption as masterfully as his albums and videos. I certainly began to feel this when word got out of him sleeping in a hyperbaric chamber or trying to buy the Elephant Man's bones, and I became almost certain this was the case when he dangled his hooded baby son over a balcony for the paparazzi, to say nothing of his alleged darker impulses. At what point, we have to wonder, did the line blur for him between Dr. Jacko and Mr. Jackson, between Peter Pan fantasies and predatory behaviors? At what point did the Man in the Mirror turn into Dorian Gray? When did the Warholian creature that Michael created to deflect access to his inner life turn on him and virally rot him from the inside?

Real Soul Men eat self-destruction, chased by catastrophic forces from birth and then set upon by the hounds of hell the moment someone pays them cash-money for using the voice of God to sing about secular adult passion. If you can find a more freakish litany of figures who have suffered more freakishly disastrous demises and career denouements than the Black American Soul Man, I'll pay you cash-money. Go down the line: Robert Johnson, Louis Jordan, Johnny Ace, Little Willie John, Frankie Lymon, Sam Cooke, James Carr, Otis Redding, Jimi Hendrix, Al Green, Teddy Pendergrass, Marvin Gaye, Curtis Mayfield. You name it, they have been smacked down by it: guns, planes, cars, drugs, grits, lighting rigs, shoe polish, asphyxiation by vomit, electrocution, enervation, incarceration, their own death-dealing preacher-daddy. A few, like Isaac Hayes, get to slowly rust before they grow old. A select few, like Sly, prove too slick and elusive for the tide of the River Styx, despite giddy years mocking death with self-sabotage and self-abuse.

Michael's death was probably the most shocking celebrity curtain call of our time because he had stopped being vaguely mortal or human for us quite a while ago, had become such an implacably bizarre and abstracted tabloid creation, worlds removed from the various Michaels we had once loved so much. The unfortunate blessing of his departure is that we can now all go back to loving him as we first found him, without shame, despair, or complication. "Which Michael do you want back?" is the other real question of the hour: Over the years, we've seen him variously as our Hamlet, our Superman, our Peter Pan, our Icarus, our Fred Astaire, our Marcel Marceau, our Houdini, our Charlie Chaplin, our Scarecrow, our Peter Parker and Black Spider-Man, our Ziggy Stardust and Thin White Duke, our Little Richard redux, our *Alien vs. Predator*, our Elephant Man, our Great Gatsby, our Lon Chaney, our

Ol' Blue Eyes, our Elvis, our Frankenstein, our ET, our Mystique, our Dark Phoenix.

Celebrity idols are never more present than when they up and disappear, never ever saying goodbye, while affirming James Brown's prophetic reasoning that "Money won't change you/But time will take you out." JB also told us, "I've got money, but now I need love." And here we are. Sitting with the rise and fall and demise of Michael, and grappling with how, as dream hampton put it, "The loneliest man in the world could be one of the most beloved." Now that some of us oldheads can have our Michael Jackson back, we feel liberated to be more gentle toward his spirit, releasing him from our outright rancor for scarring up whichever pre-trial, pre-chalk-complexion incarnation of him first tickled our fancies. Michael not being in the world as a Kabuki ghost makes it even easier to get through all those late-career movie-budget clips where he already looks headed for the out-door. Perhaps it's a blessing in disguise both for him and for us that he finally got shoved through it.

Michael Jackson

An Appreciation of His Talent

Jason King

Anyone who has reason to doubt Michael Jackson's cultural importance in the wake of his untimely death from cardiac arrest on June 25th, take note: entertainment website TMZ.com reported that so many people around the world logged online Friday afternoon to get updates about the pop superstar's status that the Internet itself nearly buckled.

Indiana-born Jackson had his first #1 hit in 1969 at eleven years old. No young singer ever sang, or has ever sung to this day, the way Michael Jackson sang on record. It is not an exaggeration to say that he was the most advanced popular singer of his age in the history of recorded music. His untrained tenor was uncanny. By all rights, he shouldn't have had as much vocal authority as he did at such a young age. Had Jackson sounded mature by simply being gruff or husky, he would have remained a precocious novelty. But his tones were full-bodied clarion calls; his pitch was immaculate, and his phrasing impeccable. He had a fluid lyricism and plenty of range, and he could find emotional nuance in challenging pop-soul material. Listen, for instance, to the way he skillfully maneuvers those tricky, Bacharach-esque harmonics on 1971's "Got to Be There."

Though he was capable of gritty soul, Jackson was more Diana than Gladys, more Dionne than Aretha. His muted, contained fervor, honed on the amateur night circuit rather than in the Pentecostal church, allowed him to handle precious ballads like 1970's "I'll Be There" with equal parts aplomb and sensitivity. It's challenging for any singer to deliver authentic emotion without resorting to melisma or other vocal crutches. Singing the original melody as written while also conveying the emotional subtext behind a lyric requires great interpretive skill. Moving between tenor and falsetto, Jackson was a fantastic song essayist. Saccharine "Ben" and "Maybe Tomorrow" became sentimental opuses under Jackson's feathery touch. Achingly slow jams like 1979's "I Can't Help It" and 1982's "The Lady in My Life" were templates for 1990's neo-soul. It's easy to forget how minimalist a balladeer Jackson was until you hear other singers—even skilled ones—attempt to cover his songs and fall flat: Cassandra Wilson's live cover of 1993 weeper "Gone Too Soon" comes to mind.

Jackson preserved his lithe tenor into adulthood. Critics claim he was trying to sound younger as he got older. But Jackson's voice became more feminine as he got older. He and Patti Austin were often mistaken for each other on the crediting of Quincy Jones tracks. And it took me months before I realized that Jackson had a female duet partner, Siedah Garrett, on 1987's "I Just Can't Stop Loving You," given their indistinguishable vocal registers and timbres. If Jackson deliberately cultivated vocal femininity, he could also sound aggressive, and even carnal, as on the opening of 1982's explosive "P.Y.T."

Jackson often draws comparison to Sammy Davis Jr.: both were preternaturally gifted pre-teens hawking song-and-dance routines. Other influences included Jackie Wilson and James Brown, dynamos for whom singing and dancing emerge from the same bodily impulse. Jackson's trademark theatrical dancing bore traces of Jack Cole's modernist angularity, The Nicholas Brothers' sinewy virtuosity, Gene Kelly's balletic grace and Fred Astaire's rhythmic flow. By the early '70s Jackson had incorporated into his repertoire West Coast popping and locking; I wonder if he witnessed those moves firsthand when the family migrated to Los Angeles after signing with Motown.

But Jackson didn't simply model his dancing after others. He somehow emulsified all his influences and created his own idiosyncratic movement vocabulary. Latter-day song and dance stars like Justin Timberlake, Usher, Chris Brown and Ne-Yo have skillfully followed in Jackson's footsteps. But they often do so too literally. While I always felt

Jackson had to dance out of the necessity of sheer ecstatic release, his younger counterparts, happy to imitate their idol, have yet to find their own original moves. Nor have any of them found a real sense of personal abandon in dance. It's been said that Jackson did not pick up choreography easily (nor did Gene Kelly for that matter). But when he danced, he did so with fierceness, with creative risk. It was as if his life depended on it.

By the end of 1969, The Supremes had unraveled. Diana Ross's solo career was set to launch. Motown CEO Berry Gordy identified his next entrepreneurial fixation in Jackson and his four talented brothers. To begin the artist development process, Gordy ratcheted up the funk missing from the brothers' 1967 efforts on local Gary record label *Steel-town*. He concocted a production & songwriting dream team he cheekily called The Corporation (Freddie Perren, Fonce Mizell, Deke Richards and Gordy himself). Their job, drawing heavily on Frankie Lymon and probably The Cowsills, was to handcraft for The Jackson Five G-rated pop tunes like "I Want You Back." *Diana Ross Presents the Jackson Five*, their 1969 debut, was released a week before Christmas and only 12 days after the Stones' ill-fated Altamont concert put a bottlecap on '60s optimism. The Jackson Five's day-glo ditties were miles away from the darker, socially conscious soul of producers like Norman Whitfield and Curtis Mayfield. But they were still more sophisticated than they're given credit for under the misleading banner "bubblegum soul." I can't recall the Osmonds ever attempting anything half as transcendent or effervescent as "The Love You Save."

Matriarch Katherine sewed gaudy costumes for her sons, drawing liberally from the look of Sly's pre-*Riot* Bay Area boho hippie couture. Stage Dad Joe, projecting his failed musical ambitions on his boys, forced them to rehearse using methods that probably contravened child labor and human rights laws. And over at the label, Gordy had set in motion an unstoppable juggernaut of early branding, licensing the J5 image to anyone who would shell out green bucks. These collective efforts resulted in mass female hysteria not seen since Beatlemania. In 1970, unassuming "A.B.C." was so immensely popular that it knocked the Beatles' epochal "Let it Be" off the top chart spot. The Jackson Five scored three number one singles before they ever even made a live appearance. And in 1971, when Cynthia Horner jump-started her black teen magazine *Right On!*, it's been reported that every single cover for the first two years was devoted to a Jackson.

The Jacksons marketed themselves as pop culture's ultimate functional nuclear family. Their seemingly unimpeachable vision of black kinship as upwardly mobility flew in the face of The Moynihan Report and inner city turmoil that defined the 1970's. The Jacksons helped spawn TV's insufferable white Partridge Family and, years later, TV's black middle-class Huxtables. Around 1987, a new cynicism crept in, and dysfunctional families became the representational norm. Satires like *The Simpsons* and *Married with Children* ruled. By the time 1989 album *2300 Jackson Street* flopped, The Jacksons had already begun rebranding themselves as the ultimate dysfunctional family. In 1991, brother Jermaine enlisted L.A. and Babyface to produce "Word to the Badd!," a vitriolic criticism of Michael that he refused to retract; eighteen years later, it would be Jermaine who would give the first live press conference to confirm his brother's death.

Michael Jackson's talents as a songwriter and producer wouldn't come to light until he left Motown in 1975. He found a degree of artistic freedom several records into his tenure with CBS Records: "This Place Hotel" from The Jacksons' 1980 *Triumph* remains a personal favorite. But Jackson truly reached creative nirvana on 1979's *Off the Wall*, his fifth studio album, by collaborating with musical journeyman Quincy Jones. Jones's production contributions to Jackson's albums were sometimes exaggerated. But he did help Jackson develop the musical DNA that would define each of his successive albums. Deep-pocket grooves with polyrhythmic percussion ("Workin' Day and Night"). Wistful ballads ("She's Out of My Life"). Pop hooks that sear into your cerebellum ("Off the Wall"). Jazzy chord progressions ("I Can't Help It"). Swirling strings ("Don't Stop 'Til You Get Enough"). State-of-the-art synthesizers ("Get on the Floor"). Michael's vocal ticks, squeals, and yelps (inserted wherever possible). Savvy songwriters like Heatwave's Rod Temperton ("Rock with You") brought their A-game, and genius sidemen from George Duke to Greg Phillinganes delivered brilliant rhythm tracks. With *Off the Wall*, Jackson finally found a way to capture the visceral thrill of his live concerts on record.

Then, the game seriously changed.

Drawing on the monumental success of the 1979 *Saturday Night Fever* soundtrack, 1982's *Thriller* redefined the pop album as a blockbuster mega-spectacle. It did for music what *Jaws* and *Star Wars* did for film, turning an art form into an event. Throughout his career Michael Jackson had an aesthetic affinity for all things spectacular. I'd call him a *spectacularist*, if that were a legitimate word. He was the thriller he sang about; he wanted to leave you constantly enthralled by every aspect of the artistic experience. The music was no exception. Each song on *Thriller* was a self-contained, high concept deliberately directed toward a desired demographic. Rockers like Paul McCartney and Eddie Van Halen made cameos; Jackson embraced Quiet Storm on "The Lady in My Life"; and the Toto-esque "Human Nature" delivered MOR soft rock. Record label Epic, under Walter Yetnikoff's maniacal direction (or lack thereof), poured money into getting the word out about the album, leaving no marketing or promotional tool untried, including the then emerging music video format.

Jackson always harbored film star ambitions but they would never materialize (save for his featured performance in Sidney Lumet's 1978 *The Wiz* and years later, a passing cameo in *Men in Black II*). But Jackson transferred his celluloid ambitions into the music video arena, grabbing the baton from UK innovators Godley and Crème and completely revolutionizing the artform. With *Thriller* he turned video into mega-spectacle. At first, MTV refused to play Jackson's videos, but as his popularity became undeniable the network ultimately had to swallow crow, as it were. Video directors Jon Landis and Bob Giraldi and others deserve a good deal of the credit for the artistic successes of these works, but one of the unsung heroes in Jackson's meteoric rise was Michael Peters, the late Dreamgirls choreographer, whose iconic moves in videos like "Beat It" and "Thriller" became a definitive part of Jackson's iconography. In 2007, when the surreal YouTube clip of orange-cloaked inmates of the Cebu Provincial Detention and Rehabilitation Center in the Philippines restaging Peters's moves from the "Thriller" video became one of the top pass-around Internet videos, it served as a reminder of how deep Jackson's presence had permeated global culture in the last 30 years.

In the mid '80s, as *Thriller*'s sales skyrocketed and Grammys piled up, Jackson emerged as the most famous person on earth, instantly recognizable through his eccentric iconography: aviator sunglasses, royal jackets with epaulets, bleached white socks, and a single jewel-encrusted glove. *Thriller* exploded the concept of pop stardom, what was possible in the construction and maintenance of global celebrity. It also exploded the concept of racial crossover. In the edited collection *Freakery*, David Yuan mentions how Jackson surpassing Elvis's sales records was as seminal a moment in black American history as previous breakthroughs by Joe Louis in boxing and Jackie Robinson in baseball. Long before Obama, Jackson raised the bar for black exceptionalism. He transformed how people around the world perceived blacks, and just as importantly, how black people began to perceive themselves.

I can vividly recall seeing Jackson perform the moonwalk on *Motown's 25th Anniversary TV Special* when it first aired in 1983. Though Jackson did not invent the move, that breathtaking moment, in the context of his larger performance, started to change my entire sense of self. Back in the day, we did not just want to be like Michael, we wanted to be Michael. We practiced moonwalking and kick-pushing our legs in our bedrooms. We tried to jheri-curl our hair or at least make it look as slick and wet as his had become. We cut the fingers off our gloves in the effort to look cool. Moving and singing with total energy, total freedom, absolute strength, and aesthetic openness, Michael Jackson seemed to be a divine revelation made manifest here on Earth. Though it now seems impossible to believe, Jackson seemed, in that cultural moment, to become the instantiation of total artistic and human perfection. It was an impossible standard to uphold.

Off the Wall and *Thriller* remain the greatest pop soul albums ever released. Some find *Thriller* too calculated and too shlocky, and it is. But I've always looked at it as a lovingly crafted, detail-obsessed, musically-rich work of authentic rhythm and blues. Not to mention, there are few albums more wildly fun and eminently danceable ("Wanna Be Startin' Something" still electrifies).

In pop music, nobody has ever duplicated the commercial or artistic success of those two successive albums. For this reason, Jackson's death might be a symbol of the end of the recorded music era as we know it.

At a time in which the Internet and peer-to-peer sharing programs have made it difficult for music aspirants to sustain careers selling records, it is unlikely that anyone will ever again top *Thriller*'s enormous fifty million plus sales feat.

As the 1980's wore on, Jackson could not compete with hip-hop's street cred demands. But he found ways to match its machismo by amplifying his own sexual aggression. He began incessant crotch-grabbing and Tourette's-like yelps, directed, it seems, at no one but himself. *Bad*, the 1988 follow-up to *Thriller*, introduced persecution and paranoia themes, like on guitar-heavy "Dirty Diana" and CD-only track "Leave Me Alone." Critics like to say that Jackson's career precipitously declined after *Thriller*, but I wonder if they remember *Bad* was some serious mega-spectacle itself. Plus, it had five number one singles and sold more than thirty million copies—hardly a paltry sum by any standard. Except, perhaps, Jackson's own.

I get the sense when some critics bemoan Michael's post-*Thriller* work, they really haven't listened to much of it very closely. I always considered *Bad*, as well as 1991 *Dangerous* and even 1995 greatest-hits-plus-more double album *HIStory* to be superb albums, characterized by the same care and attention to musical detail as Michael Jackson's earlier solo efforts. Maybe you couldn't stomach *Bad*'s silly title track, but you could certainly acknowledge the synth jazz-funk of "Another Part of Me" (Anita Baker even covered it in her live shows). Maybe you couldn't stomach *Dangerous*' sentimental "Will You Be There," but you could certainly acknowledge sinuous groove masterpieces like "Remember the Time," "Jam," and "Keep it in the Closet." Jackson's last studio release, 2001's *Invincible*, could summon neither the mega-spectacle, nor the artistic brilliance, of earlier releases. But it still has its share of prizes, like sleek lead single "You Rock My World" and tremblingly romantic "Butterflies."

At the time of his death, Jackson had spent nearly 42 years making records; that's a staggering sum considering he was only 50 years old. Jackson made plenty of artistic missteps on the way (especially 1997's "Blood on the Dancefloor"; the remixes are off the hook, though) and he was clearly unable to reinvent his brand in ways that would keep him fresh in the commercial marketplace. But Jackson at his worst is still in better shape than much of what is currently on the radio. Propulsive "Sunset Driver," an unreleased track originally recorded for 1979's *Off the Wall* and available on 2004 box set *Michael Jackson: The Ultimate Collection*, stands superior to much of the musicianship in pop today. And gorgeous Babyface-penned ballad "On the Line," little known as the opening credit track from Spike Lee's 1996 *Get on the Bus*, stands among Jackson's best work.

If Michael Jackson redefined pop music as mega-spectacle, he also redefined the surreal weirdness of celebrity culture. What started off as simple eccentricity in the early '80s—plastic surgery touch-ups, carrying Bubbles the chimp on his arm to events, carrying Emmanuel Lewis on his arm as if he were Bubbles!—soon devolved into full-blown horror. Jackson began to transform in ways that you could neither turn away from nor condone. He drastically lightened his complexion and surgically altered his facial features in ways that looked grotesque, not to mention racially problematic. He seemed to become the kind of monster he had once pretended to be in videos.

The reasons he effected this transmogrification are complex, psychological, and psychosocial. Jackson spent his life in abject fear of being perceived as normal and ordinary. He was, according to reports, by turns humble and megalomaniacal. He surrounded himself with aging legendary celebrity friends like Elizabeth Taylor and Gregory Peck and claimed in interviews that the only artist he wanted to collaborate with was Debussy, who died in 1918. Jackson wanted to be among the greatest of all legends, and he wanted you to know of his elite status. Like a black Willy Loman, he also lived in fear of becoming irrelevant. He had never known a life in which he wasn't universally relevant. By publicizing his abnormality, whether real or manufactured, Jackson could kill two birds with one stone: he could remain both talked about, and aloof, different than the everyman.

During his tenure at Motown, Jackson witnessed how to manufacture buzz through falsehood. To launch the Jackson Five in 1969, Berry Gordy had cooked up the white lie that label superstar Diana Ross (rather than Gladys Knight or Bobby Taylor or Suzanne dePasse) had discovered the Jackson Five. Even though the public largely knew it was not true, Jackson was forced to repeat this blatant lie over and over in interviews, until he himself probably believed it, or at least saw its effectiveness, particularly when the group's success did materialize. The lies and manufactured shams continued in the '80s and beyond as his solo career exploded. Jackson soon realized he could become a tabloid fixture by leaking manufactured stories to the press. We learned that he liked to sleep in a hyperbaric oxygen chamber—but who exactly took that picture? We learned that he wanted to buy The Elephant Man's bones—for what purpose, exactly? Jackson managed to turn himself into the tabloid junkie fodder he purported to despise on songs like "Leave Me Alone" and "Tabloid Junkie." Eventually the public could no longer tell what was real and false. Even Jackson's short-lived marriage to Lisa Marie Presley, which possibly might have had a genuine impulse in it, appeared to be nothing more than a desperate publicity stunt to prove his heterosexuality in the face of child molestation allegations.

Jackson also feared, to his core, being abjectly lonely. His self-esteem had long evaporated, likely the result of years of verbal and physical abuse from his father and rumored sexual abuse from older men. Jackson desperately wanted to be liked and understood. But being understood meant being accessible. Being accessible in turn meant being seen as normal, so that was not an option. Jackson had entrepreneurial talent: he bought the lucrative Beatles catalog in the 1980's and launched MJJ Records in the 1990's, a Sony imprint in which he made some bold creative choices. But Jackson wanted people to perceive him as an eccentric, tragic billionaire like Howard Hughes (with whom he was fascinated), so he lived beyond his means and ended up in a mountain of bad business decisions and staggering debt.

Over time, physical ailment, prescription drug use, endless court cases and a revolving cast of shady characters compounded Jackson's neuroses and self-destructive behavior. He found friends, and possibly lovers, in children, since he claimed they came to him with no agenda— but he was a fool to think their parents wouldn't. To stave off depression, Jackson surrounded himself with the most expensive of spiritual advisors, like Deepak Chopra. He desperately searched for the spiritual life that he had once known as a Jehovah's Witness, even reportedly joining Islam in his last years. But Jackson never again found his center.

Jon Pareles notes in his *New York Times* obit that Jackson had internalized Motown's crossover aesthetic and upward mobility imperatives. It was clear that Jackson feared the idea of being pigeonholed—not just in music, but in life. He wanted to appeal to everyone but to also remain elusive. So, throughout his career, he wedged himself in spaces of ambivalence. He did not want to look black or white. He did not want to look male or female. Though he was twice married, it was hard to tell if he was straight or queer or something else altogether. Jackson had become freakishly androgynous, and yet, he continued to crave mainstream success and public acceptance.

In 1985, in a prophetic essay in *Playboy*, James Baldwin discussed the "problem" of androgynous singers like Boy George and Michael Jackson. Baldwin predicted that Jackson's bold pursuit of mainstream androgyny would be his undoing. He said: "The Michael Jackson cacophony is fascinating in that it is not about Jackson at all. I hope he has the good sense to know it and the good fortune to snatch his life out of the jaws of a carnivorous success. He will not swiftly be forgiven for having turned so many tables, for he damn sure grabbed the brass ring, and the man who broke the bank at Monte Carlo has nothing on Michael."

Because of the way Jackson destabilized our understanding of race, gender, and sexuality as fixed categories, he became the figure that many of us academics cut our teeth on as cultural critics. I published academic articles about him, I taught his albums in my classes at NYU, and I spoke about him on panels, including a Yale conference on Jackson's life and work in 2004. Jackson emerged as a major figure in cultural studies because at the end of the day he was a frustrating, fascinating contradiction of a human being. Like the famous 1988 Jeff Koons sculpture *Michael Jackson and Bubbles*, in which the star and his chimp are rendered in cold white ceramic, the superstar became a frozen vessel onto which you could project your hopes, fears, desires, your anger and your delight.

Jackson's racial and sexual androgyny project might have succeeded had he aimed at becoming either/or. Operating in a trans third space, Jackson might have strategically challenged our ideas about stereotypes as he did on 1991's trite but heartfelt "Black or White" from *Dangerous*. Jackson could have ridiculed the notion of false opposites, without becoming ripped apart by them. But Jackson didn't want to be either/or. He wanted to be neither/nor, which is a very different thing. Jackson didn't want to be black or white; he wanted to be some other thing that nobody could recognize, some other category that kept him unique and totally different from everyone else—and he had the money and the wherewithal to effect those changes on his body to make it a reality.

In the end, wanting to be neither/nor means you can end up being nothing to anybody, and that is the recipe for an alienated, lonely life. No pop star in history, with the exception of Madonna, has ever been so open or willing to completely reinvent themselves over the course of their career in the public eye. But Madonna managed to commit to her identity reinventions without ever fully inhabiting any one for any length of time. She also seemed to understand that at the end of the day, some semblance of normalcy is desirable. Jackson did not. That Jackson used his body, not always his art, as a canvas to effect his transformation is what is ultimately so disturbing and fascinating about his career.

Still, it's comforting that someone as lonely as Michael Jackson brought together so many people through his work. One aspect that is often overlooked in American television coverage of his death but frequently mentioned in other countries where Jackson's stardom never dropped off the radar is his long legacy of humanitarian and charitable work. Perhaps only Bono has bested Michael Jackson's charitable contributions in pop. I can recall in 1991 being revolted by Jackson's "Heal the World," an inspirational treaclefest that seemed wildly out of step with gangsta, grunge and bleak chic aesthetics that dominated the airwaves. Jackson's earnesty bordered on serious naiveté.

But in retrospect, it's clear that throughout his career Michael Jackson held steadfast to a vision of one love-planetary humanism on par with the most heartfelt sentimentalists our time. Like Princess Diana (she was also a controversial figure), Jackson really did inspire people to believe that they could change the world, and that is not something to scoff at nor take lightly. Michael Jackson used art to teach many of us how to care very deeply for other people. As a child, I can recall crying in my room as a child listening to 1987's "Man in the Mirror," so powerful was his performance of Glen Ballard and Siedah Garrett's vision for personal transformation and global communion. I can recall how moved I was by the music video in which Jackson takes a backseat to scenes of world conflict, not even appearing until a brief glimpse at the end. I was struck by his ability to take himself out of the equation in the service of a greater social cause. I suspect there are people all over the world who could share their stories of how that particular song moved them.

One Michael Jackson song stands out for me. 1993's "Gone Too Soon," produced by Jackson and written by Larry Grossman and Buzz Kohan, was dedicated to late Indiana AIDS patient Ryan White, a young student who had been kicked of his school because he carried the virus. One can never choose to forget how much vitriolic hate was spewed against AIDS patients at the height of the virus's transmission. Jackson released his tribute at a time in the 1990's when I can't recall many if any hip-hop artists willing to talk about or discuss AIDS publicly. "Gone Too Soon" may have been schmaltzy, but it was authentic, it was tender and terribly moving, a genuine expression of Jackson's passion and care for a young person who had been victimized. As Carl Wilson discusses in his superb book on Celine Dion, *Let's Talk About Love*, we need to rethink the politics of schmaltz, particularly in the way it generates community through emotional expression.

If the punditry on CNN in the wake of his death is any indication, controversy is how many will remember Michael Jackson. He left this earth with numerous legal and financial entanglements that will keep his name in the press for some time. He may have also left us with more questions than answers.

I often wonder if the three children he raised, none of whom seem to look anything like him, are his real biological children. And yet, by all accounts to date, he was an excellent father.

I have always wondered about his skin lightening, which he chalked up on his 1993 Oprah appearance to the disease vitiligo, which can leave the skin with patches of depleted melanin. Many did not and do not believe that he had the disease, given this country's racist history in which black people have used bleaching creams to change their complexions. It is possible that Jackson did have vitiligo and used bleaching creams on his skin to create a more uniform complexion. But, I have always wondered why he did not darken his skin to create a uniform complexion, rather than lighten it. In the end, I'm more likely to believe that Jackson really did have vitiligo and he also decided to bleach his skin out of self-hatred. He was just that complicated. Unless a tell-all diary emerges, the contradictions with which Jackson lived may keep us guessing about him for years.

In the past few days, I have been questioning if the passing of any other public figure alive could elicit the seismic global response that we have seen in the aftermath of Jackson's death. A president, a worldwide spiritual leader, perhaps? Wherever he is, Jackson must be smiling to think that he ended up in such rarified company.

Living on the Radio

The-Dream Is Everywhere

Sasha Frere-Jones

One way to understand social-networking sites like Facebook and MySpace is to consider that younger digital natives are not necessarily being exhibitionists when they post photographs of themselves and share personal details there. Instead, these users are living a life in which consciousness is spread out evenly over two platforms: real life and the Web. Rather than feeling schizophrenic or somehow pathological, digital natives understand that these two realms divide the self much as speech and the written word divide language, a division that humans have lived with for a long time without going bonkers. One relationship that closely mirrors this new digital life is that of the professional songwriting team—the platinum assembly-line workers who write for a variety of artists, including themselves. Whether it's Leiber and Stoller, in the fifties, Goffin and King, in the sixties, or Terius (The-Dream) Nash and Christopher (Tricky) Stewart, in the aughts, there are duos whose work is spread across the charts the way a tween is distributed across multiple platforms. Right now, you could find yourself thinking that you're listening to a wide variety of songwriters only to discover that Nash and Stewart have written and produced a big chunk of the songs you're hearing. The many can be the one, and it may be that the invisible hand is more important than the faces out front. Nash and Stewart are currently two of the biggest hands in R. & B. and pop, and Nash is also making a reasonable run for it as a solo artist, The-Dream.

Nash and Stewart met in the late nineties in Atlanta, where Stewart was already an established record producer. Nash had written several songs for minor R. & B. groups, but he and Stewart trebled their yield by teaming up a few years later. Their first collaboration was "Me Against the Music," a 2003 single for Britney Spears. It stands out now, as it did then, for sounding little like other Spears or other songs on the charts. It is an unusually fast pop song, around a hundred and twenty B.P.M., and combines the humming impact of a Roland TR-808 drum machine, some clattering live drums, and an acoustic guitar. Spears's vocals move around from rapid-fire speak-singing to her typically restrained harmony vocals and a few strange ad-libs. The song wasn't a monster hit so much as an announcement that Nash and Stewart weren't scared to step up to a major artist and do something unexpected.

Stewart is generally responsible for "the track"—all the music beneath the vocals—and Nash writes the lyrics and the "top line," the melody driving those words. (Nash occasionally works on the track as well, but he's mainly in charge of the singing, sometimes in concert with the artist whom the duo is writing for.) This team is most comfortable in R. & B., and that's where the two began developing their signature sound. J. Holiday's "Bed" was one of 2007's biggest slow and sexy songs. Until Nash started releasing records as The-Dream, toward the end of 2007, you wouldn't have known that J. Holiday was singing almost exactly like Nash himself, who can be heard in the background singing "eh eh eh eh." "Bed" seems like a standard slow jam, but Nash does two things to set it apart. In a field of callow sex songs that are generally celebrations of the singer's skills, "Bed" is genuinely sweet. The singer runs his fingers through his partner's hair, and sums up his aims with the nicely ambiguous "I'm trying to put you to bed." The singing moves between traditional melodic passages and sequences in which Holiday sounds like he's splitting the difference between talking and singing, a trick that R. Kelly has made great use of. And then, as the song goes on, this one sound keeps returning: "eh eh," and its slant rhyme "bed, bed, bed." The word repeats over and over, but doesn't rise or change: the singer is looping himself, like a machine.

That "eh eh" and its cousin "ella ella" were part of a song released a few months earlier, considered by many to be the biggest of 2007: Rihanna's "Umbrella." Nash wrote the first two verses and the chorus, over a rough sketch by Stewart that was nothing more than slow, trashy drums and a keyboard line. "I usually don't do second verses," Nash told me. "I just do the first verse and do the hook." He continued, "I went ahead and finished the record because I wanted to send it out to a label as soon as possible, because I felt like it was a smash record. I put the second verse on it and the bridge, and it was a ballgame."

After Britney Spears turned down the song, it eventually reached Rihanna, who grabbed it and probably doubled the magnitude of her career. What the writers and the singer ended up doing will likely define them even a decade from now. The final version is dominated by dark swaths of synthesizers that are anything but cheerful, moving from single hits on the downbeats to long, sustained notes in the chorus that sound more than a little like distorted electric guitars. Nash's vocal line, though, is straight out of a musical, as sweet as "Bed," though more PG. "Now that it's raining more than ever, know that we'll still have each other, you can stand under my umbrella, you can stand under my umbrella." And then: "ella, ella, eh eh eh," which Nash has called "the dumb part" in interviews. It's pretty easy to get, even on first listen.

Rihanna, not a spectacularly gifted singer, does something essential to Nash's melody. Nash is a nimble singer with a sheer, flexible falsetto, able to sound completely carefree, no matter what the topic. Rihanna flattens out Nash's lyrics in "Umbrella," making them feel a little less anodyne. The song is a promise to protect and love, which Rihanna turns into a moment of both dedication and doubt. It's a sappy song that sounds totally unsappy, a feat that many people have paid Nash and Stewart to repeat.

The closest they've come is by, naturally, avoiding "Umbrella" altogether. Beyoncé's "Single Ladies (Put a Ring on It)" is the duo's runner-up hit, though it may be more surprising musically. While "Umbrella" brilliantly plays doubt against devotion, "Single Ladies" combines a jumble of feelings and sounds that don't resolve but also never become tiring. What is all that clapping? What is that ascending whistle in the background? Why is Beyoncé singing a little bit like she's leading a boot-camp maneuver? The lyrics seem to express anger that Beyoncé's man failed to "put a ring on it," though the song is generally jubilant, and even the synthesizer swells sound more excited than ominous. Beyoncé also can't be written out of her own, pure, glimmering voice, no matter whose cadence she's hired.

More typical of Nash and Stewart's work is Mariah Carey's "Touch My Body." Carey is able to sing in exactly the same paper-light range as Nash, who has a tendency to upend expectations. "Touch My Body" is a modified slow jam, certainly about sex but slightly quicker in tempo and goofy in approach. Carey brackets her singing about touching and wrestling and wrapped thighs with a promise that if her bedroom encounter ends up on YouTube she will hunt her lover down. It skips and chimes and sounds as if it would evaporate if it touched a solid surface. And that is how Nash and Stewart like to play it when Nash steps forward as The-Dream.

I am partial to The-Dream's first album, "Love/Hate," from 2007. The first single, "Shawty Is a Ten," was a bubble that refused to burst. Nash is a branding fiend, and so the song is full of "eh's" (some of which cut verse lines into odd little pieces) and the name of his new label, Radio Killa Records. Stewart limits himself to a tiny clump of rhythm and a piano chord marching gently on each beat. Nash's voice swirls as he sings about a series of tens who have come and gone: Keisha, Sonya, Tanya, Kiki. One of the moodier songs on "Love/Hate," "Nikki," evokes the breakup of Nash's marriage to the singer Nivea. It's a dark song that stays dark, and Nash's trick here is to leave his voice lower than usual and avoid the prettier range he goes to so easily. His old love is in a new house, which he calls "awful cold," but then he boasts that he's already "making love to Nikki." It's unusually callow for a Nash song, and sounds an awful lot like the template for Kanye West's forlorn "808s & Heartbreak" album.

West appears on "Love vs. Money," the latest The-Dream album. And in their collaboration, "Walkin' on the Moon," you can hear that Nash and Stewart, while steeped in hip-hop, have been generally detaching R. & B. from hip-hop and returning it to its softer roots. (When I heard Nash sing part of Lenny Williams's epic seventies ballad "'Cause I Love You" over the phone, I realized it takes a tough man to embrace the tender stuff, and that's Nash's wheelhouse now.) There is a little bit of rapping on both The-Dream albums, and on some of Nash and Stewart's hits, but it has steadily diminished in presence over the years, and the song West raps over is basically a disco tune. Hip-hop allowed R. & B. singers to become aggressive again, to make the language blunt, and to admit a little bit of selfishness into the nice-guy routine. Having run that particular program, R. & B. is now following Stewart and Nash to a more subtle and complex area, where aggression and tenderness are equally represented.

Twitter & The Death of Rock Criticism
Christopher R. Weingarten

Speech given at the 140 Characters Conference,
New York City, June 16, 2009.

Hi, everyone. I am Christopher R. Weingarten. I am a freelance writer for RollingStone.com, *The Village Voice, Revolver* magazine, *Decibel* magazine, the website Idolator and more. By this time next year, I'm going to need a new job.

I'm a music writer by design, because I live to give my opinions on things. I'm a music writer by trade because I've been paying my rent for 10 years with it. . . . That's going to stop. Venues are drying up, magazines are going away. And people are firing geeks like me and hiring a bunch of 19-year-old kids that will blog for concert tickets and a pat on the head. And any of you guys out there who care about music, if you haven't stopped listening to guys like me, you probably will soon.

And before I get into why, let me tell you about my project. It's @1000TimesYes. And I'm reviewing 1,000 new records on Twitter right now, over the course of 2009. 1,000 records over the year. I updated numbers 400, 401 and 402 out in the hallway. I'm trying to carve out a space where people can still use a music critic's opinion. But before I get into the Twitter stuff, I'm gonna tell you a little about why no one's listening to me anymore.

Before the Internet, critics had this image of the gilded geekazoids sitting in their ivory towers tossing down opinions. And even if you didn't agree with them, you had to sort of respect them 'cause they were the guys with all the promo records and heard all this music in mighty gulps. And their opinions were *so important* to the success of a record that labels plied them with cocaine and hookers and vacations. And this is all before I got in the game, so. . . . Things were a little different when I started. I started around 1999, around the time that music websites started coming out, like Stylus and Pitchfork and PopMatters. And they started appearing and they were more amateurish and D.I.Y. and homegrown, and most importantly *young*. And they pulled this curtain away and they showed that anyone could do this if they put in the time and effort. And these sites were like consumer guides, basically, for a while. They hipped people to records they couldn't have discovered on their own. Thank you, website, for separating the wheat from the chaff. And it was cool.

And then around 2004, 2005 *everyone* got a music blog. And I'm sure many people in this room got a music blog. And opinions and MP3s sprayed around like lawn sprinklers. Guys like me got scared, and editors were getting scared because people were doing our job for free. This was our job to tell people about records and now people are just *doing it*. And they were younger and they were less jaded, so you could find out about new bands without all the cranky, snarky B.S. that we have. Just, "This is good! thumbs up!" Magazines and websites around 2004, 2005 stopped separating the wheat from the chaff and just started reporting on what blogs were saying. Music writers and editors became a filter for trends on blogs. If you guys know bands like Deerhunter or Dan Deacon or Vampire Weekend, a lot of people probably heard about them first in Pitchfork or Spin magazine. That's stuff blogs were talking about for months. For nothing. Magazines and websites don't "discover" bands, they just report on trends. The bloggerhivemind does the filtering and the critic reported on it.

Now we're on the third stage. Promo CDs leak *immediately*. They show up on message boards and leak blogs and your friends send them to you. Internet connections are super-fast. People don't need a filter anymore, they can just listen to everything. And if you don't listen to everything, you probably have a friend that listens to everything. You don't need a critic to tell you if something's good, you can listen to it. There's a Twitter service called @diditleak, and it just reports on leaks.

It tells you if a record leaks. If you want a leaked record, you don't have to wait for me to tell you if it's good. You can type the name of the album and ".rar" into a search engine and get pretty much any album you want. It's easy. Try it when you get home. Or many of you appear to have computers right now, do it now. Download some records right now while I'm talking to you. Try it, it's awesome!

The only reason that the movie industry isn't falling down a shit spiral like the music industry is because downloading a movie is hard. You have to learn how to use a torrent program and build a ratio and *"Oh this fucking sucks."* You know, Google's easy! My grandma fuckin' uses Google! It's easy! So, why do you need my opinion? Now it's not a game of hearing the right records, it's hearing the leak the fastest. Music websites report on *leaks*—and they still don't cover them fast enough 'cause Twitter people cover the leaks. When Animal Collective's last album leaked a month ago, everyone was talking about it. So when the reviews came a month later, it was completely pointless. All that a music review does now is reinforce the opinion that somebody already has. And it's not like music writing on the Internet is especially interesting or good or insightful or worth reading. People have this open maw, this endless abyss and they just write for 3,000 words. And if it doesn't fit into 140 characters it's not worth saying. We don't need 3,000 words of twaddle on a record. Sometimes it requires less and editors aren't there copy-checking it.

So, one of the unfortunate side effects of the lack of critic culture is that people are getting more stratified and separated in their listening habits. If you read *Spin* or *Rolling Stone* in '96, you'd get an article on Nine Inch Nails, an article on Chemical Brothers, an article on Snoop Dogg. And the Internet doesn't work that way. If you're into rap, you go to rap twitters. If you're into metal, you go to metal twitters. Bands build audiences for themselves, you just follow the bands you like. You don't stumble across this stuff. And that's a problem. It's harder to get exposed to stuff that's not in your comfort zone. I have friends that are so deep into indie rock that they don't know what the fuck Katy Perry is, or Lady Gaga. And these are the most ubiquitous songs in the country. Number one on Billboard for 14 weeks: "I don't know what it is."

So guys like me, the eclectic music dorks, we're all looking for new careers because people are going to the hip-hop expert, the African music expert, the reggaeton expert. And that dude [BusinessWeek.com editor-in-chief] John Byrne was up here saying that Twitter makes it easy to find stuff that pertains to *you*. And he thinks that's awesome. That's the fucking *problem*. I can *always* learn about stuff that's important to me—that's easy. I want to learn about stuff that isn't important to me. I want to be exposed to things.

Crowdsourcing killed punk rock. Hands down. Crowdsourcing kills art. Crowdsourcing killed indie rock. It's bullshit. You wanna know why? Because crowds have terrible taste. People have awful taste. Once people start talking about indie rock on the Internet, it's all this music that rises to the middle. This boring, bland, white-people guitar music. It fucking sucks! I hate it! This NPR bullshit. And NPR is forced to write about it over and over again because it's the "link economy" and people are gonna click on it if it says "Fleet Foxes." Well, Fleet Foxes fucking sucks. It's not the music that's the best, it's the music that *the most people can stand*. The music the most people can *listen to*. If you let the people decide then nothing truly adventurous ever gets out, and that's a problem.

I was at Bonnaroo yesterday. I was very tempted to get a henna tattoo on my face and show up to the Twitter conference. And there were 80,000 people there. And it was a really eclectic lineup. There was an African music stage for the first time which was really cool; and an extreme metal stage which is really fun; and the usual hippy-dippy jam bullshit; and soul and indie rock. It was great, I had a great time. And the magazines weren't covering what they wanted to cover. They were pretending to care about Phish because Phish was a trending topic. These places you would go to ignore bands like Phish now have to pretend they love Phish. And I watched as the twitters rolled in, and you have this platform where Merle Haggard fans and Snoop Dogg fans were all posting the hashtag "#bonnaroo" and reading each other's posts.

And it was all very self-centered. *I'm* having a great time. *I'm* having so much fun. This band is great for *me*. What a fun show *I'm* having. It was all very self-centered. And no one was trying to convince anyone to see anything. No one said *why*. No one said why these bands were great. No one stopped to say, "Everyone at #bonnaroo, you should see my favorite band *because. . . .*" And that's what we're missing in a world without critics, the "because."

#Musicmonday is another example. It's just artist names and song titles—lots of "who," but no "why." And I've done 402 record reviews over Twitter right now, and I can say with authority there's enough room in 140 characters to not only elaborate, but have good writing. People think you need some long Internet rant to express appropriate enthusiasm—it's not true. I try to make every one of my twitter record reviews poetic as well as informative, which is something everyone should think about no matter what you're tweeting about. Be a critic in whatever you do. Let people know the why, let people know the how. . . . Just don't expect to get paid for it ever.

On "Jay-Z ft. Alicia Keys— Empire State of Mind"

Erika Villani

Works for me, John. It's been my walking-home-from-work track for a few weeks now.

Set aside the autobiographical bragging (old news, Jay) and it's just a montage of quick cuts from image to image—Brooklyn, Tribeca, Dominicans outside the McDonald's on Broadway, a gleaming white Lexus on 8th St., Knicks/Nets at the Garden, a sea of blue at the Yankee game, drug dealers on the corner, the gang kids dreaming about hip-hop, yellow cabs in Midtown, gypsy cabs in Washington Heights, dollar cabs coming back from the airport, dice games out on the stoop, red white and blue parades, the Statue of Liberty, September 11th—hurtling you from one edge of the island to the other, from the buoyant and vivacious to the sinister and grieving, from poor to rich and back again, moving fast and disorganized and detached like a subway ride, with that feeling when you emerge aboveground that the place you are has nothing to do with the place you were, and that you'll be leaving this spot just as quick as you left the last. And yet I made it here, so I can make it anywhere, you can tell by my attitude that I'm from New York, there's eight million stories out there in the naked city and it's a pity half of *y'all* won't make it. Half the stories here are tragedies, but not *mine*, so build up and bring in the big soaring hook, for fuck's sake: these streets will make you feel brand new, these lights will inspire you.

But then there's that vignette about little girls in the big city—the same lights that inspire you can blind you, will have you shutting your eyes and ducking your head each time they flash over your face in the club, giving in to temptation, just out of curiosity, just became some guy told you to. Champagne, money, guys behind your back talking about how they want to ride you, and you're half-naked in a miniskirt standing on the curb outside the club, shivering in the mid-January wind and waiting for him to hail you a cab, taking drugs to keep you up all night, taking drugs to bring you down. You're probably one of the half who won't make it. You probably thought you weren't, when you first got here. And the in-crowd / in style / in the winter / in vogue bit? Take the lyrics as written, and he's just continuing to paint the picture: those girls you see cold and underdressed outside the big clubs. Now take the lyrics as they sound, and it adds another layer: they're models, or they want to be, they're just fashionable accessories who aren't allowed to have names or voices. Bonus points for fashion magazine wordplay in a song about New York, which can feel like it lives and breathes magazines and models.

Say what you will about him losing his edge, and yeah there's some weak shit and misogyny on this track in particular (Does he say he's *up* in Brooklyn before heading down to Tribeca? Is there any portion of 8th Street that it's possible to cruise *down*? That good girl gone bad comes out of nowhere—and if the city never sleeps, why does he want to slip her an Ambien? Wouldn't that make it even *more* difficult for her to keep up with the godless life that's currently running her into the ground? Does he want her out of it and unable to defend herself? Or is he just concerned and telling her to take a nap? And how come it's cool, it's just a step to bigger things, when a guy gets caught up with the wrong crowd—but when a girl does it, there's no redemption? Oh, because any girl who has sex with multiple partners is used (*like a bus route*) but he's still one of the finest lyricists in mainstream hip-hop.

If I had managed to pull this shit together enough to make a blurb out of it, I probably would have given this a nine.

Kanye West

Back to Reality?

Maura Johnston

Six-ish hours later, and I'm still unsure if the Kanye West/Taylor Swift brouhaha at tonight's Video Music Awards was a work or a shoot. That is, whether it was the result of a genuine outpouring of emotion on Kanye West's part, or just a way for the VMAs to sneak up behind the rest of the cable lineup and command the television-watching nation's attention—no small feat on the night of competing entertainments like regular-season football, the *True Blood* finale, the US Open women's final, etc., etc. (Apologies for my continued breaking into wrestling terminology for this, but it really fits: You have one performer who has a history of raising hell and another who has what's likely the sweetest, most innocent persona in all of Radio City Music Hall; Performer A interrupts a triumphant moment for Performer B, causing strife; audience reactions that inevitably result in "buzz" for your various media properties ensue.)

I had similar suspicions after the Britney show-opening disaster in Vegas a couple of years ago, and although they might have been sorta proven wrong then, there's something weird about West's outburst and the way it falls in line with his previous ones—particularly his previous ones at MTV-sponsored events. Recall in 2007 that MTV was trying to set up the rematch between West and Justice, which he lost originally, resulting in him freaking out at the network's European bash. Know that the VMAs pretty much exist to promote MTV's ever-more-tenuous connection to music, and that this year's awards were very lacking in buzz because of a just-off-the-mark performer lineup and a competing self-promotional push involving four blokes who first hit it big almost 50 years ago. Not to mention, doesn't Beyonce come out smelling like a rose after all this, ceding her acceptance speech for the night's big award to the wronged teenager? It just all feels so . . . calculated.

I'm going to sleep on figuring out just what about this whole thing was "real," and what became "real" after Kanye's initial outburst unfurled across the Radio City stage–slash–the Internet, and what was merely a way to distract from a lineup that was lacking many of the biggest pop acts in America right now, dispensing with them in favor of the likes of Adam Brody and That Hills Chick. (Because, you know, who cares about pop music.) But if you haven't read it, Kelly Clarkson's open letter to Kanye is pretty amazing, both because she articulates the rage that Kanye's ego inspires in people—"I like everyone. I even like my asshole ex that cheated on me over you . . . which is pretty odd since I don't even personally know you," she writes—and because I suspect that her irritation with Kanye West is of a piece with so many Internet readers' willingness/desire to believe that "Kanye Campaigns for Title of King of Pop" ridiculousness a few months back. (Which, btw? Is still going strong.) Celebrity! Even celebrities can get into the game.

Selected comments in response to
Kanye West: Back to Reality?

Maura | Posted on Sep 14th, 2009
Or maybe he was just drunk? Oh I don't know, I have to sleep.

BrandonSumthin | Posted on Sep 14th, 2009
It did seem rather calculated, from her Westside Story ad, to the syrupy train performance which preceeded her syrupy ass Rhapsody commercial to Beyonce's side steppage. Her team should be kissing Kanyes balls for all this, because the rich will keep getting richer.

As He said on his blog, he and Taylors Mom "talked", I just wonder what about.

By the way I'm sure Kanye doing a country album will come as no suprise now.

neonvampyre | Posted on Sep 14th, 2009
Just imagine if Kanye replaced Paula Abdul on American Idol.

Lucas Jensen | Posted on Sep 14th, 2009
@neonvampyre: YES.

Chris Molanphy | Posted on Sep 14th, 2009
MTV's somewhat panicked reaction after it all happened—Taylor's mic cut out as they tried to switch to a pretaped Tracy Morgan skit (the intro of which they played twice)—makes it impossible for me to believe this was planned. It's way different from the Eminem "storm-out" at the Movie Awards, which to anyone with a brain was fully staged and obvious. This was way, way too chaotic.

Also, West wants to be loved too much to do something that would inspire that much all-night-long hatred and booing. (And wouldn't Diddy have been briefed if it was staged?) Sorry, I just don't buy that this was planned.

Dickdogfood | Posted on Sep 14th, 2009
Two things to consider:
Kanye's ALL-CAPS off-the-cuff spontaneous-outburst personality makes his stage-rush rather believable, and MTV was smart for recognizing this—if it was planned.
Kanye's ALL-CAPS off-the-cuff spontaneous-outburst personality makes him unlikely to keep a secret like this for long, and MTV was STUPID for recognizing this—if it was planned.

Dickdogfood | Posted on Sep 14th, 2009
. . . which is to say that ummm it probably wasn't planned. But if it was, man, MTV are even more cynical than I initially took credit for.
When he goes out of his way to make you understand his hunger and his rage, Kanye's ego is a wonderful thing. Otherwise . . .

mmmcoffee | Posted on Sep 14th, 2009
I, too, felt there was something a little too . . . buzzy? about Kanye's outburst. Really, it just happened to be at the beginning of the tele-cast? On a year when they're really pushing the whole interactive

social media blahblah? Maybe they didn't outright choreograph the moment, but perhaps didn't stop it/tried to encourage it? Maybe I've been watching too many reruns of Lost with Ben manipulating people, but I don't think it would take a lot of work for a drunken Kanye to get it into his head this is a) his idea and b) a good one at that. For what it's worth, if it was MTV's plan, it worked—after Mad Men, I logged onto facebook and read everyone's comments so turned on the VMAs.

LostTurntable | Posted on Sep 14th, 2009
@Maura: Or maybe he's just a big giant douchenozzle.

Lampbane | Posted on Sep 14th, 2009
@mmmcoffee: I was thinking about how interesting it was that it happened so early in the broadcast, because "Single Ladies" was up for Video of the Year too, and Kanye wasn't content to wait for the results of that, either because he knew she would win and that wouldn't give him stage time, or that maybe, secretly he thought the "Single Ladies" video wasn't as good as he claimed it was and didn't think it would win Video of the Year and complaining about that one would just make him look even stupider.

Chris Molanphy | Posted on Sep 14th, 2009
I keep forgetting to mention this—which actually strengthens my belief that this wasn't planned . . .
    Anyone remember the 1994 stage bum-rush on behalf of the Beasties' "Sabotage"? I believe it was Yauch, in his "Nathaniel Hornblower" drag, interrupting Michael Stipe to protest the shutout of "Sabotage" from not only the big category but, I think, everything that year. (It lost to the overrated, hasn't-aged-all-that-well Aerosmith clip for "Cryin'." R.E.M. had won Director or Breakthrough or something for "Everybody Hurts," hence the Stipe interruption.)
    Story here: http://new.music.yahoo.com/blogs/awards/14199/the-only-vmas-category-that-matters/
    In both that case and last night's episode, the bum-rusher was a bit rude but totally, totally correct on artistic grounds.

(Actually, Yauch's complaint was even more justified; "Sabo-tage," one of the all-time three or four best examples of the music-video medium, period, winning no Moonmen was truly insane. Last night, Kanye was just being impatient; it was only Best Female Video, after all, and B took the big prize.)

Maura | Posted on Sep 14th, 2009
@Chris Molanphy: WAIT. "Sabotage" DID win last night!
See? SEE?
Meanwhile, this photo makes me want to blow up the world.

Audif Jackson Winters III | Posted on Sep 14th, 2009
@Maura: There are moments when I regret getting older and slowly, inevitably, losing touch with pop music.
And then I see something like that and it makes me feel better.

Shabutie | Posted on Sep 14th, 2009
As kids will be kids—Kanye is clearly just being Kanye. I'm just stoked that P!NK and Kelly came out and gave him a good online lashing. Keep it up girls.

brownie | Posted on Sep 14th, 2009
Maura, I want more wrestling lingo thrown into these posts—per-haps something about the internet being a bunch of marks for be-lieving this if it turns out to be a work.

memento | Posted on Sep 14th, 2009
Kanye was not just a little drunk, but was actually carrying a damn bot-tle around the red carpet (not to mention sharing it with Joe Jackson):
    http://pics.livejournal.com/ecctv/pic/00rf0qd5
I expect people to get hammered at industry 'dos most of the time, but this is just ridiculous. And it's really, really odd Kanye made a total embarrassment of himself in this way too and yet this fact is omitted from most accounts of the events of last night. Being drunk is by no means an excuse for boorish behaviour, but think about it this way: had it been a woman doing the same thing, every headline this morning would have trumpeted what a "trainwreck" she was.

The End of White America?

Hua Hsu

The Election of Barack Obama is just the most startling manifestation of a larger trend: the gradual erosion of "whiteness" as the touchstone of what it means to be American. If the end of white America is a cultural and demographic inevitability, what will the new mainstream look like—and how will white Americans fit into it? What will it mean to be white when whiteness is no longer the norm? And will a post-white America be less racially divided—or more so?

"Civilization's going to pieces," he remarks. He is in polite company, gathered with friends around a bottle of wine in the late-afternoon sun, chatting and gossiping. "I've gotten to be a terrible pessimist about things. Have you read *The Rise of the Colored Empires* by this man Goddard?" They hadn't. "Well, it's a fine book, and everybody ought to read it. The idea is if we don't look out the white race will be—will be utterly submerged. It's all scientific stuff; it's been proved."

He is Tom Buchanan, a character in F. Scott Fitzgerald's *The Great Gatsby*, a book that nearly everyone who passes through the American education system is compelled to read at least once. Although *Gatsby* doesn't gloss as a book on racial anxiety—it's too busy exploring a different set of anxieties entirely—Buchanan was hardly alone in feeling besieged. The book by "this man Goddard" had a real-world analogue: Lothrop Stoddard's *The Rising Tide of Color Against White World-Supremacy*, published in 1920, five years before *Gatsby*. Nine decades later, Stoddard's polemic remains oddly engrossing. He refers to World

War I as the "White Civil War" and laments the "cycle of ruin" that may result if the "white world" continues its infighting. The book features a series of foldout maps depicting the distribution of "color" throughout the world and warns, "Colored migration is a universal peril, menacing every part of the white world."

As briefs for racial supremacy go, *The Rising Tide of Color* is eerily serene. Its tone is scholarly and gentlemanly, its hatred rationalized and, in Buchanan's term, "scientific." And the book was hardly a fringe phenomenon. It was published by Scribner, also Fitzgerald's publisher, and Stoddard, who received a doctorate in history from Harvard, was a member of many professional academic associations. It was precisely the kind of book that a 1920s man of Buchanan's profile—wealthy, Ivy League–educated, at once pretentious and intellectually insecure— might have been expected to bring up in casual conversation.

As white men of comfort and privilege living in an age of limited social mobility, of course, Stoddard and the Buchanans in his audience had nothing literal to fear. Their sense of dread hovered somewhere above the concerns of everyday life. It was linked less to any immediate danger to their class's political and cultural power than to the perceived fraying of the fixed, monolithic identity of whiteness that sewed together the fortunes of the fair-skinned.

From the hysteria over Eastern European immigration to the vibrant cultural miscegenation of the Harlem Renaissance, it is easy to see how this imagined worldwide white kinship might have seemed imperiled in the 1920s. There's no better example of the era's insecurities than the 1923 Supreme Court case *United States v. Bhagat Singh Thind*, in which an Indian American veteran of World War I sought to become a naturalized citizen by proving that he was Caucasian. The Court considered new anthropological studies that expanded the definition of the Caucasian race to include Indians, and the justices even agreed that traces of "Aryan blood" coursed through Thind's body. But these technicalities availed him little. The Court determined that Thind was not white "in accordance with the understanding of the common man" and therefore could be excluded from the "statutory category" of whiteness. Put another way: Thind was white, in that he was Caucasian and even Aryan. But he was not *white* in the way Stoddard or Buchanan were white.

The '20s debate over the definition of whiteness—a legal category? a commonsense understanding? a worldwide civilization?—took place in a society gripped by an acute sense of racial paranoia, and it is easy to regard these episodes as evidence of how far we have come. But consider that these anxieties surfaced when whiteness was synonymous with the American mainstream, when threats to its status were largely imaginary. What happens once this is no longer the case—when the fears of Lothrop Stoddard and Tom Buchanan are realized, and white people actually become an American minority?

Whether you describe it as the dawning of a post-racial age or just the end of white America, we're approaching a profound demographic tipping point. According to an August 2008 report by the U.S. Census Bureau, those groups currently categorized as racial minorities—blacks and Hispanics, East Asians and South Asians—will account for a majority of the U.S. population by the year 2042. Among Americans under the age of 18, this shift is projected to take place in 2023, which means that every child born in the United States from here on out will belong to the first post-white generation.

Obviously, steadily ascending rates of interracial marriage complicate this picture, pointing toward what Michael Lind has described as the "beiging" of America. And it's possible that "beige Americans" will self-identify as "white" in sufficient numbers to push the tipping point further into the future than the Census Bureau projects. But even if they do, whiteness will be a label adopted out of convenience and even indifference, rather than aspiration and necessity. For an earlier generation of minorities and immigrants, to be recognized as a "white American," whether you were an Italian or a Pole or a Hungarian, was to enter the mainstream of American life; to be recognized as something else, as the *Thind* case suggests, was to be permanently excluded. As Bill Imada, head of the IW Group, a prominent Asian American communications and marketing company, puts it: "I think in the 1920s, 1930s, and 1940s, [for] anyone who immigrated, the aspiration was to blend in and be as American as possible so that white America wouldn't be intimidated by them. They wanted to imitate white America as much as possible: learn English, go to church, go to the same schools."

Today, the picture is far more complex. To take the most obvious example, whiteness is no longer a precondition for entry into the highest levels of public office. The son of Indian immigrants doesn't have to become "white" in order to be elected governor of Louisiana. A half-Kenyan, half-Kansan politician can self-identify as black and be elected president of the United States.

As a purely demographic matter, then, the "white America" that Lothrop Stoddard believed in so fervently may cease to exist in 2040, 2050, or 2060, or later still. But where the culture is concerned, it's already all but finished. Instead of the long-standing model of assimilation toward a common center, the culture is being remade in the image of white America's multiethnic, multicolored heirs.

For some, the disappearance of this centrifugal core heralds a future rich with promise. In 1998, President Bill Clinton, in a now-famous address to students at Portland State University, remarked:

> Today, largely because of immigration, there is no majority race in Hawaii or Houston or New York City. Within five years, there will be no majority race in our largest state, California. In a little more than 50 years, there will be no majority race in the United States. No other nation in history has gone through demographic change of this magnitude in so short a time . . . [These immigrants] are energizing our culture and broadening our vision of the world. They are renewing our most basic values and reminding us all of what it truly means to be American.

Not everyone was so enthused. Clinton's remarks caught the attention of another anxious Buchanan—Pat Buchanan, the conservative thinker. Revisiting the president's speech in his 2001 book, *The Death of the West*, Buchanan wrote: "Mr. Clinton assured us that it will be a better America when we are all minorities and realize true 'diversity.' Well, those students [at Portland State] are going to find out, for they will spend their golden years in a Third World America."

Today, the arrival of what Buchanan derided as "Third World America" is all but inevitable. What will the new mainstream of America look like, and what ideas or values might it rally around? What will it mean to be white after "whiteness" no longer defines the mainstream? Will anyone mourn the end of white America? Will anyone try to preserve it?

Another moment from *The Great Gatsby*: as Fitzgerald's narrator and Gatsby drive across the Queensboro Bridge into Manhattan, a car passes them, and Nick Carraway notices that it is a limousine "driven by a white chauffeur, in which sat three modish negroes, two bucks and a girl." The novelty of this topsy-turvy arrangement inspires Carraway to laugh aloud and think to himself, "Anything can happen now that we've slid over this bridge, anything at all. . . . "

For a contemporary embodiment of the upheaval that this scene portended, consider Sean Combs, a hip-hop mogul and one of the most famous African Americans on the planet. Combs grew up during hip-hop's late-1970s rise, and he belongs to the first generation that could safely make a living working in the industry—as a plucky young promoter and record-label intern in the late 1980s and early 1990s, and as a fashion designer, artist, and music executive worth hundreds of millions of dollars a brief decade later.

In the late 1990s, Combs made a fascinating gesture toward New York's high society. He announced his arrival into the circles of the rich and powerful not by crashing their parties, but by inviting them into his own spectacularly over-the-top world. Combs began to stage elaborate annual parties in the Hamptons, not far from where Fitzgerald's novel takes place. These "white parties"—attendees are required to wear white—quickly became legendary for their opulence (in 2004, Combs showcased a 1776 copy of the Declaration of Independence) as well as for the cultures-colliding quality of Hamptons elites paying their respects to someone so comfortably nouveau riche. Prospective business partners angled to get close to him and praised him as a guru of the lucrative "urban" market, while grateful partygoers hailed him as a modern-day Gatsby.

"Have I read *The Great Gatsby*?" Combs said to a London newspaper in 2001. "I am the Great Gatsby."

Yet whereas Gatsby felt pressure to hide his status as an arriviste, Combs celebrated his position as an outsider-insider—someone who appropriates elements of the culture he seeks to join without attempting to assimilate outright. In a sense, Combs was imitating the old WASP establishment; in another sense, he was subtly provoking it, by over-enunciating its formality and never letting his guests forget that there was something slightly off about his presence. There's a silent power to throwing parties where the best-dressed man in the room is also the one whose public profile once consisted primarily of dancing in the background of Biggie Smalls videos. ("No one would ever expect a young black man to be coming to a party with the Declaration of Independence, but I got it, and it's coming with me," Combs joked at his 2004 party, as he made the rounds with the document, promising not to spill champagne on it.)

In this regard, Combs is both a product and a hero of the new cultural mainstream, which prizes diversity above all else, and whose ultimate goal is some vague notion of racial transcendence, rather than subversion or assimilation. Although Combs's vision is far from representative— not many hip-hop stars vacation in St. Tropez with a parasol-toting manservant shading their every step—his industry lies at the heart of this new mainstream. Over the past 30 years, few changes in American culture have been as significant as the rise of hip-hop. The genre has radically reshaped the way we listen to and consume music, first by opposing the pop mainstream and then by becoming it. From its constant sampling of past styles and eras—old records, fashions, slang, anything— to its mythologization of the self-made black antihero, hip-hop is more than a musical genre: it's a philosophy, a political statement, a way of approaching and remaking culture. It's a lingua franca not just among kids in America, but also among young people worldwide. And its economic impact extends beyond the music industry, to fashion, advertising, and film. (Consider the producer Russell Simmons—the ur-Combs and a music, fashion, and television mogul—or the rapper 50 Cent, who has parlayed his rags-to-riches story line into extracurricular successes that include a clothing line; book, video-game, and film deals; and a startlingly lucrative partnership with the makers of Vitamin Water.)

But hip-hop's deepest impact is symbolic. During popular music's rise in the 20th century, white artists and producers consistently "mainstreamed" African American innovations. Hip-hop's ascension has been different. Eminem notwithstanding, hip-hop never suffered through anything like an Elvis Presley moment, in which a white artist made a musical form safe for white America. This is no dig at Elvis— the constrictive racial logic of the 1950s demanded the erasure of rock and roll's black roots, and if it hadn't been him, it would have been someone else. But hip-hop—the sound of the post-civil-rights, post-soul generation—found a global audience on its own terms.

Today, hip-hop's colonization of the global imagination, from fashion runways in Europe to dance competitions in Asia, is Disney-esque. This transformation has bred an unprecedented cultural confidence in its black originators. Whiteness is no longer a threat, or an ideal: it's kitsch to be appropriated, whether with gestures like Combs's "white parties" or the trickle-down epidemic of collared shirts and cuff links currently afflicting rappers. And an expansive multiculturalism is replacing the us-against-the-world bunker mentality that lent a thrilling edge to hip-hop's mid-1990s rise.

Peter Rosenberg, a self-proclaimed "nerdy Jewish kid" and radio personality on New York's Hot 97 FM—and a living example of how hip-hop has created new identities for its listeners that don't fall neatly along lines of black and white—shares another example: "I interviewed [the St. Louis rapper] Nelly this morning, and he said it's now very cool and *in* to have multicultural friends. Like you're not really considered hip or 'you've made it' if you're rolling with all the same people."

Just as Tiger Woods forever changed the country-club culture of golf, and Will Smith confounded stereotypes about the ideal Hollywood leading man, hip-hop's rise is helping redefine the American mainstream, which no longer aspires toward a single iconic image of style or class. Successful network-television shows like *Lost, Heroes,* and *Grey's Anatomy* feature wildly diverse casts, and an entire genre of half-hour comedy, from *The Colbert Report* to *The Office,* seems dedicated to having fun with the persona of the clueless white male. The youth market is following the same pattern: consider the Cheetah Girls, a multicultural, multiplatinum, multiplatform trio of teenyboppers who recently starred in their third movie, or Dora the Explorer, the precocious bilingual 7-year-old Latina adventurer who is arguably the most successful animated character on children's television today. In a recent address to the Association of Hispanic Advertising Agencies, Brown Johnson, the Nickelodeon executive who has overseen Dora's rise, explained the importance of creating a character who does not conform to "the white, middle-class mold." When Johnson pointed out that Dora's wares were outselling Barbie's in France, the crowd hooted in delight.

Pop culture today rallies around an ethic of multicultural inclusion that seems to value every identity—except whiteness. "It's become harder for the blond-haired, blue-eyed commercial actor," remarks Rochelle Newman-Carrasco, of the Hispanic marketing firm Enlace. "You read casting notices, and they like to cast people with brown hair because they could be Hispanic. The language of casting notices is pretty shocking because it's so specific: 'Brown hair, brown eyes, could look Hispanic.' Or, as one notice put it: 'Ethnically ambiguous.'"

"I think white people feel like they're under siege right now—like it's not okay to be white right now, especially if you're a white male," laughs Bill Imada, of the IW Group. Imada and Newman-Carrasco are part of a movement within advertising, marketing, and communications firms to reimagine the profile of the typical American consumer. (Tellingly, every person I spoke with from these industries knew the Census Bureau's projections by heart.)

"There's a lot of fear and a lot of resentment," Newman-Carrasco observes, describing the flak she caught after writing an article for a trade publication on the need for more-diverse hiring practices. "I got a response from a friend—he's, like, a 60-something white male, and he's been involved with multicultural recruiting," she recalls. "And he said, 'I really feel like the hunted. It's a hard time to be a white man in America right now, because I feel like I'm being lumped in with all white males in America, and I've tried to do stuff, but it's a tough time.'"

"I always tell the white men in the room, 'We need you,'" Imada says. "We cannot talk about diversity and inclusion and engagement without you at the table. It's okay to be white!

"But people are stressed out about it. 'We used to be in control! We're losing control!'"

If they're right—if white America is indeed "losing control," and if the future will belong to people who can successfully navigate a post-racial, multicultural landscape—then it's no surprise that many white Americans are eager to divest themselves of their whiteness entirely.

For some, this renunciation can take a radical form. In 1994, a young graffiti artist and activist named William "Upski" Wimsatt, the son of a university professor, published *Bomb the Suburbs*, the spiritual heir to Norman Mailer's celebratory 1957 essay, "The White Negro." Wimsatt was deeply committed to hip-hop's transformative powers, going so far as to embrace the status of the lowly "wigger," a pejorative term popularized in the early 1990s to describe white kids who steep themselves in black culture. Wimsatt viewed the wigger's immersion in two cultures as an engine for change. "If channeled in the right way," he wrote, "the wigger can go a long way toward repairing the sickness of race in America."

Wimsatt's painfully earnest attempts to put his own relationship with whiteness under the microscope coincided with the emergence of an academic discipline known as "whiteness studies." In colleges and universities across the country, scholars began examining the history of "whiteness" and unpacking its contradictions. Why, for example, had the Irish and the Italians fallen beyond the pale at different moments in our history? Were Jewish Americans *white*? And, as the historian Matthew Frye Jacobson asked, "Why is it that in the United States, a white woman can have black children but a black woman cannot have white children?"

Much like Wimsatt, the whiteness-studies academics—figures such as Jacobson, David Roediger, Eric Lott, and Noel Ignatiev—were attempting to come to terms with their own relationships with whiteness, in its past and present forms. In the early 1990s, Ignatiev, a former labor activist and the author of *How the Irish Became White*, set out to "abolish" the idea of the white race by starting the New Abolitionist Movement and founding a journal titled *Race Traitor*. "There is nothing positive about white identity," he wrote in 1998. "As James Baldwin said, 'As long as you think you're white, there's no hope for you.'"

Although most white Americans haven't read *Bomb the Suburbs* or *Race Traitor*, this view of whiteness as something to be interrogated, if not shrugged off completely, has migrated to less academic spheres. The perspective of the whiteness-studies academics is commonplace now, even if the language used to express it is different.

"I get it: as a straight white male, I'm the worst thing on Earth," Christian Lander says. Lander is a Canadian-born, Los Angeles–based satirist who in January 2008 started a blog called Stuff White People Like (stuffwhitepeoplelike.com), which pokes fun at the manners and mores of a specific species of young, hip, upwardly mobile whites. (He has written more than 100 entries about whites' passion for things like bottled water, "the idea of soccer," and "being the only white person around.") At its best, Lander's site—which formed the basis for a recently published book of the same name (reviewed in the October 2008 *Atlantic*)—is a cunningly precise distillation of the identity crisis plaguing well-meaning, well-off white kids in a post-white world.

"Like, I'm aware of all the horrible crimes that my demographic has done in the world," Lander says. "And there's a bunch of white people who are desperate—*desperate*—to say, 'You know what? My skin's white, but I'm not one of the white people who's destroying the world.'"

For Lander, whiteness has become a vacuum. The "white identity" he limns on his blog is predicated on the quest for authenticity—usually other people's authenticity. "As a white person, you're just desperate to find something else to grab onto. You're jealous! Pretty much every white person I grew up with wished they'd grown up in, you know, an ethnic home that gave them a second language. White culture is *Family Ties* and Led Zeppelin and Guns N' Roses—like, this is white culture. This is all we have."

Lander's "white people" are products of a very specific historical moment, raised by well-meaning Baby Boomers to reject the old ideal of white American gentility and to embrace diversity and fluidity instead. ("It's strange that we are the kids of Baby Boomers, right? How the hell do you rebel against that? Like, your parents will march against the World Trade Organization next to you. They'll have bigger white dreadlocks than you. What do you do?") But his lighthearted anthropology suggests that the multicultural harmony they were raised to worship has bred a kind of self-denial.

Matt Wray, a sociologist at Temple University who is a fan of Lander's humor, has observed that many of his white students are plagued by a racial-identity crisis: "They don't care about socioeconomics; they care about culture. And to be white is to be culturally broke. The classic thing white students say when you ask them to talk about who they are is, 'I don't have a culture.' They might be privileged, they might be loaded socioeconomically, but they feel bankrupt when it comes to culture. . . . They feel disadvantaged, and they feel marginalized. They don't have a culture that's cool or oppositional." Wray says that this feeling of being culturally bereft often prevents students from recognizing what it means to be a child of privilege—a strange irony that the first wave of whiteness-studies scholars, in the 1990s, failed to anticipate.

Of course, the obvious material advantages that come with being born white—lower infant-mortality rates and easier-to-acquire bank loans, for example—tend to undercut any sympathy that this sense of marginalization might generate. And in the right context, cultural-identity crises can turn well-meaning whites into instant punch lines. Consider ego trip's The (White) Rapper Show, a brilliant and critically acclaimed reality show that VH1 debuted in 2007. It depicted 10 (mostly hapless) white rappers living together in a dilapidated house—dubbed "Tha White House"—in the South Bronx. Despite the contestants' best intentions, each one seemed like a profoundly confused caricature, whether it was the solemn graduate student committed to fighting racism or the ghetto-obsessed suburbanite who had, seemingly by accident, named himself after the abolitionist John Brown.

Similarly, Smirnoff struck marketing gold in 2006 with a viral music video titled "Tea Partay," featuring a trio of strikingly bad, V-neck-sweater-clad white rappers called the Prep Unit. "Haters like to clown our Ivy League educations / But they're just jealous 'cause our families run the nation," the trio brayed, as a pair of bottle-blond women in spiffy tennis whites shimmied behind them. There was no nonironic way to enjoy the video; its entire appeal was in its self-aware lampooning of WASP culture: verdant country clubs, "old money," croquet, popped collars, and the like.

"The best defense is to be constantly pulling the rug out from underneath yourself," Wray remarks, describing the way self-aware whites contend with their complicated identity. "Beat people to the punch. You're forced as a white person into a sense of ironic detachment. Irony is what fuels a lot of white subcultures. You also see things like Burning Man, when a lot of white people are going into the desert and trying to invent something that is entirely new and not a form of racial mimicry. That's its own kind of flight from whiteness. We're going through a period where whites are really trying to figure out: Who are we?"

The "flight from whiteness" of urban, college-educated, liberal whites isn't the only attempt to answer this question. You can flee into whiteness as well. This can mean pursuing the authenticity of an imagined past: think of the deliberately white-bread world of Mormon America, where the '50s never ended, or the anachronistic WASP entitlement flaunted in books like last year's *A Privileged Life: Celebrating WASP Style*, a handsome coffee-table book compiled by Susanna Salk, depicting a world of seersucker blazers, whale pants, and deck shoes. (What the book celebrates is the "inability to be outdone," and the "self-confidence and security that comes with it," Salk tells me. "That's why I call it 'privilege.' It's this privilege of time, of heritage, of being in a place longer than anybody else.") But these enclaves of preserved-in-amber whiteness are likely to be less important to the American future than the construction of whiteness as a somewhat pissed-off minority culture.

This notion of a self-consciously white expression of minority empowerment will be familiar to anyone who has come across the comedian Larry the Cable Guy—he of "Farting Jingle Bells"—or witnessed the transformation of Detroit-born-and-bred Kid Rock from teenage rapper into "American Bad Ass" southern-style rocker. The 1990s may have been a decade when multiculturalism advanced dramatically— when American culture became "colorized," as the critic Jeff Chang put it—but it was also an era when a very different form of identity politics crystallized. Hip-hop may have provided the decade's soundtrack, but the highest-selling artist of the '90s was Garth Brooks. Michael Jordan and Tiger Woods may have been the faces of athletic superstardom, but it was NASCAR that emerged as professional sports' fastest-growing institution, with ratings second only to the NFL's.

As with the unexpected success of the apocalyptic Left Behind novels, or the Jeff Foxworthy–organized Blue Collar Comedy Tour, the rise of country music and auto racing took place well off the American elite's radar screen. (None of Christian Lander's white people would be caught dead at a NASCAR race.) These phenomena reflected a growing sense of cultural solidarity among lower-middle-class whites— a solidarity defined by a yearning for American "authenticity," a folksy realness that rejects the global, the urban, and the effete in favor of nostalgia for "the way things used to be."

Like other forms of identity politics, white solidarity comes complete with its own folk heroes, conspiracy theories (Barack Obama is a secret Muslim! The U.S. is going to merge with Canada and Mexico!), and laundry lists of injustices. The targets and scapegoats vary—from multiculturalism and affirmative action to a loss of moral values, from immigration to an economy that no longer guarantees the American worker a fair chance—and so do the political programs they inspire. (Ross Perot and Pat Buchanan both tapped into this white identity politics in the 1990s; today, its tribunes run the ideological gamut, from Jim Webb to Ron Paul to Mike Huckabee to Sarah Palin.) But the core grievance, in each case, has to do with cultural and socioeconomic dislocation—the sense that the system that used to guarantee the white working class some stability has gone off-kilter.

Wray is one of the founders of what has been called "white-trash studies," a field conceived as a response to the perceived elite-liberal marginalization of the white working class. He argues that the economic downturn of the 1970s was the precondition for the formation of an "oppositional" and "defiant" white-working-class sensibility—think of the rugged, anti-everything individualism of 1977's *Smokey and the Bandit*. But those anxieties took their shape from the aftershocks of the identity-based movements of the 1960s. "I think that the political space that the civil-rights movement opens up in the mid-1950s and '60s is the transformative thing," Wray observes. "Following the black-power movement, all of the other minority groups that followed took up various forms of activism, including brown power and yellow power and red power. Of course the problem is, if you try and have a 'white power' movement, it doesn't sound good."

The result is a racial pride that dares not speak its name, and that defines itself through cultural cues instead—a suspicion of intellectual elites and city dwellers, a preference for folksiness and plainness of speech (whether real or feigned), and the association of a working-class white minority with "the real America." (In the Scots-Irish belt that runs from Arkansas up through West Virginia, the most common ethnic label offered to census takers is "American.") Arguably, this white identity politics helped swing the 2000 and 2004 elections, serving as the powerful counterpunch to urban white liberals, and the McCain-Palin campaign relied on it almost to the point of absurdity (as when a McCain surrogate dismissed Northern Virginia as somehow not part of "the real Virginia") as a bulwark against the threatening multiculturalism of Barack Obama. Their strategy failed, of course, but it's possible to imagine white identity politics growing more potent and more forthright in its racial identifications in the future, as "the real America" becomes an ever-smaller portion of, well, the real America, and as the soon-to-be white minority's sense of being besieged and disdained by a multicultural majority grows apace.

This vision of the aggrieved white man lost in a world that no longer values him was given its most vivid expression in the 1993 film *Falling Down*. Michael Douglas plays Bill Foster, a downsized defense worker with a buzz cut and a pocket protector who rampages through a Los Angeles overrun by greedy Korean shop-owners and Hispanic gangsters, railing against the eclipse of the America he used to know. (The film came out just eight years before California became the nation's first majority-minority state.) *Falling Down* ends with a soulful police officer apprehending Foster on the Santa Monica Pier, at which point the middle-class vigilante asks, almost innocently: *"I'm the bad guy?"*

But this is a nightmare vision. Of course most of America's Bill Fosters aren't the bad guys—just as civilization is not, in the words of Tom Buchanan, "going to pieces" and America is not, in the phrasing of Pat Buchanan, going "Third World." The coming white minority does not mean that the racial hierarchy of American culture will suddenly become inverted, as in 1995's *White Man's Burden*, an awful thought experiment of a film, starring John Travolta, that envisions an upside-down world in which whites are subjugated to their high-class black oppressors. There will be dislocations and resentments along the way, but the demographic shifts of the next 40 years are likely to reduce the power of racial hierarchies over everyone's lives, producing a culture that's more likely than any before to treat its inhabitants as individuals, rather than members of a caste or identity group.

Consider the world of advertising and marketing, industries that set out to mold our desires at a subconscious level. Advertising strategy once assumed a "general market"—"a code word for 'white people,'" jokes one ad executive—and smaller, mutually exclusive, satellite "ethnic markets." In recent years, though, advertisers have begun revising their assumptions and strategies in anticipation of profound demographic shifts. Instead of herding consumers toward a discrete center, the goal today is to create versatile images and campaigns that can be adapted to highly individualized tastes. (Think of the dancing silhouettes in

Apple's iPod campaign, which emphasizes individuality and diversity without privileging—or even representing—any specific group.)

At the moment, we can call this the triumph of multiculturalism, or post-racialism. But just as *whiteness* has no inherent meaning—it is a vessel we fill with our hopes and anxieties—these terms may prove equally empty in the long run. Does being post-racial mean that we are past race completely, or merely that race is no longer essential to how we identify ourselves? Karl Carter, of Atlanta's youth-oriented GTM Inc. (Guerrilla Tactics Media), suggests that marketers and advertisers would be better off focusing on matrices like "lifestyle" or "culture" rather than race or ethnicity. "You'll have crazy in-depth studies of the white consumer or the Latino consumer," he complains. "But how do skaters feel? How do hip-hoppers feel?"

The logic of online social networking points in a similar direction. The New York University sociologist Dalton Conley has written of a "network nation," in which applications like Facebook and MySpace create "crosscutting social groups" and new, flexible identities that only vaguely overlap with racial identities. Perhaps this is where the future of identity after whiteness lies—in a dramatic departure from the racial logic that has defined American culture from the very beginning. What Conley, Carter, and others are describing isn't merely the displacement of whiteness from our cultural center; they're describing a social structure that treats race as just one of a seemingly infinite number of possible self-identifications.

The problem of the 20th century, W. E. B. DuBois famously predicted, would be the problem of the color line. Will this continue to be the case in the 21st century, when a black president will govern a country whose social networks increasingly cut across every conceivable line of identification? The ruling of *United States v. Bhagat Singh Thind* no longer holds weight, but its echoes have been inescapable: we aspire to be post-racial, but we still live within the structures of privilege, injustice, and racial categorization that we inherited from an older order. We can talk about defining ourselves by lifestyle rather than skin color, but our lifestyle choices are still racially coded. We know, more or less, that race is a fiction that often does more harm than good, and yet it is something we cling to without fully understanding why—as a social and legal fact, a vague sense of belonging and place that we make solid through culture and speech.

But maybe this is merely how it used to be—maybe this is already an outdated way of looking at things. "You have a lot of young adults going into a more diverse world," Carter remarks. For the young Americans born in the 1980s and 1990s, culture is something to be taken apart and remade in their own image. "We came along in a generation that didn't have to follow that path of race," he goes on. "We saw something *different.*" This moment was not the end of white America; it was not the end of anything. It was a bridge, and we crossed it.

Paisley's Progress

Robert Christgau

Fifteen seconds of tune-up precede a partying rock riff that's corny even by Nashville standards. But it sure does rock, and soon it takes on virtuoso flourishes. Finally, 40 seconds in, there's a rather un-Nashville lyric: "She's got Brazilian leather boots on the pedal of her German car / Listenin' to the Beatles singin' 'Back in the U.S.S.R.'" Thus begins the lead and title cut of Brad Paisley's *American Saturday Night*. So optimistic it's intrepid and shameless at the same time, *American Saturday Night* rejects the anxious escapism and dark undercurrents of actually existing country, pop, and rock convention. As it strives to touch every human being in a nation Paisley knows is less unified and forward-looking than he pretends, the farthest it deviates from message is two breakup songs of uncommon tenderness and dignity. There's not a bum track on it—unless you're one of those sophisticates who's a priori nauseated by tunes more memorable than striking, lyrics that parse, pitch-corrected vocal harmonies, waveform compression, and strawberry ice cream.

Serving up an enjoyably crafted, commercially successful album in the warm months of every odd year, Brad Paisley has tasted fine to me since 1999, when I admired how confidently he opened for Loretta Lynn at Town Hall. A 26-year-old newcomer riding a good little debut few in Manhattan knew existed, he seemed more at home than she did. But I never expected he'd headline Madison Square Garden a decade later. As happens in Nashville, the hits that kept on coming were soon indistinguishable from genre exercises. Beyond the funny stuff—

great in "Me Neither," where he disavows a series of lame pickup lines as each is shot down, not so great in "Celebrity," where he lobs paintballs at a reality-show jerkola—what stood out most was his guitar, which got a showcase instrumental every time out. Genre exercises work fine in the country market as such, where "repository of tradition" is part of the job description. But the real America—right, I'm being arch, punch in "the typical American music consumer" if you like—expects forceful identities from its standard-bearers, and that goes double for dudes from the sticks.

So although Paisley was my favorite young male country artist, I pigeonholed him as a likable pro, thought of him seldom, and didn't notice when he got married in 2003. From the perspective of *American Saturday Night*, however, the marriage was a turning point. According to publicity myth, which I'm happy to believe, New York–born actress Kimberly Williams appeared to the young West Virginian as in a dream way back in 1995, when he went to see *Father of the Bride II* in the vain hope that he'd run into his high school sweetheart and was entranced by Williams's portrayal of the bride. After obsessing for a good long dry spell, during which he gathered material for songs like "Me Neither," Paisley invited Williams to co-star in the 2002 "I'm Gonna Miss Her" video, where the girl demands that Paisley choose between fishing and her and he chooses fishing. In the real America, however, he got both—far from giving up fishing after he tied the knot, he took the missis camping. The couple split their life between a farm near Nashville and a house in Malibu. They have two sons, the oldest born in 2007 and christened William Huckleberry—Huck for short.

Those nauseated by meet-cute stories should rest assured that a political angle is coming, one that culminated in Paisley entertaining an Obama soiree with bluegrass progressive Alison Krauss, his duet partner on the atypically tragic 2004 "Whiskey Lullabye," and Charley Pride, country music's only African-American star ever. (Paisley's Twitter response to the invite: "Sure we'll play? what time? Now where's your house again? 1600 Pennsylvania? Got it . . . do you have a p.a.? What about food?") Politics got me started on this album—the lead track, which only begins celebrating the ongoing mongrelization of America with the lines I quoted, and then "Welcome to the Future," inspired by

Barack Obama's victory and going out on a cross-burning tale in which a high school football star tries to date the homecoming queen. But the politics that kept me going were sexual politics, which proceed from a marriage that helped him put the genre exercise behind.

Paisley is remarkable among country stars for writing his own songs. But of course, that doesn't mean they're autobiographical. For one thing, he almost invariably collaborates, usually with buddies he's known since winning an ASCAP fellowship to Belmont University in Nashville. Paisley's 1999 breakthrough "He Didn't Have to Be," for instance, is based on Kelley Lovelace's experience as a stepfather, not either man's experience as a stepson. But don't think Paisley was just making nice when he promoted the artistic benefits of marriage to *Good House-keeping:* "Before, I had nothing to write about but failed relationships and life on the road. Now, I feel emotions more deeply in every sense."

There have always been country guys women swoon for—like Garth Brooks, paunch and all. And in a time when bad-ass macho powered Nashville new jacks like Montgomery Gentry and Toby Keith, Paisley's romantic come-ons had an appealing self-deprecation about them. But 2005's *Mud on the Tires* delivered something stronger: "Waitin' on a Woman," a song about how long they spend getting dressed, gender-based mortality rates, and if you stretch a little the elusiveness of female orgasm. Since then, Paisley has made the woman-friendly a mission—in a narrative voice more definitively his own.

That voice emerged on the two lookbacks at his naive youth that anchored 2007's *5th Gear:* "All I Wanted Was a Car," which does its partying with a fiddle and sets up "Letter to Me," where an older and wiser Brad assures his teenage self that the bad stuff is temporary, though he really should learn Spanish and give Aunt Rita some extra hugs. Both songs promised domestic satisfactions that included an SUV in the driveway. Deeper in came "If Love Was a Plane," about an American divorce rate Paisley reckons at 60 percent, and "It Did," about the ongoing perfection of love. Even the broad-jumping punch line of "Ticks"—"I'd like to walk you / Through a field of wild flowers / And I'd like to check you for ticks"—is more the kind of thing a husband murmurs to his wife on a fishing trip than a practical way for a singles-bar jerkola to get a butterfly tattoo into his vehicle.

5th Gear is the work of a master craftsman inspired to think about the shape of his life. Among its genre pieces are several born B sides and a soppy love duet with Carrie Underwood. But it establishes the foundation of a forceful identity. *American Saturday Night's* politics help flesh out that identity, but an even bigger breakthrough is a maturing craftsmanship that's learned how to address familiar themes in unfamiliar ways. If the breakup tales don't suit his happily married persona, their calm, loving substratum does. The marriage proposal "I Hope That's Me" knows it's him, promising the kindness already in place; "You Do the Math" works the same for sex. There's a lookback that mourns a grandpa as it fulfills Paisley's one-Christian-track-per-album quota, and another that looks ahead to Huck's mistakes. The boys'-day-out rumpus "Catch All the Fish" is counterbalanced by the almost metaphysical "Water." And then there are the three feminist songs.

Ideologues, cynics, and disappointed office seekers may balk at this characterization, especially as regards "Then." Its narrative hooked to the endlessly evolving refrain "I thought I loved you then," the album's first single updates "It Did." My wife Carola and I, together 30 years longer than Brad and Kimberly, had had a bad day when Paisley played the Garden October 21, but not with each other, and as he topped the show off by explaining how now he loved his spouse even more, we gripped each other's arms like teenagers in love. Avers Ms. Carola Dibbell, author of the groundbreaking "Inside Was Us: Women and Punk": "He notices all the things about marriage women are always complaining men don't notice." Given how many hits Paisley has, we forgave the omission of "She's Her Own Woman," a theme only strengthened by its unbraggadocious "and she's mine." But Carola was disappointed when the concert went out on Don Henley's "The Boys of Summer" instead of brandishing "The Pants," the subject of which is who wears them: "In the top drawer of her dresser there's some panties / Go try on that purple pair with the lacy frill / With your big old thighs I bet you can't get in 'em / With that attitude of yours, hell, I bet you never will."

Complete with the rowdy male choral farewell "You wear the pants / Buddy good for you / We're so impressed / Whoop-de-doo," "The Pants" is a typically sidelong gambit from an artist who knows how to sell simple truths to a resistant audience—a master of the catchy chorus, the phrase ratcheted up a notch, the joke only a teabagging jerkola could resent. And though that's easier with marriage songs, those soppy country staples that sometimes come as well-honed as Loretta Lynn's "One's on the Way" or Garth Brooks's "Unanswered Prayers," no country artist has ever been sharper about what connubial bliss entails. In part because it's untainted by the dread sentimentality and in part because it comes less naturally, the political stuff gets ink, as when Paisley got to tell *The Los Angeles Times*: "You can name the reasons why you feel America is the greatest country in the world, but the fact of the matter is that pretty much anything you name, aside from American Indian customs, was not indigenous—it was brought here." Note, however, that the title track of Tim McGraw's new *Southern Voice* is in-your-face biracial, that Toby Keith's new *American Ride* highlights a heartbroken tribute to his departed African-American buddy Wayman Tisdale—and that both trend-spotters, avowed Democrats unlike the "staunchly moderate" Paisley, purveyed jingoistic trash post-9/11. I say Paisley's sidelong pro-Obama songs proceed from a less opportunistic place, and that that place owes his particular marriage big-time.

It's not just that Kimberly Williams donated the max to Obama, but that this New Yorker was the woman a clear-eyed, fair-minded dude from the sticks wanted to share his life with—and even more important, helped turn that life into an American dream come true, a dream the marriage embodies and signifies. Paisley isn't pie-eyed. He tells the world that if love was a plane no one would get on; he even took marital counseling with his prospective bride. Yet by some grace of upbringing, good sense, and body chemistry, success has only intensified an optimism that preceded and enabled it. The dark and the anxious seem foreign to him, yet he's never smug—he's so self-deprecating, so funny. I've watched too many kids grow up to think all their lives turn out like "Letter to Me." But Paisley evinces so much more reach and imagination than the hard-ass thrice-removed of roots-rock convention. I love Johnny Cash. I love the Drive-By Truckers. But right now, as a decent, intellectually gifted chief executive struggles to keep hope alive, I love and need Brad Paisley even more.

The Madison Square Garden show was a two-hour knockout—amazing video, and even when Paisley was catching his breath and making jokes, he never stopped extracting riffs from his guitar, like Jimi Hendrix at the dinner table. But the top balconies were empty, and though "Welcome to the Future" went number 10 country—doubly remarkable given a shamelessly and intrepidly multicultural video that a priori nauseated some of his market—its sales didn't approach those of "Then." Like Paisley's nine previous singles, "Then" went number one, a record. Admittedly, Paisley shares that record with the anodyne likes of Alabama and Ronnie Milsap. But if us sophisticates don't figure out that optimism isn't always anodyne, this nation will never be as unified and forward-looking as we supposedly want—and hope.

Mexican Bands Hear Success Calling

Josh Kun

One of the biggest Latin hits of the past year arrived on the Billboard charts all the way from Caborca, a small desert hill town in the Mexican state of Sonora, mostly thanks to a cellphone.

Last year Los Pikadientes de Caborca recorded "La Cumbia del Río"—a bare-boned singalong about dancing and partying by the side of a local river—on a home computer, uploaded it to their cellphones and, with help from Bluetooth and Memory Sticks, shared it with friends. The song quickly went viral, and its grass-roots popularity led to heavy rotation on radio stations across Sonora; before long, cellphone videos of people dancing to the song were flooding YouTube.

Los Pikadientes had no record label, but suddenly they were the digital darlings of regional Mexican music, with a hit on both sides of the border.

Sony offered the band a record deal and rereleased "La Cumbia del Río," which spent six weeks at No. 1 on Billboard's Regional Mexican chart. The song's ring tone sold more than 150,000 copies in the United States, and the band released a debut album, "Vámonos Pa'l Río," which was nominated for a 2008 Grammy. The song is still on the Latin charts.

"We have to be honest; we wouldn't exist without cellphones and ring tones," said Francisco Gonzalez (who goes by the single name Pancho) of Los Pikadientes, whose new album is scheduled for June, complete with an elaborate ring-tone marketing plan. "We ended up doing eight months of promotion in the United States because of that one song. We're the ultimate cellphone success story."

As most sectors of the music industry scramble to cope with the way the Internet and online stores like iTunes have changed how music is distributed and consumed, the regional Mexican industry is focused elsewhere, on the power of the cellphone as both a one-stop music source and a symbol of working-class immigrant identity. This is no small news, considering that in the United States regional Mexican music—the term is an industry label that groups together norteño, ranchera, banda and other traditional styles—is responsible for close to 70 percent of all Latin sales, outperforming all other genres of Latin music, including pop and tropical.

"Our songwriters used to only want to write for pop artists," said Delia Orjuela, assistant vice president for Latin music at the performing rights organization BMI. "Now they all want to write for regional Mexican artists. This is a direct result of demographics. Mexicans are everywhere now."

Because fans of regional Mexican music tend to be working-class immigrants and their United States–born children, they don't fit the typical musical consumption patterns of the digital age. They are less likely to own a home computer, less likely to use a credit card for online purchases and less likely to have broadband at home, all prerequisites for an iTunes account. Instead they buy prepaid phone cards with cash and use their cellphones as mobile, personal jukeboxes, often downloading ring tones from their cellular providers for about $3 each, three times the price from iTunes or Zune.

"This audience has adopted the mobile phone as their primary means of communication," said Oliver Buckwell of the marketing agency Tribal Brands, which has set up deals between Verizon and regional Mexican acts. "It is also now their primary means of getting music."

In the Anglo market the majority of digital sales takes place online; in regional Mexican music an estimated 85 percent of digital music is purchased on cellphones.

"This is a very mobile population," said Michael Grasso, a former vice president for consumer marketing at AT&T, where he set up sponsorships with Mexican artists like Joan Sebastian and Marco Antonio Solis. "As consumers their behaviors depend on communication with family who might not be in the same state or same country as they are. They have national and international behaviors, local lines and shared content that go between countries on a daily basis. Phones are the easiest way to keep those family connections together."

Sensing the rising power of regional Mexican music's fan base and keeping an eye on general Latin consumer trends (Latinos were twice as likely as non-Latinos to purchase ring tones in 2008), every major phone company has made deals with regional Mexican acts: sponsoring concert tours, offering "mobile tickets" to shows, bundling song downloads and ring tones with phone subscriptions and selling phone cards emblazoned with the faces of popular bands like Los Temerarios everywhere from Wal-Mart to weekend swap meets. (Call to collect your minutes, and a member of the band greets you.) While AT&T began sponsoring tours in 2004, only now is there unanimous agreement among phone companies that regional Mexican is central to the future of mobile music.

"We see regional Mexican fans as the gateway to educating all U.S. consumers about mobile music," said Ed Ruth, the director of digital music at Verizon, which is expected to announce a new mobile music deal this month at the Billboard Latin Music Conference. "Because they have a higher tendency to access content on their phones, they are more open to trying new products and to new ways of engaging with their favorite artists."

Late last year Verizon—which introduced its V Cast mobile music platform in 2006—spearheaded a deal with the popular telenovela "Fuego en la Sangre," precisely because of its regional Mexican fan base. The show starred the singer and heartthrob Pablo Montero, and its opening theme was "Para Siempre," a popular ranchera ballad by the Mexican star Vicente Fernández. Verizon held concerts with Mr. Montero in its stores, where select customers could appear with him in a music video, shot against a green screen and then sent directly to their Verizon phones.

"Phone carriers are more interested in regional Mexican than any other genre," said Skander Goucha, vice president for digital at Universal Music Latin Entertainment. "No other genre has that kind of mobile sales." He added that the sales of a ring tone for a single by Alacranes Musical, a popular Mexican act from Chicago, were in the Top 20 of all Universal ring tones, which "puts them right up there next to Akon and Fall Out Boy."

Of course fans of Alacranes Musical might also be fans of Akon and Fall Out Boy, especially if they're second-generation and raised on a steady binational diet of Mexican and American sounds. For these younger listeners, born in the United States, keeping regional Mexican songs on their cellphone is an easy way to maintain family roots.

"Feeling like you're close to home is so important for Mexican audiences," said Leila Cobo, Billboard's executive director for Latin content. "In recent years it's stopped being taboo to be Latin or Mexican. Assimilation is not the only option. For the younger fans it's cool to like these artists and be proud of where you're from."

That phone companies and ring-tone providers are paying attention to this trend is a change from what many in the Mexican music industry characterize as years of willful, often culturally biased neglect from marketing and advertising agencies. Despite their commercial success, few norteño or banda artists—with their cowboy hats, horses, accordions and tubas—typically end up with the kind of major marketing and advertising deals that go to artists like Shakira or Enrique Iglesias, who embrace a more cross-cultural look and sound.

"The decision makers who sit atop the major marketing companies tend to be people who do not understand the depth and importance of this community," said Peggy Dold, a freelance marketing consultant and former international vice president at the Spanish-language media giant Univision. "With cellphones that's all starting to change."

This summer, Verizon will release a new EP from Los Tigres del Norte, the Northern California group that has been a regional Mexican institution for decades, that will only be available on mobile phones. Back in 1992 Los Tigres recorded what was probably the first Mexican tribute to the cellphone, "El Celular." The lyrics treated the new device as both status symbol and social nuisance, and in the song's video a primitive cellphone the size of a sneaker upstaged the band everywhere from the golf course to the nightclub.

"In those days not everyone could afford a cellphone," said Jorge Hernández, the band's singer. "Now all of our fans have them, and they're a big part of their identity. They've made us change the way we think about our music.

"Before we worried about getting the physical CDs into the little neighborhood stores. Now we worry about getting our songs onto those phones."

BeauSoleil
Beau Brothers

Geoffrey Himes

Back in 1986, when BeauSoleil was first starting to tour a lot outside Louisiana, back when the Doucet brothers still had a bit of hair atop their heads, the band played at the Kennedy Center, Washington's red-carpeted bastion of high culture. BeauSoleil was just a quartet in those days—Michael Doucet on fiddle, David Doucet on acoustic guitar, Errol Verret on accordion and Billy Ware on triangle and rubboard—and when the four musicians looked out over the East Coasters sunken in their seats, the Louisianans shook their heads.

"It's okay to dance," Michael joked. "This is dance music." The audience smiled but didn't budge. Most of them knew little about Cajun music; they had come to see the touring Newport Folk Festival package, and BeauSoleil was just an exotic attraction they were checking out. Michael made another joke, but beneath the humor was nervousness. It wasn't just that the listeners weren't dancing; they were paying rapt, quiet attention, which can be unnerving for a band used to Louisiana dance halls.

After all, if you're playing a dance, you don't have to worry about the subtleties of the music because they'll get lost amid the chatter and the bustling bodies. What really matters is the energy and the thump. But at the Kennedy Center, every nuance was suddenly exposed in the eerie quiet. The energy and the thump could work for a few songs, but if people aren't dancing, they want to hear something else before too long. It was an intimidating situation, but it was also an opportunity.

"We realized we could reach a new audience," David says. "We'd been playing for Cajun dancers and your folk music types, but when we played these performing arts centers, we had a more diverse audience, so we wanted our music to be more diverse. We wanted to sound like a Cajun band on stuff that wasn't the usual Cajun band material. We had to work at it, but the effort paid off. Even though we're still pegged as a Cajun dance band today, people are surprised when they hear what we can do."

Every Louisiana act that tours a lot outside the state faces the same dilemma: Should they stick to their dance-band roots, refusing to compromise on the social nature of the state's music, or should they expand their scope, giving themselves a chance to grow as composers, arrangers and improvisers? No one has finessed this challenge better than Beau-Soleil, which in its 35th year, manages to shine as both a dance band and a concert act.

Nothing better demonstrates the group's duality than the new album, *Alligator Purse*, BeauSoleil's first release on the roots-rock label, Yep Roc Records. It was another gig outside Louisiana that led to the album. Michael Pillot, an old friend of Michael and Tommy's from the University of Southern Louisiana, had gone on to become a successful producer of music TV and film. When the levees buckled beneath Katrina in 2005, Pillot organized a "Build a Levee" benefit concert at Bard College in New York's Hudson River Valley for December 3. Pillot asked Michael to join an eclectic group of players that included Merchant, Sebastian, Rudd, Crooked Still's Rushad Eggleston, Hot Rize's Nick Forster, Artie Traum and Dr. John.

"It was a magical night," Michael says. "I didn't know these people, but if you wanted to play with someone, you just sat in. And when you did, it felt real comfortable. So when some of them played on the new album, they didn't feel like guest artists, because they were people I'd already played with and hung out with."

It seemed natural to return to the Hudson Valley to cut the new tracks with Pillot as producer. It was good to get out of Louisiana, David claims, because when you're away from home it feels more like work.

You can concentrate on the job at hand without worrying about the busted plumbing or crying kid at home. The challenge, though, was how to differentiate this release from the 21 albums that came before it. This is always the hurdle for acts with an identifying sound: If listeners already have an album with that sound, why do they need another?

"It's like that quote from *Rolling Stone*: 'Ho hum, another great Richard Thompson record,'" says Michael. "How could they say that? But that's what you're facing. Why do another BeauSoleil record when the record industry's collapsing? So you push yourself into territory you've never been before. You record with people you haven't recorded with before. I wasn't worried about them throwing us off because we're so strong. We always have a groove, so when people come in they get absorbed into that groove, like spice absorbed into the gumbo."

Michael wanted more songs in English this time, but he didn't want to translate traditional Cajun songs into English. Instead, he wanted to take pre-existing English songs and Cajunize them. Bobby Charles' "I Spent All My Money Loving You" was a natural because Charles' swamp pop was merely a new extension of Cajun music, just as BeauSoleil's music has been. J.J. Cale may be from Oklahoma, but his music has always had a swampy tinge. And "Little Darlin'" was almost a Cajun song already.

"Our ancestors came down from Nova Scotia with a fiddle," declares Joel Savoy, the Red Stick Ramblers' ex-fiddler and current head of the Grammy-nominated Cajun label, Valcour Records. "Eventually they met up with German people who played the accordion and they added that to Cajun music. Then they met some Texans who played country swing music, and they added that, too.

"Now that a lot of people are coming to Louisiana to learn Cajun music, they get caught up in preserving Cajun music as it is rather than letting it become what it wants to be, which will always be a product of what's happening in Louisiana at the moment. Michael can play just like any of the old masters he learned from, but at the same time if he wants to add something to his improvisation, he can draw from all those things he has in his head from a lifetime of listening to all kinds of music."

"It's gone beyond, 'Oh, let's play another traditional song,'" Michael says. "That's been done. I did all that work in the '70s, reestablishing this tradition and that's great. People think these songs just fell out of the sky, but a lot of work went into them—and there's still a lot of work left to be done in continuing to develop our music and our history. It's not like we said, 'This is the concept; let's do this.' You just sit back and see what happens. When you do that, it just opens up."

Michael's point is a crucial one: Allowing new influences into Louisiana music is not the unnatural, gimmicky thing to do; keeping them out is. If you're a virtuoso fiddler you don't stop yourself from playing bebop changes or Haitian syncopation just because earlier Cajun fiddlers didn't. If you're a virtuoso guitarist like David, you don't stop yourself from playing lead breaks just because Cajun guitarists never did that before. If you're a virtuoso drummer like Tommy Alesi, you don't stop yourself from adding embellishments to the primary thump out of fear some dancer will lose track of the counting he or she learned at a Cajun dance camp in West Virginia. If Cajun music is meant to reflect the people of South Louisiana, it has to change as those people change.

"If you add a jazz solo or a funk beat to a Cajun or zydeco song," David argues, "you're not betraying the music. You're adding to it. That's how you serve the music. You don't encapsulate it in a certain time; you help it grow. Texas swing wasn't a part of Cajun music until musicians in the 1930s started adding it, and before long everyone was doing it. It's not leaving the past behind, it's adding to it. Not every idea works. When I'm playing solo, I tell myself, 'Let's see if this works.' If it works, you keep it. If it doesn't, you finish the song and move on."

When bringing new influences into a tradition, however, it is essential that musicians follow the principle of addition rather than substitution. If you substitute a new practice for an old one—substituting "Quiet Storm" R&B for 6/8 ballads, say, or "Dirty South" rap for carnival street chants or jazz violin for Cajun fiddle—you often lose far more than you gain. But if you keep the old as you add the new—and do the necessary work to make the two blend, *then* you've made a step forward. If you tackle a terrific piece of Americana such as Julie Miller's "Little Darlin'" and invite Natalie Merchant and John Sebastian to add vocals and harmonica respectively, it's necessary to hold on to what you had before: the push-and-pull of Tommy's two-step beat, the swampy drone of Michael's fiddle and the springy bounce of David's guitar breaks. That's just what BeauSoleil does on *Alligator Purse.*

That's also just what it did when it played the "Grand Reopening" of the New Orleans Mulate's after Katrina on April 27, 2006. It was Mitch Reed's first show with the band as the official new bassist and second fiddler (replacing Al Tharp, who was devoting himself to his first love, old-time Appalachian music—the band's first roster change since 1989). Filling out the line-up were the Doucet brothers, Billy Ware, Tommy Alesi and button accordionist Jimmy Breaux. Michael wore a loud, blue-print beach shirt and faded jeans; his shiny bald dome was flanked by two snowy tufts above his ears and anchored by a pointy white goatee. Behind him was the restaurant's famous logo: a painting of the early-1980s BeauSoleil when the Doucet brothers had darker hair and more of it.

The sextet quickly demonstrated how they could appeal to active dancers and seated listeners at the same time. Surrounding the dance floor on three sides were tables where diners, mostly out-of-towners, sat entranced by the dizzying solos from the Doucet brothers and Jimmy Breaux.

Standing just outside of the kitchen door off to the band's left was Bob Dylan. He slouched within his jacket, his curls stuffed inside a brown stocking cap, as if no one would recognize him, and standing next to his longtime bassist Tony Garnier. His Bobness didn't join the dancing, but he seemed as mesmerized by a Cajunized "Baby, Please Don't Go," as the tourists lingering over their bread pudding.

The song, an old blues that Dylan himself had often played early in his career, had slowed down so all those minor-key chords had time to bleed into the forlorn cry of first Michael's high-register fiddle and then his voice: "Baby, please don't go back to New Orleans; you know I love you so." Jimmy's button accordion squeezed out the droning, hypnotic riff, while Michael played jazzy lines on top. For all the deliberate tempo and ominous harmonies, however, Tommy, Billy and Mitch still delayed the beat a split second and then pounced on it with a syncopated snap, keeping the couples moving on the floor. How many other bands could satisfy dancers, tourists and Bob Dylan all on the same song?

"Last year we played this gig at Nunu's in Arnaudville, north of Lafayette," David says. "I was sitting there eating gumbo after the gig, and this guy came up to me and said, 'I never listened to you guys before. I thought you just played that traditional music that no one likes.' I had to laugh because we'd just played a bunch of traditional tunes on traditional instruments. Sure, you borrow licks and ideas from other music, and you blend those in with what you already know. It's always going to sound a little Cajun, because you inevitably put yourself into it and you're a Cajun.

"People don't know why we sound different, but that's why it is. When you learn a song, you don't have to play it the way you learned it. It wouldn't have been as fun for the past 35 years if we had just played the songs the way we'd learned them. I don't think the guys before us played the songs the way they learned them. You can't tell me Dewey Balfa played songs the way he learned them. Or Nathan Abshire."

BeauSoleil is doing what Cajun musicians have always done: they're listening to the radio in their heads and turning it into new Cajun music. But it has a different playlist than the radio in Dennis McGee's head or D.L. Menard's head. The radio in their heads plays rock 'n' roll, Caribbean music, jazz, swamp pop and more, so why shouldn't they make Cajun music with Garth Hudson and Roswell Rudd or with a Bobby Charles song?

"The cats I learned to play from—Dennis McGee and Canray Fontenot—are gone," Michael points out. "We paid homage to them for years—we were the first modern Cajun band to record a Dennis McGee song, to play an Amede Ardoin song, to play zydeco—but we're getting older; we're speaking in English now. The world here in Louisiana has changed; it's not the same place it was even 30 years ago."

It's a measure of the way the Doucet brothers think that when they heard a version of "Les Oignons" by Don Vappie, they immediately heard the connections between this New Orleans street chant in Haitian French and Michael's own composition, "Valse a BeauSoleil," a blues waltz in Cajun-French. If John Sebastian of the Lovin' Spoonful could play harmonica on the latter for the new album, why couldn't jazz trombonist Roswell Rudd play on the former?

After all, Rudd had been a Dixieland revivalist before playing with such avant-gardists as Cecil Taylor, Steve Lacy and Archie Shepp. Rudd understood how Dixieland contained the potential for free jazz just as Michael understood how South Louisiana's dance halls contained the potential for concert music. They got along so famously that Rudd invited BeauSoleil to play on two tracks for his next album. It's these unexpected connections that keep the band pushing forward into new music rather than resting on familiar ways. They can try anything because they never have to worry about their essential identity.

"Bands are not just the type of music they play," insists David. "It's how they play. Michael Pillot told us, 'You're known as a Cajun band, but you play a lot more than that.' We do, but we're still a Cajun band because that's *how* we play. Michael may like Caribbean music; Tommy may like jazz; Jimmy may like country; I may like old-time acoustic music, but when we play together, we sound like a Cajun band because we play this other music in our own way. We can have John Sebastian singing backup on a rock 'n' roll song that Michael translated into French, and it still sounds Cajun. How cool is that?"

On the Road to Burma

Globetrotting with Ozomatli, Unlikely U.S. Diplomats

Randall Roberts

Four days into a five-day tour of Rangoon, Burma, we thought we'd had our fill of weirdness. But after Ozomatli are led through Kawechan School for the Blind's darkened hallways and up a flight of stairs, the sound of a flailing guitar solo and the thump of a bass drum punch through the corridor. Around a corner, standing on a stage, four conservatively dressed men wearing sunglasses and matching pink-and-blue polo-type shirts are banging out a rock song. They look like a '60s surf band, the Ventures or something—square and stiff.

Ozomatli, a band born in Los Angeles in 1996, are scheduled to perform a few songs for students, orphans and disabled kids as part of an outreach program arranged by the U.S. Department of State. They didn't count on any competition, and they watch from the side as a band called Blind Reality, facing 100 people of varying degrees of disability, creates a chaotic, freakazoid sound that only four sightless rock dudes living in the pocket of one of the world's most beaten-down countries could possibly make.

New-genre alert: Burmese blind-metal.

Ulises Bella's jaw drops. Wil-Dog Abers gasps, and Raúl Pacheco, a thoughtful former Tom Hayden political intern with "Chicano" tattooed on the back of his hand, witnesses, eyes agape, as the guitarist does a double-fingered fret run that would make Eddie Van Halen shift uncomfortably in his seat. The members of Ozomatli have a catalog of mind-blowing images stored from the two years they've been working as musical diplomats for the U.S. Department of State, but this one surely ranks: an expert Blind Reality guitarist whose main influences, he will tell the band, are fretboard gymnasts Yngwie Malmsteen and Steve Vai.

As if Blind Reality couldn't take it any further, after a mean cover of a Bon Jovi song, a lady guest vocalist, also wearing sunglasses, is led slowly to the microphone stand. She touches it with her hand and, the room silent, moves into Creedence Clearwater Revival's "Have You Ever Seen the Rain?" She sings the words in Burmese: "Someone told me long ago / There's a calm before the storm / I know, it's been coming for some time / When it's over, so they say / It'll rain a sunny day / I know, shining down like water."

"Getting up there and seeing these four blind dudes just killing it? I never witnessed anything like that in my life," says Ozo percussionist and MC Justin "El Niño" Porée a few days later.

Ozo sets up, still buzzing from that lightning-bolt moment. Even in a little corner of the world with way bigger concerns than one-up-manship, pride enters the equation when an opening band smokes it. Soon the seven in Ozomatli—guitar, bass, percussion, drums, keyboard, saxophone, trumpet—are playing hard, their rhythms running through the room. A row of children with Down syndrome bounce and fidget; blind kids in middle rows direct their ears at the music and absorb it. Nurses in the back smile.

It's after the first couple of songs that a man sandwiched in the second or third row starts making a commotion. It's not clear whether he's having problems or is somehow disturbed. He's contorted with what looks to be cerebral palsy, and is struggling to stand. Ozomatli watch from the stage, swinging to their poppy hit "After Party." Grasping his neighbors' shoulders, the guy pushes his way toward the aisle, arms taut, legs and torso cockeyed, and moves to the empty space in front of the stage. Bella bursts forth with a tenor-sax solo.

Then, as if plugged into a socket, the man starts flailing his arms with the rhythm, a look of joyful determination on his face, bouncing at his knees, punching as he fights to remain balanced while tabla player Jiro Yamaguchi, Porée and longtime Ozomatli drummer Mario Calire offer a cumbia rhythm. You know the iconic image of the man facing down tanks in Tiananmen Square? Imagine the opposite: An observer standing before an invisible force, willfully getting plowed over.

After the gig, the handshakes and the photos, Ozomatli load back in the van and wave goodbye, a little bit different in the head from before.

When you drive along the boulevards of Rangoon in a white late-model Chevy van, you might as well be rolling in a polka dot Rolls Royce. Monks in saffron robes rubberneck and nudge their companions. At stoplights, as we idle next to old pickup trucks retrofitted to be people-movers, riders in the back and on the bumpers crane their necks to look with kind but curious eyes. In a country in which even a junky compact car costs $25,000 and anything new will run you at least $100,000 after licensing fees and kickbacks, a fresh U.S. government–issue Chevy is something to behold.

The van moves in dense traffic through roundabouts and curving lefts and rights, past Inya Lake, where, three days earlier, an American named John Yettaw had been arrested on its southern shore after swimming to Aung San Suu Kyi's compound. A few kilometers later, the Schwedagon Pagoda, constructed a few millennia ago to house eight strands of the Buddha's hair, appears like a hallucination. Shimmering in the morning sun with a new coat of gold leaf, the bell-shaped pagoda looks like it was on loan from another—better—planet.

The first stop of an early-May, three-country U.S.–sponsored tour that ultimately takes Ozomatli to Vietnam and Thailand, Burma will jar even the most jaded travelers. One of our guides warns us that the country is at least 20 years behind the rest of civilization; soon thereafter we drive past a billboard excitedly advertising the arrival of a new Yellow Pages. The name of the country's most beloved leader, Aung San Suu Kyi, is forbidden from being spoken aloud; rather, she is known simply as "The Lady." The exchange rate of American currency is based as much on the cleanliness of the bill as on what numbers are on it. Hand the hotel receptionist a crinkled or torn $100, and you may as well have just handed her a leaf.

In addition to the moment-to-moment oddities, it has been a strange few days for the band—and the country. On the same day that Yettaw is pulled from the lake and Ozomatli arrive in Burma, two American journalists traveling in Mandalay, to the north, are detained by Burmese immigration authorities. The week of Ozomatli's tour of Burma is also the first anniversary of Cyclone Nargis. The storm, thought to be the most deadly natural disaster in the country's recorded history, killed an estimated 100,000 people.

And if that weren't enough weight, the house-arrest sentence of Suu Kyi, the leader of the National League for Democracy, who has been confined to her compound on Inya Lake for 13 of the past 19 years, is up for renewal in a few weeks. The Lady won the Nobel Peace Prize in 1991. She's a living symbol of the prodemocracy movement in Burma but is imprisoned under the orders of the military junta that controls the country. She is allowed no visitors, save for her doctor, and her home is guarded 24 hours a day. This is one reason that many nations refuse to recognize the legitimacy of the junta, or the new name it has chosen for the country—Myanmar.

Richard Mei, chief public-affairs officer in Burma for the U.S. Department of State, doesn't know whether any of these factors—the swimmer, the journalists' detention, the anniversary—are connected, or whether Ozomatli's visit has anything to do with any of it. But news and rumors of the curious happenings have wormed their way into the heads of the American visitors, their State Department guides and the two Burmese translators assigned to serve as Ozomatli's attachés.

Mei, a tall Asian-American born in Queens, has a simple catchall explanation for anything that occurs in his oft-baffling station: "This is Burma. Strange things can happen."

Ozomatli have already traveled the world a few times over, and Burma is just the latest hot spot. Since 2007, the Grammy winners, born of protest rallies in East L.A. in 1996 as a 10-piece salsa/cumbia/ hip-hop/rock amalgam, have been playing cultural-outreach gigs at the behest—and with the support—of the U.S. government. On past travels, they've been escorted in a bulletproof SUV through a Palestinian refugee camp in Jordan and asked by a little boy, who confused the band with U.S. soldiers: "How come you let your friends kill my little brother?" They've played songs to kids rescued from an Indian orphanage that was a front for a child-prostitution ring. Guitarist Pacheco was nearly electrocuted onstage in Madagascar.

These tours occurred during the Bush administration, at a time when the last thing a left-leaning Chicano/Jewish/Black/Whatever band from the hood wanted was to be known as enablers for an embattled Republican government.

But if there's one thing the band has learned on these State Department–organized tours, it's that the closer you are to situations, the more murky the so-called "politics" become. When Ozomatli were first approached to participate in these outreaches, some of the most forceful U.S.-government advocates for Asian cultural and democratic efforts were former first lady Laura Bush and then–Under Secretary for Public Affairs Karen Hughes.

The fact that longtime Bush cheerleader Hughes once danced to your band in D.C. isn't something you want the Ozoheadz in Boulder to catch wind of. When the band hit the ground on their first missions, though, they were greeted by America's midlevel public-affairs officers, outreach organizers and charity workers, and realized that left, right and center mingle more than they imagined.

Jack Healey was president of Amnesty International for 12 years, founded the Washington, D.C.–based Human Rights Action Center, which works with the U.S. Campaign for Burma, an advocacy group. In April 2008, Healey met with the National Security Agency at the White House. What he saw surprised him: "The Bush people—and I hate the sons of bitches—but on this topic, they were as good as you could be."

Wil-Dog Abers first hooked up with his eventual Burma entourage at Ozomatli's debut outreach program there, at the tiny Gitameit Music Center in the Moe Kaung Yankin township, a labyrinthine, *Slumdog*-type neighborhood in Rangoon. The building is surrounded by a tangle of dirt pathways and makeshift avenues lined on both sides by one- and two-story homes that look like rural fruit stands.

The posse thing was bound to happen. Ozomatli's bassist and co-founder, Wil-Dog, as he's known to everyone (his mom goes by Mom-Dog), is a big personality and loves playing to kids. Wil-Dog perhaps knows more about Mexican music than any other Jew on the West Coast, but his first love was punk rock. He got a taste of a future when, as an 11-year-old with a Mohawk, he was taken by his Communist-activist parents to see the Clash at the Hollywood Palladium. "That was it," he says. "I knew that night I would be doing this." He treasures the notion that he could be a Joe Strummer to some Burmese kid.

Wil-Dog spots his Rangoon posse, a half-dozen 5-year-old students, in a second-floor recital room that feels like a jungle tree house. Five girls and a boy, they're poised before music stands, with baby violins on their shoulders. The lessons here cost $15 a month, which seems a pittance until you learn that the average annual income throughout the country is less than $300, and probably far less in this neighborhood. They stare at the sheet music, and with great concentration they scratch out an oblong melody. When it's done, the band applauds, and Wil-Dog is officially smitten.

Afterward, Ozomatli and the students walk down to an adjoining performance space about the size of an Appalachian church. It isn't Glastonbury, Coachella or Kathmandu, but when the band, standing on a small stage, begin their "Ya Viene El Sol," a melodic, Latin-tinged pop song with rolling rhythms and the joyous and eruptive voice of lead Ozo vocalist Asdru Sierra, the eyes in the audience emit a warm glow, and the little boys and girls immediately become enrapt, as though they're watching a favorite movie. Soon, Wil-Dog is in front of them, playing bass and doing funny dances along with the song, bouncing and clapping like a clown and making the six giggle.

After the show, the kids and their teacher, an elegant Burmese woman carrying a sun umbrella, take the band on a tour of the neighborhood, and the reality of the children's situation reveals itself. Seldom do the residents of this village see Westerners, let alone Latinos, and as we walk dirt paths lined with open sewers, skinny dogs tromp alongside and people peek out of their doorways and look at the Americans blankly.

We learn later that what we did during the hourlong stroll—videotape and photograph the state of the Burma ghettos—was dangerous. Unaware, we pointed and shot, waved as we walked the paths, an eerie silence giving the feel of some sort of postmeltdown dystopia. Ozo's sound guy, Eduardo "Mack" MacKinlay, remembers the silence, but even more, he was struck by the mysterious theraminlike music emanating from somewhere within many of the homes and food stands, like the soundtrack of some horror movie.

Music is perfectly legal in Burma, as long as any song you write or perform is first approved by the Scrutiny Board—the state censors. But video cameras are a dangerous technology here, one used as a weapon by the junta's minions to document dissident activities; shoved in the faces of protesters in a malicious attempt at quelling dissent; smuggled out of the country by democratic activists to document protests—and aimed at American bands walking through alleyway markets by men straddling mopeds.

"That was the most surreal moment, walking through that neighborhood," recalls sax player Bella, talking about our guides' concern that operatives were watching us. "It almost seemed unbelievable, to a degree. Like, 'Bullshit, there's people keeping track of us through this neighborhood? Yeah, right.' But then, that's not our reality."

The regime has a right to be paranoid, as do its people, because their reality is different. Our two translators, a man and a woman, were careful about what they said. In the restaurant on our first night, our male guide was very nervous. Ozomatli manager Amy Blackman recalls saying something and the guide replying quietly, "People are watching and listening." In the hotel, he'd hardly say anything. At an outdoor market restaurant, and especially in our vans, however, both were much more talkative.

During one window of opportunity, the male guide told the band that when Cyclone Nargis hit last year, none of the Burmese people knew of its impending arrival, even though satellite images predicted its path. Nargis was all the more destructive because of the suddenness of its arrival. Along Burma's 1,200-mile coastline, few saw it coming. It hit, then passed, and time stopped.

Over the following days and weeks, the State Peace and Development Council, the name of the 11-general junta that governs the country, refused all offers of foreign aid. In the Count Basie Room at the American Center in Rangoon, there are of the disaster children's drawings that will hurt your heart: of big stick figures stranded in palm trees and littler figures drowning in scribbled water below. In a country where one in three children is chronically malnourished, the cyclone was a hit matched only by the blowback realization that its rulers care more about perceived threats from abroad than helping their people.

Eight months before the natural disaster, the SPDC was on the butt end of a political disaster. In September 2007, the Buddhist clergy marched through Rangoon in an unprecedented show of civil disobedience to protest the government's gasoline price hikes. Over the next two weeks the monks created a sea of saffron robes along the roads surrounding the Schwedagon Pagoda. The monks were soon joined by citizens, who marched to Aung San Suu Kyi's residence.

Then came the obligatory shielded-soldier crackdown, troops locked in rows marching at unarmed monks. In the ensuing violence, captured by renegade video journalists and uploaded to networks across the globe (the subject of the Academy Award–nominated documentary, *Burma VJ*), security forces breached a line they had never before crossed: They beat monks. In the weeks to follow, SPDC officers arrested a few thousand more, many of whom remain locked up.

Human Rights Action Center's Healey says that the cyclone and the military actions reveal the potential for change. "Any respect that was left for the military, among the young soldiers in particular, and among the young in general, is gone. That they didn't take care of the people drowning? Huge loss of respect. When they hurt the monks, chased them to the border, tortured them, that's a big break. So there's a tipping point possible that isn't seen outside. The people are ready to go."

Guitarist Raúl Pacheco knows a little bit about organizing The People. Before joining Ozomatli, he spent nearly five years in Sacramento, working for politicians. In the early 1990s he landed a job in Willie Brown's state Assembly office, and interned with former state senator and democratic activist Tom Hayden. The word Chicano, written in neat cursive on Pacheco's left hand, makes him look like a gangbanger. But he's the polar opposite, warm and soft-spoken. He toured Burma while reading Gabriel Garcia Márquez' autobiography and letters Aung San Suu Kyi wrote in the mid-1990s.

While Suu Kyi was crafting those letters from a home prison, Pacheco was getting resettled in L.A., intent on writing about Chicano politics. He started volunteering at the L.A.-based People's Union for Democratic Rights, organizing an afterschool program for kids, and decided to play music again. So he called up Ozomatli's then-drummer and asked about a gig. "He said, 'Come to the Peace and Justice Center. We're gonna start making music.'"

Asdru Sierra, who was a kid in South-Central when they sent the National Guard in, was there. Sierra started singing when he was young, then moved on to trumpet and keyboards—music was always around. His grandfather had been signed to RCA-Victor in Mexico, his father and uncles were professional musicians. Sierra followed the music to CalArts. Ozomatli's mission fit right in with his aesthetic: "It was raw and undefined, but it had so much passion, and it was fun. We could bring any instrument, any idea and any style of music and no one would judge you."

Ulises Bella grew up a trench-coated punk rocker in the blue-collar East L.A. township of Bell and fell in with the ska crowd in his teens. He played saxophone with Yeska, whose stated goal was "to be the Latin *Skatalites.*" Yeska was getting great gigs in the mid-'90s, and Ozo was Bella's second band. The two outfits would gig together at the Viper Room, and as Ozo's star rose, Bella quit Yeska to commit full-time.

Wil-Dog had followed Joe Strummer's lead, moving from punk to hip-hop, and became the persistent center of the band, one whose dubby and funky bass-playing is the perfect reflection of his demeanor, open and honest, filled with enthusiasm for the adventure of it all. He invited percussionist Porée to jam with Ozo, but Porée was skeptical. "The thing that caught me, though, was when he said, 'I got turntables and tablas,'" Porée says. On practice day, he walked in to see Yamaguchi and DJ Cut Chemist, one of the city's preeminent turntablists, practicing. "I was, like, this is insanity, but this is dope. How can I not be a part of this?"

From early protest gigs, Ozo sold out residencies at the Viper Room and Opium Den with lines stretching down the Sunset Strip. The band signed to a label called Almo Sounds, the post-A&M project of Herb Alpert and Jerry Moss, and released their anthemic, self-titled debut, which established them as one of the go-to bands of the so-called "Latin rock" scene. They've won two Grammys and a Latin Grammy. The awards have fed more opportunity, especially in a changing media landscape trying to adapt to the much-belated realization that the Spanish-speaking markets were not only demographically ignored but also that television shows need funky Latino music to support certain scenes.

Blackman says when the band is feeling jaded, they call their demographic niche "Spanish-language music for gringos," a truth that they've all had to grudgingly accept. The band itself has appeared in an episode of *Sex and the City* and performed on last season's *Dancing With the Stars*. "NBC loves their stuff," Blackman says. They've done *CSI, Ugly Betty, Shark, Las Vegas*. HBO used "Saturday Night" for their fall promos; the Los Angeles Lakers use their song "City of Angels" a lot. Last week they performed "Afterparty" on *The Today Show*, and Al Roker did his funkiest dance.

"They've become their own paradigm," Blackman says. "Supervisors will say, 'I need some upbeat, Latinesque, party-sounding Ozo-like music in this scene.' It's like they are their own genre, in a way."

It was this so-called paradigm that attracted the State Department's Bureau of Public Affairs, via a broadcast on one of America's most popular gringo news outlets, National Public Radio. A department official had heard an interview with the band, and was looking for an act to perform in different parts of the world where the bureau believed it might send a message.

Blackman did a little research on the history of the government's cultural-diplomacy efforts, and what she learned helped her to make a case to the band. Beginning in the 1950s, President Dwight D. Eisenhower started what was to become a landmark series of globetrotting musical programs sponsored by the Department of State. Among those who traveled on the 20-year program were Dizzy Gillespie, Duke Ellington, Count Basie and Louis Armstrong.

"The State Department still kind of looks back and admires what they did in the '50s and '60s with Gillespie and Louis Armstrong, and Dave Brubeck and all these people," says Tim Receveur of the Bureau of International Information Programs at the State Department. "It was really effective with sending jazz musicians over, but we're trying to evolve, see what people are listening to now, younger kids, hip-hop/rap and rock."

Blackman took the idea to the band in early 2007, and was ready to argue her point: "Our mantra in general has been to say yes to most opportunities. Just say yes. And this was just one of those things. It was like, 'Okay, this sounds cool and kooky and weird—and let's try it!'"

It was a polarizing pitch.

"I was, like, 'Fuck this shit,'" Porée says. "I was totally against it." When the band started, he says, he wasn't that politically active. But he learned and absorbed, and became part of an L.A. musical movement that was based on protest and consciousness. So his reflex response at the time was, "Basically, they're just using us, and we're like puppets. The U.S. government's image around the world is shit, and they're just using us to soften the blow."

Pacheco, though wary, paid close attention to his moral compass, one that gets tested a lot in a business where the best-paying gigs often come from the cigarette companies. "We had contradictions within ourselves even without going to the State Department. We've played music for booze companies. People say we sold out—but we sold out when we signed a record deal. Do you know what it means to start caring about money coming in every month?"

Plus, he adds, "We were the only band they could ask. We're mixing up way more stuff. We're rocking, using beats that are Middle Eastern, playing reggae music over cumbia beats and all this type of fusion."

Ultimately, it came down to a vote. Over the years, the band has supported as many as 15 full-time touring musicians. A core of six remain from the initial lineup, along with drummer Calire, and though it hasn't been all roses, and the band has nearly disintegrated a few times for reasons either financial, chemical or personal, they banged out a deal among the half-dozen members that splits all publishing rights evenly, which creates a democracy among them. It's a bitch being in the studio with six equal voices—apparently they nearly break up every time they step near a mixing board. (In fact, the band is in the beginning stages of recording a new full-length for the New York–based Mercer Street label, an offshoot of the high-flying Downtown Records imprint.) The democracy makes for a lively discussion when something like songwriting structure, sequencing or "representing the Bush administration" gets thrown in the mix.

They decided to give it a try. Pretty quickly, the band realized that the black-and-white of political right and wrong goes gray once you meet your perceived antagonists face to face.

Blackman remembers the first time she met Karen Hughes, in 2008, at the Latin Museum in Washington, D.C. By then, the band had toured

India, Nepal and the Middle East, and the longtime George Bush confidante had been getting positive feedback regarding Ozomatli's trips. But she had never seen the band, and she wanted to meet them.

Hughes and her staff showed up at 7:30 p.m.—"on the dot, of course," Blackman says with a laugh. Hughes, whose steely demeanor and forceful opinions Blackman and the band had watched on TV as she defended Bush's positions, admittedly had preconceptions. "She was actually very pleasant to talk to," Blackman recalls. "She isn't smarmy, which is so weird. She is kind. She asked me a ton of questions about the band and where they came from, who they were and what makes them tick and what parts of the trip struck them the most."

"She was really into Ozomatli," confirms Receveur at the State Department. "It was really pretty cool." He adds that as a rule, the State Department doesn't insist on any restrictions regarding what Ozomatli can say onstage, "and this was the Bush administration. Ozomatli did interviews where they were talking about how they were antiwar, that they didn't like the Bush administration, but that they were there to represent America."

Despite the many public-policy disasters of the Bush administration, even some of its most vocal critics acknowledge that, in specific countries, the administration provided a much-needed injection of both attention and funding for public-diplomacy programs.

"Laura Bush—as good as you could be. She knew the issue, she could talk about it," says Human Rights Action Center's Healey on the government's Burma policy.

Hughes' replacement as under secretary of Public Diplomacy is Judith McHale. Before being nominated by the Obama administration to fill the position, she was president and CEO of Discovery Channel. At her Senate confirmation hearing last month, McHale discussed her goals in the job, at least one of which alarmed advocates for Ozomatli-style outreach programs. "New technology, used effectively and creatively, can be a game-changer," she told the committee, citing communications advances that offer opportunities to engage people more efficiently.

Whether this sort of diplomacy would work in Burma is debatable. Most citizens don't have access to computers. For those who do, however, only one social network, Facebook, is allowed, and it's closely monitored. Despite Big Brother, the network is incredibly popular in

Burma, and Ozomatli have a lot of new friends in the country. The downside is, every single status update, photo or video posting runs through servers controlled by the Scrutiny Board.

Hence, ground-level outreach like Ozomatli's is a vital tool.

The American Club is an oddly juxtaposed chunk of tennis courts, swimming pools, softball fields and a clubhouse built on property owned by the U.S. government, and tonight Ozomatli will perform. By Burmese law, any public gathering of more than five people is illegal, so any large event requires permission from the authorities. Because tonight's concert is being held on the grounds, though, it wasn't necessary for the State Department to ask permission. Still, the office informed the Burmese foreign ministry of its plans via a diplomatic note, so it wouldn't be surprised.

The day before, Richard Mei and Burmese Regional Security Officer Bill Mellott had convened the band for a briefing. He told them that they have to be particularly careful about how they act and what they say. If they mention Aung San Suu Kyi's name, he explained, not only will they jeopardize themselves and risk being deported but they could also endanger anyone who attends the concert. He advised them not to mention "The Lady" at all.

Mei had explained as much on the morning the band arrived in the country. He gathered the 11-member entourage in a hotel meeting room, and spoke very specifically about the proper way to move around Rangoon: quietly and anonymously, except when you're onstage. After they had left the country, he encouraged them to say whatever they wanted, and to tell what they saw. But here, delivery of an incendiary message wouldn't help. "They hear the music, but I'm not sure if they're going to get too much of the message. But that's what we're interested in, and we want you to do your normal thing." His voice lifted a little bit as he stretched to explain his next point: "It's just that because of this country, and the way that you have to operate in this country, you have to be sensitive of certain things. And that means not being overt about the political situation."

Twenty-four hours before the concert was scheduled, representatives of the local township gave a note to the guards at the American

Club that said the State Department had not informed the township of the event. The department responded on Friday morning by sending a copy of the earlier diplomatic note, which seemed to satisfy them.

By this point, news has started to spread about Yettaw, the American who was captured in the lake on the morning the band arrived in Burma. On the evening of May 4, he sank into Inya Lake with homemade fins, toting with him a strange collection of items that he wanted to get to Suu Kyi. Uninvited and seemingly unconcerned that his visit would violate the terms of The Lady's house arrest and jeopardize her possible release, Yettaw swam to the shore of her home and, carrying what state news reports say included a video camera, two black Muslim robes, veils, sunglasses and several books, including the Book of Mormon, he entered her compound and met with her. She urged him to leave immediately, but he said he was too tired. He left two days later, and was arrested on May 6 on the opposite shore.

Suu Kyi, her two caretakers and her doctor were all arrested and charged soon thereafter. Suu Kyi remains at Insein Prison, where she was taken after the incident, and with the recent removal of the security surrounding her house, which included drop-down gates, barbed-wire fences and full-time guards, it appears that the government has no intention of releasing her back into house arrest. (Yettaw has since been dubbed "The American Fool" by the *Bangkok Post*.)

By 5:30 p.m., a few hundred people have gathered, many of them Western expats desperate for something, anything to do. The locals start trickling in, and the second of two opening acts performs—a local rapper named J-Me, who, while forbidden to rap about politics, focuses on the universally understood language of, in his words, "bitches, money and weed."

Wil-Dog's six-student entourage from the music school arrives. Wide-eyed and wearing their best clothes, they look a little frightened, especially the little boy, who hasn't smiled once. This is the first time they've ever been out of their neighborhood.

They take a spot standing in the front row, their heads peeking just above the stage. J-Me the rapper prowls around, at one point nearly stepping on the children's fingers. The crowds keep coming, and the concrete space, about the size of two tennis courts, is soon filled.

Ozomatli step onstage right at 6 p.m., and pretty quickly it's clear that the Scrutiny Board hasn't screened the lyrics to "Saturday Night," as Porée rhymes the lyrics: "People to places the message basic / from raised fist to sit-ins resist to change shit / Peep this scenario / to the future, bro / 2020 and some number of years ago / people rose up, governments froze up / worldwide block party, everybody shows up."

If only it were that simple. Sing a song with words of hope, the crowd hears them and decides that tomorrow night the revolution will begin.

Nobody's naive enough to believe in that, not least Ozomatli. But that doesn't stop the band. During the encore, Wil-Dog runs over to his little posse and motions them up. They look confused. He smiles, takes one of them by the hands, lifts her up onto the stage and outfits her with maracas. Soon all six are up, and they're jumping and playing in rhythm. The boy, nervous down below, has a confused smile on his face. He looks around, takes a shaker, and starts jumping enthusiastically while staring at the crowd before him.

As the final song winds down, Ozomatli do their signature move. Each of the band members grabs a portable instrument, and as the crowd continues to dance, the band descends from the stage into the citizenry and starts a dance train. The trumpet and the saxophone blare through the night as the rest of the band bangs on tablas, maracas and tambourines and the crowd bounces and claps along, laughing and dancing behind the best Latin/cumbia/salsa/hip-hop drum corps ever to grace a Burmese stage.

The Passion of David Bazan

Jessica Hopper

At the Cornerstone Christian rock festival, a fallen evan-
gelical returns to sing about why he broke up with God.

"People used to compare him to Jesus," says a backstage manager as
David Bazan walks offstage, guitar in hand. "But not so much anymore."

It's Thursday, July 2, and Bazan has just finished his set at Cornerstone, the annual Christian music festival held on a farm near Bushnell,
Illinois. He hasn't betrayed his crowd the way Dylan did when he went
electric—this is something very different. The kids filling the 1,500-
capacity tent know their Jesus from their Judas. There was a time when
Bazan's fans believed he was speaking, or rather singing, the Word.
Not so much anymore.

As front man for Pedro the Lion, the band he led from 1995 till
2005, Bazan was Christian indie rock's first big crossover star, predating
Sufjan by nearly a decade and paving the way for the music's success
outside the praise circuit. But as he straddled the secular and spiritual
worlds, Bazan began to struggle with his faith. Unable to banish from
his mind the possibility that the God he'd loved and prayed to his whole
life didn't exist, he started drinking heavily. In '05, the last time he
played Cornerstone, he was booted off the grounds for being shitfaced,
a milk jug full of vodka in his hand. (The festival is officially dry.)

I worked as Bazan's publicist from 2000 till 2004. When I ran into
him in April—we were on a panel together at the Calvin College Festival
of Faith & Music in Grand Rapids—I hadn't seen him or talked to him
in five and a half years. The first thing he said to me was "I'm not sure

if you know this, but my relationship with Christ has changed pretty dramatically in the last few years."

He went on to explain that since 2004 he's been flitting between atheist, skeptic, and agnostic, and that lately he's hovering around agnostic—he can't flat-out deny the presence of God in the world, but he doesn't exactly believe in him either.

Pedro the Lion won a lot of secular fans in part because Bazan's lyrics—keen examinations of faith, set to fuzzed-out guitar hooks—have a through-a-glass-darkly quality, acknowledging the imperfection of human understanding rather than insisting on the obviousness of an absolute truth. As the post-9/11 culture wars began to heat up, Pedro the Lion albums took a turn toward the parabolic: an outraged Bazan churned out artful songs about what befalls the righteous and the folly of those who believe God is on their side.

Bazan's relationship with the divine started out pretty uncomplicated, though. Raised outside Seattle in the Pentecostal church where his father was the music director, he hewed closely to Christian orthodoxy, attended Bible college, and married at 23. Now 33, he didn't do a lot of thinking about politics until the 1999 WTO protests. "Growing up, Christianity didn't feel oppressive for the most part, because it was filtered through my parents. They were and are so sincere, and I saw in them a really pure expression of unconditional love and service," he says. "Once I stepped away, I could see the oppression of it."

Bazan's *Curse Your Branches*, due September 1 on Barsuk, is a visceral accounting of what happened after that. It's a harrowing breakup record—except he's dumping God, Jesus, and the evangelical life. It's his first full-length solo album and also his most autobiographical effort: its drunken narratives, spasms of spiritual dissonance, and family tensions are all scenes from the recent past.

Bazan says he tried to Band-Aid his loss of faith and the painful end of Pedro the Lion with about 18 months of "intense" drinking. "If I didn't have responsibilities, if I wasn't watching [my daughter] Ellanor, I had a deep drive to get blacked out," he says. But as he made peace with where he found himself, the compulsion to get obliterated began to wane. On *Curse Your Branches* Bazan sometimes directs the blame and indignation at himself, other times at Jesus and the faith. He's mourning what he's lost, and he knows there's no going back.

"All fallen leaves should curse their branches / For not letting them decide where they should fall / And not letting them refuse to fall at all," he sings on the title track, with more than a touch of fuck-you in his voice. On "When We Fell," backed by a galloping beat and Wilson-boys harmonies, he calls faith a curse put on him by God: "If my mother cries when I tell her what I discovered / Then I hope she remembers she told me to follow my heart / And if you bully her like you've done me with fear of damnation / Then I hope she can see you for what you are."

The album closer, "In Stitches," may be the best song Bazan's ever written. It's the most emotionally bare piece on the album and as close as he comes to a complete thesis:

> *This brown liquor wets my tongue*
> *My fingers find the stitches*
> *Firmly back and forth they run*
> *I need no other memory*
> *Of the bits of me I left*
> *When all this lethal drinking*
> *Is hopefully to forget*
> *About you*

He follows it with an even more devastating verse, confessing that his efforts to erase God have failed:

> *I might as well admit it*
> *Like I've even got a choice*
> *The crew have killed the captain*
> *But they still can hear his voice*
> *A shadow on the water*
> *A whisper in the wind*
> *On long walks with my daughter*
> *Who is lately full of questions*
> *About you*
> *About you*

The second "about you" comes in late, in a keening falsetto, and those two words carry his entire tangle of feelings—anger, desire, confusion, grief.

Since the jug-of-vodka incident, Bazan has kept a pretty low profile, doing a couple modest solo tours and releasing an EP of raw-sounding songs on Barsuk. Pedro the Lion was a reliable paycheck—most of its albums sold in the neighborhood of 50,000 copies, and the group toured regularly, drawing 400 to 600 people a night. His most recent tour couldn't have been more different: Bazan doesn't have a road band put together yet for his solo stuff, but he couldn't afford to wait for *Curse Your Branches* to come out. So he found another way to keep in touch with his most devoted fans, booking 60 solo shows in houses and other noncommercial spaces. He played intimate acoustic sets to maybe 40 people each night, at $20 a ticket, and took questions between songs—some of them, unsurprisingly, about the tough spiritual questions his new material raises.

Despite his outspokenness on those questions, he was invited back to Cornerstone for the first time this year.

"I know David has a long history of being a seeker and trying to navigate through his faith. Cornerstone is open to that," says John Herrin, the festival's director. "We welcome plenty of musicians who may not identify themselves as Christians but are artists with an ongoing connection to faith. . . . We're glad to have him back. We don't give up on people; we don't give up on the kids here who are seeking, trying to figure out what they don't believe and what they do. This festival was built on patience."

At Cornerstone, where I catch up with him behind the fair-food midway, Bazan laughs when I suggest that he's there trying to save the Christians. "I am. I am really invested, because I came up in it and I love a lot of evangelical Christians—I care what happens with the movement," he says. "The last 30 years of it have been hijacked; the boomer evangelicals, they were seduced in the most embarrassing and scandalous way into a social, political, and economical posture that is the antithesis of Jesus's teaching."

With *Curse Your Branches* and in his recent shows, he's inverting the usual call to witness: "You might be the only Christian they ever meet." He's the doubter's witness, and he might be the only agnostic some of these Christian kids ever really listen to.

When I talk to some of those kids in the merch tent the day after Bazan's set, many of them seem to be trying to spin the new songs, straining to categorize them as Christian so they can justify continuing to listen to them. One fan says it's good that Bazan is singing about the perils of sin, "particularly sexual sin." Another interprets the songs as a witness of addiction, the testimony of the stumbling man.

Cultural critic and progressive Christian author David Dark, who since 2003 has become one of Bazan's closest friends, claims that Bazan's skepticism and anger are in line with biblical tradition. "I doubt this is what your average Cornerstone attendee means, but when David is addressing his idea of his God, the one that he fears exists but refuses to believe in, when he is telling him, 'If this is the situation with us and you, then fuck you—the people who love you, I hope they see you for who you are,' when he's doing that, he is at his most biblical. If we are referring to the deep strains of complaint and prayers and tirades against conceptions of God in the Bible—yes, then in that way he's in your Christian tradition. But I disagree that he's an advocate for the biblical."

When I tell Bazan that there are kids at Cornerstone resisting the clear message of his songs, he's surprised. "That someone could listen to what I was saying and think that I was saying it apologetically—like, in a way that characterizes [doubt] as the wrong posture—bums me out, but that's pretty high-concept given how I'm presenting this stuff. So I have to hand it to someone who can keep on spinning what is so clearly something else." He pauses for a long moment, then adds, "I don't want to be that misunderstood."

During the two days I follow Bazan and his fans around the Cornerstone campus, though, it becomes clear that he isn't really misunderstood at all. Everyone knows what he's singing about—what's happening is that his listeners are taking great pains to sidestep the obvious. "Well, his songs have always been controversial," one says, but when asked to pinpoint the source of the controversy suggests it's because he swears— nothing about not believing in hell or not taking the Bible as God's word. Bazan's agnosticism is the elephant in the merch tent.

Fans rhapsodize about Bazan's work: they love his honesty, they love how they can relate to him, how he's not proselytizing, how he's speaking truth—but they don't tend to delve into what exactly that truth might be. Brice Evans, a 24-year-old from Harrisburg, Illinois, who came to Cornerstone specifically to see Bazan's set, dances artfully around it. "He's showing a side of Christianity that no other band shows," Evans says. "He's trying to get a message across that's more than that."

It's hard to say if anybody is conscious of the irony: the "side of Christianity" Bazan sings about is disenfranchisement from it.

"I think with *Curse Your Branches* David expands the space of the talk-about-able," says Dark. "It's not confessional in the sense that he's down on himself and trying to confess something to God in hopes of being forgiven. I think that's what crowds are trying to make of him, but they're going to have a tougher time when they get the record."

Bazan is known for his dialogues with fans, and during his set he's affable, taking questions from the crowd. Tonight's audience, openly anxious and awed, keeps it light at first: "Would you rather be a werewolf or a vampire?" Then he opens with the new album's lead track, "Hard to Be," a sobering song with an especially hard-hitting second verse:

> *Wait just a minute*
> *You expect me to believe*
> *That all this misbehaving*
> *Grew from one enchanted tree?*
> *And helpless to fight it*
> *We should all be satisfied*
> *With this magical explanation*
> *For why the living die*
> *And why it's hard to be*
> *Hard to be, hard to be*
> *A decent human being?*

By the time he finishes those lines I can see half a dozen people crying; a woman near me is trembling and sobbing. Others have their heads in their hands. Many look stunned, but no one leaves. When the song ends, the applause is thunderous.

After Bazan plays a cover of Leonard Cohen's "Hallelujah," reinstating the sacrilegious verses left out of the best-known versions, someone shouts, "How's your soul?" Bazan looks up from tuning his guitar and says, "My soul? Oh, it's fine." This elicits an "Amen, brother!" from the back of the tent.

Following Bazan's set a throng of fans—kids, young women with babies on their hips, a handful of youth pastors—queues up around the side of the stage to talk to him. Some kids want hugs and ask geeked-out questions, but just as many attempt to feel him out in a sly way. "I really wished you had played 'Lullaby,'" says one kid, naming a very early Pedro the Lion song that's probably the most worshipful in Bazan's catalog. A few gently bait him, referring to scripture the way gang members throw signs, eager for a response that will reveal where Bazan is really at.

During discussions like this Bazan doesn't usually get into the subtle barometric fluctuations in his relationship with Jesus, but that still leaves room for plenty of postshow theological talk. "This process feels necessary and natural for these people," he says. "They're in a precarious situation—maybe I am too. To maintain their particular posture, they have to figure out: Do they need to get distance from me, or is it just safe enough to listen to? I empathize as people are trying to gauge, 'Is this guy an atheist? Because I heard he was.'"

Bazan has chosen sides, but old ideas linger. "Some time ago, we were discussing [the Pedro the Lion song] 'Foregone Conclusions,'" Dark says. "I told him I was impressed with the lines 'You were too busy steering conversation toward the Lord / To hear the voice of the Spirit / Begging you to shut the fuck up / You thought it must be the devil / Trying to make you go astray / Besides it could not have been the Lord / Because you don't believe He talks that way.' I thought, what a liberating word for people who've been shoved around by all manner of brainwash. But also Dave's doing something even more subtle, as many interpret the unforgivable sin to be blasphemy against the Holy Spirit—confusing the voice of God for the voice of the devil—so there's a whole 'nother level of theological devastation going on in the song.

"When I brought it up, he laughed and told me he still worries about going to hell for that one. He knows that it's horribly funny that he feels that way, but he won't lie by saying he's entirely over it. He's both 100 percent sincere and 100 percent ironically detached. He's haunted even as he pushes forward, saying what he feels even though he half fears doing so will be cosmically costly for him."

After a long few years in the wilderness, Bazan seems happy—though he's still parsing out his beliefs, he's visibly relieved to be out and open about where he's not at. "It's more comfortable for me to be agnostic," he says. "There's less internal tension by far—that's even with me duking it out with my perception of who God is on a pretty regular basis, and having a lot of uncertainty on that level. For now, just being is enough. Whether things happen naturally, completely outside an author, or whether the dynamics of earth and people are that way because God created them—or however you want to credit it—if you look around and pay attention and observe, there is enough right here to know how to act, to know how to live, to be at peace with one another.

"Because I grew up believing in hell and reckoning, there is a voice in me that says, 'That might not cut it with the man upstairs,' but I think that that has to be enough. For me it is enough."

The Decade in Indie

Nitsuh Abebe

"I opened up the door, and much to my surprise
The girls were wearing formals, and the boys were
wearing ties
And I feel that I should mention that the band was at
attention
They just stood there, oh so neat, while they played their
swinging beat. . . .
It's been long overdue—we've been needing something new—
Sophisticated boom boom!"
—The Goodies, 1964

So have you heard? Indie rock is the choice of a new generation! Allegedly! Don't let the exclamation points fool you into thinking I'm being sarcastic! Just *try* selling iPods or straight-leg jeans without knowing what fresh-faced guitar band is the hip new thing; just try telegraphing to audiences that a character on your television show is quite special and interesting. Stephenie Meyer, author of *Twilight*, not often accused of lacking insight into the hearts of America's young, just told the world what her favorite records were this summer—Grizzly Bear and Animal Collective among them. (Do you think that's awesome, or does it make you want to listen to nothing but rap mixtapes and noise?) I just read an article by a pretty likeable 57-year-old who'd decided indie rock was really interesting, that older people should check it out, and that Wilco were probably its godfathers. (That makes more sense than you'd think.) And it's not like charts mean what they used to, but still: they're home to the Shins (#2 record), Wilco (three records in the top 10), Arcade

Fire (17 weeks), Interpol (24 weeks), and Death Cab for Cutie, who went to #1—as in, knocking off Neil Diamond and being replaced at the top by 3 Doors Down, *that* #1—without even much changing their sound from a decade ago. Toward the end of the 1990s the Flaming Lips were the kinds of weirdos who released an album you had to play on four different stereos at once, and now they get considered for Oklahoma's state song and soundtrack moving funeral scenes in Mandy Moore movies. Let's not even start on movies: Natalie Portman said the Shins would change your life, and she was in *Star Wars*.

It's not just music, either. I don't know quite when it happened, but at some point a certain vague strain of "indie" dropped its last vestiges of seeming weird and became a commonplace—sort of like in Britain, where "indie" has long been synonymous with the normal guitar bands people find fashionable. When those I'm-a-Mac, I'm-a-PC commercials came out, I even saw some ad critic describe Justin Long's Mac guy as an "indie type." Why? He's just a young middle-class-looking white guy with a haircut. (I'd be more aghast, except it's actually *not* hard to imagine him telling you about the New Pornographers.) And soon enough any film, book, or cultural product that came anywhere near a certain sensibility—anything anyone would describe as "quirky" or cleverish or tender—fell in the indie bucket, too: *Garden State* with its hilarious Shins scene, Wes Anderson movies, Dave Eggers (??), *Juno*, Zooey Deschanel's general existence, private colleges, button shirts, the Internet, IKEA, Miracle Whip, literacy, you tell me. The sensibility used to seem rarer, and then, I suppose, half the people attracted to it grew up and got creative jobs and now it floats everywhere. So huge swathes of twentysomethings, like anyone with a college education or a Mac or a strummy guitar record: indie, apparently? Which is allegedly quite the thing these days.

I'm actually not mocking or complaining. I have an ulterior motive. I mention all this because I'm positive that some of you read the above in a neutral, casual way, while others of you, having gotten through it, are right now actively gagging and fuming and experiencing some very visceral squirming, and if you check your reflection in the computer screen you will look approximately like Homer Simpson when he's choking Bart. Because you hate this stuff. And what I want to tell you today is why that split—the neutral reading versus the visceral tooth-grinding hate-that-stuff feeling—is precisely why I'm really, really excited about what might happen to indie over the next decade.

Here's the thing: "indie" has always been a baggy, contingent word, and the whole loose umbrella of stuff that gets considered "indie" has usually included huge splits and tensions. Back in the 1980s, for instance, there was a major difference between hardcore punks and what kids in my hometown would continue to refer to as "wavers," as in new wave: fans of stylish British bands and synthesizers, drama-club Morrissey types. But by the end of the 80s, as it happened, there had emerged this crop of bands that seemed to *resolve* some of that punks-versus-wavers tension, bringing together parts of both camps—a little thrash/trash/noise and a little arty/stylish/pop—under one big tent. I don't think it's an accident that some of those bands, like Sonic Youth or Pixies, are still big tentpoles of what we now think of as indie: They're part of what brought together that audience, that category, in the first place. This is a big simplification, just one way of wrapping a narrative around what's ultimately only a bunch of individuals buying records. But there's truth in it. When different people are standing under the same umbrella, there's bound to be some elbowing, some argument about who's taking up too much space and what direction everyone's walking. There's tension and then things shuffle and rearrange.

So if you want to know where today's popular indie comes from, I can offer you a similar narrative about that. Consider that in the early 1990s, "alternative rock" became very popular, very suddenly. It wasn't like indie's slow creep toward normality this decade: Alt-rock more or less party-crashed the mainstream, and mainstream audiences party-crashed it right back, and that sent everyone under the indie umbrella elbowing and shoving for new space. The kinds of alt-rock that got popular tended to be very straightforward: fuzzy, glossy rock songs; brash, masculine grunge; blocky, bright, and ironic pop. It could, and did, get old. Again: It's probably no accident that if you look at the things the "indie" world turned toward over the following years, a lot of them can be read as straight-up reactions to those qualities. I mean, if you happened to be tired of that stuff, or object to where it was headed, then something like post-rock—sedate, studious, un-macho—was a lot more likely to smell like fresh air, right? Same with trippy electronic pop, scrappy homemade lo-fi, twee, slowcore, IDM, lounge-record re-issues, or a lot of other things people got into in the late 1990s. A lot of the people *making* this fresh-air music were people who used to play loud, simple punk and were shooting for something fresh.

And after a while of that, as everyone settled from the shake-up of the alt-rock boom, this whole "indie" audience really did regroup around liking certain types of things: think, for example, of Elliott Smith, Belle & Sebastian, Air, Cat Power, latter-day Flaming Lips. This music was pleasant, accessible, and aesthetically interesting, but without making a whole lot of noise or sudden moves about it. There were things about the songs that were comfortable and traditional, which was how con-sensus got built around them: They were easy to like. But there were also things about them that, in the context of their time, seemed rare and special and worth getting behind. Some acts were soft-spoken and wry, which was a big contrast not only from pop but from buzzy, earnest alternative. Some, like Belle & Sebastian or Cat Power, had a sense of privacy and withdrawal to them, like they lived in your bedroom instead of blaring everywhere—like there was something precious about them. There was a level of fantasy and whimsy around a lot of records, a light psychedelia, that hadn't been heard in a while and couldn't be gotten elsewhere—this sense, when listening to the Lips or Stereolab or Ele-phant 6 bands, that the artists were picking up different aspects of pop music and painting swoony little dreams out of them. It felt *thoughtful*, a quality that's hard to define but a very big part of what made it appeal. Thoughtful and, of course, different. Music your parents *could* like, but probably found strange: This could feel subversive, somehow, in a world where youth culture was presumed to be aggressively loud. This stuff wanted to be *nice*; it wanted—rather unusually—to be subtle, maybe even a bit quaint. You can see this reflected in the new influences and heroes it took up and began lionizing: Nick Drake (patron saint of qui-etude, privacy, and obscurity), Brian Wilson (big-eyed innocence and lush imagination), Antonio Carlos Jobim (effortless, breezy cool), Serge Gainsbourg (louche, but suave, aloof) . . .

Quiet, wry, quaint, imaginative, thoughtful, nice—all of these are qualities that seem like part of whatever vague, ambient "indie" sensi-bility is attached to movies and advertisements and t-shirts now, right? I'm not writing to argue that you should like it, only to explain what shaped it. I know that a lot of you, in today's context, won't see those qualities or that music as at all a positive thing; hell, I *liked* a lot of those records, and sometimes *I* can't see those qualities as positive anymore. But I'm also sure that plenty of you in this decade had a very similar experience—chafing at the nu-metal or buzzy alt/emo on the radio, and then experiencing something like the dorky, semi-fantastical Decemberists as fresh air.

The first cracks in this arrangement started to show at the turn of the millennium. The status quo accumulated discontents. Suddenly the big rap on indie was that it was po-faced and insular and lacking in passion, a self-congratulatory system of people in plaid shirts playing to audiences with their arms crossed. The songs were tasteful, polite, and predictable, and no one, allegedly, danced. No noise, no sudden moves, just a comfy, private bubble where everything tried to be so clever and cerebral and *nice*. The Internet only furthered this complaint. The amount of online chatter about music was on a huge upswing, and the sheer variety of viewpoints made it pretty hard *not* to feel insular and over-comfortable. The sudden availability of mp3s, of just about any sort, also meant there was a lot less excuse for not looking outside your own bubble. And besides, why should "indie"—which had, at various points, been a joyously weird dumping ground for loads of misfit sounds—suddenly become codified and narrow? Why should it camp out around music that, increasingly, looked rather settled, timid, and polite? Why *should* it be so damned nice?

You heard that complaint a lot back then, and at the start of the decade, certain trends seemed to present as antidotes. Personally, I was totally taken with new electro, which felt like everything mainstream indie was not—trashy, party-focused, danceable, dumb and simple, vibrant and exciting. So was greasy garage rock, for some people, even in its least greasy, most popular incarnations; I can still remember a summer in Chicago where the nearest cafés all switched from playing post-rock to non-stop White Stripes. The Strokes seemed like a breath of fresh air, and people started leaping at snappy, upbeat, big-tent guitar bands as some kind of Return of Rock moment. This should tell you something: The Strokes were not exactly hard rockers, but in indie's 2001 they somehow came off as *surly*! Even the Hives presented, in indie-world, as a burst of potential excitement—nothing against the Hives, who kicked out some killer singles, but this seems like evidence of some kind of *very* deep psychic need. This was the other kind of indie that got really popular: The snappy guitar bands extroverted enough to shoot for excitement and fans—Interpol, Strokes, Yeah Yeah Yeahs, Franz Ferdinand, Bloc Party.

More importantly, those years saw indie types paying more attention to things outside the indie world—this website's coverage, for instance, widened significantly—and indie, in its thieving magpie way, started seizing at things, assimilating them. People embraced house acts, got excited about the possibility of "dance punk," dabbled with underground rap. At first, plenty of folks derided these trends as faddish, embarrassing, or somehow even elitist, like the people who went for them were trying to fool someone. But as far as I can tell, things changed. You can see it just visually: Neon t-shirts and skinny pants and fashion and "hipster"ism—the stuff some indie kids recoiled from when new electro came along—won out. Daft Punk and M.I.A. have big old parking spots reserved for them in the indie world. All sorts of new things wound up getting absorbed into indie's sensibility, because indie is a superb thief: It gets into things and then picks up their trappings. Electro, minimal techno, French house, the production on hip-hop and R&B singles—at this point you probably don't think twice when an indie act grabs something from these genres; you don't think twice about whether the result is "indie" or not. It's assimilated, just another option.

It's funny how umbrellas work, though. Because the more some people wanted to dig down toward something fresher and rowdier—noise, metal, club music, weirdo back-shed clangers—the more they left that *other* indie sensibility, the allegedly polite and earnest and po-faced one, to sail its course. And its course was to get really, really popular. It became the kind of thing an average American teenager might casually listen to without feeling there was *too* much meaningful or different about that choice: It's just guitar-pop, right? People who'd always followed it got older and kept listening. The combination of sounds in it—the blend of strong, accessible songwriting with aesthetics just stylized enough to be head-turning—brought more listeners into its fold.

Eventually you could hear about it on National Public Radio, read about it in *The New York Times*; if you followed a certain variety of "middle-brow" media, or even just watched the bands showing up on late-night shows, you'd quite possibly hear *more* about indie acts than platinum-selling rappers or country acts.

"Indie" got ever more widely adopted as pop music for the "thought-ful" person—the *sophisticated* boom-boom. And be honest: Why *wouldn't* loads of everyday non-music-geek people hear a good Iron & Wine song and think not just "hey, that's really pleasant," but also "hey, that's kinda different and interesting"? Why not, if you put it in front of them? The sheer fact that it was available made a huge difference. I'll spare you a long, old-mannish digression about the things I had to do, pre-Internet, to engage with the music I wanted to hear; it was a constant and hilariously archaic scramble. But these days, these things float past you everywhere, and I'm hard-pressed to think of many acts I'd recommend that you couldn't very casually, within two minutes of web-searching, check out right on your computer. More and more, we define ourselves—or pride ourselves, or at least "express" ourselves—via our skills in picking interesting things out of that cloud of options. We probably shouldn't be surprised that somewhere in this process, "indie" completed its trip from being the province of freaks and geeks to some-thing with cachet—something that appeals to people's sense of them-selves as *discerning*. Something that is, in some quarters, enough of a staple of "cool" that people begin to feel oppressed by it, to the point where some people's defense of liking it is no longer a defense against being weird, but a defense against being trendy.

Well. There are major issues and tensions involved in one variety of indie being that popular. Big ones. This website experiences some of them. Pitchfork has spent most of its existence covering both cate-gories: both mainstream, populist indie records and weirder, rowdier sounds. Most of the time, those things have gone together really well; the sense has been that the average "indie" listener would like a bit of both, some pop records to sing along to and some stranger ones to be wowed by, plus plenty in between. That's probably still true of most of you! But now, more than ever, there's also this tension between the two, and a feeling of sides-taking.

On one side, there's a pleasingly large audience who listens to popular indie as a matter of course, looking more for solid records and strong songs than any huge feeling of strangeness or experiment. On the other side, there's a pleasingly large group who feel like the "indie" umbrella is looking beige and boring, and crave more mystery, strangeness, and noise; who lament that some of its punk energy is gone, now the province of a whole other teenage realm of screamo, emo, and white-belt metal; who miss indie's being defined by a weird risky energy, and not being too "nice" or "thoughtful." This website can get a writer angry mail from both positions, sometimes over the same piece: One message that says you're an elitist hipster snob for enjoying a noise band or "pretending" to like a pop single; another message that says you're a corny, predictable lamer for liking a conventional indie band.

So long as you get a few of each, things seem okay. Both impulses can coexist just fine. We can listen to both and neither. But when that tension's felt—when it starts to feel like something's at stake—it affects what people *want* to like, what they feel like giving a chance; it affects where they go to learn and talk about music; it affects the music that gets made. People situate themselves in relation to what's at stake.

What's great is that there's loads of real love and passion around this split, and the arguments I see about it indicate that people still care a ton about what they think indie *should* be like. I was pretty charmed with Vampire Weekend's debut, but I was also charmed by the way that some people who hated it didn't just dislike the music: some of them objected, viscerally, to the very idea that indie bands would even be like that. I liked the way a lot of people heard No Age and remembered that they enjoyed indie rock being a little slack and thrashy—a quality that used to be everywhere and had somehow fallen out of earshot—and I liked the way other people sat sneering and pointing out that there was far more slack and thrashy stuff beyond that. I like that people can rally around Animal Collective as something honestly interesting and forward-facing, and I like that other people can still complain that they've become too mainstream. Indie still does the thing I care about most, which is providing a reasonably open-minded audience and space for people—like Antony Hegarty or Max Tundra or the Tough Alliance—who make popular music that's just a bit odd and stylized; all you magpies pick and choose from everywhere. But I like that now, more than ever, I keep seeing that old punks-versus-wavers type of tension surrounding things—a real tension, a real desire for things to go in opposite directions.

I'm not here to make predictions: The last thing I want is for the music I follow to be predictable. But what this adds up to is a feeling that something is coming—some kind of spasm, some rearrangements of where things stand. Yet another big shuffle of who stands where under indie's umbrella, and where indie's umbrella stands in the first place. Maybe that sounds improbable, but it seems right. Maybe it'll involve sounds we think of as "indie" lapsing over into mainstream taste— the mainstream is even more of a magpie assimilator than indie!—and an underground digging more and more for new fresh-air directions to travel. Maybe some kids who grew up on screamo and Animal Collective both with come around and mix up audiences in bizarre new ways. Maybe something game-changing will crawl out of a Hot Topic somewhere; I don't know if you follow these things, but there are weirdnesses and genre collisions coming out of those scenes that make indie look kinda square. I don't know what, precisely, to expect, but I can't think of another time in my life this "indie" world has looked quite so ripe for shaking itself up. I'm excited for it—I think we'll *all* enjoy it. It'll be awesome. I promise. You'll be there.

My Hilarious Warner Bros. Royalty Statement

Timothy Quirk

I got something in the mail last week I'd been wanting for years: a Too Much Joy royalty statement from Warner Brothers that finally included our digital earnings. Though our catalog has been out of print physically since the late-1990s, the three albums we released on Giant/WB have been available digitally for about five years. Yet the royalty statements I received every six months kept insisting we had zero income, and our unrecouped balance ($395,277.18!)* stubbornly remained the same.

---

* A word here about that unrecouped balance, for those uninitiated in the complex mechanics of major label accounting. While our royalty statement shows Too Much Joy in the red with Warner Bros. (now by only $395,214.71 after that $62.47 digital windfall), this doesn't mean Warner "lost" nearly $400,000 on the band. That's how much they spent on us, and we don't see any royalty checks until it's paid back, but it doesn't get paid back out of the full price of every album sold. It gets paid back out of *the band's share* of every album sold, which is roughly 10% of the retail price. So, using round numbers to make the math as easy as possible to understand, let's say Warner Bros. spent something like $450,000 total on TMJ. If Warner sold 15,000 copies of each of the three TMJ records they released at a wholesale price of $10 each, they would have earned back the $450,000. But if those records were retailing for $15, TMJ would have only paid back $67,500, and our statement would show an unrecouped balance of $382,500.

I do not share this information out of a Steve Albini-esque desire to rail against the major label system (he already wrote the definitive rant, which you can find

Now, I don't ever expect that unrecouped balance to turn into a positive number, but since the band had been seeing thousands of dollars in digital royalties each year from IODA for the four indie albums we control ourselves, I figured five years' worth of digital income from our far more popular major label albums would at least make a small dent in the figure. Our IODA royalties during that time had totaled about $12,000—not a princely sum, but enough to suggest that the total haul over the same period from our major label material should be at least that much, if not two to five times more. Even with the band receiving only a percentage of the major label take, getting our unrecouped balance below $375,000 seemed reasonable, and knocking it closer to −$350,000 wasn't out of the question.

So I was naively excited when I opened the envelope. And my answer was right there on the first page. In five years, our three albums earned us a grand total of . . .

$62.47

What the fuck?

I mean, we all know that major labels are supposed to be venal masters of hiding money from artists, but they're also supposed to be *good* at it, right? This figure wasn't insulting because it was so small, it was insulting because it was so stupid.

WHY IT WAS SO STUPID

Here's the thing: I work at Rhapsody. I know what we pay Warner Bros. for every stream and download, and I can look up exactly how many plays and downloads we've paid them for each TMJ tune that Warner controls. Moreover, Warner Bros. *knows this*, as my gig at Rhapsody is

---

here if you want even more figures [www.negativland.com/albini.html], and enjoy having those figures bracketed with cursing and insults). I'm simply explaining why I'm not embarrassed that I "owe" Warner Bros. almost $400,000. They didn't make a lot of money off of Too Much Joy. But they didn't lose any, either. So whenever you hear some label flak claiming 98% of the bands they sign lose money for the company, substitute the phrase "just don't earn enough" for the word "lose."

the only reason I was able to get them to add my digital royalties to my statement in the first place. For years I'd been pestering the label, but I hadn't gotten anywhere till I was on a panel with a reasonably big wig in Warner Music Group's business affairs team about a year ago.

The panel took place at a legal conference, and focused on digital music and the crisis facing the record industry.* As you do at these things, the other panelists and I gathered for breakfast a couple hours before our session began, to discuss what topics we should address. Peter Jenner, who manages Billy Bragg and has been a needed gadfly for many years at events like these, wanted to discuss the little-understood fact that digital music services frequently pay labels advances in the tens of millions of dollars for access to their catalogs, and it's unclear how (or if) that money is ever shared with artists.

I agreed that was a big issue, but said I had more immediate and mundane concerns, such as the fact that Warner wouldn't even report my band's iTunes sales to me.

The business affairs guy (who I am calling "the business affairs guy" rather than naming because he did me a favor by finally getting the digital royalties added to my statement, and I am grateful for that and don't want this to sound like I'm attacking him personally, even though it's about to seem like I am) said that it was complicated connecting Warner's digital royalty payments to their existing accounting mechanisms, and that since my band was unrecouped they had "to take care of R.E.M. and the Red Hot Chili Peppers first."

That kind of pissed me off. On the one hand, yeah, my band's unrecouped and is unlikely ever to reach the point where Warner actually has to cut us a royalty check. On the other hand, though, they are contractually obligated to report what revenue they receive in our name, and, having helped build a database that tracks how much Rhapsody owes whom for what music gets played, I'm well aware of what is and isn't complicated about doing so. It's not something you have to build over and over again for each artist. It's something you build once. It

---

* The whole conference took place at a semi-swank hotel on the island of St. Thomas, which is a funny place to gather to talk about how to save the music business, but that would be a whole different diatribe.

takes a while, and it can be expensive, and sometimes you make honest mistakes, but it's not rocket science. Hell, it's not even algebra! It's just simple math.

I knew that each online service was reporting every download, and every play, for every track, to thousands of labels (more labels, I'm guessing, than Warner has artists to report to). And I also knew that IODA was able to tell me exactly how much money my band earned the previous month from Amazon ($11.05), Verizon (74 cents), Nokia (11 cents), MySpace (4 sad cents) and many more. I didn't understand why Warner wasn't reporting similar information back to my band—and if they weren't doing it for Too Much Joy, I assumed they weren't doing it for other artists.

To his credit, the business affairs guy told me he understood my point, and promised he'd pursue the matter internally on my behalf—which he did. It just took 13 months to get the results, which were (predictably, perhaps) ridiculous.

The sad thing is I don't even think Warner is deliberately trying to screw TMJ and the hundreds of other also-rans and almost-weres they've signed over the years. The reality is more boring, but also more depressing. Like I said, they don't actually owe us any money. But that's what's so weird about this, to me: they have the ability to tell the truth, and doing so won't cost them anything.

They just can't be bothered. They don't care, because they don't have to.

"$10,000 IS NOTHING"

An interlude, here. Back in 1992, when TMJ was still a going concern and even the label thought maybe we'd join the hallowed company of recouped bands one day, Warner made a $10,000 accounting error on our statement (in their favor, naturally). When I caught this mistake, and brought it to the attention of someone with the power to correct it, he wasn't just befuddled by my anger—he laughed at it. "$10,000 is nothing!" he chuckled.

If you're like most people—especially people in unrecouped bands—"nothing" is not a word you ever use in conjunction with a figure like

"$10,000," but he seemed oblivious to that. "It's a rounding error. It happens all the time. Why are you so worked up?"

These days I work for a reasonably large corporation myself, and, sadly, I understand exactly what the guy meant. When your revenues (and your expenses) are in the hundreds of millions of dollars, $10,000 mistakes are common, if undesirable.

I still think he was a jackass, though, and that sentence continues to haunt me. Because $10,000 might have been nothing to him, but it was clearly something to me. And his inability to take it seriously—to put himself in my place, just for the length of our phone call—suggested that people who care about $10,000 mistakes, and the principles of things, like, say, honoring contracts even when you don't have to, are the real idiots.

As you may have divined by this point, I am conflicted about whether I am actually being a petty jerk by pursuing this, or whether labels just thrive on making fools like me *feel* like petty jerks. People in the record industry are very good at making bands believe they *deserve* the hundreds of thousands (or sometimes millions) of dollars labels advance the musicians when they're first signed, and even better at convincing those same musicians it's the bands' fault when those advances aren't recouped (the last thing $10,000-Is-Nothing-Man yelled at me before he hung up was, "Too Much Joy never earned us shit!"* as though that fact somehow negated their obligation to account honestly).

I don't want to live in $10,000-Is-Nothing-Man's world. But I do. We all do. We have no choice.

THE BORING REALITY

Back to my ridiculous Warner Bros. statement. As I flipped through its ten pages (seriously, it took ten pages to detail the $62.47 of income), I

---

* This same dynamic works in reverse—I interviewed the Butthole Surfers for *Raygun* magazine back in the 1990s, and Gibby Haynes described the odd feeling of visiting Capitol records' offices and hearing "a bunch of people go, 'Hey, man, be cool to these guys, they're a recouped band.' I heard that a bunch of times."

realized that Warner wasn't being evil, just careless and unconcerned—an impression I confirmed a few days later when I spoke to a guy in their Royalties and Licensing department I am going to call Danny.*

I asked Danny why there were no royalties at all listed from iTunes, and he said, "Huh. There are no domestic downloads on here at all. Only streams. And it has international downloads, but no international streams. I have no idea why." I asked Danny why the statement only seemed to list tracks from two of the three albums Warner had released—an entire album was missing. He said they could only report back what the digital services had provided to them, and the services must not have reported any activity for those other songs. When I suggested that seemed unlikely—that having every track from two albums listed by over a dozen different services, but zero tracks from a third album listed by any seemed more like an error on Warner's side, he said he'd look into it. As I asked more questions (Why do we get paid 50% of the income from all the tracks on one album, but only 35.7143% of the income from all the tracks on another? Why did 29 plays of a track on the late, lamented MusicMatch earn a total of 63 cents when 1,016 plays of the exact same track on MySpace earned only 23 cents?) he eventually got to the heart of the matter: "We don't normally do this for unrecouped bands," he said. "But, I was told you'd asked."

It's possible I'm projecting my own insecurities onto calm, patient Danny, but I'm pretty sure the subtext of that comment was the same thing I'd heard from $10,000-Is-Nothing-Man: all these figures were pointless, and I was kind of being a jerk by wasting their time asking about them. After all, they have the Red Hot Chili Peppers to deal with, and the label actually owes those guys money.

Danny may even be right. But there's another possibility—one I don't necessarily subscribe to, but one that could be avoided entirely by humoring pests like me. There's a theory that labels and publishers deliberately avoid creating the transparent accounting systems today's

---

* Again, I am avoiding using his real name because he returned my call promptly, and patiently answered my many questions, which is behavior I want to encourage, so I have no desire to lambaste him publicly.

technology enables. Because accurately accounting to my silly little band would mean accurately accounting to the less silly bands that *are* recouped, and paying them more money as a result.

If that's true (and I emphasize the if, because it's equally possible that people everywhere, including major label accounting departments, are just dumb and lazy),* then there's more than my pride and principles on the line when I ask Danny in Royalties and Licensing to answer my many questions. I don't feel a burning need to make the Red Hot Chili Peppers any more money, but I wouldn't mind doing my small part to get us all out of the sad world $10,000-Is-Nothing-Man inhabits.

So I will keep asking, even though I sometimes feel like a petty jerk for doing so.

---

* Of course, these two possibilities are not mutually exclusive—it is also possible that labels are evil and avaricious AND dumb and lazy, at the same time.

Biscuits and Jam
With a Side of Mud

Evie Nagy

The Disco Biscuits liked to play festivals, so they made their own. Now they run it—come hell and high water.

The night of Monday, July 13, Jonathan Fordin couldn't sleep. It was three days until Camp Bisco—the annual three-day music festival hosted by jam band scene stalwarts the Disco Biscuits—and Fordin's Meatcamp Productions was almost $750,000 behind where it needed to be for its biggest event of the year. "I was lying in bed thinking, 'This might be it,'" he says. "'This whole thing might be over a week from now.'"

MCP took a big risk on this year's Camp Bisco, the eighth for the band and the fifth for the company, increasing total expenses 30% from last year to $1.4 million and upping the talent budget 40% to $650,000. Fordin and his business partner Brett Keber started with a $225,000 budget when they took over the event in 2005, steadily increasing it every year to attract more people and bigger talent. "What we've tried to do is build this brand that's almost bigger than the band itself, to lay the grounds for the band to grow with it," Fordin says.

So far it had been working, with revenue, profits and attendance growing by 20% or more every year, and scoring major artists like Snoop Dogg in 2008 and Nas and Damian Marley this year. But as the week went on, and ticket sales remained slow in a down economy, Fordin and Keber thought attendance might barely reach last year's levels.

Then on Thursday, festival day one, the rain came.

JAM-PACKED

As Camp Bisco's founder, hosts and six-set headliners, the Disco Biscuits—drummer Allen Aucoin, bassist Marc Brownstein, guitarist/ MIDI keyboardist Jon Gutwillig and keyboardist Aron Magner—are the festival's biggest draw. But the addition of electronic and hip-hop acts helped expand the event beyond the band's hard-core fans and exposed these other artists to the committed, camp-out community that defines the jam band scene.

As the festival's owners, the Biscuits are paid a guarantee by MCP. Then, after the promoters meet their costs, profits are shared between MCP and the Biscuits in a partnership arrangement. Even before the final numbers were in for this year's event, Brownstein estimated that the single Camp Bisco weekend would account for at least 8% of his band's annual gross.

Camp Bisco began in 1999 "out of necessity," Brownstein says. "When the Biscuits started as a young Philadelphia band in the '90s, we were in the festival circuit, and like any young band we started playing at noon. We knew within a year or two that we weren't the noontime band anymore, that our fan base had outgrown that, but the promoters still didn't necessarily believe it."

Brownstein says the last straw came at the 1997 All Good Festival in Brandywine, Md., when the Biscuits played at noon to a field of 1,500 people, which promptly emptied when the next band arrived. "That was the first time we saw that there was a differential between the way we were being treated by the industry and the reality of what our band was," he says. "When you can't seem to crack through but you know that you have something special in terms of a community, the only thing you can really do is do things on your own. We were fans of the Grateful Dead and Phish, and they had control of everything—nothing mattered to them except them and their fans; no one was calling the shots except for [Phish frontman] Trey [Anastasio]. And we knew that model was going to be good for us because we played in that same style, we didn't have pop songs, we weren't the best singers back then, but that's not what people were coming for. They were coming for the interaction and the improvisation."

In 1998, the band held a small festival in western Pennsylvania called Melstock, and from that the idea for a multiday camp-out was born. The band hired its own production and security teams for the first Camp Bisco in 1999, which drew about 800 people for "unknown and extremely affordable bands," Brownstein says. All Good promoter Tim Walther pitched in for Camp Biscos II and III in 2000 and 2002, which drew 1,600 and 2,600 fans, respectively.

By then, Phish had run several festivals, starting in 1996 with the Clifford Ball in Plattsburgh, N.Y. And although the Biscuits' albums had only sold 21,000 copies by that point, according to Nielsen Sound-Scan, the group's destination events became the foundation of its business. Even so, Camp Bisco was "a huge undertaking, a full-time job in itself," Brownstein says, and the band put the festival on hold for the following two years.

BISCO INFERNO

That full-time job is now well-known to Fordin and Keber. By the time the promoters were pushing vans out of ankle-deep mud in the middle of the night on July 17, they looked at each other and questioned whether this was really what they wanted to be doing with their lives.

Thursday afternoon's thunderstorm already forced a set cancellation, and 12 straight hours of torrential rain on Friday turned the clay of Indian Lookout Country Club in Mariaville, N.Y., into a 200-acre tar pit.

And yet still, somehow, the numbers were looking up. "The storm kept a lot of people from coming on Thursday this year—but then Friday they just didn't stop coming, from 7 a.m. to 5 a.m., through the worst rain I've ever seen as a festival promoter," Keber says.

Moreover, the fans weren't huddling in their tents. "It was amazing—they stood at that stage and waited for Nas and Damian, who had wanted to cancel, for an hour-and-a-half in the pouring rain. Then they didn't leave for the Biscuits' set or anything," Fordin says. "It really shows how dedicated our fan base is," Keber adds. "They come for the music first and foremost."

Fordin and Keber knew this about their audience before relaunching the festival in 2005, because they were Biscuits fans themselves. Best friends at Appalachian State University in the late '90s, the two started booking bands at a rented house in Meat Camp, N.C., and eventually got to know the Disco Biscuits as pioneers of a scene and style that blended jam band rock with electronica.

"When Meatcamp took over the fourth Camp Bisco, Jon and Brett were like 25, and they said, 'Look, we can make this event better. We know what kind of music the fans like because we are the fans,'" Brownstein says. "So we said, 'Fuck it, let's let these guys do it. They seem really passionate about it.' So it really became a family event—these kids who started out as fans became friends and turned into promoters."

Camp Bisco IV: The Trance-Formation was held at Skyetop Festival Ground in Van Etten, N.Y., and included such jam band favorites as Umphrey's McGee and John Brown's Body, plus DJs and other acts that incorporated dance and electronic influences. MCP took heavy losses—which they say they expected in the first year of rebranding the festival—but attendance grew to 4,400.

What makes Camp Bisco unique among festivals is how the daytime jam fest merges with the late-night rave communities that had overlap in their fan bases—and in the Biscuits' music itself.

"[Fordin and Keber] did such a fantastic job of realizing our vision," Brownstein says, adding that the band handpicks at least the first few tiers of acts. "That's really what it's all about—we know what we want to do. It's just a matter of being able to find competent people to help you do it because we also have to write songs, record them and tour. But there are hundreds and hundreds of phone conversations."

There sure are, Fordin says. "Most festivals deal with a band and they're gone. We deal with this band every year for three days. We have to build an RV headquarters for them. We have to listen to all they want, and there's four different band members and they never agree and they all call me separately—and it starts in November and goes through July."

A big change to the dynamic occurred this year when the Biscuits signed with Red Light Management, which represents dozens of acts including Dave Matthews Band, Alanis Morissette, Phish and the Decemberists. "Their new management has helped connect the dots that the band could not connect when they didn't have a manager," Fordin says. "The four of them need to worry about playing music and coming together; someone else needs to worry about making the decisions."

Still, the added personnel didn't necessarily always help Fordin's and Keber's stress levels. "For the past five days, all day long, I would get text messages from management, saying, 'What are the counts? How many tickets have we sold?'" Fordin says. "I would respond back, 'I get my counts at 10 a.m. If I look at them before that, I will not sleep. You want us to produce your $1.4 million event, let us produce it—whether 1,000 or 10,000 people show up, we still have to put on a smile and a quality event.' Whether we're losing $200,000 or making $200,000, we still have to produce the event. Artists look at it differently, but they're understanding it more and more."

ANGELS AMONG US

The venue is an all-important production detail that has been rocky in the history of Camp Bisco. Camping for three days to hear live music takes a level of commitment far above hitting the local rock club, and MCP has moved the festival around as trial and error and event expansion came into play.

In 2007 MCP found what it believes is the festival's long-term home, 30 miles northwest of Albany, N.Y.: the Indian Lookout Country Club, built and maintained by the bikers who run the Harley Rendezvous Classic, one of the largest annual gatherings of motorcycle enthusiasts in the country. This move from nearby Hunter Mountain Ski Resort was an unpopular decision, Fordin and Keber say, as stories of the infamous clash between hippies and Hell's Angels at the Altamont (Calif.) Speedway festival in 1969 floated among Biscuits fans. But the fear was unfounded, and the bikers have proved to be invaluable partners.

"I like the security with all the bikers, it's a different feel—very safe but democratic, very chill," says Will Stroud, a Philadelphia Biscuits fan. "This one lady over there cleaned the bathroom every time someone used it."

He says this while standing steps away from the Harley Rendezvous headquarters, where two wayward campers just have been ushered sternly into an office with a cardboard sign labeled "Rehab" in magic marker. Two five-foot wooden statues of phalluses adorn the porch.

"Everyone thinks it's a strange thing to see a bunch of bikers taking care of a bunch of hippies," says Frank Potter, Indian Lookout's president. "But we all want the same things they want. Bikers want to have fun and keep their families safe, and sometimes there's arguments over turf, but it's no different than in the music industry." It's especially important for the bikers to crack down on bad behavior, he says, because they fought the state and county for more than 10 years for the permits to build the site and host their annual rally.

Having a consistent venue eases one headache, but Fordin and Keber still feel the pressure to meet their numbers and keep everyone happy. As Fordin says, it gives him "more gray hairs than anyone my age should have."

By Saturday afternoon, however, the sun is holding and the single tow truck from town is slowly making the campground rounds, hauling up cars trapped in the mud. More important, though, the Disco Biscuits are playing their 3 p.m. set, and the field in front of the stage is full enough that Keber estimates there are 10,000 people. This would meet the growth goals from 2008's attendance of 8,000 and prove the effectiveness of the pricing strategy.

"We've always believed in keeping our prices as low as possible and try to be one of the cheapest festivals in the country every year," Fordin says. This is particularly important because the Disco Biscuits and the electronic/hip-hop lineup draw an overall younger crowd, many student-aged with less disposable income, than some of the other jam band festivals, such as Gathering of the Vibes, held this summer in Bridgeport, Conn., with headliners moe., Bob Weir & Ratdog and Crosby, Stills & Nash.

Camp Bisco's initial presale began in January—with only the Disco Biscuits and dates announced—and was set at $115 for three-day tickets and camping, up from $110 in 2008. Those 300 tickets sold out in 48 hours, after which the price rose to $125 through March, unchanged from last year.

When the lineup was announced, tickets rose to $145, also unchanged from 2008, and the gate price was $165, up from $160. Several weeks before the festival, a one-day option was added for $75 ($85 at the gate), and this is where much of the count was ultimately made up on Saturday.

In total, 8,000 three-day passes were sold for this year's event, up 20% from 2008, while sales of Saturday one-day tickets increased 50% to 1,500. The remaining 1,500 people at the festival, for a total attendance of 11,000, were guests and media.

"Where we saw pricing backfire was in our VIP," Fordin says, referring to an additional $250 charge for premium camping facilities that include a lounge and special viewing areas, VIP-only showers, flushing toilets, shopping services, catered meals, discounted drinks and other amenities. In 2008, 700 people upgraded, but this year MCP sold only about 300 VIP tickets. "People still came, obviously; they just chose this year to spend $160 instead of $400."

Ticket sales account for 80% of Camp Bisco revenue, with the remaining 20% coming from the VIP upgrades, travel packages, alcohol sales, food and craft vending, RV parking fees, event merchandise and sponsorships from brands including Asics, Flip Video, Sirius XM and imeem, some of whom provided high-visibility in-kind promotional sponsorship.

But the ancillary prices are also held in check, with vendors being much more of the fairground family business than corporate variety. "The prices here are great," says Will Stroud, waiting in the long line for the site's one ATM. "At Bonnaroo I spent $21 on a beer and a pack of cigs."

In addition to pricing, a big factor in MCP's risk/reward equation for Camp Bisco is the booking. "It took a while, but I think we hit the nail on the head last year when we booked Snoop Dogg—all these people were like, 'This is an awesome festival, and I don't even like the Disco Biscuits,'" Fordin says. "If we go too big with the band, Biscuits fans aren't going to come because it won't fit. One of their agents wanted us to book the Black Crowes, and we said, 'We might gain 200 locals who want to see the Black Crowes, but we're going to lose 200 Biscuits fans, and we won't get the 10,000 Crowes fans that we should.'"

Where much of the investment goes is into international electronic acts, some of whom make their first significant U.S. appearances at Camp Bisco. This was true for Younger Brother, a U.K. duo that first performed stateside at Camp Bisco IV.

"In the U.K. there is no jam band scene, but over here it kind of spills into the trance scene, which is where our fans are in Europe,"

Younger Brother's Simon Posford says. "The people themselves are very similar. They all like to take psychedelics, they like psychedelic music, and they're generally very musical."

Electronic acts also get huge exposure at Bisco when featured at the late-night tent, where campers retreat after the headliners. This year, LCD Soundsystem's James Murphy played a set at the main stage on Saturday night, and then curated a late-night Disco Tent for his label DFA Records.

HIGH-WATER MARK

When the weekend was over and the tractors were pulling the last cars out of the still-sopping clay, MCP estimated revenue at $1.6 million, a 30% growth over 2008 and $200,000 more than expenses.

For Fordin and Keber, thoughts can now turn to their smaller events, which include club shows and other outdoor events closer to their Asheville, N.C., headquarters, with the optimism that next year, their goal to grow Camp Bisco by another 30% could be a reality.

"We've learned that we can almost make a better living by not touring and concentrating on the big events, although our fans hate that, so we go out and pound the pavement when we need to," Brownstein says. "We built our business around touring out of necessity. We have an extremely loyal and growing customer base, and when the record industry fell out from under itself, unbeknownst to us, it didn't affect us in the slightest.

"This is our life together; us and our fans are intrinsically connected, and if we can find a way to maintain that, then it doesn't really matter what happens anywhere outside of our little bubble," he says. "If 10,000 kids come here, or 7,000 kids come to an event we play at Red Rocks [in Colorado], that's all that matters to us. And if we can grow this festival to 20,000, it's game over."

Stompin' at The Grand Terrace

Excerpts from a Jazz Memoir in Verse

Philip S. Bryant

Picture two black Chicago working-class men living on the South Side of the city just after the midway point of the last century, slowly but steadily easing their way into middle age. They are part of that vast post-war army of working men and women who labored at the various factories, steel mills, slaughterhouses, auto plants, and other blue-collar industries that paid relatively well, but demanded grit, muscle, and endurance. Their class and race permanently marked their status, designated largely by an outside (white) world that surely welcomed their muscles and backs, but otherwise disdained and relegated them to the strict and closed confines of their ethnic and racial ghettos. The ghetto largely and at times narrowly defined the men and women who dwelled there. How they passed their time; what deep thoughts, hopes, dreams, visions, and aspirations they had; what lives they led; and what music they created, played, and listened to went mostly unnoticed and was usually dismissed as having little or no consequence or significance for the wider world that lay just beyond the borders of the ghetto. But for them, their Blues, Gospels, and Jazz were vital and of utmost importance, as seen here through these two aging African American men: Chicago Southsiders fated to a mostly obscure workaday life, trying to eke out a living in order to take care of families, wives, and children, while at the same time striving to kindle and nurture a deeper and more passionate sense of their own inner lives and the immediate worlds they inhabited—

which for them was defined, expressed, and reflected in the jazz they collected, listened to, and loved. Music was their haven and oasis, for better and for worse. It gave them (if ever so briefly) a true sense of who they were as human beings. It affirmed a spirit flowing within and between them and throughout the world where they lived and would soon depart and vanish from forever. This spirit they rarely tried to articulate in words or speak of directly. But both men believed in it, in the same way they believed in the music they heard. This is the story of James and Preston—friends, confidants, and companions—in whose dark faces reflects this light and life, lifting and spinning and shining ever forth like music itself across the infinite.

COOK!

They were in the living room one Friday night listening intently to Booker Ervin's *Blue Book* album. Booker's scratchy, big Texas drawl of a solo was in mid-flight when all of a sudden, exactly on the downbeat, Preston shouted, *"Cook!"* James looked startled at first, then smiled and nodded as Booker began to descend the summit he'd just climbed.

I used to love to hear the sound of that word when Preston or my dad would shout it in the middle of *The Sermon* by Jimmy Smith or Rahsaan Roland Kirk's biblical version of *All the Things You Are* or Shirley Scott's appropriately named *Slow Blues in the Kitchen.*

"Cook!" my dad would holler in the middle of her funky organ romp late at night, and I'd get a terrible hunger in the pit of my stomach. I thought I smelled my mother's simmering collard greens and ham hocks on the stove, though she'd put away the food from dinner hours ago.

STOMPIN' AT THE GRAND TERRACE

My father was playing something by Earl Hines—old—probably from the early '30s, when he was still with Louis Armstrong. He mentioned the old Grand Terrace Café, where Hines and the great ones used to play. Preston was snapping his fingers and nodding along with the beat. "That reminds me of a dream I had the other night. It was beautiful, man, in the sense of lights and music. Fatha Hines and Satchmo was *burnin'*. Outside, a soft glow from the streetlights seemed like a Canadian sunset, while inside the crystals of the great chandelier were lit up like a thousand stars. Bean took a chorus. Then Prez. Then Bird. Then Diz. Art Tatum was there. Teddy Wilson, Bill Basie, Lady Day, Don Byas, Duke Ellington, and Baby Dodds. Big Sid Catlett and Little Jazz Roy Eldridge himself. Everybody was diggin' it. People were dancin', not to show off, but to put into movement what the musicians were playin'. Everyone was there. You were there, James, with all these egghead-lookin' white cats. They weren't lookin' too hip, but could somehow dig it. The place got more crowded. You said, *Look, Preston, it's Bach, Beethoven, and Brahms returned from the dead to check out the scene!* I turned and saw these cats in gray powdered wigs, all steadily diggin' the show. Pops and Fatha kicked it into high gear. The place became so crowded I went onto the terrace to get some air. A cool breeze was blowin' as music poured out the doors into the night. People were dancin' on the terrace now, and it began to shake and vibrate. I thought, *Oh, shit, this muthafucka's about to crumble!* And it was a long way down, too—certain death if you fell. Then there was this big crackin' sound, and I thought, *Well, that's it.* We began to list like the *Lusitania* or *Titanic*, and I shouted, *We're all goin' down together!* And then a miraculous thing happened—the music swung that much harder! Pops and Diz were approaching the stratosphere on the bandstand! We righted and were lifted up by the sound. We were saved! The music held us up, James! And that's when I woke up." My father reset the needle on the Fatha Earl Hines album. This time they listened and did not speak.

LIVER & ONIONS: THE PIANISTS

My father was alone.
Preston was supposed to come,
but sometimes without a prior call
wouldn't show.

My father had the weekly selections
picked out—piano players today.

He started at their regular time,
drinking malt liquor and playing
Unit Structures by Cecil Taylor.

My mother, meanwhile,
hated Cecil's music and hated Preston more.
She was furiously chopping up onions
into a skillet of frying calf's liver.

"Liver, again?" I protested. She looked up
and flashed a warning flare, pointing
the knife at me. "Don't complain.
Some kids don't even have this to eat."

My father had gone through three of ten
selections he'd picked out. From Cecil
to Red Garland to Kenny Drew. Now
he was playing Tatum's *Humoresque*
—that choppy beginning—
still hoping the doorbell would ring.

Tatum was almost mocking the
classical Dvořák, before he got down to
hard swing.

My dad looked out the window,
then at his watch, and took
another sip of his malt liquor.

The overpowering smell of
frying liver and onions
and my mother's curses
filled the room.

DISCOVERING A NEW STAR: SONNY STITT

Preston removed
the album's cellophane wrapper.
A bright gem?
A dark, precious sapphire?
He held the unplayed
shiny black diamond
disc carefully between
the palms of his hands.
"James," he said, "I have
just discovered a new star
in the constellation Orion."
He set it on the record changer.
They listened,
charting its exact course
and position in the vast infinite cosmos.
"What shall we call it?"
my father asked as
they heard the fading echo
of a beautiful alto.
Preston looked toward the heavens.
There was absolutely no question.
"We'll call this star
Sonny Stitt."
"Sonny Stitt, it is!"
my father said, reaching
to turn over the record
as if gently adjusting the lens
of a telescope.

SWINGING HARD

It was snowing so hard outside you could barely see the houses across the street—a thick, heavy, wet snow that sounded like gravel being thrown against the windows. Preston and my dad were having a fierce argument over which pianist could swing harder: Kenny Drew or Hank

Jones. Drew was on, playing his part on *Blue Train*. My father said, "You can't tell me Jones ever dreamt of swinging this hard, much less playing it." Preston waved him off. "Shit, James, anybody who plays with Trane is bound to swing hard. Trane would *make* 'em swing. Hell, my grandmother could swing behind Trane, Mr. PC, and Philly Joe." My father said, "And your grandmother could probably jam a lot harder with The Drew than Jones." Preston shook his head, called him out. "Jones is a lyricist," he said. "He ain't in there sweatin' in the kitchen tryin' to cook no collard greens and ham hocks. He don't have to. His playin's more like a Cuban cigar and French cognac after a fine meal." My father walked to the window and watched the snow piling up on the street. Trane had started his solo on *Moment's Notice*. "Cognac or no cognac," he said, "the essence of jazz is to swing, so whether you're cooking French cuisine or black-eyed peas and cornbread, somebody's got to be in the kitch—" but then stopped. "Hey, Pres, we better go out there and see if we can dig your car out." Preston got up and peered through the glass at the snow fallen nearly a foot since they'd started playing records earlier that day. "Damn, it's a muthafucka out there!" He gathered up his records, and both of them put on their coats and boots and went downstairs. My father stood behind the car, pushing while Preston gunned the accelerator, spinning his wheels in the deep snow. "Rock it back and forth," my father hollered. "Ease up a little, then push it down." Preston did, and after a lot of rocking and grunting, the car finally started to free itself from the curb. "Yeah, now swing it hard!" he shouted, and Preston's Corvette fishtailed out into the street. As it started to pull away, my father laughed and yelled, "Yeah, you played that just like Drew—swinging hard! If you'd done it like Jones, you'd still be spinning your wheels!" Preston beeped his horn, flashed his lights, and slowly slid down the snow-packed street.

SAVING THE TRUMPET KINGS

Preston worked at the steel mills and made good money at the time, was twice married and divorced, paid alimony and child support, and with the rest of his money bought records, hi-fi equipment, and brand-new Corvettes—which, like his marriages, he would then proceed to wreck. My father said he drove like a lunatic, and had vowed never to get in or near a car that Preston drove. One day, he came over with one record instead of his usual armful and with head and hands bandaged.

"What happened?" my father asked.

"They burned up when I went into a viaduct trying to avoid some fool in front of me. (Everyone—*else*—on the road was a *fool*.) I was all right, but the gas tank ignited, and the whole car caught fire. The police came by the time I remembered I'd left my records in the trunk. Only managed to get one—this rare Emarcy release of *Rex Stewart and The Trumpet Kings*. Ran back, put my hand in the blazin' car, got the keys, opened the trunk, and rescued it. Police just about locked me up.

"Boy, yer crazy! Yer brand-new Vette is burnin' up, and all you can think about is a damn phonograph record! Well, I've seen it all.

"And I knew then and there how that story would be goin' 'round in some cop bar in Cicero later that night:

"Yeah, Joe, this crazy nigger went back into his burnin' Vette to get some damn record album. And you wonder why they don't have nuttin' to shake a stick at.

"Nothin' but this." Preston slowly pulled the plastic off the record jacket, obviously in pain with his bandaged fingers.

"Will you be all right?" my father asked, really concerned.

"Oh, yeah. Once you open me a beer and put on The Trumpet Kings."

MILES: PRINCE OF DARKNESS

I remember my father's stories
about him being cold, fitful,
reproachful, surly, rude, cruel,
unbearable, spiteful, arrogant, hateful.
But then he'd play
Some Day My Prince Will Come
in a swirl of bright spring colors
that come after a heavy rain
making the world anew again
and like the sometimes-tyrannical king
who is truly repentant of his transgressions
steps out onto the balcony
to greet his subjects

and they find it in their hearts
to forgive him for his sins
yet once again.

BASEMENT APARTMENT:
BLUES AND THE ABSTRACT TRUTH

My dad did not go to Preston's much. He mostly came to our place. On one occasion, one cold, rainy, gray November afternoon, he invited both of us. He had some old Race records by Duke Ellington to show us. Preston lived in the basement unit of a big apartment house on 80th and Drexel Avenue. He opened the door dressed in a long navy-blue terrycloth robe and black stocking cap—like a Trappist monk letting us in the heavy gate of a secluded monastery. He greeted us, but then apologized for the way his apartment looked. His most recent wife had taken all his furniture in the divorce settlement. He'd meant to clean up, but had worked overtime at the mill, so he was just getting up. The living room and dining room were spartan—couch, coffee table, television set, easy chair. That was it. Fireproof canvas work clothes were piled on the floor. A half-eaten bowl of popcorn sat on the coffee table and could have been there all week. The small kitchen contained a metal table, two chairs, refrigerator, a few dirty dishes in the sink. It looked like a stark motel room where you'd stay only the night, glad to check out first thing in the morning. We passed the first bedroom—a queen-size box and mattress on the floor, covers askew, the walls bare except for a cross over the bed. The room had a small table lamp and an electric alarm clock. We continued down the narrow hallway to the "master" bedroom, where Preston kept his record collection and stereo equipment. There, records on shelves completely took up the four walls of the large room. A conservative estimate would be more than twenty thousand albums. These were broken into fifty or so sections, each meticulously ordered and numbered. A card file cataloged all of them. The section on Johnny Hodges contained nearly 150 albums. The first shelf held old 78 Vocalions of Count Basie and Jimmie Lunceford. Deccas and Columbias, Okeys in original sleeves and in pristine condition. No one had spoken in the inner sanctum. I remember hearing the hum of a dehumidifier and then sinking into the berber carpet. Track lights lit and warmed the room. His stereo system was state-of-the-art—Thorens turntable, Klipsch woofer and subwoofer system, McIntosh amp and pre-amp—housed in a custom-made oak stand. Oliver Nelson's *Blues and the Abstract Truth* lay there. We were in the vaults of the Louvre or The Prado, staring out at the twenty thousand albums—years' worth of American music, culture, and history. Preston, hunched over, looked older and more feeble than his real age. I wondered what would become of all these treasures. His children barely knew him; his wives, he said, were only interested in his money. They'd all told him to keep his goddamn records. We listened to *Lester Leaps In*, a mint-condition 1939 original Vocalian recording of the timeless Lester Young. It sounded as if he might have recorded it the day before. Preston showed us the record sleeve: *Best to you always, Pres, Chicago, August 9, 1951.* Lester leapt while outside an early winter gale blew. Prez was spinning around an infinite black universe on the turntable. The music was perfect, crystal clear, and true.

PREZ

Lester's
Sound
Insinuated
That
There
Would
Always
Be
A
Door
Somewhere
That
We'd
Find
Already
Unlocked
If
We

Ever
Tried
To
Open
It.

THE TERRACE: REVISITED

Ben Webster was on, playing *Autumn Leaves.*
Preston came into the living room, shaken.
He'd dreamt about The Grand Terrace again.
"It was the night after King was assassinated.
All the musicians were gathered to play a memorial tribute,
but niggers were riotin', burnin', and lootin' all over.
We came outside and said, "This is no way to remember
Dr. King and his work!" There was this brother carryin' a big
color TV down the street. *Fuck that. This is what's king now!*
Then they started burning down The Terrace!
Reverend King came out of the flaming building
to get them to stop. Told them they were burnin' their own
history, everything that was good about 'em as a people.
One of 'em just pushed him out of the way.
Nigger, you dead. You had your time, now it's our time,
so get out the way!
With that, he lit a Molotov cocktail and threw it into
the already-burnin' building. All the musicians who got out
stood with their instruments and watched it burn. Prez, Bean,
Bird, Duke, Lady Day, Don Byas, Louis, Art Tatum,
Count, Diz, Roy, Rex Stewart, and so many more appeared
in the crowd, watchin' as it burned, as siren and glass broke the air.
After a while, one of Jelly Roll's kin pushed to the front.
It's over now, folks. You can all go home.
The burning Terrace lit up the night sky.
Then I woke up."
My father got up and put on the other side of Ben Webster.
"A sad dream," he said, handing Preston a beer. "A very sad dream,
indeed."

WORKING OUT AT THE CORNER LOUNGE

7th & King Drive

Spilling out onto
the quiet streets
the Hammond B
tumbles and
somersaults
followed by a complete
drum set and
red Gibson
hollow-body guitar
and maybe a
funky old
tarnished saxophone
that just happened
to be sitting out
followed by a large
black woman
—dress hiked up
over her brown
padded thighs—
raucously laughing
and spilling out
herself more than just
a little drunk.

Still III

Timmhotep Aku, Carl Chery, Clover Hope,
Rob Markman, Starrene Rhett, and Anslem Samuel

*In spring 1994, a chip-tooth kid outta
Queensbridge released a 10-song debut
album that set a new standard for hip-hop
lyricism. Fifteen years later, XXL takes
a trip down memory lane to get an
in-depth look at the making of a classic.
It's* Illmatic. *Yeah.*

They called him prophet. Poetry was a part of him. And on Tuesday, April 19, 1994, when 20-year-old Nasir Jones released *Illmatic*, his debut album on Sony Music's Columbia Records, true-believer hip-hop heads rejoiced. It felt like revelation.

The journey began three years earlier, with Main Source's 1991 posse cut "Live at the Barbeque." On it, the rap world was introduced to an upstart MC from Long Island City's Queensbridge Houses. Queensbridge, the largest housing project in the U.S., was home to Marley Marl, MC Shan and the mighty Juice Crew, who'd fallen to the Bronx's Boogie Down Productions in the famous "Bridge Wars" of the late '80s. The son of jazz trumpeter Olu Dara, Nas was discovered by Main Source's Large Professor—and was still in his teens when he stole the "Barbeque" single with lines like, "Verbal assassin / My architect pleases / When I was 12 / I went to hell for snuffin' Jesus!"

New York streets were buzzing heavy. 3rd Bass rapper MC Serch signed Nas to his Serchlite Publishing and started shopping for a record deal. Not all of the industry's honchos were as enthused (Russell Simmons, for example, at Serch's own label, Def Jam Recordings, turned him down for fear of commercial failure). But Sony Music A&R Faith Newman-Orbach eventually signed Nas to Columbia Records.

With an all-star team of New York beatmakers abetting Large Professor's production, work began on hip-hop's perfect album. Nas's first recorded solo track, "Halftime," appeared on the soundtrack to the 1992 indie flick *Zebrahead*, whetting fans' appetites for what was to come. In the years leading up to the album's release, overzealous DJs began liberating unguarded tracks via mixtapes and the college-radio circuit. In the face of such early bootlegging, Columbia rushed a short, 10-song *Illmatic* to stores in '94—nixing original plans to include more material.

New York purists and the rap press raved, but Russell was right: The album was not a huge commercial success, selling a mere 330,000 copies its first year out. Its cultural impact, though, has proved to be immeasurable, marking Nas's messiah-like arrival and the beginning of a nine-album, multimillion-selling career. A decade and a half after its release, *XXL* assembles the people who were there to bear witness.
—*ROB MARKMAN*

REPRESENTERS

Nas: Queens rapper, a.k.a. the Prophet
Jungle: Nas's Brother, one-half of rap duo Bravehearts
Faith Newman-Orbach: Executive producer, former Sony A&R
MC Serch: Executive producer, one-third of Queens rap trio 3rd Bass
DJ Premier: Brooklyn (by way of Prairie View, Texas) producer, one-half of rap duo Gang Starr
Large Professor: Queens producer, rapper, member of rap group Main Source
L.E.S.: Queens producer
AZ: Brooklyn rapper
Olu Dara: Nas's father, jazz trumpeter
Pete Rock: Mount Vernon producer, one-half of rap duo Pete Rock & CL Smooth
T La Rock: Bronx rapper
Busta Rhymes: Brooklyn rapper, former member of rap group Leaders of the New School

Grand Wizard: Queens rapper, one-half of rap duo Bravehearts

Q-Tip: Queens rapper, producer, member of rap group A Tribe Called Quest

[1] "THE GENESIS"

Conceived by Nas and Faith Newman-Orbach

Jungle: Nas picked the beat for us to talk on in the background. I remember I didn't like the beat. I was like, "Off this beat, man? This is garbage." I was mad young. I didn't even understand what he was doing.

Nas: I always loved all the breaks in the *Wild Style* movie. [This session] wasn't in the beginning of recording [the album], it was closer to the end. I brought a VHS tape of the movie and had the engineer just loop it.

Faith Newman-Orbach: Wild Style was, like, his first introduction to hip-hop. His father took him to see that when he was a kid.

MC Serch: The most difficult sample [to clear] was with [*Wild Style* director] Charlie Ahearn, believe it or not. We had made a deal with Charlie, and then Fab 5 Freddy got into the mix and started getting into Charlie's ear like, "Nah, you didn't get enough [money]." The funny thing was, Fab 5 Freddy was about to direct the "One Love" video. So I'm calling Freddy like, "What are you telling your man? I'm about to cut you a check. You're about to direct a video. Get on the same page." [Freddy said,] "Are you threatening me?" I'm like, "Nah, it's not a threat. I'm just saying, you don't take care of this, you're not gonna be directing no video." I haven't spoke to Fab 5 Freddy since.

[2] "N.Y. STATE OF MIND"

Produced by DJ Premier

DJ Premier: That was actually the second beat that I did [for *Illmatic*]. The first one was "Represent." I just had the drum pattern going with the funny little—it sounds almost like an astronaut signal at the beginning. . . . I found that Joe Chambers sample ["Mind Rain"], which is where that's from. I usually don't disclose my samples, but I cleared it, so it's all good. Found the sample, and when they heard that melody, Nas and them was in agreement, like, "Yo, hook that up, that's hot." So I hooked it up, and Nas started writing.

Nas: I had most of it already written, and the original [rhyme] was probably close to 60 bars, so I just broke it up. When I got in the studio, we heard that record. We were just listening to records. I would sit with Premier for hours on end in D&D Studios. When he started putting it together, I just pieced the stuff that I had and wrote a couple of new things in there, too.

DJ Premier: Right at the beginning of the record, when he says, "Straight out the dungeons of rap, where fake niggas don't make it back." And then there's kind of like a silence, where the music is building up, and you hear Nas go, "I don't know how to start this shit." He just wrote it, and he was trying to figure out how to format it, like when to come in. I'm waving at him in the control room like, "Look at me, go in for the count." So right when he looks up and sees me counting, he just jumps in. He did the whole first verse in one take, and I remember when he finished the first verse, he stopped and said, "Does that sound cool?" And we were all like, "Oh my God!" It was like, I don't even care what else you write.

[3] "LIFE'S A BITCH"

Produced by L.E.S.
Co-Produced by Nas
Featured Vocals: AZ
Trumpet: Olu Dara

Nas: I asked L.E.S. to bring [a copy of Mtume's "Juicy Fruit"]. I wanted to sample "Juicy." He didn't have the record, so he brought the Gap Band's "Yearning for Your Love" instead. Looped it up, and I was like, "Yo, it ain't 'Juicy,' but it's a whole 'nother monster!" Once we looped it up, I didn't even care about "Juicy." Of course, when Biggie dropped, I was like, "Oh my God." I lost my rhyme books [the day we recorded "Life's a Bitch"]. When we got to the studio and realized that I lost my books, we realized I left it on the train. Everybody was mad, like what we left on the train was a winning lotto ticket. [Laughs] We were like, "Oh man, it's over!" That was years of writing, but the good thing was that I had memorized a lot of it.

L.E.S.: You know, AZ was there. Nas was like, "A, you got something for this?" A just went in the booth and spit it, and Nas came right behind him. AZ had a chorus. They vibed, and before I even blinked, I left the studio, went back to the projects, and niggas was like, "We love that Nas joint." I was like, Damn. Word? How they get that?

AZ: The hook I had written. . . . After the hook was there, they was like, "Damn, you gotta spit, dawg." I was like, "Aight, fuck it. If you like it, you like it. You don't, you don't." I did it, and everybody liked it. That was it. It was history made. I didn't know who the hell Nas's father was, but I was introduced to him there, and pop was getting it on.

Olu Dara: Well, I had my horn with me, and Nasir said, "Just play 'Life's a Bitch.' Could you play a little at the end?" I remember his brother, Jungle, was there, and we had our Hennessy and our Champagne and everything.

[4] "THE WORLD IS YOURS"

Produced by Pete Rock

Pete Rock: We were in my basement. Large Professor had brought him over. That's when I actually first met Nas, when Large brought him up to Mount Vernon. We went through beats and stumbled across that one. It wasn't like I made it then. It was already made, so I just popped the disc in, and he was like, "Yo!" Next thing you know, we in Battery Studios knocking it down. When I was doing the scratches, Preemo was there. He was just standing there, looking in amazement, and I was like, "Come on, nigga! You that dude, too."

Nas: At the time, getting a beat from Pete Rock was like getting a beat from Kanye or Timbaland or fuckin' Dre. I fought to get that [T La Rock] sample on there. Pete had a way of doing his beats, and he was Pete Rock, so I didn't wanna interfere that much. But I had "It's Yours" in my head, and I thought it would sound ill. At the last minute, he fit it in there, I think at the mix. I didn't know how he was gonna fit it in there, but it was perfect how he did it.

T La Rock: When I first listened to Nas, I thought he sounded like a combination of T La Rock and Rakim. . . . Anyone that can rhyme and make sense and not make me wanna just skip to the next track I consider a really good lyricist. And Nas is that. I was kinda blown away by the song itself, and then Pete Rock putting in that "It's Yours" sample.

MC Serch: There was one hiccup—with Pete Rock's brother Ruddy. We were really coming close to the end of the album, and Pete and Nas had done a lot of work together, and the week that they were mixing, my grandmother passed away. And in the Jewish religion, you have to sit shiva, and my day to sit shiva was Friday. When you sit shiva, you basically sit on a box, and you do nothing the whole day. So I get a call from Ruddy, his lawyer and my lawyer telling me that they're due a $5,000 check for the album. And I explain to them, "No problem, I'll get it to you Monday." And they had that session that day, and they're like, "Well, we'll go into the studio on Monday and record Monday." I was like, "No, no, no. You gotta get it done [today], because mastering is on Monday." We had a lot of pressure on us to release this album before the streets got flooded with bootlegs. So there was no way I could miss this date. I'm trying to explain to Ruddy, "Look, it's shiva, it's respect to the dead." And he's like, "I don't care about your grandmother, I don't care about shiva, I want my effin' money, or we're not going in the studio." To this day, I don't mess with Pete Rock. I don't have any words for Pete Rock. Even if Pete said to me, "I had no idea, I didn't know," that's still your manager. You still should be involved. And if you're not involved, you're catching an L for his loss. This was not Nas's beef. It was my beef. I didn't even want Nas knowing anything about it. I didn't even tell Nas about it until this past year.

Pete Rock: I don't even remember that shit. I mean, it might have happened, but it was so long ago. Niggas still remember bullshit? All I was concerned with was making a dope-ass record for this new nigga Nas at that time. I don't know what Serch is talking about.

[5] "HALFTIME"

Produced by Large Professor

Large Professor: The session for "Halftime" was hot, 'cause he was gettin' his big chance. And it was like, he had his weed already, Big Bo was there, Jungle was there, Wiz was there. I came through. I had the beat already. And we sat there, cooled out a lil' bit. And he was takin' it easy, 'cause he was like, "This is my turn now, and I'm gon' make it count." So we would roll up an oowop and shit and sit back, listen to the beat. And he was real cool with that shit, like, real smooth with that shit. He'll sit there for a little while and then be like, "Yo, aight, I'm ready." And then he go in the booth and start sayin' the words, and then everybody's up, shit is lit up. And shit is connecting, and everybody is in the live room like, "Wow!"

Busta Rhymes: I went over [to Large Professor's house], and he made the "Halftime" beat in front of me, and he was gonna give it to me at the time. I didn't know what to do with it. I didn't know why I didn't know what to do with it, because I loved the shit out the beat. Then I heard it on "Halftime," and I was like, Goddamn, I was a stupid ass for not touching this beat!

Nas: I remember one time Busta Rhymes stopping by [Chung King Studios], and I met him. I guess he knew me from being with Large Professor. . . . And my brother told him that he should leave Leaders of the New School and go solo. [Laughs]

Jungle: Oh yeah, the first time I met Busta, he was still down with Leaders of the New School and shit. And I was like, "Yo, man, you tight. I think if you went solo and left your peoples alone, you would blow up." And Nas and everybody was like, "What the fuck are you talking 'bout?" It's like I insulted the rest of his crew and shit. But then he went solo, and he blew up.

Busta Rhymes: I just took it in stride. I was feeling good that niggas was feelin' that way about me. I just appreciated Jungle when he told me that.

[6] "MEMORY LANE (SITTIN' IN DA PARK)"

Produced by DJ Premier

DJ Premier: Nas wanted to help me pick a sample for that, and he heard the Reuben Wilson sample [from "We're in Love"], and he was like, "That's it." I wasn't really into that one. But he was like, "Yo, that's it, Preem. Cook that up." So I just hooked it up, because he asked me to. I was in competition with the other producers on the album, so I wanted to be funkier than what they had. I had just seen Q-Tip, and he played me a cassette, and he had a rough [version of "One Love"]. He pause-mixed the record in order to let Nas hear it before he put drums and stuff to it. And when I heard the sample and the way he had it hooked up, I was like, Oh my God, everybody is coming with shit harder than mines. But Nas was like, "Man, I really wanna do this one." And he wrote it right on the spot. Once we cut the vocals, I heard what he was saying. I wasn't mad at it, I wasn't against it, I just thought I could have done better.

Nas: I just felt like all the shit I saw in Queensbridge, it meant something. For some reason, I knew this ain't the average shit a kid my age is supposed to be seeing. I knew it was something special about what I was seeing, and it wasn't all good. This was real life. It's situations—whether it's welfare, or my friends' havin' dope-fiend parents, or teenagers being chased by cops.

Grand Wizard: Every word that was spit came from something that happened or something that everybody was a part of. My man got shot for his sheep coat. Every word was happening all around us.

[7] "ONE LOVE"

Produced by Q-Tip

Large Professor: He was like, "Yo, you think Q-Tip would give me a beat?" That's really when I was gettin' up with Tip a lot, so I was like, "Yo, of course. Just roll through with me out to Jamaica one time, and we'll just sit down." And we did. We rolled out there, back when Tip had all the stuff in Phife's grandmother's basement.

And we sat down, and Tip was like, "Oh word? I don't really have no beats done right now. But I'ma show you the record I'ma use for you." And he played this record [The Heath Brothers' "Smilin' Billy Suite Part II"], and it was just like, "Oh shit! That shit is crazy!" He hooked it up and did his thing, and it was on.

Even though dudes already knew who Nas was, and they wouldn't have fronted on him, but just kinda makin' it more natural feelin', where he's not going through Sony or Faith or Serch. It was like, We gon' stay right here on the street and roll through to they street. We not goin' in a cab or one of the cars that Sony gets you. We goin' street style, and go right up to they door. Things like that make all the difference in the world to me.

Q-Tip: Just from when you heard Nas initially, you knew he was ill. When I first heard him rhyme, I knew he was ill. Everybody knew he was ill. But I told Faith, "You guys got somebody special." Because he has vulnerability in his rhymes. A lot of niggas who MC, you don't hear the vulnerability. He keeps it relatable, but he has a lot of depth. He can keep it gangsta, he can keep it educated, he can keep it thoughtful. He can tell you that he's the shit, and he can tell you when he fucks up. And that's what makes Nas endearing to everybody.

[8] "ONE TIME 4 YOUR MIND"

Produced by Large Professor

Large Professor: We got this kinda attitude. It wasn't like, "Yo, the budget," and all that type of shit. It was cool, 'cause it was a little quick rhyme that he had. Some shortie-to-the-store shit, like that. Not like he was tryin' to go too hard or lyrical. It was just like, "Yo, I'm a regular dude. I'll kick some cool, around-the-way, corner shit for you."

Nas: Honestly, that song was just like, "Hey, we chilling." That song, I didn't give a fuck—it was just, go in there and have fun. I wanted Wiz's voice on that. Out of everybody around, I thought that he had a voice that can be on a record and come off. I always wanted him to rhyme and shit, and that was my way of pushing him into that shit.

Grand Wizard: At the time, we were just listening to the beat, and Nas was like, "Come in [the booth] with me and help me with the hook." So I get on the mic and say, "One time for ya mind, one time. . . ." And Nas comes in with, "Yeah, whatever. . . ." He just knew how to bounce off of me.

[9] "REPRESENT"

Produced by DJ Premier

Jungle: That was one of the days Nas let everybody get in the mic booth and talk and shit. I don't know why he used to do that shit, 'cause none of us was—we only had one or two rappers [in the crew]. Like, everybody who was in the studio was in the booth, but none of them would even wanna be a rapper. They just wanna roll with the rapper. The whole project was happy to just be out the projects and shit. Everybody was packed up in D&D studio.

Nas: That was a serious weight, representing Queensbridge. I was honored to do it, because of what Shan and Marley had already done. I just wanted to grab the flag and hold it up as high as ever. I felt like they had already paved the way, and now they needed an unbeatable soldier to hold that flag up high. After the battle with BDP, you can't ignore the doubt that people had in my hood. So it was like, I'm here now, and I got it, and I'ma hold it down to the death.

Jungle: That era was the era where you thought you wasn't gonna make it to 20 years old. You thought you was gonna die. So when he was making that album, I didn't know it was gonna go further than Queensbridge. I didn't know we could actually go to L.A. and see other famous people and make money.

[10] "IT AIN'T HARD TO TELL"

Produced by Large Professor

MC Serch: "I'm a Villain" and "It Ain't Hard to Tell" [were on his demo]. "It Ain't Hard to Tell" changed a little bit. Not much. First verse and most of the second verse was changed, but the Large Professor's beat, with the horns in it, it pretty much stayed the same. Russell Simmons said, "He sounds like G Rap, and G Rap don't sell no records. I'm not fuckin' with Nas." That's exactly what he said to me. I said okay, and I left, never looked back. I never told Nas, because by the same day I went to Columbia and saw Faith. Her and David Kahne pretty much locked me in a room and said, "Whatever deal you wanna make, let's make it."

Faith Newman-Orbach: "It Ain't Hard to Tell" was on the original demo that I got from him. Then there was another song ["I'm a Villain"], where he sounded just like G Rap on it, which is why Russell didn't wanna sign him.

Nas: We did the original version in Large Professor's apartment. And once there was a deal in place, we were able to use a real mic and a real studio [to re-record]. After me, SWV did "Right Here" with the same sample [from Michael Jackson's "Human Nature"]. I felt like I was responsible for that record, but the reality is that "Human Nature" was such a beautiful-ass song that people wanted to replay that. When the SWV record came out, I was pissed, because if I was to have a record for the radio, that was the perfect one. And when SWV took the shine, it was like, "Oh no!" Of course, it was my first album. I was like, Wait, how am I gonna get Michael Jackson to clear this? And then I realized, Oh shit, we're label mates! So we made it happen.

We had an in-store [at Tower Records at Fourth and Broadway]. And I'd never been to one. I expected to sign maybe 40 autographs at the most. [Before we left,] my record company kept telling me what a scene it was down there. I had no idea what they were talking about. It was me and the crew. We were excited, happy, celebrating. And we went to the in-store, and when I saw the crowd, it really let me know that this is gonna be something. This is not a tape that comes out and they just play it for a little while. When we left, it was kids screaming, crying and chasing the car. It was like 'N Sync. And this is my first album. It was a mob scene. That's when I knew. I was like, Yo, this is gonna be all right. I looked around, and I was like, This is gonna be all right.

The Revolution Will Be Harmonized

Barry Walters

Keyboardist Lisa Coleman was 19 when she started working with Prince on his 1980 album *Dirty Mind*. Her childhood friend, guitarist Wendy Melvoin, was also 19 when she joined Prince in 1983 for *Purple Rain*. Known from that point on as Wendy & Lisa, Melvoin and Coleman became key members of the Revolution, Prince's band at the peak of his musical powers and multi-platinum popularity. After they left the group in '86, the pair continued as a recording duo and as composers for such hit TV shows as *Heroes*. Shimmering with bright surfaces that complement its complex depths, their latest album, *White Flags of Winter Chimneys*, showcases sophisticated strains of rock and jazz that definitively assert their serious chops. To celebrate that achievement, Melvoin and Coleman cast aside their usual privacy and gave *Out* their most candid interview ever.

Out: *People who know about you as players in Prince's band may not know about the music you've composed for film and TV, or all the records you've appeared on, like k.d. lang's* Invincible Summer, *or last year's incredible Grace Jones comeback album,* Hurricane.

Wendy: We had an amazing month with [Jones] in our home writing "Williams' Blood," becoming friends, and being bizarre divas. We had to pick her up when she woke up in the morning, and the morning to her was like 6 PM.

Lisa: She gets in the back seat of the car and of course we have to stop to buy bottles of champagne. She wanted to play the bass. She kind of couldn't, but she could groove like nobody's business on one note. She started to sing and I wish I could've seen my own face. I was like—
Wendy and Lisa in near unison: Oh my God, it's *Nightclubbing*! [Jones's classic 1981 disco-punk album with the hit "Pull Up to the Bumper"]

Like Hurricane, *your new album has a cinematic quality, and you compose background music for film and TV as well. How do you go about creating music that's inherently cinematic?*

Wendy: It's trying to compose the song so that you can see it better in your head. Choosing specific notes to enhance a certain line that you're singing, or using a particular instrument that would evoke a visceral response from a listener. My girlfriend is a film director and writer and asks me a lot of these kinds of questions. [She's Lisa Cholodenko, the acclaimed filmmaker behind *Laurel Canyon* and *The Kids Are All Right*.]

Lisa: When Wendy and I score, we aren't accompanying the lead singer. Instead, there are the actors and the narrative. You have to be invisible and only enhance what's there. So it's kind of like drawing outlines and shadows on things that make it more three-dimensional. In a pop song, especially when you write it yourself, you become the actor. Then you add the landscape, the environment in which the situation is taking place.

I imagine that your history with Prince has been both a blessing and a hindrance to getting TV and film work. How has that played out?

Lisa: A lot of people take meetings with us and the whole meeting will be, "What was Prince like? What is he doing now?" So it opens a lot of doors, but it doesn't fill the room with anything substantial to do with us.
Wendy: We've had to get on a soapbox every time a door gets opened and convince the world that we're viable. That's sort of been a pathology

for us. We've been composing for film and TV for almost 20 years now, and we just in the past maybe 10 years have gotten away from only being called to do black movies. Now we're working on a show that's run by all lesbians and we're thrilled to be doing it. It's on Showtime, *Nurse Jackie*, with Edie Falco. It's fantastic.

Why did the two of you decide to keep working together after you left the Revolution?

Wendy: We were married and I was her biggest fan. Everything that she played broke my heart and still does and I wanna own it and covet it and make it mine.

Lisa: [*Laughs at that*] Yeah, we're chained together. We're shackled. No, I love Wendy. We've known each other our entire lives practically. Once she was finally hired into Prince's band, it was like a dream for me. I had fallen in love with Wendy, my childhood friend, and suddenly we were looking at each other differently, but I had to leave on the road all the time. It was always just torture. Finally Prince met Wendy and there was some trouble with the other guitar player [Dez Dickerson], and providence moved in such a way that Wendy ended up on the road with us.

Was the image you projected in Purple Rain *a function of who the two of you were together? Or did it come from Prince, or the director?*

Wendy: I don't think the director had anything to do with it. I think Prince saw us as the couple that we were and used that relationship to add more mystery to him. And I think Lisa and I were willing to go there because at that time we felt mysterious. We were young and it was the thing, so we went with it, not knowing what the result of that would mean or imply later in life. We didn't think about it in those terms. We just thought, *Wow, this is cool!*

Before we continue, I have to ask: Have you come out before? Is this it?

Wendy: We've never done a "Let's come out" interview. We've never been in the closet, but we never said, "Let's get an interview with

The Advocate. Let's get an interview with *Out.*" I didn't want to be a lesbian musician. I felt really uncomfortable with that role. I was already fighting, being a guitar player in a man's world and to have that on top of it—Lisa and I were so very married at the time, it just didn't seem like something I could handle.

Lisa: With Prince and the Revolution, I think that it was just taken for granted that we were supposed to be the gay reps in the band. [*Laughs*] The blacks, the whites, the gays. And people would say, "Gee, do you think this lesbian thing is going to work for them?" [*Everyone laughs*] So, after the band kind of split up, the record labels would be like, "You need to be wearing fur coats and sitting on motorcycles and long fingernails . . . "

Wendy: It was just horseshit.

Lisa: "And why don't you wear that lingerie like you used to?"

Wendy: Which I never did.

Lisa: I did.

Wendy: But you wore it in a very different way.

Lisa: Yeah, it was more punk, like a fuck-you thing, not, "I'm a sexy girl."

How did the process of asserting your own identity as a duo conflict with the record company's perception of your marketability based on the Revolution?

Wendy: To be honest with you, it kind of manifested itself in every aspect of our career at the time. From the songs we were writing to the pictures we were taking to the videos that we wanted to do to the places we wanted to perform to the print that we wanted to give interviews to, it was all in constant contrast to what the business wanted from us. It was extremely frustrating because we were in such a minority as musicians and as young women. We weren't even considering coming out because we were already dealing with so much adversity coming away from Prince. That on top of it just seemed insurmountable. I don't think either one of us were prepared at that age to have that be the ultimate battle.

Were the record companies aware that you were lesbians and in a relationship together?

Wendy: They'd never talk to us about it. I think everybody knew, but nobody said to us, "But you're a lesbian couple. We could work the Lilith Fair angle. We could work the Olivia Records angle." No one used that kind of language with us.

Lisa: We were so hung up on the fact that these people wanted us to be Prince. It didn't matter what our sexuality was. After we would leave the record company offices, I remember one of our managers mentioning that the art department people would comment on the way Wendy and I would talk to each other. Like I would say, "Yes, dear," and they would be all like whisper-whisper after we would leave the room. "They're gay, aren't they? They're like an old married couple." At that point, we had already been a couple for 10 years. It was very normal for us and very precious.

Wendy: I saw a lot of other women coming out at the time and I didn't want that on my plate. I wanted my life with Lisa to be so much more private and so much more conventional than that.

Lisa: You know, Wendy, I don't know if you'll mind me saying this, but we did slightly differ on our consciousness about it. We would do interviews together and people would ask us questions like, "What is it like living in LA?" And I'd start talking about living in a house together and literally get a kick from Wendy under the table like, "You're going too far."

Wendy: Lisa, at the time we were talking to bullshit magazines. I just didn't want the judgment from people who didn't know about us or the struggle it takes for gays to fucking live a normal life.

Lisa: I know, but I felt that you had to teach by example instead of making some statement.

Wendy: I disagreed at the time. You can hear it still. Lisa and I are so much on the same page as older women, but at the time it was like, "Fuck that!" I'm not gonna go there. I want more control of this. I just simply do. I lead the way for Lisa and I to be closeted.

You were dealing with this during the Reagan years when the AIDS crisis was exploding and the progressive attitude regarding gays started reversing. It must've been hard to contend with that while the music industry pushed you to be the next Mary Jane Girls.

Wendy and Lisa, nearly in unison: That's exactly what they wanted.

Wendy: We couldn't have been more opposite of that. We were just geeky musicians. We still are. We did a record 10, 11 years ago with Trevor Horn that was never released. We were hoping that we would have the next fucking Grace Jones "Slave to the Rhythm" extravaganza. We thought, "This is going to be genius! We're going to be musician freaks and experiment." And he, honest to god, wanted us to be the Spice Girls. My heart was broken.

Lisa: Not only that, but he was so homophobic. I hate to say it, but he wouldn't even let us eat off of his silverware on Friday because he was Jewish. It turned into this nightmare. He and his wife, oh God, I don't want to talk disparagingly about anybody, but it made us very uncomfortable.

Wendy: Our homosexuality became quite an issue for them.

That's especially disturbing coming from the guy who produced Frankie Goes to Hollywood and Grace Jones and the Pet Shop Boys.

Wendy: And Marc Almond and ABC and t.A.T.u. You name it.

Lisa: He would come in and start talking, "Well, I asked my rabbi about homosexuality and my rabbi said it's comparable to being born a mass murderer. You can be born a mass murderer, but if you practice mass murder it's sinful." I was like, "Okay, you can be born gay, but if you practice being gay, you might as well be a mass murderer?" Oh, thanks Trev. Let's record this song now.

That must've been a shock after what you'd experienced in the Revolution. How conscious was Prince of assembling for the Revolution that racial and sexuality rainbow you described?

Wendy: He was incredibly conscious of it. Look at the way he looked during *Dirty Mind* and *Controversy* and *1999*. He was so androgynous. He didn't care if you were [paraphrasing Prince's "Uptown" lyric] "black, white, straight, gay, Puerto Rican, just a freakin'." That guy wanted fans. So anyway he could get them—and a more interesting way he could do it—appealed to him. The Sly and the Family Stone mentality, that whole black/white/freaky thing on stage appealed to him.

Lisa: I'll give you an example. We had a photo shoot for the Purple Rain poster. We were all in our different positions and he at one point walked over to me and Wendy and lifted my arm up and put my hand around Wendy's waist and said, "There." And that is the poster. That's how precise he was about how he wanted the image of the band to be. He wanted it to be way more obvious. We weren't just the two girls in the band.

Wendy: We were the couple.

Lisa: We were the gay girls in the band. It was very calculated.

Wendy: And how did it make us feel? I felt slightly protected by it, which is really ironic. There was so much mystery around him and he never had to answer to anybody or anything and I was so young and dumb that I thought I could adopt that philosophy.

Lisa: It was validating. It was just, "Here you go. This is the name of the story and this is what it looks like." And it was all the more reason why we didn't feel as though we had to talk about it. People just saw it. They bought the records and we were successful, so it wasn't that big a deal. It's like hip-hop today. It's dangerous, but every little kid in the Midwest is rapping.

So Prince knew the full extent of your relationship?

Wendy: He wouldn't spend the night at our house. He was very much aware of it. [During the mid-'80s, Prince dated Wendy's twin sister, Susannah Melvoin, who sang the Family's 1985 version of "Nothing Compares 2 U."]

How far back had you known each other before the Revolution?

Wendy: Lisa and I had known each other since we were two years old. Our families grew up together. We had bands together. We went to the same schools together, the whole thing. And then during those pivotal teenage years, we spent a few years apart. I turned 16 and fell in love with her, and we were a couple for 22 years starting when I was 17. We fell in love in 1980, and we were a full-blown couple from 1981 to 2002.

Did you first think Prince was gay?

Lisa: He was little and kinda prissy and everything. But he's so not gay.
Wendy: He's a girl, for sure, but he's not gay. He looked at me like a
gay woman would look at another woman.
Lisa: Totally. He's like a fancy lesbian.
Wendy: I remember being at that "Sexuality" video shoot and him on
stage with that little black jacket and that tie thing around his neck
and his black pants with white buttons on the side. And we looked
at each other for the first time and I thought, "Oh, I could so fall in
love with that girl easy." It doesn't matter what sexuality, gender
you are. You're in the room with him and he gives you that look and
you're like, "Okay, I'm done. It's over." He's Casanova. He's Valentino.

*Prince certainly played up the ambiguity of his sexuality, and yet many
straight men have a certain kind of relationship with lesbians that a
gay man doesn't have: It's a turn-on for them. Did you feel at any point
as though you were being exploited to assert Prince's heterosexuality?*

Wendy: Yes. Towards the very end of our relationship together as a
working triumvirate, yes. It felt more like he had used up all he
needed from us and he was going on to something else.
Lisa: But do you think that was connected to sexuality?
Wendy: Well, it might've been because he got Cat the dancer and
Sheila E. to be in the band and be more sexually irreverent on stage
with him, and that kind of played to his heterosexual side. Because
as a lesbian couple, we weren't playing that sexuality with him
specifically, and I think that maybe he needed more of that playfulness, and that probably came from him wanting to exploit his heterosexual side more. Maybe it was unconscious, but yeah, for sure.

*All the women on Prince's record label, Paisley Park, were really at-
tractive. And as time went on, it became more of an issue whether or
not they were picked for their musical talent.*

Wendy: Prince liked to be your savior. He liked to promise the world
to you and he liked to be the guy who could deliver that to you and

make you feel bigger than life. And I think he continues to do that with certain artists who would never be signed to a regular label and would never be played on radio and could never sell a record. I think that he actually believes that the women were all worthy musicians in his eyes, but I do probably think that there was a sexual component to it. That's just my psychology and I could be dead wrong, I don't know.

Regardless of what you went through and what came after, I'm sure there is a generation of women who saw you two in Purple Rain *and went, "Huh, maybe this is what I am."*

Wendy: I remember getting a lot of letters from young girls: "I wanna play guitar just like you," and you could tell in some of the writing that they were little young lesbians and their parents were freaked. And I would write back and just be like, "Just go for it. Live it. You'll work it out." It doesn't come our way much anymore except from people who are just a few years younger than us. You know, "You made such a difference to me growing up and I wanted to be just like you. A lot of straight girls are like, "You're the only gay girls who I'd wanna screw."

How does your musical partnership sustain your relationship and challenge it?

Wendy: We're so merged that we can either function incredibly high or really fuckin' low and not get shit done. So we do our best now because we're both mothers with different women, but you can't help but have all the other shit try and drag you down. We fight everyday, so it's hard to answer that question.

Lisa: [*Nervously giggling at Wendy's admission*] There was so much of it that was so incredible. To be able to share that with the person that you're in love with, to be on stage and play music that you wrote together and look over at each other and be like "Wow, look how cool this is!" We had our sisters in the band and our brothers on the road with us in the crew or helping out in the studio. We had this great life and a big house. We didn't lock the door for 15 years. People were in and out of the house and it was really utopian in a lot of ways. At the same time, it's really difficult, not having enough privacy sometimes.

Wendy: We started to need different things as far as intimacy [goes] and we knew each other our whole lives. So we decided that it was best to be our higher selves and be where we're at now.

Lisa: Our marriage ended, but our soul relationship will never end. We're a couple of sick puppies, basically.

Are you hitting a point in your career where things are finally turning around for you?

Lisa: Now it's kinda just fun. I actually find myself enjoying my memories more.

Wendy: But we'll end up getting more calls from Prince because he can't stand when we talk about him.

Lisa: He's always like, "Could you just err on the side of privacy?" Well, it was our life too, pal! Whatever. It's okay.

Wendy: Trust me, Barry. He will read this article and we will get a phone call and he'll be pissed. Somewhere in this article he'll find something to be pissed about.

Won't he be proud of you too?

Wendy: No. No. No.
Lisa: He's not very generous like that.

Well, I'll do my best.

Lisa: Make it crazy! I don't care.
Wendy: Holy shit, Lisa. I don't wanna get that call.
Lisa: I'll take the call.

The Orange Line Revolution
Aaron Leitko

Before the McMansions and the Cheesecake Factory,
Arlington was home to some of the region's
most storied punk residences.

Collin Crowe is a lucky guy. He got to turn the lights out on 13 years of D.C. indie rock and punk history.

Crowe, 26, the guitarist for Buildings, was among the final tenants of Kansas House, a tiny single-family home on the corner of N. Kansas Street and Wilson Boulevard that was among Arlington's last underground art spaces.

Over the years dozens of musicians lived there, generations of bands practiced there, and countless concerts were hosted in the house's cramped, increasingly grimy living room.

But Crowe's place in D.C. punk lore comes at a cost.

In mid-October the landlord sold the property to a Northern Virginia–based development company and told the tenants they had one month to find new accommodations. Graciously, she agreed to pay back everybody's security deposit, so long as Crowe and his remaining housemates emptied the house, including the basement.

It was a messy place, the basement in particular. An astute punk-rock archaeologist could probably have found junk down there dating all the way back to the early '90s.

The dust and mold "probably took a couple of years out of my life," Crowe says. "There was old furniture, old clothes, some Savage Boys and Girls seven-inches." And a few saucier items, too. "Actually, I found a nude Polaroid of some people."

Every burgeoning arts scene needs a safe, cheap, and relatively care-free place in which to set up shop. Baltimore had its bottle cap factories. Brooklyn had its loft spaces. D.C. had the close-in 'burbs.

The '80s and '90s were a golden era for the D.C. music and arts community. But many of those artists lived in places like Arlington and Silver Spring. Because they were cheaper. Because you were less likely to get your face punched in. Because you could play loud music all night.

DIY record labels like Teenbeat, Dischord, and Simple Machines, as well as activist groups like Positive Force, cleverly repurposed Arlington's middle-class workforce housing, then available as cheap, safe rentals, into small businesses, design studios, and rehearsal rooms.

Now that Kansas House is kaput, that time is effectively over. Those houses have been repurposed again, this time by developers who have built condominiums, restaurants, and shopping centers.

Here's a look back at a time when driving over Key Bridge could get you more than a plate of tapas. When it was a place where you could live cheap, play loud, and, evidently, take naked Polaroids of yourself without shame. A look back at when Arlington was punk.

POSITIVE FORCE HOUSE

Location: 3510 N. 8th St.
Years Active: 1988–2000
Notable Occupants: Mark Andersen, Jerry Busher, Tomas Squip, Joe Lally
Cultural Exports: Good works, alternative lifestyles, Riot Grrrl
Then: The home base of Positive Force, a nonprofit leftist political action group that has raised more than $200,000 for various charities since its inception in 1985. P-Force's group house was a live-in community, a touring band crash pad, and a place for the organization's members to meet up and organize. "In a sense, it was a commune, an experiment in radical democracy," says founder Mark Andersen, who lived in the house all 12 years that it existed.
Why Arlington? One aspect of Positive Force's mission was to establish a link between the suburbs—where most of its members lived—and

the city—where the organization did the majority of its charity work. According to Andersen, it was easier for young punks to get permission to mobilize in Virginia than in D.C., a place that scared the bejesus out of their parents. "The location in Arlington enabled us to build this bridge," he explains. "There was a real anxiety about letting kids go across that imaginary line." Also, it was cheaper.

The Neighborhood Vibe: Even in liberal Arlington, a vegan, straight-edge, punk commune was not inconspicuous. But according to Andersen, the neighbors—who included a major Republican party activist—didn't make much of a stink. "Did everybody love us? I'm sure not. But we managed to work pretty well within that neighborhood," says Andersen. Which isn't to say P-Force didn't raise a few eyebrows every now and then. "That's the house where Riot Grrrl was born," recalls Andersen. "There was a basketball court there. There was some topless basketball being played. The idea was that, 'Well, if men are going to take off their tops, we're going to take off our tops too.' It was not the smartest idea."

Suffering for Your Art: "I lived in the basement for a while; it was $100 a month," recalls Andersen, 50. "The basement came with some special features—for instance, it had running water. That is to say, it had water that ran in through the walls." It was close to nature in other ways, as well. "One window was missing a pane of glass, which I thought that was fine because it could be a little musty down there," Andersen recalls. "One night I awoke to discover myself with a mother possum and her brood. After the possums had moved along, I fixed the window."

Now: Positive Force's original Arlington location, 2600 N. Fairfax Drive, is the only surviving single-family home on a block that has otherwise been dramatically redeveloped. The N. 8th Street location, however, was not so lucky. After Andersen and company vacated in late '00, the property was sold to new owners who erected a grand multistory home on its footprint. In Andersen's opinion, this was not an improvement. "Every inch of the lot is taken up by this garish gargantuan house. It is the epitome of monstrosity, of McMansion," he says. "The house had a lot of structural issues, I wasn't surprised that they tore it down, but they also pulled out three beautiful trees. They could have built a big home and preserved the trees, but I guess they wanted their third level."

TEENBEAT HOUSE

Location: 715 N. Wakefield St.
Years Active: 1992–1998
Notable Occupants: Mark Robinson, Andrew Beaujon, Rob Christiansen, Evan Shurak
Cultural Exports: Indie rock, dead rats.
Then: The house behind Robert J. Murphy funeral home served as the headquarters for Teenbeat, a record label founded by Mark Robinson, and as a rehearsal space for the label's roster—bands like Unrest, Eggs, and Blast Off Country Style. "That's the one thing I loved about it," says Robinson. "In most other cities bands rent a space. It was great to have it there in your house, to not to have to go anywhere. Pretty much everyone who lived in that house put out a record on Teenbeat. Or they worked for it."
Why Arlington? Robinson and Beaujon, both now 42, are Arlington natives. "We hadn't started out thinking, 'This will be a house that will be associated with our record label'," says Robinson. "We just wanted to move out of our parents' houses."
Suffering for Your Art: "It was super run-down," says Robinson. The basement leaked, and so did the roof. "We would have to put buckets in the roof. To catch the water." The elements weren't the only thing getting in, either. "We had mice. Then, after the mice, we had rats. We put out poison for the rats and then, unfortunately, you can never find the rats," says Robinson. "The kitchen stunk like you would not believe for months. There was a huge stack of old copies of the *Washington Post*—it must have been 4 feet high. When we finally moved it, the dead rat was sitting under there."
The Neighborhood Vibe: Robinson and Beaujon, now managing editor of *Washington City Paper*, originally found the house while driving around with Robinson's mother, a real estate agent. "Driving down that street—it was just this otherworldly place. It was all shacks, essentially," Robinson recalls. "It looked totally weird. There were real Virginia people there with old school Southern accents. Even back then, you didn't see that [very often]." But there was a neighborhood artistic tradition, of sorts. "There was a guy a couple houses down, supposedly his dad had drawn the Smokey the Bear logo and he was

living off of residuals from that," says Robinson. "Every six months he would go sit in the back yard with his amp playing these incredible solos for hours."

Now: In 1998 Robinson's landlords decided that they wanted to sell the property off to developers, so Teenbeat had to go. "It was pretty quick after that," says Robinson. "I guess they couldn't alter the foundation, but they rebuilt the entire house. So it looks totally different." Robinson relocated the operation to Wilson Boulevard before moving to Cambridge, Mass.

SIMPLE MACHINES HOUSE

Location: 3813 N. 14th St. (1992–1995), 510 N. Monroe St. (1995–1998)
Years Active: 1992–1998
Notable Occupants: Jenny Toomey, Kristin Thomson, Pat Graham
Cultural Exports: Indie rock, booklets about how to distribute indie rock, photographs of indie rock
Then: The two houses that Simple Machines occupied in Arlington served as label HQs and practice spaces for Toomey and Thomson's group, Tsunami. Photographer Pat Graham also lived there and worked for the label filling mail orders. "It was one of those classic 1950s peaked-roof houses," says Thomson. "It had a wooden front porch and lovely floors on the inside." Simple Machines put out full-length records by Tsunami and Lungfish, myriad seven-inch singles, the "Mechanics Guide" to running record labels, and one very popular cassette tape by Dave Grohl.
Why Arlington? They were already there. Toomey and Thomson originally started running Simple Machines out of the Positive Force House before striking out on their own.
Suffering for Your Art: Aside from the occasional flood or the living room filled with cardboard mailing tubes, Simple Machines House was a pretty pleasant place to live. "It was never a bother, and it was always exciting to be around creative people," says Thomson, now a Philadelphia resident. "I try not to put on my rose-colored glasses, but I think it was OK."
The Neighborhood Vibe: Thomson, 42, recalls the neighborhood as being pretty humble, aside from the odd office building crammed with

military contractors. "It wasn't a house where you could do shows. We had parties. One time Rocket From the Crypt [came on tour] and we all played that dice game kuriki. It was a band plus all sorts of extra people playing kuriki," says Thomson. Then everybody passed out for the night. "There was a litter of bodies around, some of them outside. It probably looked like we'd been overcome by poison."

Now: In 1998 Toomey, now 41, and Thomson decided they were ready to move on from the record business and brought Simple Machines to a close. The houses the label occupied—save for the original Positive Force house—have been leveled. "I looked on Google Street View; they had knocked it down and put up some sort of brick thing," says Thomson. The Monroe Street house "was also demolished and the lot was split in two. Now there are two condo-ish houses there."

DISCHORD HOUSE

Location: 2704 N. 4th St.
Years Active: 1981–present
Notable Occupants: Ian MacKaye, Jeff Nelson, Cynthia Connolly, Joe Lally, Eddie Janney, Tomas Squip
Cultural Exports: Punk
Then: The poky bungalow has served as the headquarters for Dischord records since Ian MacKaye and Jeff Nelson first rented it in 1981. But more than that, the four-bedroom dwelling has been retrofitted into a sort of DIY one-stop—including a practice space, a design studio, and, for a while, a darkroom. "It was an intentional house, in the true sense of the word," says MacKaye, 47. "There was a shared interest that defined it. We were punks; we lived in a punk house."
Why Arlington? After graduating high school, MacKaye and Nelson, then playing in Minor Threat, decided to leave their parents' houses in Northwest. "We were looking for . . . a place that we could practice, somewhere safe, somewhere we could have equipment, and have lots of people coming and going. And it had to be affordable because we were dirt-poor," says MacKaye. "That ruled out most of [Washington] at that time."

Having never looked for a house before, they settled for the first place they stumbled into, a $525/month four-bedroom next door to a

7-Eleven. "So we sat down with [the landlords] to sign the lease," MacKaye recalls. "It was a boilerplate one-year lease and, being a native Washingtonian, I was really struggling with the idea that I was going to live in Arlington. I drew a line through 'one year' and wrote 'six months.' I was there for 21 years."

Suffering for Your Art: When you're broke, even cheap rent is pretty expensive. "We only needed to come up with $105/month [each] for rent, but that was almost impossible for us," says MacKaye. And footing the bill for the house's archaic oil heat system was pretty much out of the question. "The first winter was brutal, and if it got really cold the pipes would burst. So if it got really cold we would buy five gallons of diesel fuel and throw that into the spout. The rest of the time we would have to sit in our sleeping bags while we watched television."

The Neighborhood Vibe: To this day, MacKaye can recall meeting only a handful of the neighbors. Those interactions were not particularly rosy. "The next-door neighbor called the cops on us regularly," he says. "She told the cops we were selling drugs, which was absurd, but that was her MO. We were tough guys, too. We would get into some pretty serious arguments with her." But over the years, the hostilities mellowed a little bit. "Eventually she stopped drinking and stopped being so insane," says MacKaye. "I actually went to her funeral." Connolly and Amy Pickering went, too. "Even after all those years of torturing us, we were still there to see her off."

And while Dischord bands may have practiced in Arlington, performing there, at least during the early '80s, was another matter. "Everything was in the city. There was only one show I can remember in Arlington. It was in the summer of 1981," says MacKaye. "There was a place called the Branding Iron House of Beef, and somebody had convinced them to let us do a show there. Minor Threat was supposed to play." MacKaye was in the recording studio producing Government Issue, but they all knocked off early to head over. "When we got there, things were a little bit punchy. I don't remember exactly how things proceeded—I think people were out front [of the restaurant] throwing bottles at a construction site. But this was three blocks from the police headquarters. The cops just descended on us—they just went insane. They had dogs and everything," he recalls. "That was the only show."

Now: MacKaye purchased the property from his landlords during the mid-'90s and, although he no longer resides there, he continues to use his old room as an office. Dischord's offices across the street are low-profile, but there's no denying that the label has left its mark on the neighborhood. "See that street lamp over there?" MacKaye says, and gestures toward the parking lot at the 7-Eleven. He points to a piece of sheet metal welded to the lamp's fixture, blocking some irksome light pollution. "I made [the county] put that there," he says. "One time it blew down. I made them put it back."

KANSAS HOUSE

Location: 900 N. Kansas St.

Years Active: 1996–2009

Notable Occupants: Derek Morton, Bob Massey, Anne Jaeger, Jason Hamacher, Jason Barnett, Collin Crowe

Cultural Exports: Records, concerts, goat-meat smells

Then: During the mid-'90s local musician Derek Morton moved into the house—then just a normal group home—hoping to use the basement as a practice space for his band Ex-Atari Kid. Since then, numerous D.C. musicians have passed through Kansas House's walls. In '96 Bob Massey, then of Telegraph Melts, started hosting concerts in the living room, a tradition that enhanced the house's legend tenfold, but didn't do much for its decor.

Why Arlington? Kansas House had the virtue of being out of the way but still close to the Metro. And the $250-per-person rent didn't hurt either, even if your room was only 6 feet wide and 12 feet long.

Suffering for Your Art: Early on Kansas House was a pretty nice place to live. But more than a decade of house shows and parties put some serious wear and tear on the place.

"The house was getting kind of run-down," says Jason Barnett, who ran the record label Paroxysm out of the house in the early '00s. "The shower would leak, and the kitchen wasn't in the greatest shape." A neighboring halal meat market didn't do much for the neighborhood ambience, either. "They would take their goat meat and throw it on the ground."

The Neighborhood Vibe: On Kansas Street, do what thou wilt was the whole of the law. Jorge Pezzimenti—then bassist for D.C. ska group the Pietasters—moved in next door in '01 just to take advantage of the neighborhood's freewheeling environment. "I knew if I moved in there I would be able to play music all night and nobody would say shit," he says. "I consider myself fairly open-minded, but there was some No Wave shit coming out of Kansas House at night and nobody ever cared. I just thought, 'This is the best street in the world.'" It couldn't last forever, though. By the middle of the decade, some people actually wanted to sleep at night. Near the end of his tenure on the block, Pezzimenti's '80s cover band, the Legwarmers, played a show at Kansas House that was subsequently broken up by the cops—possibly the only time such a thing has happened to an '80s cover band, ever. "But, yeah, until we played 'Eye of the Tiger' that night, we never had any trouble at all," he says.

Now: In October, landlord Margarita Metaxatos announced that she was in negotiations to sell the property to an Arlington-based development firm. Tenants were given one month to leave the premises. They left at the end of November.

One on One with Maria Schneider

Eugene Holley, Jr.

Maria Schneider's music has been described as evocative, majestic, magical, heart-stoppingly gorgeous, and beyond categorization. Born in Windom, Minnesota, Schneider arrived in New York City in 1985 after studies at the University of Minnesota, the University of Miami and the Eastman School of Music. She immediately sought out Bob Brookmeyer to study composition, and at the same time became an assistant to Gil Evans, working on various projects with him. The Maria Schneider Jazz Orchestra came into being in 1993, appearing at Visiones in Greenwich Village every Monday night for a stretch of five years. Subsequently, her orchestra performed at festivals and concert halls across Europe as well as in Brazil and Macau. The CD *Concert in the Garden* won the 2005 Grammy Award for Best Large Ensemble Album and became the first Grammy-winning recording with Internet-only sales. It also received Jazz Album of the Year from the Jazz Journalists Association and the *Down Beat* Critics Poll. Both also named Schneider Composer of the Year and Arranger of the Year. "Cerulean Skies," from her newest fan-funded ArtistShare recording, *Sky Blue*, won a 2008 Grammy Award for Best Instrumental Composition.

On January 11, 2008, PMP brought Maria Schneider and music writer and radio producer Eugene Holley together for an intimate discussion about her work. The talk coincided with the Maria Schneider Jazz Orchestra's regional debut at the Philadelphia Museum of Art that evening, presented by the PMA's "Art After 5" series with support from PMP.

Eugene Holley: *When do you as an artist realize that you're sounding like yourself?*

Maria Schneider: Well, I could start out by saying that when I finished college in 1985, my biggest frustration was I felt like my music could be just about anybody's, you know. I was writing a piece here and there that was influenced by Thad Jones, and a piece influenced by Gil Evans, and I didn't really know who I was. We had had many guests come through the Eastman School of Music and one of them was George Russell. When George was in front of the band playing "All About Rosie," it was like he was just rising out of this music. Keith Jarrett came. He's got a personality, but his music, no doubt, it's Keith Jarrett, you know? And I remember Dave Holland came and when he played, I realized all the music that I loved, it was infused with personality.

When I started studying with Bob Brookmeyer, I would bring music in, it might be a tune with a solo, and he'd look at it and say, "Why is there a solo there?" And I'd say, "Well, you know, this is something from Mel Lewis' band, and there's a tune, and then there's this little sendoff and now comes the solo." And then he'd say, "A solo should only happen when the only thing that can happen is the solo." And I'd kind of say, "Okay. Yeah, yeah I know what you mean." I really didn't quite understand what he meant. And then it would be, "Well, why are there chord changes here?" "Well, you've got a solo over the chord changes." The more I looked into every aspect of the music, I realized kind of subliminally, we've developed this template from the history of jazz: you have a tune structure; everybody solos on that tune; there are chord changes; the bass line has its functions—so it almost becomes, for a lot of people. . . .

A script?

A script—a template—almost like a prefab house: these are the walls you have to choose from, and then okay, some people can do some really creative things by putting it together in a different way. But if all of a sudden you really break down every aspect and you say, "Well, I can do anything. Why does someone have to solo using chord changes as the context? What if it's a motive, or what if it's something else?"

And so the more that I asked myself, "Why did I do that? What else could I do?"—without even realizing it, my music, I think, became my own, because suddenly you're not accepting somebody else's dictum for what you should do. Then over time, more and more influences. . . . I went to Brazil. Of course you cannot go to Brazil without having every aspect of your life changed.

That's true.

And it changes you molecularly, you know? And the shift, the biggest shift that came to my music in Brazil—these are things you don't even realize when you're going through it—you realize it two records later. All of a sudden I realized joy came into my music after I went to Brazil. Before Brazil my music was dark, intense, dance heavy, minor, Phrygian, with small intervals towards the bottom. Brazil happened to me and all of a sudden everything started to lift and be light and. . . .

The Carnival effect.

Yeah, absolutely.

What really blows me away about what you do; you have this natural counterpoint that goes on. In "Hang Gliding," from your Allegresse *CD, the way you voice your horns in certain. . . .*

There ain't nothing natural about it! It is hard work!! I remember I really suffered. I mean, so many things are going through my head, and then I was looking at myself and going, "You're insane! Who are you?" All the shifting of the keys and keeping it constantly moving, I remember, "Okay, should I go up a half step there, or should I go up two steps? I need to clean the sock drawer. Now I gotta eat. Oh man, a manicure, then I'll feel good." You know, it's so crazy how much avoidance I go through, and those decisions, it's like, "Okay, if I go up a whole step *and* a half step instead of a half step for that last key, what if I regret it?" You know, so I can spend three days worrying about if I regret it. It's insane.

*How did the training that you got from studying classical music help
you to at least make the contrapuntal stuff sound easy?*

Okay, when I was back at the University of Minnesota, first of all they
didn't have a jazz program. They had a big band there, and I wrote for
their big band, but I had no jazz training whatsoever, except I studied
with Manfredo Fest, who's a Brazilian pianist, a blind man. Those lessons were amazing, but I learned the jazz thing just by listening and
studying on my own.

How?

I studied out of this *Inside the Score* book that Ray Wright had written,
who eventually I studied with, but basically was analyzing scores by
Thad Jones, Bob Brookmeyer, and Sammy Nestico. And then I studied
the *Lydian Chromatic Concept* by George Russell. I remember just
getting into that book. And then I just listened like crazy. Listened to
Mingus try things, listened to just everybody I could. My classes at the
University of Minnesota were fantastic; I had such great teachers. My
orchestration teacher was phenomenal, Dominick Argento. He was such
a great teacher: classy man, funny, intellectual. And then I had this fantastic counterpoint teacher, Paul Fetler, who had studied with Hindemith.
I was kind of shunning my classical because I just got so into jazz. I just
wanted to do jazz and he was teaching my comp lessons, and he said,
"You know, you're listening to so much jazz, why don't you go write for
the big band and watch them rehearse? But in the meantime, you know,
take my advanced counterpoint class." His class was amazing. It was a
whole year of going through Bach's *Art of the Fugue*. All those fugues
are all made with the same subject. They all have the same motive. But
they all use a different technique. One stretches it out longer, and it's
like putting it through different mathematic formulas. Finally, by the
end, it's a mirror fugue, you can turn it upside down and play it backwards
and forwards and I forget how many ways. And every technique we
studied, we'd have that week to then write a fugue. It was difficult, but I
learned so much, and I loved it.

I feel like jazz really suffers from "voicing-itis." I remember this guy
I was taking lessons with once, and I wrote some kind of structure. He

said, "Oh, why don't you throw in one of these boys?" One of those boys? I mean, I can't relate to that. You know, because to me, a voicing isn't just a voicing. The beauty of Gil Evans . . . everybody thinks Gil Evans is about voicings and woodwinds and mutes. Well, he is about woodwinds and mutes, but he's not about voicings. It's all about lines. Lines on the bottom—the tuba's always playing the melody. And it's how those lines converge, and everything's always moving. There's never anything that's not part of almost a stepwise line coming in contrary motion and sometimes parallel motion, and then it goes like *this*, and *that*, and because of the logic of how every single part is moving, something that might be startling if you just took a slice, just like if you took a picture from a film of some beautiful actress, but you caught her in a weird moment, she might look odd. A voicing can be like that too. If in music, all you are concerned with is every voicing sounding strong or powerful, then you get this sort of milk toast effect.

Right, exactly.

And everything becomes "ba doop ba ba ba ba doop ba." I call it testosterone big band. I like nuance and beauty and lightness. That does come from classical music, and more and more jazz musicians are getting hip to doing that, and yet maintaining whatever we perceive as being "jazz."

I want to add something to this because, one thing about your music, you adhere to dynamics. I can't tell you how many times as a reviewer that I listen to big bands and somehow there's a green light just to be loud all the time, and I guess this is what you've gotten from studying with Gil.

Well, my whole reason for doing music—it's expression. It's not to make cool sounding music or hip tunes—it's storytelling. It's sharing something through music. The problem with big band music is so few writers are writing with that serious intent that the music really means something beyond just being a really cool sounding chart, so the players are going to play like that because there's not that other level to play from. But it's also come through years. My first music was much more bombastic. You know, it's become softer and part of it is I'm just so tired of that sound in my ears.

Audience member: Could you talk about your creative process? Do you use pencil and manuscript, or a computer?

I have a board on my piano and a huge piece of score paper, with clips so I can expand the paper, and I use score paper that has lots of little staves with no bar lines because I don't want anything to pin me down. I think if you see bar lines you tend to start thinking in a set meter. I want my ideas to just flow freely and then figure out where the bar lines need to be in order to make the music sound like what I'm hearing. And then I just usually throw down an idea, fool around playing what I'm hearing, writing it down. When I find an idea I really like, I try to go off of it spontaneously.

Audience member: Are the ideas melodic?

They might be melodic, or could be a rhythmic thing, or could be a vamp, harmonic, a chord texture . . . and I just try to go spontaneously off of it. And when I get stuck I try to analyze it and say, "What's inside this?" Because I believe if you love something or it resonates with you, it has math inside of it. We live in this mathematical universe. Everything has order. I believe our intuition does too. I always tell students, you don't have to sit and write from math from the beginning. In the end, analyze. If you analyze your ideas, you will find out that you're a mathematical genius. And then once you understand that, you can pop your intuition to another level. So I go back and forth between this intuitive—pushing it, writing myself into a corner, go back, analyze it, and develop it.

Audience member: Is it in sections, or do you see and hear the piece in its entirety?

I wish. It's like a puzzle, so I've got this little chunk, and I'm like, "Shit, how do I break out of this?" It's like you have a puzzle and no one told you what the picture is going to be, and you have five billion pieces and most of them are shades of yellow, brown and black, and then there's a few red pieces, and you're like, "Okay, find all the red pieces," because otherwise what are you going to do? So you find the red and put them together and you see it's a scarlet tanager—okay, it's a bird, so maybe it's trees and grass. Sometimes you have these miraculous days where everything fits perfectly together, and you're like, "Oh my God, the key just miraculously modulates to this, and look, this is a motive of this upside down." And then you're like, "I'm a genius." Then you become cocky as all hell, and like, "I'm going to get a pedicure!"

Conducting 101

Mark Swed

Gustavo Dudamel hones his skills without
a harsh spotlight in Sweden.

On Thursday night, for the first time in his career, Gustavo Dudamel conducted Verdi's grandly operatic 90-minute Requiem here with the Gothenburg Symphony. Afterward I visited the 28-year-old conductor in his modest dressing room in the Concert Hall, a Swedish functionalist auditorium that was built in 1935 and stands proudly as part of a sternly imposing arts complex at the end of the city's main avenue. He greeted me with a sheepish smile and blurted out, "Sorry."

There had been unmistakable thrills and the occasional moment of sudden, stunning beauty, but Dudamel was thinking about the many mistakes. He had misgauged some tempos. He hadn't managed to fully hold together a long, segmented, operatic score. He hadn't realized how differently the soloists, with whom he had never worked, would sing under the pressure of a live concert from rehearsal. And he needed more time with the chorus, which was a well-prepared amateur body that sang from memory. But the members have day jobs and are available to rehearse only in the evening. Dudamel had arrived in town only two days earlier, having just made his debut with the storied Concertgebouw Orchestra in Amsterdam, and may have still been changing gears.

But he was, nonetheless, infectiously happy. He was ending his second season as the orchestra's music director and knew things would get better with what he called "this crazy opera" over its three-day run. They did.

Saturday afternoon I was again in Dudamel's dressing room, this time after a spectacular final matinee performance. Players filed in to thank their ebullient young maestro. The seasoned concertmaster Christer Thorvaldsson, a member of the 104-year-old ensemble for 36 years and something of a legend in Swedish orchestral circles, announced that Dudamel was the finest conductor he had ever worked with. Dudamel brought out a bottle of old Scotch.

As the classical music community well knows and as a rapidly growing general audience has been finding out, Dudamel is a sensation and pretty much still always a surprise. When he begins as music director of the Los Angeles Philharmonic in the fall, he is expected to generate a huge amount of attention, no matter how celebrity-saturated the city. But even a conducting sensation has to learn the music director business somewhere, to say nothing of a broad repertory of pieces. That's where Gothenburg comes in.

Being music director of the Simon Bolivar National Youth Orchestra in the Venezuelan capital of Caracas for a decade is far different from heading an orchestra in Europe or America. At home Dudamel can rehearse nonprofessional young players as much as he likes, unconcerned with union regulations—or any regulations. He knows these youngsters intimately; he grew up with many of them. They are family.

Sweden's second city, though, is a great distance geographically and culturally from Caracas. The Gothenburg Symphony is a relatively traditional institution, and its concert hall was built to be a temple to music. You enter through a very long, mundane cloak room and ascend a marble staircase, to the higher realm of art.

But Gothenburg is also a relaxed, pleasure-loving place that seems to suit Dudamel remarkably well. Cafe society is a central part of its charm. The student community is large. Sea and mountains are nearby. It is a culinary capital. This town of a half-million residents on Sweden's west coast, halfway between Copenhagen and Oslo, boasts an astonishing five Michelin-starred restaurants.

Obviously, on some level, Dudamel's presence here was a business decision. His high-powered London management is pleased to have him in this relatively obscure post where he can learn and experiment outside the international limelight.

For the orchestra—which Neeme Jarvi headed for 22 years followed by a short three-year term with Mario Venzago—Dudamel offered a huge dose of much-needed glamour and vitality, and it is willing to forgive a lot knowing what the final results can be. Had he given Thursday's performance in London, he would have been slaughtered by the critics. In Gothenburg, all three performances were sold out and audiences stood and cheered with the same degree of enthusiasm for each of the radically different performances.

But what Gothenburg really offers Dudamel is respite from constant attention. His guest-conducting stints in European capitals and in America draw a media circus. In Venezuela, he and his wife, Eloisa Maturen, need armed security with them at all times because of kidnapping threats.

And though Dudamel says he is not crazy about Sweden's dark, cold winters, it was sunny and warm during my stay, turning dark around 11 p.m. Here he can walk the streets, interrupted only by the occasional friendly greetings of well-wishers. He is also left in relative peace to study and work.

In a curious way, Dudamel may have been destined for this orchestra, which is the most convivial large professional ensemble I have encountered. After Saturday's matinee, Dudamel, flashing a conspiratorial grin, told me I had to see the bar. I thought I had seen the bars in the lobby, where one could have a drink while mulling over a somber bust of an obscure Swede. He meant a private bar for the players, where outsiders are rarely welcome and only orchestra members are permitted to buy drinks. Dudamel bought me a beer and hung for half an hour with his fellow musicians.

Nearly all the players come by after each performance, and Dudamel always shows. On this afternoon he was practically as chummy with his Swedish players (most of whom are quite a bit older than he is) as he can be around the Bolivars. Later that night, Dudamel's wife would cook a Mexican dinner for the family of a Danish member of the orchestra with whom the couple has become friendly.

I'm assuming that the trust the Gothenburgers feel for Dudamel explains what happened over these three performances of the Verdi Requiem, since I have no other explanation. Although this was his first time with any Verdi score, Dudamel conducted from memory.

The impression over three days was like that of being in an optometrist's chair. Each click of the apparatus brought greater focus.

Dudamel always began and ended in theatrical silence, which felt gimmicky the first two times but worked brilliantly at the last performance. After he walked onto the podium, he waited until the hall was entirely still and then coaxed the cellos to come so quietly that you couldn't tell when they first began playing. When the Requiem reached its final peace, he ever so slowly lowered his baton, holding an audience ready to burst at bay. Thursday and Friday, the crowd couldn't take the final silence for more than a minute, but on Saturday he got away with an extra 30 seconds. At the bar, a number of player commented on this. Like me, they too had begun timing the baton-lowering act.

Saturday, he had also been able to bring instrumental details into superb relief while still maintaining the grand sweep (earlier it had usually been one or the other). Dudamel, of course, raised the roof in the Dies Irae section, where God's wrath is unleashed in magnificently thunderous brass and timpani outbursts. Instead, Dudamel represented this as just one more, if particularly exciting, expression of an irrepressible life force.

The earthy Ekaterina Semenchuk was terrific all the time, her expressive Russian mezzo sounding ravishing. But the other soloists—soprano Erika Sunnegardh, tenor Dominic Natoli and bass Julian Konstantinov—were nervous and unreliable in the first performance and still in trouble the second. By Saturday, Dudamel found exactly what they needed in order to let loose but not lose control.

The result reminded me of something one might hear in a pirated recording from Italy in the 1930s, where the singing may not be pitch perfect but the expression carries you away. In fact, I wouldn't be surprised if a pirate of this performance begins making the rounds someday.

When Saturday's performance was over I began to wonder just who was teaching whom. Dudamel came to Gothenburg to learn. And to the extent that all experience is learning, he undoubtedly has learned a lot. The next time he conducts Verdi's Requiem will be with the Los Angeles Philharmonic in November. He says he can't wait, and he is surely more ready for this than he was a week ago.

Still, I left Sweden with the distinct feeling that you can take the boy out of Venezuela—well you know the rest. Gothenburg may actually be reinforcing Dudamel's habits of comradeship and his tendency to conduct for the moment.

"I have to set something like this up in Disney Hall," he said, flashing another conspiratorial look as we left the players' bar. As far as Dudamel is concerned, the orchestra is family and that is all there is to it, be it Caracas or Gothenburg.

And L.A.?

Drake
Rookie of the Year

Lola Ogunnaike

Toronto MC Drizzy Drake has the Internet stans, a pretty boy pedigree and a recording contract far from industry standard. But can the young spitter—who already has a shelf for his future Grammys—deliver a product that matches the hype machine?

"The view from up here is amazing," says Drake late one fall evening. "You can see all of downtown Toronto, the Royal Ontario Museum, Fifth Avenue. . . ." Dressed down in a gray sweat pants, house slippers and a simple white T, hip-hop's hottest freshman is taking me on a tour of his new apartment, a sprawling, 4,000-square-foot bachelor pad made for the type of wild nights men like to gloat about in their golden years.

The Canadian-born rapper has shown me his cavernous living room, his in-house studio, and shiny, stainless-steel kitchen, which doubles as a weed- and wine-scented playground/boardroom for his crew, a multi-culti cast of characters with backgrounds as diverse as a UN assembly roster. (His business partner and product manager Oliver El-Khatib is Lebanese-Scandinavian.) He's also shown me a hallway of empty shelves that he hopes will one day be filled with awards. "This is where I'll put my Grammys," he says only half-jokingly. "This is where I'll put my BET Awards."

The place is sparsely decorated—drapes, a piano and more are on their way, he promises. "I'm going to definitely be getting my *House & Home* swag on."

Now we're outside on the swagalicious balcony. The air is crisp and the wind is making itself heard as Drake looks out over the town that raised him. It's a real "I'm the king of the world" moment, but he's not channeling his inner DiCaprio. "Sometimes when I'm up here I feel the burden of an entire city," he says quietly. "But most of the time I'm looking out and thinking about all the people I have to make proud. It keeps me motivated and also reminds me that I have to keep going. There's no time for celebration. There's too much work to do."

A little more than a year ago, Drake, 23, was on the ground floor of the rap game, a virtual unknown as a musician outside of his native country. These days he's elevated to the top tier, on the strength of his third mixtape/mini-album, *So Far Gone*, and its hit single, "Best I Ever Had," 2009's summer anthem. Since debuting on iTunes in June, the track has sold more than 1.5 million paid digital downloads, hit No. 1 on *Billboard*'s R&B/Hip-Hop Song and Ringtones charts, and peaked at No. 2 on the Hot 100. Before *So Far Gone* had a price tag, it was already an online phenomenon. Released in February, the mixtape was downloaded by more than 8,000 people in less than two hours. Since then another 200,000 have paid for the EP on iTunes, although it's still available as a free download. After *So Far Gone* dropped, Drake's performance offers went from $7,500 per show to $30,000. "By the time he re-injured his knee, I had an offer for as high as $75,000," says Nina Packer, vice president of Bryant Management, which handles his bookings.

By all measures, Drake is the unlikeliest of choices for hip-hop's rookie of the year. He hails from Canada, a country better known for its bacon and maple syrup than its MCs. The last and only rapper to make it big out of the Great White North was Snow, an early '90s one-hit wonder who topped the *Billboard* charts with the painfully catchy track "Informer." Another potential strike against Drake: He was a child actor—starring in the hit teen drama *Degrassi: The Next Generation* as Jimmy Brooks, a basketball player confined to a wheelchair after a school shooting. One need only recall the unremarkable rap career of *Beverly Hills 90210* alum Brian Austin Green as evidence of how these re-inventions often turn out. Strike three? Pretty boy Drake looks like he should be fronting a bubble-gum pop band, not rhyming alongside Lil Wayne, a self-professed goblin. He's got no gangster tales either, having been raised in Forest Hill, an affluent, predominantly Jewish enclave of Toronto.

And yet, despite all of the above, Drake decided to actually do what so many others in hip-hop only pretend to: keep it real. "I knew having some fake persona would never work anyway," he says. "I grew up on television. Google me. My worst hairstyles and worst outfits, it's all documented." Since so many rappers have similar come-up-from-the-streets stories, he figured he was so different, it just might work. "I thought if this shit works, it's going to be super big," he says. "And I'm thinking I could eventually become one of the most well-known rappers in the world. But it's like betting it all. You take a risk and hope you win big."

So far so good. Drake's already notched an impressive number of collaborations: Jay-Z, Mary J. Blige, Justin Timberlake, Young Jeezy and Bun B. Kanye West directed the video for "Best I Ever Had." In October, Jay welcomed Drake to celebrate his birthday in a private room at The Spotted Pig, a restaurant Hov co-owns in New York. When Jay was performing in Toronto a week later, he invited Drake to join him onstage. Drake spent the earlier part of the year as the opening act for Lil Wayne, who's given Drake an invaluable co-sign, tons of exposure and a generous deal with his Young Money imprint. "Drake is scary," says Wayne. "He can sing, rap and act. You have to sign someone like that."

On the same day as Drake's birthday party, Wayne was in a New York courtroom pleading guilty to criminal possession of a weapon that will reportedly send him to prison for eight to ten months. (He's due to be sentenced in February 2010.) Though he missed most of the festivities, Jay-Z popped by the party at the end after jetting in from a show in Cleveland. "That made my birthday," Drake says. "I was super drunk at that point and I was like, 'Please, no long conversations tonight.' I don't want to say anything crazy and make a fool of myself."

Drake has his haters, of course. There's now a Facebook page for those who think he's lame. "He sounds like Lil Wayne and Young Jeezy had a baby and Drake came out," wrote one of the unimpressed. And a prominent industry executive, unwilling to go on the record, calls him "overrated. He'll be so far gone by next year."

The sniping didn't stop labels from offering Drake deals that would make any newbie salivate. After an intense bidding war that the rapper claims reached as high as "four to five million," he ultimately signed with Lil Wayne's Young Money label. Drake's long-time manager, Cortez Bryant, told the *Los Angeles Times*, he "received a $2 million advance. He retains the publishing rights to his songs and cedes only around 25 percent of his music sales to the label as a 'distribution fee.'"

"In the 18 years I've been in the business I've never seen a new artist get a $2 million advance," says Wendy Day, founder and CEO of Rap Coalition, a non-profit artist advocacy organization. She's credited with negotiating deals for Cash Money Records, No Limit Records and Eminem. "Typically a new artist gets an advance on the low end, $100,000, high end, $500,000." Day compares him to an NBA phenom. "Like LeBron, there was a lot of hype surrounding him, but LeBron lived up to the hype and I hope Drake can too," she says. "The music industry needs him. We need someone to come in and hit a home run."

The rabid fans, the lucrative deal, the exuberant bear hugs from rap's elder statesmen, it's happened so quickly that Drake and his crew are still processing it all. "It's like we were hit by lightning," says El-Khatib, Drake's resident style guru, who recently quit his job as a buyer at Ransom to work with the rapper full time. "We knew it would happen eventually, but this is bigger than we thought and it's definitely moved a lot faster. In Toronto, people like Jay-Z, Kanye and Wayne are imaginary figures. Now that we hang out with them . . . it's like, 'Wow, holy shit!'"

"I'm just getting comfortable with the idea that I can e-mail [Jay-Z]," adds Drake. "Jay is a hero to me. . . . That's who I grew up listening to."

Even his own management admits Drake's rise has been meteoric. "I told him he's been spoiled," says Bryant. "He's flying on private jets and hasn't even put a record out. Most artists have to go platinum before they get to do that." Bryant oversees Drake's career alongside the management team Hip Hop Since 1978 (Gee Roberson and Kyambo Joshua), which also handles Kanye West and Young Jeezy. "He's stayed in all the best hotels, gotten all the perks. He didn't have the 12-year grind that Wayne had."

The story of how Drake linked up with Lil Wayne sounds like an urban fairy tale: An industry insider plays Wayne some of Drake's freestyles—including one over the beat to his hit "A Milli." Weezy, who's touring at the time, dials Drake and says, "I need you in Houston tonight." Drake jumps on the next flight and before he knows it, he's on Wayne's tour bus, face-to-face with the tattooed one.

"All of a sudden the bus pulls off and I was still on it," Drake recalls. "Now I'm on tour automatically. No choice. No nothing. My luggage had already been packed on the bus. It was like something from *Almost Famous*." He was on Wayne's "I Am Music" tour for nearly two weeks, crisscrossing the country. "The whole time I was this quiet fly on the wall," says Drake. "I was too scared to even ask for my own bunk. I would sleep sitting up in a little corner."

It's this honesty that his fans have come to appreciate and Drake has plans to be just as open on his debut album, *Thank Me Later*, due out in late February—if only he can finish it. Work on the album has been slowed by an old basketball injury the rapper aggravated during a performance this summer. "I can't write anything vivid about sitting in bed and recovering," he says, several weeks after painful ligament surgery on his right knee. "I need real experiences to rap about." As of late October, he'd only completed one song, but now that he's walking again, he has ideas for several. His long-time engineer Noah Shebib, who goes by the moniker 40, is confident that they'll meet the deadline. "This is how it always happens, and then it comes together in the end."

Another of Drake's buddies, Foots—so nicknamed because he wears a size 15 shoe—says the rapper's fastidiousness is part of what's slowing down the process. "The lyrics, the beats, the interludes, the cameos, it all has to be perfect," he explains. "He wants to give them no other option than to say something positive. He knows people are watching."

It's late fall in New York and Drake is holed away in a dimly lit photo studio, standing before a white backdrop in a T-shirt, jeans and boots by Red Wing. He's sporting little in the way of jewelry, just a small chain with two pendants no bigger than quarters. One is a circular medallion that represents his father's Christian heritage; the other, a diamond encrusted *chai*, the Hebrew symbol for life, represents his mother's Jewish heritage. After years of watching rappers parade around in gaudy crosses and Jesus pieces, the subtlety is refreshing. But Drake's so understated that he might be mistaken for plain—that is until he begins to strike a pose. As his eyes squint and lips pucker and face turns just so, the temperature in the room begins to rise. I'm reminded of my hairstylist's 16-year-old daughter, Ariel Williams, and her breathless, one-line description of the rapper: "Oh my God, he's *sooooo* cute."

It's been ages since hip-hop has had a true matinee-idol. (Most of today's MCs have faces better suited for radio.) Drake, meanwhile, is indisputably handsome in that boy-next-door sorta way, the type of guy over which both mothers and daughters can comfortably squeal. He seems slightly uncomfortable with this notion, even though on "Best I Ever Had" he rhymes: "When my album drop, bitches will buy it for the picture / And niggas will buy it too and claim they got it for they sister."

"I'm not a sex symbol," the rapper declares days later during lunch at a popular bistro in his hometown. "There are guys out there who take their shirts off and show off their abs. That's not me. But maybe if I got some abs. Nah, I'm kidding. I'd never do that."

Daughters would be wise to leave mom at home when attending a Drake concert. As his verse on the remix to Fabolous's hit, "Throw it in the Bag," makes clear, Drake has a thing for cougars. "I love older women," he says proudly. "I find our encounters have much more substance. I like a woman who is open to teaching me things. She's mature, she has great stories, she's in a better place professionally."

As he digs into a juicy steak, he says the oldest woman he's ever dated was a remarkably well-preserved 47. He was 20 or 21. He didn't know about the age difference at first, but wasn't going to let a few decades get in the way of a good time. "We had fun," he says with a sly grin. "It was a moment. It'll make a good movie one day."

Ask him to address rumors that he dated the young beauty Rihanna after her bruising breakup with Chris Brown and he coyly offers an, "I'm not dating anyone right now. I'm totally single." Okay, but what about before right now? "I'm not saying that I've never been around her and that we've never hung out, but we weren't dating," he says. Well, what about a little kiss here and there? He laughs nervously and lowers his head. "Um, maybe so," he says, smiling. Any touching? "My memory, um, it's all a blur. My mind is conveniently, um, foggy." Tell him he and Ri-Ri would make a cute couple, and he chuckles. "I could see it."

He's young, single and the man of the moment, but Drake claims he's not really partaking in one of music's evergreen perks: the groupie. "Me and my crew like to go out to dinner with a woman, have a real conversation with a woman," he says. "We're not really into the cliché of having sex with nine women in one night and forgetting them all the next day. If you listen to my music you can tell that I really take interest in the whole woman, not just her body, but her mind too, her thought patterns. I like to meet a woman that I can be with on more than just a physical level. Probably has to do a lot with my mother. She taught me to really respect women."

Aubrey Drake Graham says his formative years were far from idyllic. His parents, who co-owned a floral business in Toronto, divorced when he was five. His dad would return to his hometown of Memphis, but not before leaving years of drama in his wake. "I knew my dad was not doing great as a father," he says as we cruise around downtown Toronto, aka "T Dot," in a Maybach he's test-driving for the day. "He was reckless, going to jail, having the police constantly coming and looking for him, trying to get by, but doing it in such a poor way. He's such an intelligent man, a great cook, a great writer, but it's the Memphis in him. Even when he comes to Toronto, he brings the Memphis in him. He'll find a way to get arrested, somehow some way, even in the winter time. He will bring that Memphis. Growing up, I used my dad as a reverse role model. What not to do. Watching him made me want to do better."

Nevertheless, Drake's fond enough of his father to feature him on the song "Successful." He's the voice on the telephone saying "You need to go for the money, and not the honey, you know what I'm sayin'?" He credits his father—a former drummer for Jerry Lee Lewis and a nephew of Larry Graham—with introducing him to soul music. Drake spent summers in Memphis and on the long rides down from Canada, they'd bond over music. "He'd allow me to listen to like half an hour of rap," says Drake. The rest of the time they'd listen to pop's Spinners and Marvin Gaye tapes.

It was his mother who first introduced him to acting, enrolling him in theater camps when he was a child. He landed the role on *Degrassi* when he was 14 and quickly became one of the more popular cast members. Two years later, he dropped out of high school.

"I was sitting in history class one day, just looking up at the teacher, and it hit me that I didn't need to be here," he recalls. "This is not going to help me with my life. I'm not going to university. I'm not getting a regular job. I packed my bag and started to leave. The teacher stopped me and said, 'If you make this decision, make sure you never come back.' I said, 'Don't worry, I won't.' And never did."

Once Drake graduated from his high school TV show, he began to pursue a music career in earnest. He was living in his mother's basement, rhyming at local clubs for little money. Reaction to his aptly named 2006 mixtape *Room for Improvement* was tepid. "People didn't want to accept him," Foots says. "It wasn't like 'Drake sucks.' It was like, 'Who is his mixed kid from *Degrassi* trying to rap?'"

In an effort to build a fan base, he started posting music online. Blogs started giving him shine. Later on, the twitterati took to him. "We cut out the middleman of a label," says 40. "We record it, mix it, put it on the Internet, keep it moving." The same strategy worked for *So Far Gone*. "I didn't care if it was for free," says Drake. "I just wanted people to listen, duplicate it, sell it if you want to make money off of it. Just listen, so when I come to your city I can perform before 2,000 people and set the mic down for the entire show because everyone in the audience knows and is yelling all the words."

Shania Twain, Avril Lavigne, Nelly Furtado, Céline Dion, Alanis Morissette, Jim Carrey, Sarah McLachlan, Pamela Anderson—just a sampling of the Canadians who have made it big in recent years. But the country can't claim one true rap star, which is both a gift and a curse for Drake. He can no longer walk through a mall without over-the-top fanfare. "When he first released his mixtape, we used to be able to go out in peace because the only people who really knew him were *Degrassi* fans or Internet fans," says CJ Gibson, his road manager, a quiet presence who also works closely with Lil Wayne. "Now it's not really such a good idea."

"I encounter some extreme reactions going out," Drake says. "Either people are extremely attached to you and they're like, 'I need a picture of you. I love you.' Or it's like, 'Drake's here. Let's try and rob him.

Nothing really serious or dangerous has happened, but you hear of things brewing. We've never had rappers from Toronto be able to do what successful rappers do, flying private, riding around in Maybachs. It's never happened, so it definitely leads to a lot of awkward moments."

Nowhere is this more evident than at the luxury high-rise where Drake currently resides. It's a building filled with moneyed, older White people who don't know what to make of the rapper and his motley multiracial friends in sagging jeans and fitted caps. Unlike the U.S., where Russell Simmons, Diddy and Jay-Z have become the establishment—hobnobbing in the Hamptons with Martha Stewart or in D.C. with President Obama—hip-hop hasn't come close to infiltrating Canada's upper echelons.

"I don't like this building," says El-Khatib one early evening as we stand in the lobby. "They're always looking at us like, 'How'd you all get in here?'" No sooner does he say this than Drake storms in and launches into an angry diatribe that includes heavy use of the f-bomb. The valet has just informed him that some neighbors are complaining about his cars idling too long in the front of the building. It's a petty gripe and the rapper believes he knows exactly where it stems from.

"I'm young, Black and I live in one of the best apartments in the building," he says later. "They feel a little bitter."

Back in his fabulous crib, Drake's safe from meddling valets and resentful neighbors. Most of his crew have headed home. Toronto is asleep.

Drake, however, is wide awake and out on his balcony, taking in the view, contemplating his bright future. "When I finish my album, I'm going to stand out here and listen to it from beginning to end," he says. He takes a deep breath. "I can't wait."

50 Cent

One Dethroned King Out to Reclaim His Crown . . .

Phillip Mlynar

He's candid, you've got to give him that: "All of my albums have im-perfections, man. 'Get Rich Or Die Tryin',' I would have trimmed it down, like drop the bonus cut at the end. And 'The Massacre' I feel was over-written—it was 21 cuts, the maximum play time, technically it's a double CD. And I regret giving Game the hit records I wrote in the same period—that shit came out just a couple of weeks before my album—just because of the disrespect following that. For the 'Curtis' record, I should have pulled away from it. I shouldn't have made a whole album where I reached out to artists I like and appreciate: I put *everyone* on the record, so it's me and Justin Timberlake, it's me and Robin Thicke, it's me and Mary J Blige, it's me and Akon, it's me and Nicole from the Pussycat Dolls, and what happened was because there was more hit RnB artists than real hip-hop artists, the album became more light-hearted."

Perfectly candid then. But with Interscope-stamped album number four on the horizon—the rumored last contractual obligation, after a greatest hits package, before he's courted as a free agent—there's a new question: Can 50 Cent get open?

There are meant to be no second acts in American lives, and hip-hop, despite its yearning towards a rebel-rousing 'tube, has been a pretty faithful student of the credo. You might get away with hushing up an aborted image from the past—Lupe's painful wannabe gangsta phase, most recently forgiven—but few rappers ever return to the top after a deflating career move. Now 50 Cent is faced with just that. The king of the entire rap realm for the best part of a half-decade, the merciless general in complete and smooth control of the game, he's now gearing up to the prospect of a battlefield where he isn't guaranteed to win by virtue of his name alone; where his brand of straight outta Southside gangsta rap doesn't strike the same notes of frenzied excitement and terror—and accompanying ching of sales registers—as it once did. He's no longer the first thing that comes into the average bloke in the street's mind when they think 'rap,' seeing that title very publicly gaffled up by Kanye West and his Louis Vuitton army last album around, and now witnessing the title pass to Lil Wayne and his cackling gaggle of bugged-out followers. In 2009, 50 Cent is no longer bulletproof.

"The biggest challenge facing a hip-hop artist these days is just making a traditional rap record," he decrees, suddenly sounding to all the world like a hip-hop purist, almost—whisper it—back-packerish in devotion to a bricks-and-mortar notion of rap. "If you look at the records they consider hip-hop right now, it's real sing-songy records. Like TI's record has a lot of melody to it, [singing] 'You can have whatever you like'; Kanye West's 'Love Lockdown,' that's an RnB record in my perspective, you know what I'm sayin'? So you got a lot of hip-hop artists making music that fits into another genre; like when you got the T-Pain voice, the vocoder—they call it the T-Pain voice but it's Roger Troutman—it's more a traditional RnB sound than it is hip-hop, right? So you got rap artists with the vocoder on them all the time and then they're sounding more like RnB records to me.

"The situation isn't frustrating to me, it's just something for me to cut through," he continues, seeming to confirm that Curtis's RnB leanings weren't what the public wanted from him. "So now of course I'm going to go against the grain and make a hit hip-hop record that they can't deny. The current situation just creates a bigger space for *my* record."

The space for a back-to-basics hip-hop record may physically be there—we're still secretly fiending for that top-to-toe Premo produced Nas joint, even though it's never going to appear—but is the crowd?

However you want to coin rap cycles, 2009 is coming off the back of a year when macho, straight-edged, balls-to-the-curb gangsta rap was roundly suffocated by svelte figures wearing rainbow colors, slipping into ball-squashingly tight jeans, admitting to—of all things!—liking dance music, and talking in tones that wanted to show that being a nerd, being a wimp, being a student of unisex couture, was *cool*. (Hell, current prince darling Weezy has a catalogue of pictures and rumors suggesting intimacy with the hairier sex—imagine the audacity of that flying five years ago in hip-hop's openly homophobic world!) The history books will show that it was one of these supra-nerds who finally toppled Fif' (though chinks in the General's armor were rumored at before confirmation of first-week figures from his Soundscan war with Kanye came in, with speculation about disputes with his label—office-wrecking allegations and all—and the unceremonious public-flip of 'Before I Self-Destruct' (version one) into 'Curtis'), but now, in 2009, it's not about the fall any more. After going from figuratively and theoretically bulletproof—has there ever been another rapper to cause so many others to dig their own career graves?—to wounded, can 50 Cent embrace the change? Can the bulletproof bravada, the closed but impenetrable shell that took him to the very top, be opened up to capture the public's imagination again? He's cashed in on their vicarious lust for the gangsta, but can he get their hearts?

"At one point I would be looked at as one of those animals that it's okay to take a look at on safari—just don't get out and get too close 'cos they'll hurt you," he starts to answer, talking about the side of him that so effectively captured the whole world's attention. "But I come from a place where the actual price of life is cheap, where it don't mean much to people if they blow your head off. So the vibe, everything about me, it's different.

"So when they all get ready to go to their judgment—'cos people pass judgment on me all the time—they'll just always define me by financial success," he continues, defensively. "But I'll always look at that success as having no true significance 'cos I keep looking back and focusing on the struggle, saying look how far I came.

"It's amazing," he says, now moving comfortably towards that favorite offensive tic of his, taking shots at others, "'cos every time I get ready to write I'm going to be writing from the perspective of the have-nots even though I have most of it, but the guy who doesn't have anything is writing from the perspective of luxury! You know half of the fuckin' hip-hop population has on fake jewelry? And these are the same people who keep screaming 'Keep it real'! Come on, man. This is what makes me significant—me being who I am and where I'm from and still being able to articulate it in a way that's entertaining enough for people to listen to. People may be able to beat you at being a different kind of artist, but they won't ever be able to beat you at being you. You got guys out there that can write great songs, but they can't write the kind of songs I'm writing better than me."

For an off-the-cuff self-analysis of the way people look at him, it's on-point, well broken down, and with requisite overtones of more general frauds in hip-hop. But does it promise anything new that is going to get those mythologized 872,000 early endorsers back on his side?

If there are meant to be no second acts in American life, then it's also said that the truly great manage to rise and fall and then rise again. They're tested, and the second ascent is the most noble of all, being the one that solidifies their standing. This return from the collective conscious abyss is one that very few rappers ever carry off. Fellow Queens icon LL restored himself perhaps better than most with 'Mama Said Knock You Out,' openly battering those who'd earlier pelted him with piss rockets for his loverman escapades, and Ice Cube seemed to feed off the controversy that his early solo albums raised, each time coming back more prickly than the last. Taking the other route, old man Jay-Z extended his career another five or so tax cycles by giving the impression that his introspective side went beyond thoughts of the morals of the hustle with 'The Blueprint.' So, with 50's stock as low as it's ever been since his blockbuster breakthrough moment, with even his reality TV show, *The Power and the Money*, getting cancelled, and with the sky-high sales expectations he's burdened himself with meeting, where next? Where next for the rapper so familiar with priding himself on being able to manipulate the very game of rap?

Maybe we'll see the level-headed façade dropped and an unleashing of the truly beastly, demonic side of 50 Cent—that predatory big cat hunger he alluded to earlier, uncaged and allowed to devastate the entertainment world's moral constitution. ("'Fuck you 50!'"/Yeah, I'm the rapper you love to hate!" anyone? The ad libs on his 'Heartless' freestyle—"Niggas from the hood ain't supposed to wear no retro shit—I'm a tell my little niggas to start kickin' your fuckin' ass, if we see you out there with that funny shit on"—suggest the anger's definitely within him to come back meaner than ever, and album track titles like 'Need Your Hate' and 'Norman Bates Motel,' featuring Em, hint that things might just get a whole lot darker.) But it's hard to recreate the phenomenal frenzy of excitement that attaches itself to breakthrough moments, so maybe this time around he needs to do something offering a bit more intrigue. Maybe he'll come good on the promise given in the run up to 'Before I Self-Destruct's original 2007 release, when he talked about it being the album where he opens up—his 12-bar confessional on the 'Hate It Or Love It' remix expanded across an album. Maybe he'll change his mind on the declaration that rap's too competitive to be vulnerable: after all, who can't relate to being a kid and waking up to the universe-stopping discovery that someone has stolen your bike?

At times, it seems like he's acutely aware of the situation he's approaching. Looking back on 'Curtis,' he says, "I take full responsibility for that album's performance. Not to take away from the album and say it isn't good, but that's the actual album that people consider my weakest effort because I didn't give them the aggressive content. So it's a catch-22—they'll complain about you writing the aggressive material and the harsh realities, but I don't get a response from writing the light-hearted stuff.

"It's like on 'The Massacre' when I wrote 'God Give Me Strength',"he continues. "If you write a record with that content it's almost impossible for it not to be radio ready, but they'd rather hear Kirk Franklin during the inspirational hour than to hear 50 Cent. It's not like I don't believe in God—I believe in God. God's the only way that I can be fuckin' sitting here talking to you. I've been hit nine times and all type of shit's going on in my life, so I feel like I must have a bigger purpose than sitting here having this conversation."

Maybe that's it. Right there. Maybe that's what he needs to show the world next: the tensions and turmoils that come with being the one-time biggest superstar in rap now more familiar with being criticized than applauded, forever held to higher standards than his contemporaries. Maybe that's the line of sympathy he needs to inspire to see him back on top.

"I'm comfortable in accepting a failure at this point, musically," he admits on the eve of his most precarious move yet. "A project from me today that doesn't directly connect on the highest level possible would be considered a failure. So if I go on what I chose to deliver, I can accept it, but if I'm following someone else's idea or instruction then I'd be fuckin' devastated, I'd be mad.

"So I'm always gonna make what I want to make," he vows, delivering his parting shot. "I'll accept constructive criticism from Em and Dre, but other than that I'm about the most hard-headedest person you know."

Regret, Divorce, Compromise

Greg Pratt

It's not all good times with the New Kids on the Block.

Donnie Wahlberg, he's got my back against the wall. I'm about halfway through a shockingly candid and interesting interview with the New Kid on the Block/actor and I ask him if he wants to write more serious lyrics than those found on the band's comeback disc, the Block. I bring up a particularly taste-offending couplet in "2 in the Morning," where Wahlberg sings "I gotta know if you're mad at me / before Grey's Anatomy."

"What do you mean?" Wahlberg asks after a silence; I don't really know what to say. I mutter, "It just seems so . . . kind of . . . " I fear this could be the end of the interview, but Wahlberg sets the record straight.

"It was written about my wife and my break-up," he says. "We basically spent a summer not communicating. Pretty much every night we wouldn't talk until two in the morning. I was sleeping on the couch and she was up in the bedroom. I'd send her a text saying, 'Are we gonna talk or do you wanna sleep?' And most nights she said, 'I'm going to sleep.'" Wahlberg sounds distant and intense; I realize I've brought up the wrong lyric. "I just couldn't compete with Grey's Anatomy that summer," he says.

He admits that although the lyric I mentioned is not a good example, there are plenty of "goofball lyrics" on the disc. It's something he feels the band didn't really think about: people might not want to hear a 39-year-old man singing about being "your boyfriend."

"Music comes on certain stations and it's young people listening to it; some of them are gonna like it and not care, and some of them are going to say, 'I don't wanna hear those guys singing it, I want to hear the Jonas Brothers sing that shit.' But if we do another [album], I think your point is well taken and we may take a different approach, but certainly not because we have regret."

Regret: something Wahlberg does feel about some of the decisions the band made when they were younger. Not that, say, pillow cases negate musical credibility, but . . . they didn't help.

"We tried to stay as on top of things as possible," he says. "It's just . . . it was so big, you know? When something gets that big it's really out of control; you have to do all you can just to keep your sanity and not forget who you are. Our mentality started to be, look, it may not last forever but we'd like to have some dignity when it's done. So enough with the bullshit. Enough with the pink slippers and the cereal and the cartoons. It's enough . . . it's enough. We made enough compromises and did enough things that we look back on with some regret . . . " Wahlberg pauses, sounds intense again; I find it hard to believe this is the once-teen heartthrob of a time past; he sounds like a man whose eyes are locked in the thousand-mile stare as we speak; a man who may be talking about his divorce or may be talking about his band's past when he finishes his sentence: "at some point we said enough is enough." And he says it with such intensity that I just leave it at that.

The Fighter

The Life & Times of Merle Haggard

Jason Fine

Some afternoons, when his kids are at school and he doesn't feel like practicing with his band, Merle Haggard will load a pipe, climb onto his John Deere golf cart and take a ride around his property, 200 acres of rugged California ranch land at the northern edge of the San Joaquin Valley. He'll check on projects that are always underway but never seem to get finished—the mending of a fence in his sheep pen; planting redwood trees; the construction of a waterfall—or he might park on a wooden bridge that crosses the lake where he fishes for bass and catfish, and smoke some weed.

On a perfect summer evening, as the electric-blue sky fades to glowing orange, Haggard's golf cart strains and lurches up a steep incline on the north perimeter of his property. The hillside is covered in waist-high yellow grass and twisted manzanita. Haggard, coughing frequently and speaking with a low, syrupy twang, points out that the grass looks soft but is actually razor sharp—better than any fence to keep out trespassers. He also says it's full of rattlesnakes, some as big around as his calf.

Just below the crest of the hill, Haggard pulls into a clearing where he's thinking about building a new house—a place the 72-year-old country singer would like to pass on to his family after he's gone. "I've lived in houseboats and motor homes and band houses and cabins," he says.

216

"But I'd like to build me a home with some sanity, where it's totally green. I think that's a necessary project for me right now." Below us, workers haul lumber and pour concrete at construction sites. I ask Haggard if he takes part in the work. "I need to keep my hands tender," he says. "I'm the ideas man."

Haggard fishes a plastic M&M container of weed from the pocket of his camouflage shirt, shrinks low on the seat and lights a black glass pipe. As he smokes, two fawns wander by, not intimidated by our presence. He watches them silently, his head cocked in concentration. "Residents," he says finally, as they disappear into the trees. He doesn't mention the view, which is incredible: purple mountains rippling all the way to Mount Shasta, its snow-covered 14,000-foot peak shining in the dusky light.

Haggard bought this land in 1980. He was 43 years old, twice divorced and 14 years into an amazing streak of 26 Number One country singles, with another dozen to come in the next decade. Haggard's early hits—"The Fugitive," "Branded Man," "Mama Tried," "Hungry Eyes," "Workin' Man Blues," "Okie from Muskogee," "Sing Me Back Home"—form the backbone of one of the greatest repertoires in all of American music, plain-spoken songs populated by the kinds of working people Haggard grew up with: farmers, hobos, convicts, widows, musicians and drunks. Mostly, though, Haggard's early songs narrate the difficult circumstances of his own life: The son of Dust Bowl migrants from Oklahoma to the San Joaquin Valley, Haggard lost his father at age nine, hopped his first train a year later, and spent his teenage years in and out of juvenile institutions, military schools and, eventually, San Quentin. "Johnny Cash once told me, 'Hag, you're the guy people think I am,'" Haggard says. He spent nearly half of his first 21 years "running away or behind bars," he says. "I would've become a lifetime criminal if music hadn't saved my ass."

Haggard's songs look on his early life with a mixture of pride and regret, and they are sung in a warm, rangy baritone, strong but hinting at a deeper vulnerability, with little of the cornball sentimentality that characterized much 1960s country. "Merle Haggard has always been as deep as deep gets," says Bob Dylan. "Totally himself. Herculean. Even too big for Mount Rushmore. No superficiality about him whatsoever.

He definitely transcends the country genre. If Merle had been around Sun Studio in Memphis in the Fifties, Sam Phillips would have turned him into a rock & roll star, one of the best. I'm sorta glad he didn't do it, though, because then he'd be on the oldies circuit singing his rock & roll hits instead of becoming the Merle Haggard we all know and love."

Haggard's property is several miles off the highway, at the end of a curving blacktop that passes ranch-style houses with ornate gates and horses grazing under giant oak trees. Haggard once owned 900 acres back here, but he was forced to sell most of it, along with his entire publishing catalog, when he declared bankruptcy in 1993 following a string of failed business ventures and costly divorces. In the 1970s, before the interstate was built, this was about as isolated a place as you could find in California. Now the land is being sold off in five-acre parcels to weekend cowboys and wealthy retirees. "I'm sure the minute I go, they'll subdivide my place, too," Haggard says. "I'm trying to prevent it by making this a game refuge—I don't want this to become a trailer camp." The thing that bothers Haggard most is the recklessness and greed of the local ranchers, whom he says run too many cattle back here, choking with waste the creek that runs through his property. "There's certain times of day that the cowboys like to send cow turds down the river," he says. "Them fuckers piss me off. If you gotta mess up the ecology of the world in order to raise a bunch of cows, well, eat somethin' else. I'm not a fan of some of these cowboys around here."

There are other problems, too. Haggard's ranch sits at the edge of California's Emerald Triangle, the country's most fertile pot-growing region, and during harvest season DEA and state agents run military-style raids in the mountains. Recently, a helicopter flew over low enough that Haggard could see the agents' faces. "Black helicopter. Guy hanging out the side with an automatic weapon," he says, his voice rising. "Dressed all in black. All in black. What does that mean?" Haggard's reaction was to run into the yard, wave his arms and thrust his hips—"the big 'fuck you,'" he says. "It's like, 'Hey, do you guys realize that I'm down here and I'm responsible for protecting my family?'" he continues, shouting now. "'I'm not running drugs. I'm a 70-year-old goddamn Hall of Fame songwriter.'"

Haggard fires up the cart, and we bounce along a dusty trail down the hill. He points out the black metal gate at the entrance to the ranch, near a street sign that says there's a lane, named for his fifth wife, a statuesque blonde 23 years younger than he is. "No one can get in here except through that one road," he says, "and you can see them coming around the bend—no one can surprise you.

"Johnny Cash used to really like it here a lot," he goes on. "He loved the privacy. He never spent too much time here, though. He was always in a hurry. I could never understand that. I'd always say, 'What's the hurry, Cash?' I don't like to hurry."

The property has several dwellings, including an elegant Spanish-style house where the Haggards lived until rampant mold forced them out. That house, with its mountain views and swimming pool, sits empty now. The family—Merle, Theresa and their two kids, Jenessa, 19, and Benion, 16—moved into a modest stucco bungalow where Haggard's drummer, Biff Adam, lived for many years, at a time when Haggard envisioned the ranch as a home base for his band, the Strangers. The house has a sunny stained-glass foyer decorated with Haggard's gold records, an island kitchen and a cluttered living room that's dominated by an enormous TV, usually muted on CNN or the Bloomberg network.

Haggard's business is run from a single phone line in a corner of the living room, and Jenessa and Ben can sometimes be found doing homework at the dining table a few feet from where Haggard is practicing with his band. Outside the kitchen window is a vegetable garden where the Haggards grow much of their own food—tomatoes, lettuce, cucumbers, peppers and all kinds of beans. Haggard, who stopped eating beef more than 20 years ago, loves beans. A plaque above the stove says "The Bean Man"—his nickname. "We grow purple peas in the garden," says Theresa. "It's a specialty. He'll call his sister and say, 'I want to get that taste that Mom had.' She says, 'Well, all we had back then was coffee.' 'Oh.' Then he'll work all day long on a pot of beans, getting it right. Anything he cooks is great, because it's always different. It's like his music: It's never the same."

"He's always got that pot of beans goin', exactly like he had it goin' 30 years ago," says Hank Williams Jr., an old pal. "The last time I went out to his ranch, I stayed with him about three days. I'll never forget it. He drove up in a Mercedes-Benz with a cap on his head that said asshole. He said, 'I've got one for you, too.'"

Haggard parks the golf cart in the carport and stomps, with a kind of stiff-legged shuffle, across the lawn to the front door, avoiding the stone path completely. Two wiry old fox terriers, Mabel and three-legged Blackie—the same breed Haggard has kept since he was a boy—sneak in the house behind him. Theresa asks Merle if he wants to eat inside or at the picnic table. Haggard is still riled about the pot raids and isn't listening. "What is happening to this country?" he says. "I've never been frightened, but now I feel fear creeping up my back, and what little I have, I may have to fight for—literally take up arms."

Theresa doesn't like when Merle talks this way—she worries he'll make himself and their family a target. "What am I supposed to do?" Haggard asks. "Something's seriously wrong—and someone better say something before it's too late. People don't seem to realize it. I see it."

Jenessa brings Merle a cup of tea made from hyssop, an herb that calms the nerves and that he believes is good for his heart. Haggard had heart surgery in 1997: He no longer drinks coffee or smokes cigarettes, and except for a couple of extended benders in the Eighties, he's never been much of a drinker. "What's going to be left worth saving?" he goes on. "I'm afraid that one day we're going to look up and it's all going to be gone. It's the most depressing damn thing you can imagine: to feel everything slipping away."

Haggard sits in a beat-up leather swivel chair. Everything he needs is within reach: his Rose acoustic guitar, the phone, remote control, reading glasses, a Bible, bottles of herbs and prescription medications, and his M&M canister, black pipe and two Bic lighters. In the windowsill is a model-train car and a framed fax sent by Keith Richards after he and Haggard performed at a 2004 Willie Nelson birthday bash in L.A. "If you ever need an extra hand," Richards scrawled, "call on me."

Richards says he's been a fan of Haggard's since the Sixties, but he'd met him only once or twice before they played together at the Nelson event. "This cat was next to me with a Stetson and a gray beard, and he's picking this Fender like a motherfucker," Richards recalls. "And I'm thinking, 'Who do I know who plays like that?' Halfway through the first song, I looked up to see who it is, and I go, 'Merle, right?' And he says, 'Yup. Call me Hag.'" Richards laughs. "He's such a neat player, so economical and so unflash, which I admire."

On a shelf next to the TV is a Macintosh amplifier, a stack of old country LPs and a plaque that reads nothing's easy. This is pretty much Haggard's credo. "I've got a lot of things to be proud of," he says. "But it's not easy. It never became easy. Everything that ever happened that was good, I look back and say, 'Goddamn it, it took me 40 fuckin' years to do that.'"

In his songs, Haggard often portrays himself as a free-spirited rambler, but in life he's weighed down by a complicated personality—intelligent, ornery, contrary, impulsive, always curious, with a deep worrying streak. "I've never seen anybody who can take a light load and make it a major burden the way Merle can," his manager, Fuzzy Owen, has said. "Merle's a mood man," observes his pianist, Doug Colosio. "He lives in the moment. You never know where things are going—just that it's probably not somewhere you've been before."

Being around Haggard, you get accustomed to his unpredictable rhythms: He might be quiet for long stretches, then his mood will brighten, and he'll launch into ideas for a new album, or his plan to start a business selling catfish from his lake, or a joke—often dirty—that's punctuated by a staccato, lascivious-sounding laugh that causes his whole body to shake.

Frequently, Haggard veers into tirades about what's wrong with the country. You can hear his mind working, stretching, as he spins out theories, trying them on to see if they stick. "I don't believe there's a dime's worth of difference between Democrats and Republicans," he told me a few months before the 2008 presidential election. "When we get someone new in the White House, don't you suppose they'd set him down there the first morning in the Oval Office and explain the rules? Give him orders about what to do, and if he didn't do 'em, they'd kill his kids? That's what I think. I think there's a No Shit Day, when they sit the guy down and he says, 'No shit.' And they say, 'Yeah, and it's this way, too.' 'No shit.' 'And we'll kill your fuckin' kids if you don't like it.' I think we're there."

Haggard launches a new tour two days later. There's a large desk calendar on the floor, with X's marking the dates: 31 shows in 38 days, casinos and state fairs and dinner theaters. Haggard stares silently at the calendar. "How am I gonna do this?" he says finally. "I don't want to die out there, and I don't want to get to the point where no one shows up. I want to quit with some dignity."

In 2008, Haggard was diagnosed with lung cancer, and he underwent surgery to remove a malignant tumor in November. He lost the upper lobe of his right lung—enough to end the singing career of a much younger man. "I was probably more scared than I let on," he says. "There was a good possibility it was over. When it hits your lungs, it's usually everywhere else. A guy's gotta think—realistically. I was just hoping I'd made the right spiritual preparations."

Six weeks after surgery, Haggard played two hometown shows in Bakersfield—"I needed that as a personal test"—and was back in the studio recording a new batch of songs, including one called "Hopes Are High," which he wrote two days before Obama's inauguration. "It was both about me and about the country getting a second chance," he says.

In addition to playing hundreds of his own shows, Haggard has in the past few years toured with Willie Nelson, George Jones, Dylan and the Rolling Stones. In June, he played Bonnaroo for the first time. "One time, somebody asked Fuzz, 'How did you get into country music?'" Haggard says. "And Fuzz said, 'How the fuck do you get out of it?' Ah ha hah hah hah ha ha! And that's really the way it is. I don't want to go on this tour. But I'll get out there and at about the 12th or 15th day, I'll start to play good again. When I get done, I'll come home, and it'll be the damnedest, most difficult change you can imagine going through—it'll just rip me apart."

Retiring is a constant theme with Haggard. He's been talking about it for at least a decade, but until recently he had to keep going: bankruptcy had put him $14 million in debt. "I had to work," he says. "It made it a job—it never was a job prior to that. Somebody my age, sixty years old and broke, with forty number one records—it didn't make sense. A lot of people figured I'd go the way of Waylon at that age, and they were probably making good calculations. But somehow I managed to keep alive and keep going."

As we sit and talk, Haggard's daughter Kelli—the third of four children from his first marriage to teenage sweetheart Leona Hobbs—stops by to visit. She's a pretty, freckled woman in her 40s, dressed in overalls and smothering her half brother Ben with kisses. She mentions that when she was a kid, Haggard threw her tape of Jimi Hendrix at Woodstock out the car window because he didn't like the cursing. "I never understood using that kind of language onstage," Haggard acknowledges solemnly.

Haggard's marriage to Hobbs was tumultuous and often violent. "It was horrible for a child to witness," Haggard's oldest daughter, Dana, has said. "I seen blood, I seen terrible things."

Haggard was touring and rarely home, and the kids barely knew their dad. "Most of the time we called him 'Hey,'" Kelli has said. Haggard carries a lot of guilt for his absence. He keeps his older kids close now—his son Noel, a country singer, opens many of Haggard's shows and operates the teleprompter during his dad's set; Kelli and Dana live nearby; his other son, Marty, is a Christian country singer based outside Nashville. Haggard has 11 grandchildren and three great-grandchildren, which he calls a "blessing" but also describes as a burden. "It's a strange feeling to be the one in charge of what some people might call a dynasty," he says. "They expect me to have answers, even when I don't."

This afternoon, Kelli is trying to persuade her father to retire. "Daddy, we worry about you," she says. "You don't have to tour—you can sing for your grandkids." Haggard frowns, sinks low in his chair. After a long silence, he says, "I think you do what you can do as long as you can. Then you weigh up and see what you've got."

Kelli reminds her dad she's come to borrow money. Haggard reaches into the pocket of his Wranglers and counts out a stack of bills. "How can I quit?" he says. "I have an expensive lifestyle."

Dinner is served at a picnic table on the front lawn, next to a patch of rosemary and black-eyed Susans. Theresa says grace and passes around plates of peppers, salad greens, fried okra and purple-hull peas, all grown in the garden. Theresa and Jenessa chat about pickling vegetables, while Ben, an expert fisherman, tells me about one Thanksgiving when the family pulled a 45-pound salmon out of the creek. Merle sits quietly, chewing slowly, lost in thought. He perks up when Theresa tells the story of a wild turkey that lived on the ranch and took a liking to Merle. They named her Hannah, and she used to ride around on the back of Merle's tractor. "One time Hank Jr. called up," Merle says, "and he said, 'Hey, you got any turkeys out there?' I said, 'Yeah! I can see 'em walking by outside the window.' He said, 'Well, what are you doing, man, get your gun!' I told him I don't want to shoot them—they're my friends! Ah hah hah!"

After dinner, Haggard drives me back to my hotel in his white Hummer, improvising a zigzagging route across dusty farm roads and interstate overpasses. A CD of songs by Cole Porter, one of Haggard's favorite composers, plays quietly on the stereo. "I can get depressed real easy," he says. "My life is not as smooth as it might appear. There are secrets that I wish there weren't, and the blue—I'm the glue, I guess, that keeps it all from falling apart. When I die, that property will die. Nobody will be there for the grandkids. The whole family will fall apart. And it's very depressing to realize that I've got this goddamn obligation of keeping the whole thing together."

He's quiet for a while. "The glue," he says. "There might be a song there."

Haggard's best songs these days deal with two things: the decline of the country and his own personal decline. "Those are the two most disturbing things in my life," he says, "my age and the aging country, and to not see more sincerity of interest in what's happening. It don't seem like anybody cares." Haggard has made 11 albums in the past decade, everything from jazz standards and bluegrass to honky-tonk classics, an album of duets with George Jones and three discs of new material. Some of his best new songs, like "Wishing All These Old Things Were New," "I Hate to See It Go" and the heartbreaking "Learning to Live With Myself," show a vulnerability and a self-awareness that's come with age; others express his outrage. Tracks like "Rebuild America First," "What Happened?" "Where's All the Freedom," "Haggard (Like I've Never Been Before)" and "I've Seen It Go Away" describe a country that has sold out its ideals and abandoned civil liberties, and where people have become timid and small-minded. "I wish I could say something in eight lines that would turn the entire country's head," Haggard says. "If there's an ambition left in my body, it's to do that: to write eight lines that will put the condition of the country foremost again before it's too late."

The next morning at Lulu's, a diner in Redding where Haggard often eats breakfast, he is still trying to explain what motivates him to keep going. "I heard a song that changed my way of thinking," he says. The song, Kris Kristofferson's "Final Attraction," describes watching Willie Nelson sing and muses that some divine purpose must keep him going night after night. "For Hank Williams, go break a heart," Kristofferson sings. "And Waylon Jennings, go break a heart." "It turned me around," Haggard says. "Suddenly, I felt like those guys who all meant something to me would be terribly disappointed in me if I didn't continue."

Haggard feels the loss of so many friends and musical peers. "It's getting pretty lonely," he admits. Most of all, he misses Johnny Cash. "We was more like brothers than the brothers we had," Haggard says. "We understood each other's problems. He was the guy every macho guy in the world wanted to be, and he wasn't happy with himself at all. I'm a lot like that."

Before Cash died, in 2003, Haggard dressed in a white doctor's coat and snuck into the ICU to see his friend one last time. "Cash said, 'What are you doing here, Haggard?' I said, 'I'm here because I love you.'" Haggard's blue eyes cloud over as he says this, but he doesn't attempt to hide his tears. He stares directly at me, elbows on the table, until the feeling passes. "When Cash died," Haggard says, "I think a lot of faces turned to look at me, and looked at Willie. We sort of moved up a notch."

Like Cash, who made some of his greatest music in the last decade of his life, Haggard is also in the midst of a late-period resurgence few would have expected a dozen years ago, when he was broke and playing second-rate casinos and county fairs. But while Cash handed over the reins of his career to producer Rick Rubin, Haggard refuses to cede control to anyone. He still has the same manager, Fuzzy Owen, he started with in 1961, and he still runs his business in what could be described as an impulsive, haphazard manner.

"I've shot myself in the foot plenty," Haggard acknowledges. "I don't even have to look back at my career to see that—I can look down at my foot. But I'm just not one to give a lot of thought to the brilliant ways to make money. I guess you'd call me a lazy thinker in that particular area, but I think more about good songs and catching a big bass than I do about how to make money. I can sit down and spend two, three weeks and make enough money for you and me both for our entire lifetimes. I'm not stupid. But I just don't find all that much satisfaction with what the money might bring. I'd just rather do what I want to do."

Haggard sees his maverick approach as a form of self-preservation. "If you compare my life to some other people who were ready to do anything they were asked to do, look where they are now," he says. "You take people who did anything to get on the Grand Ole Opry. They thought the Grand Ole Opry was the pinnacle of their life. Well, it was."

Recently, a man he describes as "a billionaire" approached with a plan to kick Haggard's career into high gear. "He has it already figured out. He wants me to do three albums, then do my 75th birthday at Carnegie Hall. But I've already been to Carnegie Hall, and he don't even know that. Fuck him. I'd rather die my own man, and if I become more successful toward the end, it'll be because of the work, the songs— not the presentation. I guess I'm stubborn. I'm gonna just do it my way, that's all."

When he's not on the road, Haggard likes to wake up early, drink some herbal tea and play old records, often those of the Texas-swing band-leader Bob Wills. Wills relocated from Texas to California after World War II, and his live radio broadcasts from Bakersfield's Beardsley Ball-room made him a hero to transplanted Southerners. From the first time he heard Wills, Haggard wrote in his 1981 autobiography, *Sing Me Back Home*, "that beautiful fiddle . . . was piercing little holes right through my head." Haggard modeled his own band, the Strangers, after the hillbilly-jazz sound of Wills' Texas Playboys, and he hired several Playboys after Wills died in 1975. One of Haggard's proudest achievements is his 1970 album *A Tribute to the Best Damn Fiddle Player in the World (Or, My Salute to Bob Wills)*. Haggard spent four months intensively learning to play fiddle, practicing Wills' solos all night on the tour bus. "He'd be listening over and over to those tapes," says Haggard's drummer, Biff Adam. "Sometimes we'd have to go back in the bunks and cover up our heads."

Haggard got to know his idol in the last years of his life. "It was like a Godfather thing," Haggard says. "I was his boy. Once he patted me on the cheek, and he said, 'I say a lot of prayers for you.'"

Listening this morning to Wills' version of "Sweet Jennie Lee"—its jumping beat punctuated by Wills' trademark "aaaaah-haaaah" hollers— Haggard taps one cream loafer and rolls his shoulders in rhythm, smiling broadly and calling out the name of each soloist. Later, I ask what he still discovers in this music he first heard more than 50 years ago. "You know, America was so gorgeous back then," he says. "The trees were still up here in the north, and the Colorado River still had water. Everything hadn't been invented. These songs are like turning on a direct message from the past. It takes me back to the way I felt when I was 16 years old. It felt real good."

Haggard is deeply nostalgic, and he often writes songs about America in some idealized past, when he believes hard work, honesty and individualism defined the national character. These traits are the same ones he ascribes to his father, James Haggard, a carpenter for the Santa Fe railroad who died of a stroke when Merle was nine. "The only thing I knew that my dad hated for sure was a liar," Haggard wrote in his second autobiography, 1999's *My House of Memories*. "I don't remember any sermons on the subject, but it was something I always knew. Everyone knew his word was good. Ever since my early childhood, I have found more importance in the trait of honesty than maybe most children."

Haggard views his father's death as the defining event in his life. "I was around 30 years old before I began to realize that things would have been different, maybe better, if he'd lived," he says over breakfast. "I'm sure that I was probably much more street-wise on account of his death—probably wound up in prison because of it."

The Haggards migrated to California from Checotah, Oklahoma, in 1935, after their barn burned down in a suspicious fire. Though they were far from wealthy, Haggard points out that they did not arrive with mattresses strapped to the roof of the car. "The Grapes of Wrath was not our story," he says. "We did not yield to the Depression."

Okies were discouraged from settling within Bakersfield city limits, so the Haggards moved to a migrant settlement across the Kern River called Oildale. James Haggard paid $500 for an old railroad boxcar, which he converted into a kind of early mobile home. The boxcar was set on a small plot of land next to some abandoned oil wells. "We lived like the Beverly Hillbillies," Haggard has said. Merle's brother, Lowell, and his sister, Lillian, were teenagers when his mother, Flossie, found out she was pregnant with Merle. "She sort of was embarrassed about it," he says. "The children were nearly up and gone. They were going to move into this new little place. And then I came along."

Merle was born on April 6th, 1937. "When he was an infant—and I mean an infant," Lillian once recalled, "Mother would turn the radio on, and when he heard what was then called 'Western music' his little feet would start keeping rhythm with the beat. We would change the station—nothing would happen. Put it back, the feet start moving again."

Merle's other childhood fascination was trains. The Southern Pacific ran less than a hundred yards from the Haggards' home, and a little farther away Merle could hear the all-night passenger trains chugging to and from Los Angeles. "There's a couple lines in 'Mama Tried' that are actually factual," he says. "'The first thing I remember knowing was the lonesome whistle blowing.' At night, you could hear the Southern Pacific, that passenger train, rolling by. Before I'd go to sleep I would hear that damn train headed out of town with all those people on it going somewhere. It was intriguing, to say the least."

Lying in bed at night, Merle also heard his parents arguing about whether to stay in California or go back home. "My daddy was a rambler, and he was never happy in California," Haggard says. "Almost every night, he'd say, 'Mom, I've been studying. I think we ought to sell out and go back to Okie.'"

I mention that this sounds a lot like Merle: always looking for somewhere else to be. "Yeah, he was probably a lot like me and me like him," he says. "Probably genetic. Probably came with the package.

"I've always had the desire to go, to move," he says, "and I probably will until the day I die. I'm a nomad."

By the time Merle's father died, Lillian and Lowell were out of the house, and Flossie took a job as a bookkeeper, leaving Merle with little adult supervision. When he was 10, Merle and a friend packed pillowcases with food and hopped their first freight train. They got caught late that night walking along the tracks in Fresno, a hundred miles away. When Merle's mother came to pick him up, she asked Merle why he'd ridden without a ticket—he'd been given a free pass as the child of a Santa Fe employee. "Mama'd missed the point completely," Haggard wrote. "I had had my first taste of adventure, and now I wanted more."

His sister believes Merle acted out of misplaced guilt over his father's death. "He somehow thought it was his fault," Lillian has said. "We could have gotten help for him, but we didn't realize what was going on in his head."

This began a pattern of what Haggard calls "illegal motion"—ditching school, hopping trains, getting caught by truancy officers and being sent to a series of increasingly strict institutions. By Haggard's estimate, he was locked up 17 times, in places like the California Youth Authority, the Fred C. Nelles School for Boys and the Preston School of Industry, one of the oldest and most infamous reform schools in the country. (Haggard has a small psi tattoo still visible on his left wrist.) The first time he saw *Cool Hand Luke*, years later, he said, "It seemed like a documentary of my young life." The institutions were brutal: He was beaten with a rake, made to run miles in boots that didn't fit and brutalized by older inmates. Haggard took pleasure in outwitting the sadistic guards, and he found a way to escape from every single place he was locked up. Asked what motivated him, he shrugs. "I don't like to be told what to do." Behind bars, he learned to be a criminal. "It was the cells I was in that corrupted me," he says. "My idols changed during those years, from Jimmie Rodgers to Bonnie and Clyde. Hell, people were after me, running me down like I was a criminal. All I wanted to do was buck hay and go to work in the oil fields. My dad was dead and my mother was old, and I just wanted to live and work. And them sumbitches wouldn't let me do it. I understand why now—the simple law of truancy. But it was hard to understand when I was young."

Haggard still gets visibly nervous around police officers. "I'll never get over that," he says. Twice when I'm with him he notices a group of cops approaching, puts his hands behind his back, and tells me he's going to turn himself in. "For what?" I asked the first time. "I'm a pot smoker," he says. "I'm sure they'll find something they can arrest me for. That's the kind of country this is now. I'm serious. It's right on the verge of Nazism."

When Merle was 11, his brother, Lowell, gave him a used Bronson guitar. "For a boy who was shy," Haggard wrote, "that guitar gave me a new and exciting way of saying something." Lefty Frizzell's "I Love You a Thousand Ways" became a hit a couple of years later, and Merle learned to perfectly replicate the pleading phrasing of Frizzell's hillbilly tenor. Haggard loved the "brilliance and clarity" of Frizzell's music, and he studied Lefty's easy charisma onstage, which came less naturally to Haggard. "For three or four years I didn't sing anything but Lefty Frizzell songs," he wrote, "and then because Lefty was a fan of Jimmie Rodgers I learned to imitate him, too." When Merle was 14, he and a friend bought tickets to see Frizzell perform at the Rainbow Gardens in Bakersfield. They got so drunk on Burgie beer before the show that they passed out on the front lawn and missed the first set. Two years later, when Frizzell returned to Bakersfield, Haggard snuck backstage. Someone told Frizzell that Haggard could impersonate him, so Frizzell gave him an audition. Frizzell was so bowled over he refused to go on unless Haggard performed first. Haggard sang two Jimmie Rodgers songs and Hank Williams' "You Win Again," and decided then and there that he wanted to be a professional country singer. "It's like the guy who catches his first fish," Haggard says. "I was really the one who was hooked."

In 1956, when he was 19, Haggard married his 16-year-old girlfriend, Leona Hobbs, a beautiful, dark-haired girl he met at a local hamburger stand. Haggard has called their relationship one of "the great battles in history"—he recounts nearly strangling her in one fight shortly before their 1965 split. Through most of his teens, Haggard never saw himself as a real criminal, just a misguided buy who got into bad jams. In *Sing Me Back Home*, he points out that often when he'd steal a car, he'd return it cleaned up, with gas in the tank. But with his new wife and no steady income, his criminal pursuits got more serious. He forged a check in Arizona, robbed a California gas station and broke into safes. On the day his first daughter, Dana, was born, Haggard, then 19, was in jail for car theft.

In 1957, Haggard and a friend were home drinking wine when they launched a plan to rob a cafe owned by an acquaintance of Merle's. With Leona and infant Dana wrapped in a blanket in the backseat, Haggard drove up to the back door of the cafe and started to pick the lock. Haggard was so drunk he thought it was three in the morning— but it was really 10 p.m. and the cafe was still open. The owner came out back, confused. "Why don't you boys come around to the front door?" he said. Haggard took off, but he got caught with his headlights off half a block away. Haggard escaped jail the next day. He was recaptured at his brother's house the following evening, with a bottle of whiskey in his hand, and returned to custody, where he was sentenced to five years in San Quentin. In San Quentin, Haggard got caught for being drunk on beer he brewed in his cell and spent seven days in solitary confinement, with just a pair of pajama pants, a Bible and a mattress that was taken away every morning at 5 a.m. During his confinement, Haggard struck up a conversation through the air vents with convicted rapist Caryl Chessman, whose case was at the center of a battle over the death penalty in the U.S. Supreme Court. Chessman's execution partly inspired one of Haggard's greatest songs, "Sing Me Back Home."

Haggard says that week in solitary was the turning point in his life. "I thought, 'You might better change your locality and get into another area of life, because this is pretty dangerous right here,'" he says. In 1959, he got a glimpse of what that new area might be when Johnny Cash came to perform at San Quentin on New Year's Day. "I didn't care for his music before that—I thought it was corny," Haggard says. "He couldn't sing a lick that day, but he had the crowd right in the palm of his hand. I became a Johnny Cash fan that day."

Several years later, Haggard ran into Cash in the men's room before a TV appearance in Chicago in 1963. As they stood at the urinal, Cash asked if they'd met before. Haggard said no but that he was in the audience at San Quentin in 1959: "I told him, 'You came in there, left, and my life changed.'" By the time Haggard was paroled from San Quentin, in 1960, the Bakersfield scene was swinging with a new style of country music—harder and rowdier than Nashville, driven by Telecaster guitars, electric bass and rockabilly beats. "Nashville was more fruit-jar drinkers, bluegrass-country than California," says Fuzzy Owen, who played steel guitar in local clubs and had a record label, Tally Records, with his cousin Lewis Talley. "We had a different atmosphere in our music. We wanted a brighter sound, and we was kind of wild."

Wynn Stewart and Buck Owens were the biggest Bakersfield stars (the Beatles covered Owens' 1963 hit "Act Naturally" on *Help!*), and Haggard found work as a fill-in guitarist at local clubs like High-Pockets, the Clover Club and the Blackboard, which he calls "the epitome of the country redneck honky-tonk." In 1960, Haggard took second place in a local talent show and landed a job playing at the Lucky Spot, along with Fuzzy Owen. "When Merle come off the stage, he come back and introduced himself, and I said, 'Boy, that's the best damn singing I ever heard,'" says Owen. "He said, 'Well, if you like it so much, why don't you record me?'" The two cut Haggard's composition "Skid Row," with one of Owen's tunes, "Singin' My Heart Out," as the B side. Owen pressed 200 copies, and the record got some local airplay. Owen told Haggard to call him when he had some new material. Soon after, Haggard landed a gig as the bass player for Wynn Stewart's band in Las Vegas. He earned $225 a week but spent far more on booze and gambling and often had to call his mother to wire him more money. After a year in Vegas, Haggard went home broke, with his marriage on the rocks. Before he left, he asked Stewart if he could record a song the star had recently written, "Sing a Sad Song." "He had it all tailored for himself," says Haggard, "ready to record. It was a big thing of him to let me have that song, and I'll always be thankful." The single, released on Owen's Tally label, hit Number 19 on the Billboard country charts. It was followed by a Johnny Cash–style novelty song, "Sam Hill," and a duet with Bonnie Owens (who had previously been married to Buck Owens and would later marry Haggard), "Just Between the Two of Us," both of which also made the charts. Haggard's next single, "(My Friends Are Gonna Be) Strangers," written by California songwriter Liz Anderson, cracked the Top 10 and helped Haggard get a contract with Capital Records. From early in his career, Haggard was more interested in being a musician than an entertainer, rarely bantering or even addressing the crowd. This caused trouble in some places. "People had a hard time accepting Merle Haggard," Jack McFadden, Buck Owens' manager, once said. "I got a call from a guy in Minneapolis one morning. . . . He said, '[Merle] walks out on the stage, picks up his guitar, he don't even say hello, he don't say nothin'. And I've never seen anybody do that before.' I said, 'Well, how's he singing?' He said, 'Oh, he sounds great.' I said, 'Well, you don't have anything to bitch about.'"

In 1966, Haggard had his first Number One song with Anderson's "The Fugitive." The song was about a TV show popular at the time, but it hinted at Haggard's story: "I raised a lot of Cain back in my younger days / While Mama used to pray my crops would fail / Now I'm a hunted fugitive with just two ways / Outrun the law or spend my life in jail." Though he sang about outlaws, Haggard was terrified to let people know about his own criminal past. "The last thing in the world I wanted to do," he says, "was walk up like David Allan Coe and say,

'Hey, I've been to prison, look at me.'" "The amazing thing about Merle," says Kristofferson, "is that he's never said, 'I'm the real thing, and these other guys are just going through the motions.'" It was Cash who eventually persuaded Haggard to talk about his past on Cash's TV show in 1969: "He told me, 'They're going to find out anyway. If you own up to it, you'll be a hero.'" As Haggard began to write about the circumstances of his life in songs like "Mama Tried," "Hungry Eyes" and "Workin' Man Blues" (which he says was his attempt to create a defining song, like Cash had done with "Folsom Prison Blues"), he came to be viewed as a rebel icon and folk hero, an inheritor of the traditions of Woody Guthrie and Jimmie Rodgers. The Grateful Dead named their 1970 album *Workingman's Dead* in tribute to Haggard, and the Rolling Stones were influenced by Haggard, most directly on 1968's *Beggars Banquet*. "I was definitely listening to Merle by then," Keith Richards says, "and when you're a songwriter and musician, what goes in your ear tends to come out of your fingers."

But if Haggard started out as a hero to the hippies, that changed with one song: 1969's "Okie from Muskogee." Released three weeks after Woodstock, the song stood up for small-town values, baiting longhairs and war protesters in lines like "We don't smoke marijuana in Muskogee / We don't take our trips on LSD / We don't burn our draft cards down on Main Street / We like livin' right and bein' free." "Okie" became Haggard's biggest hit and earned him entertainer of the year from the Country Music Association. Haggard was invited to play Pat Nixon's birthday party at the White House (which he struggled through with a raging hangover). In 1972, he was granted an official pardon by California governor Ronald Reagan. Haggard has always wavered on how seriously he intended "Okie." Soon after its release, he wrote a follow-up, "Somewhere in Between," which tried to spell out his political position more precisely, but the song was never re-leased. (It is now available on the Bear Family box set *Merle Haggard: The Studio Recordings 1969–1976.*) Haggard still struggles with how to explain "Okie." "The reason I wrote it was because I was dumb as a rock," he told a crowd recently. Then, confusingly, he added, "Another reason is it needed to be written."

Kristofferson, who as a young songwriter in Nashville idolized Haggard as "the closest thing to Hank Williams walking the streets," took to performing a left-wing parody of "Okie." "I remember saying at the time, 'Maybe that's the only bad song he ever wrote,'" Kristofferson says. "I was wrong. That song is saying, 'I'm proud to be an Okie from Muskogee,' and coming from his background in California, that's like saying, 'I'm black and I'm proud.'"

Bob Dylan sees it another way. "I always thought everybody got 'Okie from Muskogee' wrong," he says. "It's one of the funniest satires ever. If Randy Newman would have written and sung it, nobody would have thought twice." "Okie" made Haggard the most successful country artist of the early 1970s, but he resented being made into a political symbol. "I've never been a Republican, I've never been a Democrat, and I've never voted," he says. "I've never brought that up before—you're the first one to know that."

Just as he resented being made a political symbol, Haggard ran away from being a star. For his follow-up to "Okie," Haggard wanted to release "Irma Jackson," a tortured song about interracial romance (not a popular subject at country radio at the time). Capitol released the jingoistic "The Fightin' Side of Me" instead. Not long after, Haggard was invited to appear on The Ed Sullivan Show, which would have put him in front of the biggest audience of his career, but he ditched rehearsals because he thought the skit designed for his segment made him appear "fruity." "When you say, 'Who's the great California songwriter?' people say, 'Brian Wilson,'" says California guitarist and songwriter Dave Alvin. "And he is, for a particular California. But Merle is the voice of another California." Alvin singles out "Kern River"—about a girl drowning in the treacherous waters that separated Bakersfield from the Okie settlements—as one of the great evocations of place and class in the Golden State. "It's amazingly deep and complicated," he says. "I hear a lot of California in those two and a half minutes." Dylan loves "Kern River" too, but for other reasons. "Sometimes you forget about how much natural-born heartbreak there is in a Merle Haggard song, because of all the boomtown oil-well Dust Bowl honky-tonk imagery of his music," he says. "I mean, 'Kern River' is a beautiful lament, but let's not forget it's about his girlfriend dying."

In 1970, Haggard built a mansion on the Kern River, where he lived with his second wife, Bonnie Owens, and he bought a cabin up at Lake Shasta, which he'd first seen out the window of a train when he ran away from home as a teenager. He says he realized he was a celebrity one day in the early Seventies when he was shopping at Nudie's, the Hollywood Western-wear boutique: "Both John Wayne and Jimmy Stewart came up and told me how much they admired me."

Haggard drove Cadillac Eldorados and wore ostrich boots and bought several planes, which he piloted himself on late-night fishing expeditions and Vegas gambling binges. "People are still paying for the fun we had in the Seventies," he says. "One night I was in bed and the phone rang," recalls Strangers drummer Biff Adam, Haggard's longtime aide-de-camp. "It was Merle calling from Lake Shasta, and he said, 'Hey, there's a bear up here trying to break in my cabin. Will you go out to the ranch and get my .30–30, and fly it up here?' I said, 'Merle, you don't want to kill that bear.' He said, 'No, no, I just want to scare him.' I said, 'OK.' I go out and get the rifle, get the plane out of the hangar, I'm on the runway ready to take off, and the guy in the tower said, 'Hey, Biff. Hag just called. He said don't worry, they've made friends with that bear, they fed him. He said, 'You can go back to bed.'" Flying a Cessna 206 one night out of Vandenberg Air Force Base near Santa Barbara, Haggard noticed strange lights above the plane. "It looked like a big searchlight coming from behind us, and it lit up the whole cockpit," Haggard says. "The pilot called the control tower at Vandenberg and said, 'What'd you do, shoot a rocket at us?' He said, 'What you talking about?' 'Well, we saw these bright lights up here over the top of us.' 'Well, it didn't come from here.'"

Haggard came to believe the light was from a UFO, and it sparked a lifelong curiosity about extraterrestrial life. (In 2003, he started the Merle Haggard UFO Music Fest in Roswell, New Mexico, near the site of the alleged UFO landing in 1947. A guitar pick from the festival is buried in Johnny Cash's coffin.) "You'd have to be crazy to believe there's not life out there," Haggard says. "People say, 'If we find life, then we'll know that there's life everywhere.' Bullshit. We know it now if you have a brain. I think the government is extremely puzzled, and they're aware that we're not the smartest bear in the woods. There's some other intelligence around that's observing our progress. Who knows, I mean, this may be an experiment. This planet. The whole gamut may be an experiment being conducted by some superior race."

The hits slowed down in the 1980s, but the party revved up. After splitting with his third wife, country singer Leona Williams, Haggard moved onto a houseboat on Lake Shasta. In 1983, he bought a stake in the Silverthorn Resort, a marina with a cafe, bait shop and nightclub. He hosted wet-T-shirt contests, slept all day and fished at night. "I had my toothbrush tied to the boat and let it dangle in the water," Haggard wrote in *My House of Memories*. "We drank cayenne-pepper drinks and wore very little clothes. . . . There were lots of drugs, women, good friends, good music and fun."

Around this time, Haggard and his buddy Willie Nelson recorded *Pancho and Lefty*, a laid-back album about boozing, chasing girls and skipping out on responsibilities to go fishing—with a hint of the fallout to come. "We were living pretty hard in that time period," says Nelson. The album's finest track, a cover of Townes Van Zandt's "Pancho and Lefty," was cut after four in the morning. Haggard had already gone to bed, Nelson says, but they needed him for the final verse. "We went over to the condo, woke up ol' Merle and said, 'It's your turn.'" Haggard's verse on "Pancho and Lefty" is one of his greatest performances— strong, unsentimental, yet conveying all the tragedy of the lyrics about the inevitable bad end that can come from a life of rambling. "Merle is a genial old boy," says Nelson. "He did it about half in his sleep, but Hag sings pretty good in his sleep." Haggard's mother, Flossie, died in 1984, and his close friend Lewis Talley died two years later, while having sex with a woman on Haggard's boat. Haggard married a waitress named Debbie Parret in 1985, but it didn't take. "I was partyin' pretty hard. I'd canceled all my dates, and I was in heavy mourning. And I was probably smoking pot, smoking Camels and drinking George Dickel— we did that for about five months. It was an isolated time when I really lost it for a while. Losing my best friend, and bad love affairs, you know. And spending way too much money." Haggard met his current wife, Theresa, during those wild times. She was 26 years old, newly divorced, and one night her mother persuaded her to come see Haggard perform at Silverthorn, even though she was more of ZZ Top fan. After the show, Theresa met Haggard's guitarist, Clint Strong, and the two went back to Strong's room. But Haggard kept calling, inviting them to his boat. "Finally," Theresa says, "Clint goes, 'Merle wants us to come over, but I have to tell you one thing: Watch out for that guy.'" The party was in full swing, Theresa remembers. "Merle was sitting in the corner. I locked eyes with him, and I could feel my face just turn beet-red."

Strong invited Theresa to come to the show in Vegas the next night. After the gig, Haggard asked Strong to go to the bus and get a guitar. "He said, 'I'll take her up to the room, and we'll meet you up there,'" Theresa says. When Strong returned with the guitar, Haggard wouldn't let him in. "There's bangin' on the door, and it's Clint," Theresa says. "And Merle says, 'Get the fuck out of here! She's my woman now. You don't know how to treat a woman. Get the hell out of here, or I'm going to fire your ass.' I went on a month tour with him, and we were pretty much together."

Theresa didn't believe she could have kids, so when she got pregnant in 1989, she says, "It was a blessing." They named their daughter Jenessa— the name came to Haggard in a dream—and moved off the houseboat to the ranch full time. "We got worried the baby might fall overboard," Theresa says. "So Merle fixed up a cabin at the end of the property, and we moved in after he brought me home from the hospital."

Three years later, Theresa gave birth to Benion, named after Benny Binion, the colorful, criminal owner of the Horseshoe casino in Las Vegas whom Haggard says was like a father to him. The same day Benion was born, Haggard was served with papers at the hospital claiming he owed creditors $14 million. "Once again, I was paying a high price for cheap thrills and bad decisions," he wrote in *My House of Memories*. "And I was dunned at one of the most memorable moments in my life."

Despite his new family, the early 1990s was the darkest period of Haggard's career. He is unclear about exactly what happened to all his money, but he alludes to corrupt business managers and lawyers, bad decisions made under the influence of various substances, and conspiracies. "It was overwhelming," he says. "I was almost 60 years old, had one child and another just born—they kept me from going crazy, kept me from killing a few people. There were a couple of people didn't know how close they were. There was people wanting to do it for me. And all I'd had to do was wink—it was that close."

Two of Haggard's overlooked records from this period—with the uninspired titles *1994* and *1996*—tell much of the story. The production is hokey, but the best songs are heartbreaking: After all the difficult circumstances Haggard had overcome in his life he sounds as if he's finally been beaten. "In my next life," he sings, "I want to be your hero, something better than I turned out to be." And in "Troubadour," "I'll always be a minor-leaguer, probably never get no bigger / I just love to play my old guitar." If his 1990s albums were commercial duds, they paved the way for Haggard's re-emergence in this decade, beginning with the 2000 album *If I Could Only Fly*. "Merle's very emotional," says Theresa, sitting under an umbrella on the front patio one afternoon. "He takes everything so seriously, whether it's something on the news or a new song that just comes out. He's a real busy man in his mind—I'm 23 years younger than him, and I cannot keep up. I try to get him to slow down a little."

In addition to helping Haggard quite caffeine, red meat and cigarettes, Theresa introduced him to a regimen of herbs and supplements, and got him doing yoga. "He's a very good yogi. We've got our mats, and I've got his yoga pants for him. He doesn't do a lot of big stretches and stuff, but the breathing, the stretching . . . the first time we did it, he said, 'This stuff is like a high!'" "He's such a thinker," she continues, "and yoga is kind of nonthinking. It does him so much good to not think. He asked me, 'Why would you want to not think?' I said, 'Well, you might want to give your mind a rest.'"

The Strangers are the longest-running, most exciting band in country music, a wiry, daredevil outfit that specializes in a swinging hybrid of country and jazz. Haggard formed the Strangers (named for his first hit) in 1965. Three of its members—Biff Adam, steel-guitar player Norm Hamlet and horn man Don Markham—have been in the group for more than 35 years. The Strangers don't operate like most bands. Haggard does not hold formal rehearsals—the entire group will likely not be in a room together until soundcheck at the first show on a tour. He doesn't prepare set lists, either—no one knows what song is coming until Haggard starts to play it. "Merle likes to keep you guessing," says Adam. "Nobody ever knows who is going to take the next turnaround until Merle points at you, and it's 'Go!' When you play with Merle, you are never gawking at the good-looking girls. You can't."

Three Strangers—musical director Scott Joss, who plays fiddle and guitar; pianist Doug Colosio; and bassist Kevin Williams—whom Haggard calls "the Three Musketeers," live nearby, and some afternoons Haggard pays the guys $50 to come by to jam for a couple of hours.

Today, they set up in Haggard's crowded living room: Williams on a stool against the fireplace; Joss next to the TV on a chair from the dining table; Colosio wedged in behind the couch, his keyboard hidden from view so it looks like he's playing the back of the sofa. The guys are on call whenever Haggard feels like practicing or recording; their job description includes missing dinners at home, canceling vacations and adapting to any new musical circumstance that might arise. "Whatever way the wind blows in his mind, that's the way he goes," says Joss. "Sometimes we don't all understand where he's going, but that's the joy of it. He's willing to take the chance and see where it takes him."

Today Haggard is wearing a long-sleeve gray T-shirt under a camouflage jacket, blue jeans that hang loose on his skinny legs and cream-colored loafers. An identical pair of loafers sits on the bookshelf behind him. The group warms up with old favorites: Rodgers' "Blue Yodel #9," "Stardust," which Haggard considers one of the best songs ever written, and "Corrine, Corrina." When Haggard sings, he uses his whole body— his right leg shakes, his shoulders pull from side to side, his neck stretches as he reaches to hit the notes. His voice may not be as forceful as when he was younger, but it's subtler, more elegant. "Merle is one of the great interpreters of song," says singer Peter Wolf, who recently recorded a duet with Haggard for his own new album. He says the experience was "not unlike being there with Ray Charles or Sinatra. You hear that Sinatra had a way of bringing out the story in the lyrics, but I didn't realize how true that was until Merle comes in and does this song, and I just heard it in a whole new way."

Haggard is also an underrated, inventive guitar player. Today, he picks out single-note solos and riffs that at times sound like they're about to collapse onto each other, then resolve in some unusual, beautiful way. After a while he finds a Mexican-sounding chord progression he likes, and repeats it until he finds a line to go with it. "She came in with her own fandango," he tries, riffing off an old Wills line. "Da da da dee do do do da da dee deh. . . ."

Theresa, in the kitchen fixing a bacon sandwich for Ben, notices Haggard's up to something, and rushes in to add her own line: "She danced to Grappelli and Django?" "Write it down!" shouts Haggard, then adds, "She did a fine waltz and a tango!" "She had her own kind of lingo?" says Theresa.

The song goes around the room, with everyone kicking in lines, until Haggard gives up after a few minutes and starts to play Hank Snow's "I'm Moving On," another of his favorites. "Hank was a small guy," Haggard says. "But that ol' boy had a 10-inch dick. There are photos."

Soon, Haggard wants to listen to demos from a new album he's working on that the guys have been casually referring to as "the rock & roll record." "I've played this more than I've played any of my records in 20 years," he says.

One tune, called "It's Gonna Be Me," stands out with its heavy bass line and lyrics that stake Haggard's claim to singing about what's wrong with the country today. "Who's gonna say the people's mad?" he growls. "Who's gonna say the music's bad? / Who's gonna say it's lost its soul? / Who's gonna get the shysters told? / It's gonna be me." "Not sure where it came from," he says. "Anger. I'm speaking for the simple majority—not necessarily the 'silent majority' but the people that mind their business and don't bitch about nothing. I do all the bitching for 'em." Haggard invited me back to the ranch for the final sessions for the rock & roll album. But when I arrive, the first thing I notice is a van loading out equipment from the studio. The power is out while a generator is replaced, and I find Haggard in the hot, dark living room, picking at his guitar. He says he sent the musicians home early, after three days, during which they cut 14 tracks, but none he was satisfied with. "The musicians played fine," he says. "But I wasn't happy with myself." We drive to the studio to hear playbacks. Haggard listens with his arms folded, a dirty brown fishing cap resting on his knee. After three songs he tells engineer Lou Bradley to shut off the tape. "I gotta get out of here," he says, holding his stomach. "I feel queasy." He walked into the studio's musty entry hall. "It's probably just my vocal on the track that made me sick," he says.

Haggard is bothered by something that happened earlier in the day. While he was in the studio, a man with a long beard carrying a canvas bag over his shoulder wandered onto the property. Theresa met him in the driveway, and the man told her he'd traveled all the way from Martha's Vineyard to give Haggard a message: In a former life, he said, he had been John Wilkes Booth and Haggard was Abe Lincoln. He said he came to apologize for killing Merle. Haggard cocks his head as

Theresa retells the story. Theresa notes that the canvas bag was shaped like it could hold a rifle. Haggard tells her not to worry, but a few minutes later he leaps up from his chair when he thinks he sees a flash of metal on the hillside. Haggard doesn't feel like talking and asks me to pick him up at 9:30 the next morning for breakfast. At 6:47 a.m. the phone rings. "It's Haggard," he says. "Can you come get me now? I'm up, and I'm ready to get started." Haggard is quiet for most of the ride, but as we approach downtown Redding, he points out his favorite buildings and tells stories about the town's frontier history. He notices a redwood rising from the side of a crumbling apartment complex and asks me to pull over. "Would you look at that?" he marvels. "This all used to be redwood trees up through here, till the loggers pulled them all out. How can you do that—destroy something so beautiful?"

Lulu's diner is perched between old and new Redding—on the frayed edge of downtown, across the street from a big-box mall. "Right here is like much of America, I suppose," Haggard says sadly. Two teenage girls smile and wave at Haggard in the parking lot. "They recognize you?" I ask. "No. Prostitutes, I'm pretty sure. No other reason to be around this part of town." A fire engine roars past. Haggard throws his arms in the air and salutes.

Haggard eats breakfast most mornings at Lulu's and flirts with the waitress, Joan, a droll, middle-aged country girl whom Haggard seems relaxed around in a way he's not with most people. Joan brings over a pot of his usual ginseng tea—but he sends it back. "No ginseng tea today," Haggard says. "They're not gonna let me drink this anymore—bad for the heart or something."

Joan brings orange spice instead. "You sure you don't want to ask your doctor first?" she says, with a wink. "All those spices are liable to upset your stomach." "Can't have nothing that's good," Haggard says dryly. "You're finally facing it?" she says. "I'm facing it." He goes on, "Let me have a short stack and oatmeal. Thin." "So you're just going to have a bunch of starch?" She smiles. "You know, Merle, you better just grow your own everything in the garden—you want to be safe." "Hell," says Haggard, "I can't even grow a hard-on. How'm I gonna grow a garden? Ah ha hah hah hah ha ha!" A fly has been buzzing around the table and lands on my arm. "That damn fly is bugging me," Haggard says. He grabs for it and misses. "I think I hit him," he says, though the fly is now buzzing loudly against the window. "Well," he says, "at least he knows we don't like him."

As usual, Haggard is thinking about retiring from touring. "I hate to quit, but I think that's about what I'm gonna do. I'm tired of spending what little energy I've got out there with the voice, with the career—everything is for the career. The career comes first, and the family takes second place. I don't know why, but suddenly they're more valuable than the voice."

Haggard sees a lot of similarities between his son and his father. "One time I took Ben fishing when he was about six," he says. "The sun was so that you could see the fish in the water. Boy, the fish were bigger than him. He said, 'I don't want to fish here.' And I said, 'Why?' And he said, 'If I hook one of them, they'd pull me in.' I said, 'No, Ben, I'll hold on to you, go ahead.' 'No.' I said, 'Now look, goddamn it, we come down here to fish, man.' He said, 'Dad, let's not make a bad memory.' A six-year-old kid . . . I realized I was dealing with somebody that was an old soul."

Ben is a gifted guitar player who recently began touring with the Strangers. Jenessa goes to culinary school and handles much of Haggard's business. "I think these kids are more grounded than their parents," Haggard says. "Theresa and I have had a hard life. My wife doesn't know how much I care about her and how much I care for the family unit, and I'm at the place in my life where if I'm ever going to get it across to her, it's going to have to be now. She doesn't know that she's number one. I need to stick around. They need me. My wife needs me more now than she did when we met."

The next time I see Haggard is early February. He underwent lung surgery in November, and doctors did not know whether he'd ever be able to sing again, let alone go back on tour so soon. "They say it's probably more invasive than open-heart surgery," Haggard says, standing in his driveway as the band and crew prepare his new million-dollar bus for its maiden voyage. "They come in from the back and they have to cut off a couple of bars—like breaking a guy out of jail—and you don't get to put those back. I'm like a fence with a hole in it."

The bus is state-of-the-art, with cream leather seats, yellow oak cabinets ("no plywood onboard") and a custom-designed back lounge. "You could say I went ahead and bought the whole loaf of bread," Haggard says. He's dressed for the road in a long blue coat, black fedora and beat-up ostrich boots, with his guitar slung over one shoulder. Except for the six-pack of bran muffins he carries under one arm, Haggard looks every bit the rambling troubadour he's been for almost half a century.

The tour does not start smoothly. On the drive toward Sacramento, the lights in the bus keep blinking on and off, and Haggard can't get the floor heaters to work. "Everything these days is built to last about eight hours," he observes. Later, he barks at his drummer, "They gotta fix this shit, Biff. This bus is worth $1.2 million, and the lights don't work." Then, inexplicably, he adds, "Tell 'em I can't show this bus to Clint Eastwood till it's fixed right." As the bus pulls into the parking lot of tonight's venue, a rinky-dink casino in Colusa, tour manager Frank Mull informs Haggard his set time is only one hour. "They want 'em back on the gambling floor—that's their attitude," Mull says. This makes Haggard so angry he threatens to walk out. "Goddam," he says. "Tell 'em 90 minutes if they want a show."

Theresa, who was supposed to drive herself the two hours from home to the venue, does not show up. Haggard seems flustered, and every few minutes he asks Mull to call the house to find out where she is. He eats two bran muffins for dinner—absentmindedly chopping the crumbs up on the table with a card, as if they were lines of cocaine—and has trouble picking his stage clothes without her. "I guess I'll go with black," he mutters. "Funeral black." Then he changes his mind and pulls out a long, fringed blue Western shirt and a white Stetson. "Shit, I may just slap on a Lefty Frizzell jacket and a hat. They'll think I worked all day on the outfit." After all these years, Haggard is not a natural performer. He is almost bashful in front of a crowd. "He never has really been a star like some people think," says Stranger Norm Hamlet. "Merle has always been more like he just wants to be one of the guys in the band." Tonight, he strolls onstage in long, slow strides, performs a little two-step, then lifts his Stetson in greeting before launching into "I Think I'll Just Stay Here and Drink." Despite today's rough start—and the fact that the concert hall is just a linoleum-floored bingo hall, filled with plenty of senior citizens in wheelchairs and dragging oxygen tanks—Haggard puts on a spectacular show. His voice is missing a little low-end since the surgery, but once he warms up, he sounds clear and open, and he works through a set heavy on recession songs: "Workin' Man Blues," "Big City," "Are the Good Times Really Over." "It's nice to be here," he tells the crowd. "It's nice to be anywhere." After the show, Haggard holds court in the diner-style booth at the back of his tour bus. "How much you weighin', son?'" he asks Noel. "I'm up to 170. Most I've ever weighed in my life. My Theresa's got me on a diet. We're doing a protein-and-salad thing." (In fact, Haggard says his favorite food these days is raw bass, which he catches in his lake. "I wrap it up and do it like you do sushi. It's absolutely delicious.") I ask if he's slowing down on his marijuana intake since the surgery. "I don't know if quitting will make you live longer," he says. "But it'll damn sure seem like it's longer."

After the gear is packed and the last joint has been smoked, Haggard gets ready to turn in—it's a long ride to Orange County for tomorrow night's show, and there are 11 more shows on consecutive nights through Nevada and Montana after that. Haggard has traded his stage clothes for a striped rugby shirt and his brown fishing cap. Underneath his ostrich boots he's wearing dirty white socks. He looks worn out, but he says he's looking forward to getting back into the rhythm of the road. "It was a bit surprising to find that the outcome of the surgery was as good as it was," he tells me. "It's kind of like finding out there's more time on the show and you've played your best songs. I was probably ready to go, you know. I'd done about everything I knew how to do. But to get an extension is always nice." He looks up, locking his liquid-blue eyes on mine. "God was kind," he says. "But now he expects some work out of it."

A Very Dylan Christmas

Chris Willman

Going electric was one thing. But going Andy Williams?

Bob Dylan has been making records for 48 years, and deeply disappointing people for the last 44 of them. "Judas!" some disenchanted legendarily screamed during a Manchester concert in 1966—a peanut-gallery pissant who dimly knew that Dylan had traded in Pete Seeger purism for rock voltage the year before but showed up to register his protest anyway. The heckling has hardly ceased since. The next eruption was when he stopped going electric, sort of, with 1967's *John Wesley Harding*. Then came 1970's *Self Portrait*, alleged by the faithful (or various factions thereof) to be an act of self-sabotage. And the full-on embrace of female backing vocals and guy-liner in the late seventies . . . the Evangelical era, replete with walkouts when he refused to play his secular oldies live . . . the subsequent years when he played all his hits live, but audiences didn't realize it because he'd rendered them unrecognizable . . . an acting career with choices as hard to comprehend as 1986's *Hard to Handle* . . . the ad-licensing years . . . the Will.I.Am "Forever Young" remix.

In a career measured in both greatness and WTF moments, only mysterious, magisterial Teflon Bob could come out of it all as revered as ever. History would advise, then, against presupposing that Dylan might finally meet his Waterloo at the North Pole. But you'll come across no shortage of "last straw" comments concerning his 34th studio album, *Christmas in the Heart*. When I suggested to one aggrieved friend that maybe Dylan had the right to a lark, it was as if I'd told a Baptist it was high time Billy Graham got to enjoy a threesome. "You don't understand," the pal shot back at me, plaintively. "When *Another Side of Bob Dylan* came out, it changed my life, for good." What to do when your personal Jesus turns out to be Iscariot in a cardigan, betraying you with a kiss under the mistletoe?

Well . . . laugh, maybe? Although the idea of a Dylan Christmas album never struck me as inherently ridiculous, when it was first announced, I joined in the fun. What songs might he record? "Positively 34th Street"? "Don't Check Your List Twice, It's All Right"? Would the album be called *Blitzen on Blitzen? Elf Portrait? 'Nog on the Tracks?* The Photoshoppers of the world got busy grafting Santa hats onto old LP-jacket photos, as if they could take the piss out of Dylan any more than he could take it out of himself. But it struck me that Dylan really had the potential to make one of the cooler Christmas albums ever. On his satellite-radio show, "Theme Time Radio Hour," he'd done a two-hour Christmas special, trotting out obscure sides by Lead Belly, Johnny Paycheck, and Celia Cruz. Surely his own album would follow that hepcat path.

Instead, it follows Mitch Miller's bouncing ball right down Santa Claus Lane. Filled largely with the most familiar carols, *Christmas in the Heart* is a full-on embrace of the old, not-so-weird America, a tribute to the kind of mass-market holiday records that his own Jewish family might have picked up in suburban Minnesota in the fifties, as a near freebie at the gas station.

Cue up the first track, "Here Comes Santa Claus," and the first thing you'll notice, other than a certain faithfulness to Gene Autry's mild version of Western swing, is that Dylan's trading off lines with a slick male chorus right off a Ray Conniff LP. For pure distaff sweetness, he also enlists the L.A. retro duo the Ditty Bops, whose prominent parts on several tracks manage to recall the Christmas recordings of both the Andrews Sisters and the Roches.

Roughly half the album finds Dylan in his vocal comfort range, including a surprisingly smooth "Little Drummer Boy," a wonderful reprise of the World War II soldiers' ditty "Christmas Island," and the excellent polka "Must Be Santa," with a heart-stoppingly frantic arrangement openly borrowed from the group Brave Combo. It's when he gets to the hymns that things get . . . interesting. His recordings of

"Hark! The Herald Angels Sing" and a half-Latin "O Come, All Ye Faithful" are sung in a voice so ravaged, they could double as anti-smoking PSAs.

The hymnody here raises certain questions. Wasn't Dylan supposed to have converted back to Judaism? Maybe, but he has also continued to sing folk spirituals like "I Am the Man, Thomas" on tour; on the evidence of his last few albums, he's most likely just your garden-variety ecumenical Bible-as-literature liberal Christian-Jewish agnostic-mystic with a comically morbid streak. Anyway, perhaps we shouldn't look for spiritual clues in lyrics like Autry's "Let's give thanks to the Lord above / 'Cause Santa Claus comes tonight," a conflation of sacred and spiritual magic that has warped kids' religious sensibilities for decades. In *Christmas in the Heart*, Dylan's being Bing again, not born-again.

A source in Dylan's camp has said this album was not a throwaway; it's a charity project (benefiting Feeding America, in the U.S.), and he wanted to actually bring in some dough. You hear that in the arrangements, where he's done a terrific job of melding his live combo with the fifties easy-listening sound, even if the David Hidalgo–assisted "Must Be Santa" is the only time anyone rocks out. And he's clearly aware of the incongruity between the rawness of his instrument and the effectiveness of everyone else's. He milks it—not for kitschy juxtaposition but because the old-man's-prerogative, take-'em-or-leave-'em vocals and the eager-to-please slickness of the backing tracks aren't about ironic juxtaposition. Both represent honest impulses.

I get the betrayal some friends feel. With rock integrity ever waning, we want some bard to believe in, and moves like this are as if Yeats had indulged an inexplicable desire to write for *The Saturday Evening Post*. But what if the "integrity" old-school Dylan fans long for was just another phase—albeit a brilliant, culture-changing, and occasionally recurring one? As his "never-ending tour" of the past twenty years proves, Dylan really sees himself, first and foremost, as a roadhouse musician—one who happens to let collections of poetry slip through the cracks every few years.

The weirdest thing of all? The album feels . . . deeply felt. Dylan's vocals, for all their constant playfulness, have never betrayed much emotion. But to assume he's not feeling it makes an ass out of you and me. I recall an interview with Bill Flanagan in April in which Dylan claimed that when he visited cities, he liked to go stand in vacant lots. I thought, "Mmm-hmmm," and tried to picture Bob telling his driver to pull over by that batch of weeds. You know the upshot of this story: Dylan was picked up by Long Branch, New Jersey, police in July for being a suspicious person roaming the neighborhood. So should any of us doubt that he might actually have his tour bus stop alongside a meadow so that he can build a snowman and pretend it's Parson Brown? Stranger things have happened. Like, you know, that Victoria's Secret commercial.

Appropriate for Destruction
Nikki Darling

Sweetness is a virtue
And you lost your virtue long ago—"Locomotive"

I was in a relationship with Axl Rose. The boy I had waited twenty years to be with, without ever having met, the one I spent my life dreaming about, was about to stand naked in front of me. And I felt nothing. As I undressed, t-shirt—hopes of making the cheerleading team in 9th grade, jeans—father daughter dance I never went to, socks—holding my breath in the back of the auditorium, waiting to be called student of the week, bra—not going to college, underwear—the shame of never having had anyone to push me toward it. I took it off. He was here now, stringy, blonde, heavy metal hair, some cheap Sunset strip tattoos, silver, pleather chaps over ragged jeans, a flannel left over from three years earlier, not yet having come back into fashion. "Do you have *Appetite for Destruction*?" I asked, as he put his hands on me and pressed his mouth to mine.

"I don't know, maybe."

I pulled away, walked to the CD tower. "Find it." He followed. Under the lamp the body shimmer on his cheeks picked up light. "Uh, I have *Use Your Illusion*." He turned it over in his hand.

"That's perfect, actually." If it was happening now, like this, after all this time, and it was turning out to be like everything else, a built up expectation that failed upon arrival, then I would take it back. I would not let losing my virginity be one more thing to feel sad about. Slash lifted the room, came punching out of the speakers in violent thrusts.

I closed my eyes. And then I heard *him*: "Get in the ring motherfucker! And I'll kick your bitchy little ass!" His legs—long, matchsticks possessed with the power of the red slippers, he couldn't stop spinning, sliding, shifting, not having let them rest since they ran out of Indiana, until they were so tired he willed them to forget they had ever been there, his voice snarling and whining with dissatisfaction—with his place in society, with his rejection of self. His red hair a flame to grab on to, a snapping firecracker, his body a fluid line, kicking and weaving itself away from youthful expectations. I don't remember my first's name, but that's all right, because on the night of my twentieth birthday, I fucked Axl Rose.

> *But oh the taste is never so sweet*
> *As what you'd believe it is—*
> *Well I guess it never is—*"Locomotive"

Six years earlier, I had stood in line at the Tower Records in Pasadena, California, trying to remember the lyrics to a song I'd heard on the radio. *"Why do we crucify ourselves?"* I sang to the cashier with pink Betty Page bangs and L7 shirt, *"Every day, I crucify myself, nothing I do is good enough for you."* She huffed, I followed, "Amos," she said, dryly, pulling it from the middle of the "A" section and handing it over. I stared, transfixed by the cover, Tori, a confident figure in blue; a small smirk on her face, as if to signify self-awareness, *"you can't trap a voice in a wooden box."* Much later when I finally sat down and read the actual lyrics, it turned out that I had memorized many of them incorrectly, but it didn't change the terms of urgency and realness I'd felt at fourteen, coming through the speakers on the late night KROQ call-in sex show I'd heard it on, alone in my room nearing the a.m. on a school night. What was important was that I had felt the connection at all. It was the first time I recognized my fear and anxieties expressed in song: invisibility, the desire to be accepted by the popular girls, a silent distance growing, concerning my day-to-day actions, where before there had been vocalized participation. The next day I pestered my mother the entire ride home from school until finally she stopped at Tower Records, so I could find this mysterious messenger. Relenting with little argument—most likely recognizing the seriousness of the acquisition, a willingness even to venture into Tower Records, a place of much socializing for the city's junior high set, in my school uniform, which until that day I had made adamant refusals to do anywhere.

> *This is a song about your fuckin' mother—*
> "Mama Kin"

Gender roles assigned to girls by the media culture are confusing, but when inundated with images of sex and purity at lightning like speed, girls fall into the trap of emotional exhaustion—constantly having to guess what to do before you're asked to do it is bound to result in failure. But the message is further skewed and punishing, media culture assigns the failure to the person who has made the effort to conform. Never in the cycle do we point the finger back at ourselves, as party to the judgment. Websites such as Perezhilton.com, which are hugely popular among teenagers, label female celebrities, many of them underage, as sluts, or whores, for things as seemingly noxious as looking "greasy" or "gap toothed." Meanwhile Perezhilton simultaneously encourages young people to get out and vote, participate in open dialogues about GLBT rights, poverty, donate money to charitable institutions, or sign petitions—all meaningful causes, but the message then is, "I am being asked to be responsible by this source that is also participating in sexism and misogyny, if this person wants me to vote, certainly they are a reputable and trustworthy source." The whore and slut labels are absorbed as normal, the accepted burden of being female.

As Maria Raha writes in her book *Hellions*, "Sorting out that conflict can lead young women to become consumed with being desirable, especially at a time when social rejection is a daily fear. But when we begin resisting our true spirit—as layered human beings who don't always want to eat, do, wear or say the 'right' thing—the sense of mischief that seems so present in childhood slips away. Instead of embracing our complexity and imperfections and questioning the physical and behavioral standards set for us, we end up turning for inspiration to the examples we're inundated with on television, in new media, and in our daily lives."

They won't touch me
'Cause I got somethin'
I been buildin' up inside
For so fuckin' long

They're out ta get me
They won't catch me
I'm innocent
They won't break me—"Out Ta Get Me"

High school was spent caring, caring about boys, caring about parties and booze and weed and grades. Caring about where and who I sat with at lunch, about the way I smelled sitting next to Ian Hawke on the twenty-seventh through thirtieth day of each month, caring about who invited me where and who slighted me, caring about the color of the rubber bands on my braces. Caring about what other girls thought of my looks, throwing hair in my face and wiping off lipstick when they walked by for fear of being ridiculed or called a "slut" or "bitch," wishing with all my might that my face might wipe off as well, smudging all the offending features. Putting lipstick back on once the boys came around.

I turned instead into music, I turned to poetry and the Beats, I turned to Cat Stevens, Virginia Woolf and rockabilly. I turned into a sloucher and I slouched my way into the silent corners of the library, where I tried my hardest to disappear.

Eventually, I graduated. With no college to attend, no prospects to speak of outside of retail and with family issues colliding at breakneck speed, I finally dropped out of caring.

And then, just like I had heard Tori Amos's "Crucify" that faithful night, I heard Gn'R's "Welcome to the Jungle." It was in a friend's car, a new friend, she drank red wine from beer tumblers and wore bell-bottoms, and had pictures of Motley Crüe taped above her lace canopy sleigh bed. I had heard the song dozens of times before that moment, but I had never heard it like I was hearing it then. Driving down the 101 Hollywood Freeway with the palm trees obscured behind street lamps that lit pools of light like hovering spaceships, taking quick sips from a small silver flask. All the sad ridiculousness of having beat myself emotionally, raw, in order to make it out of my teens alive, suddenly came rushing to the surface. I clenched my fist around the flask, fighting the urge to throw it out the window and into the dirty, busted street. My face tilted down, so that my new friend couldn't see that I was crying. An unholy howl rising from some sulfurous pit of disillusionment had slammed me into unexpected release—the night became clearer, crisper. I heard *Axl.* The world seemed alive.

I'm a sexual innuendo
In this burned out paradise—"Rocket Queen"

There is something fragile, feminine and menacing about Axl Rose, the way he snarls at the end of a verse, the way he holds himself, eyes closed, as if trying to keep down the pain, the way he slithers across the stage or approaches the mic slowly, in rhythmic half steps, afraid of what he might say, reluctantly grabbing the mic, swinging it gently to and fro, violently yanking it to his mouth, spewing lovesick venom. The way he grabs at his cheeks, pulling on them until his hands get lost in the tips of his long red hair, where, palms open, he pushes the momentum downward, swallowing the orgasm back into the floor. His lyrics tear apart the character of women while next verse over, schizophrenically lift them back to saint-like status. Axl straddles a line of uncertainty in his love songs. The songs flirt with rejection, one can't settle in to enjoy the moment, even in "Sweet Child O' Mine," arguably his most successful ballad, there is the hint of displacement, where should they take their love, when their love is on the run?

Axl Rose has spent his life trying to escape pre-conceptions about who he was supposed to be. As he sings in the song "Don't Damn Me" off *Use Your Illusion I:* "I never wanted this to happen / Didn't want to be a man." In Mick Wall's biography *W.A.R, The Unauthorized Biography of William Axl Rose,* Axl's high school girlfriend recalls an incident in Indiana when he was harassed by cops: He had been walking down the street once, she said, "it was probably two o'clock in the morning. From the back he looks very effeminate, with his long hair— not common in that area—and very thin legs, and he had a long coat on. These police were making comments, making gestures, because they thought it was a woman. Until he turned around, and they were very embarrassed to find out it was a male. So they started hassling him because they were homophobic as hell. They questioned him and when they found out it was Bill Bailey, who'd obviously been in trouble before, they threw him in jail.'

It's this mix of unconfined gender and machismo that makes Axl, the figure, electric, unlike David Bowie, who is at once effeminate and bizarre, embracing his dual nature, his androgynous sexuality. Other hair metal bands used their make-up and feathers as a way of social buffoonery, a cabaret of the absurd. Axl, though, is charged masculinity oozing from every swarthy gesture, human oil and vinegar, unable to mix the two parts into a harmonious existence. Rather, his androgyny is not for show, but an attempt to extrapolate that part of himself he struggles to control, the patriarchal voice inside his head that calls him worthless, that tells him to conform. The self-hating part that despises his misogynist self, his own Indiana cop. His flounces of femininity then, his long hair, rings, and scarves, are organic rather than prescriptive, unlike the Poisons and Ratts that quickly picked up on his seventies boho head bands and Led Zeppelin, leather, skin-tight pants. His snakeskin boots and gypsy earrings were attempts to enmesh with the creative part of his identity he could hear calling back on the radio. His first attempts at reinvention. His closest musical and visual allies are not the other metal bands that lined the Sunset Strip, but rather the New York Dolls—those other angry, confused, broken-hearted weirdos, with glitter in their eyelashes and dirt underneath their fingernails.

You know I don't like being
stuck in a crowd—"Patience"

The Internet is overrun with young women who have picked up on Axl's androgynous energy. Youtube overflows with girls not wanting to be with Axl, but *be* Axl. Literally, dressing up in costume, hitting play on their CD players and acting out some of Guns N' Roses most famous songs. Other videos show all girl bands covering such typically male narrated songs as "You Could Be Mine," at blistering Axl-like speed. Karaoke video after karaoke video show young girls reclaiming such classics as "November Rain," "Sweet Child O' Mine" and "Paradise City," particular emphasis placed on how they spit out *"Where the girls are pretty."*

Street Train is a normal high school Gn'R cover band posting videos of their performances, with one exception, the singer is a petite, red-headed girl, no more than eighteen, who looks more like Axl Rose than Axl Rose does in 2008. Long shiny hair, and a turn with a phrase like a rabid dog on a leash. Another video shows a young woman about the same age, donning a pair of silver aviator sunglasses, bandanna and the same parted long, shiny hair, sitting in front of the monitor and holding a guitar she clearly doesn't know how to play, strumming out and lip syncing the verses to "Patience." The power of the exchange lies not in her appropriation but that the entire mood of the song, as well as Axl's persona, inspired her to add an instrument to a repertoire, where one usually does not exist. Other girls take it a step further. A female comedienne also in her late teens or early twenties dresses as Axl, and during a performance, uses the safety of this costume as an opportunity to verbally assault her audience, screaming "No pictures! I said no pictures motherfuckers!" Reenacting the Guns N' Roses St. Louis riot of 1991, when Axl jumped into a crowd to retrieve a camera from a fan, who refused to stop photographing him. Later, Axl, marched off-stage in a huff when he felt his actions were unsupported by the band. Thus ending the show, resulting in a stadium wide riot. After a long verbal rant against her own audience, in which many are seen laughing uncomfortably, our young comedienne also storms offstage, throwing her mic down behind her. Whether a planned part of the routine or not, there is an essence of authenticity to her insults, as if wearing the masque of Axl allows freedom to pontificate, to unleash an anger she was previously unable to express.

Youtube is not the only place Axl's image has been appropriated. Guns N' Roses fan fiction is in abundance, stories pick up and continue like internet round-robins. Axl dies and comes back as a ghost to profess his love and agony to Slash, ashamed of his behavior in the previous life. Axl as a victim of an internet stalker who beats and sexually abuses him, Axl as a tyrant who takes Izzy by force and rapes him. In *The Melancholy of Axl Rose* by Popcorn Rose, one of the hundreds of prolific Axl Rose fan fiction authors on the web, Axl is portrayed as perhaps his most consistent incarnation: rebellious, misfit, smart aleck, unknowingly nerdy, outcast. In each story, there is a nod to his slippery, androgynous appeal:

The teacher sounded slightly uncomfortable . . . "Er . . . You next. The girl behind him."

"I'm a fucking guy!"

Whoa . . . Sweet . . . You tell him, dude. Slash thought, smiling . . . Okay . . . I should probably look at this guy. He turned around and saw a boy . . . Actually, he did look a lot like a girl . . . With long orange hair and bright green eyes. He was probably the shrimpiest guy in the class, standing there with crossed arms and a tough-guy look on his face.

"Er . . . Right . . . Sorry." The teacher replied. Ah shit. . . . Got the two freaks in the middle of the room . . . "Would you like to present your speech?"

"Yeah, whatever." The red-head stood up and looked around the classroom. "My name is Axl Rose, and . . . Well, I don't have any time for you normal people. Honestly, you bore the fuck out of me. But if there are any espers, aliens, and time-travelers out there, please, come see me."

Sometimes I wanna cry
Sometimes I could get even
Sometimes I could give up
Sometimes I could give
Sometimes I never give a fuck—"Don't Damn Me"

"Normal people," as Popcorn Rose so eloquently refers to them, have tended to bore the fuck out of many girls. With bottled answers and abstract solutions that often have no bearing on what seems to be the monumental importance of their day-to-day issues—guidance counselors, if the girl in question is lucky—parents, and other role models available at the brink of young womanhood, fail to understand that sometimes not fitting in, after a lifetime of trying desperately to, can come as a relief. At the axis of decision-making, the fork in the road where either you embrace Raha's *Hellions* or turn to the "normal" people, i.e. media culture, for inspiration and behavioral instructions, Axl becomes an alternative to the pressure, a leak in a balloon which young women can grab onto. Young women are reflected in his complex and contradictory image: Humans who can storm offstage, curse, cry, change their minds and fall to their hands and knees at the power of indecision. Axl walks with the swagger of a man who doesn't believe he will wake up tomorrow. Exploring his deepest demons in violent songs, he taps into the fear and hatred young women turn onto themselves when their lives become too complicated to share with others: Body image, relationships, depression, and the failure to live up to expectations. Skimming the edges of health and reputation, his complete disregard for political correctness, his naked feelings flying around in the wind for all to see, his *damage*. Axl literally becomes the embodiment of feminist actualization: escaping gender, and the limits on what can be achieved—from inside the confines of a wooden box. In being himself, an anti-hero, Axl encapsulates the moment of transcendence away from self-imprisonment and toward re-birth. Axl's reinvention of himself from William Bailey to Axl Rose is of course one of mythic interpretation, but he did it, tearing off the shackles of the past and rushing out—a swearing, fighting, angry effigy.

We've been through this such a long, long time
Just tryin' to kill the pain—"November Rain"

His recently undisturbed Dorian Grey–like presence in our collective memories allowed girls to build their own stories around Axl's mythology, adding new chapters as they pleased.

It is no mistake that it is Axl Rose who has become mythologized. However, with the release of *Chinese Democracy*, it is uncertain how this myth will continue. And at the very least, the long convoluted history of its making has brought into clear daylight exactly how flawed and human he is.

Of course the last and most puzzling and perhaps disturbing piece of the tale cannot be ignored. Axl's other, all-too-real persona; alleged domestic abuser, misogynist, homophobe and racist.

As I neared my twenty-second birthday and my bad obsession (to borrow a lyric) escalated to a frenzy, I uncovered the sad truth about the real man, William Bruce Bailey, who beat his wife Erin Everly so badly that she filed for divorce, or the man who allegedly, according to court documents, dragged model and ex-fiancé, Stephanie Seymour, by the hair, through shattered glass. Revelations that shocked—I had been turning a blind eye that entire time to the other glaringly obvious, problematic issues surrounding Axl Rose and Guns N' Roses, most of all, his lyrics.

To re-read those lyrics at twenty-two, with new eyes, brought a deep and profound sadness. His humanness was no longer in my favor, and I started to wonder if it ever had been, or if Axl Rose, as I now believe, was and always had been, for Axl Rose. I could no longer reconcile the man with my own illusions about whom I had made him and what I needed him to be: a symbol of transformation, a new form of radicalized sexuality. He started to fill out with flesh and color. I started to see the real person, who lived and breathed, somewhere hidden away in Malibu working obsessively on *Chinese Democracy*, while the world continued outside his tower walls, fighting whatever demons refused to release him. I had to release him. The alternative was that I start to justify his actions, and become the very thing I had resisted in the beginning: *complacent*.

> *Honey, don't stop tryin, an' you'll get*
> *what you deserve.*—"My Michelle"

In a perfect world, the role of Axl Rose would not need to be appropriated. There are the Patti's, Debbie's and Chrissie's, but as pop culture rolls along, the list of empowered women in rock—in the mainstream— is shrinking. We need new voices to be heard, we need to pull the Marnie Stern's, Mika Miko's and Erase Eratta's out from the shadows of the underground. We need women who perform the same functions as Axl, without the repercussions or reproach. So that they can duplicate and proliferate, like the fan fiction, spun from that powerful, attractive rock 'n' roll mystique.

Help from His Friends
The Return of a Fallen Idol

Jon Caramanica

Lil Wayne. Swizz Beatz. Juelz Santana. Soulja Boy. Timbaland. Keri Hilson. Polow Da Don. Nelly. Larry King. Those YouTube wedding bridesmaids and ushers with their absurd dance routine. The writing staff of "The Office."

It will be helpful, sometime in the history-writing future, to have handy the list of people who, in actions and deed, smoothed Chris Brown's transition back from pariah. In February Mr. Brown assaulted his girlfriend, the singer Rihanna. In August he was sentenced to probation, community service and counseling.

And on Tuesday night at the Izod Center here, just two months later, he was headlining his first concert in almost a year. You can add the New York radio station Power 105.1 (WWPR-FM) to that list.

The implication at Power 105.1's Powerhouse—in essence, a revue of contemporary male R&B singers—was that Mr. Brown, 20, was fragile. "Show him that the stage is where he belongs," the radio host Ed Lover told the caffeinated crowd. "Show him that you still love him."

As if the burden of proof were somehow no longer on Mr. Brown, who appeared immune to subtext, or at least deaf to it. He opened with the new single "I Can Transform Ya," a classic power fantasy: "See potential in you / Let me mold you," he sings by way of seduction. In the video, he plays with nunchaku and dresses military style.

Mr. Brown is a sometimes sweet but largely undistinguished vocalist, and during this show he toggled easily between naïve declarations of puppy love—"No Air," "Yo (Excuse Me Miss)"—and overgrown sexual come-ons like "Gimme That." During "Take You Down" he ground himself down into the stage, to deafening shrieks, and when he sang "With You," digitized rose petals streamed down the screen behind him.

If there were ever a moment to reassess publicly, this would have been it, but Mr. Brown stuck with what he believes he does well, even when he underwhelmed. When he was singing, his microphone wasn't always on. And, unfortunately, vice versa. He was also bedeviled by shoddy camerawork and artless graphics, which gave his stage show a slipshod air.

In recent months Mr. Brown has been steadfastly inarticulate about his situation, whether on TV with Larry King, in print in People magazine or on the radio with Angie Martinez. Or maybe underarticulate: he says little and appears to be aiming to say even less. That's probably why Mr. Brown's D.J. did most of the talking on Tuesday night, lest Mr. Brown get lost in an attempted mea culpa. After asking how Mr. Brown was doing, the D.J. played a few bars of Clipse's "I'm Good" while Mr. Brown danced. Later Mr. Brown took a moment: "I wanted to thank everybody for coming out tonight, despite my past and stuff like that. I appreciate all y'all. I really am going to change for every one of y'all and be a better man."

But this crowd—filling only two-thirds of the arena—was no jury, having appeared to move past forgiveness and back to rabid lust. Perhaps in a genre where moral boundaries have already been stretched thin by the tribulations of R. Kelly, Mr. Brown has more room to maneuver.

And few in pop can move like Mr. Brown, who is a mesmerizing dancer, liquid and springy and effortless in his isolations. He's far better than anyone in his backup troupe, and all his moves required was silence.

Earlier in the night the rising R&B star Trey Songz had demonstrated his firm grip on the public's sexual imagination; without the burden of teen stardom, he was free to be more lascivious than Mr. Brown.

He was one of several opening acts in a lineup almost guaranteed not to outshine Mr. Brown, whose real competitors—Usher, Mr. Kelly—weren't here. And neither was Ne-Yo, as close as Mr. Brown has to a contemporary, who probably wouldn't have taken this stage, even if asked: Ne-Yo wrote "Russian Roulette," the dark new single from Rihanna, and seems to want to be on the other side of history.

Another Love TKO

Teens Grapple with Rihanna vs. Chris Brown

Raquel Cepeda

*An unsettling conversation, to oft-disturbing
and potentially lasting effect.*

It's hard to tell, but maybe she's pursing her lips *at* me. Or, like any other eighth-grader, maybe she's just irritated about having to spend a whole period with a bunch of seventh-graders—and in an advisory class, no less. After all, what's left to talk about, especially after the fact? There are so many other things a 13-year-old would rather be doing with her time, like tomorrow's homework, or daydreaming, or whatever.

But this Monday morning, at the Talented and Gifted School for Young Scholars in Spanish Harlem, we're going to harp—like it or not—on a subject these kids are way, *way* over: gender violence against women and girls. And so the bell rings. The kids shuffle in from noisy hallways. And the eye-rolling begins.

Many of these students aren't grasping why we're *still* riding the Rihanna-and-Chris-Brown drama so hard, more than a month after the "alleged" assault. This isn't an isolated case, or even solely a celebrity drama about the 21-year-old pop princess and her 19-year-old American-idol boyfriend, whose Grammy-eve brawl in Los Angeles resulted in two felony charges against him: It's bigger than tabloid fodder or the countless myths and speculations surrounding the incident. (Brown will be arraigned April 6.) And it has everything to do with these roughly 12- and 13-year-old boys and girls who are about to enter a danger zone: According to DoSomething.org, a New York

City–based nonprofit organization, one in three teens will become victims of relationship violence.

Seven boys have filed to one side of the room; 16 girls are huddled on the other. OK, I have a question as serious as cancer: Did Rihanna provoke Chris Brown? The boys are deadpan. And by the looks of it, the girl who was pursing her lips has something to vent, and she does: "All we see is, 'Oh, Chris Brown beat Rihanna up, so she must be *so* innocent,'" she snaps. "But she must have done something to make him mad." Some of the kids nod in agreement. "My mom told me that we really don't know what happened because we weren't there," she continues. "But as far as I know, she went back to him, so that's her problem."

The girl—whose identity, along with her classmates', is being withheld at the request of the school's principal—is hardly anomalous in her train of thought. Peruse almost any blog or major media outlet that's following the battery case, and chances are that you'll come across postings that zealously defend Brown while squarely placing the blame on Rihanna's shoulders. One such comment, from a teenager—her MTV user profile lists her as being from Washington, D.C.—insists that Rihanna "wasn't beaten to a pulp. The phrase means to beat someone until they are seriously injured and disfigured." The post-attack photo of the singer's battered face, plastered across the Internet by TMZ, evidently didn't suggest she was "seriously injured." The commenter continues, "Someone needs to sit her little tail down and tell her, 'Yes, it's a bad situation that you were abused, but you need to understand it's not OK for you to think you can control and abuse a male with no consequences.'"

An overwhelming majority of the kids here agree: In a class of 23 mostly Latino and African-American students, all but three girls think that Rihanna provoked the beatdown. And once it was rumored that she got back together with Brown after a jaunt at Sean Combs's Miami manse, the critical backlash against the Cover Girl was especially harsh, especially in the case of many of these children's parents. A seventh-grader of African-American and Latino descent slowly raises her hand. "My dad said she's a loser and retarded for going back to him," she says, almost hesitantly. Another bright-eyed seventh-grader chimes in, at lightning speed: "If they want to be, then they are on their own.

They decided to go down there together to work it out because—and they did, so it's not Diddy's responsibility if Chris Brown were to beat her again because everybody has their instincts, and if hers is to go and work it out—and it *did* work out, *so . . .* "

"We live in a society that reinforces violence as the way to handle conflict, from the government to the schoolyard," says Elizabeth Mendez Berry, a New York City–based journalist who wrote "Love Hurts," an award-winning 2005 *Vibe* feature about domestic violence in the hip-hop industry. "You might disagree with [Rihanna's] choice, but that doesn't excuse his. I think women are often socialized to empathize more with men than with other women."

Furthermore, it's a pandemic every woman will have to grapple with at some point in her lifetime, regardless of race or class. However, the economy does intersect. According to the Department of Justice, females living in households with lower annual incomes experienced the highest average annual rates of intimate-partner violence in the U.S. If this statistic holds true in the forthcoming years, violence against women will only escalate as Americans (and the rest of the world) continue to be weighed down by economic hardship.

The bright-eyed girl, like half of the students in the room, knows someone who has been battered: in this case, her mother. The girl, who was supposed to be sleeping, was awakened by a noise and found her mother and a then-boyfriend throwing punches all the way to the front door. Eventually, her mom kicked him out. "I think it's a woman's responsibility," the girl says now. "If she has to, she can fight back." Perhaps taking her cue from the grown-ups around her, this kind of backlash may be contributing to why countless other teens and women are suffering in silence.

"It's easier to blame the victim because it gives us a sense of control over our own lives," writes Pamela Shifman, Director of Initiatives for Women and Girls at the NoVo Foundation, in an e-mail. "Otherwise, we'd have to confront the fact that we, too, could be victims (which, of course, is true)." Or worse, we can find ourselves—or mothers, daughters, and friends—reduced to a sensational headline on the evening news. But on the flipside, adds Shifman, "It's also important to note that there are some men . . . like A Call to Men (acalltomen.org), for example, who are using this as an opportunity to reach young people to say that violence against girls and women is unacceptable, and that men need to take responsibility to end this violence."

Another question: So, how many of you ladies and gentlemen still listen to Chris Brown and Rihanna? The boys squirm in their seats—they don't care. But on the other side of the room, every girl save two raised their hands when asked about Brown, and waived their option to vote when asked about Rihanna. "You can't judge a person's personality, because we don't really know Chris Brown—he's just a singer," says the eighth-grader who had earlier blamed Rihanna for provoking the attack. "Chris Brown could have done this one thing and could be a really nice person." Another seventh-grader, who listened throughout without saying a word but often shook her head disapprovingly, breaks her silence: "I think a lot of girls that liked Rihanna before—all of a sudden after this happened to them, they don't like her anymore, because they say she provoked him. It doesn't matter what happened. It shouldn't change how you feel about him or her."

Author and cultural critic Joan Morgan, who coined the term "hip-hop feminism," remembers a pivotal moment in 1991, when women in the entertainment industry—led by the pre-eminent fashion model, agent, and activist Bethann Hardison—came together to support one of their own, rallying around rapper and *Pump It Up* host Denise "Dee" Barnes, who was very publicly and viciously assaulted by super-producer and then-N.W.A. member Dr. Dre at a record-release party while a bodyguard reportedly held off the crowd. (Dre eventually settled out of court.) "It was really a rallying cry for many people," Morgan says now. "And it really started to plant what became a very directly feminist commitment to analyzing hip-hop."

Since, we've moved into a viral world without boundaries, where more voices are heard, raw and uncensored, because of the anonymity the Web offers. And now, nearly two decades later, the conversation about misogyny among young people, hip-hop culture, and society in general needs to address another very real facet: the hatred of women *by* women. "By definition, misogyny is about the hatred of women. It's not gender-specific," says Morgan, who saw gender-trumping violence when covering the Mike Tyson rape trial for the *Voice* in '91. "So there are men who hate women, and other women who hate women." The teenage girls' unconditional, sometimes puzzling support of Chris Brown isn't necessarily misogynistic; their acrimonious contempt for Rihanna—their hatred—is.

One thing is clear: Educators must incorporate the issue of gender violence into the curriculum on a national scale, because many families are finding it difficult to talk about it at home. "Only two states, Texas and Rhode Island, have mandated educational programs around relationship abuse," says Mendez Berry. "But I think it's clear that young people really need to learn how to have healthy relationships and how to resolve conflict in a constructive way."

Not all the kids before me today think Brown was justified. "I disagree with the fact that she provoked him, because when you say 'provoke,' to me, that means he had a reason to hit her," says an eighth-grade Latina. "I don't think that's fair." That this opinion puts her in the minority is a major crisis. For everybody.

Let's (Not) Get It On

Or, Fucking to Songs About Fucking and Other Uncomfortable Developments in the Awkward Relationship Between What We're Going to Have to Just Agree to Call Indie Rock and Sexuality in the 1990s

Sean Nelson

Despite my decades-long love of Mickey Rourke, I had a few problems with the movie *The Wrestler*. Not least of these was the fact that if you were to mute the sound track, you'd be watching a movie about a man who'd had so much plastic surgery on his face that he was forced to be a minor-league wrestler living in a trailer park. But the film had one scene that really stayed with me. It takes place in a bar, where Rourke's and Marisa Tomei's characters are talking about the music they love most, which, not uncharacteristically, consists of bands like Mötley Crüe, Guns N' Roses, and, cue "Round and Round" on the jukebox (it's a rerecord), Ratt. Rourke talks up the good-time rock 'n' roll merits of these bands and decries the malign influence of "that Cobain fuck" who came along and spoiled everything before both characters agree that "the '90s sucked."

Whether or not the '90s did in fact suck is for history to decide (though as I recall, people began making a pretty convincing case that they did as early as 1989). What landed hardest about this scene, however, was the subtextual relationship between the wrestler, a battered

267

narcissist with no capacity for navigating emotional complexity, and the music that stirs his soul, simple songs by hedonistic bands that defiantly offer no emotional complexity to navigate. As the film unspools, the dying hero (not unmovingly) strives, and fails, to establish meaningful human interactions with his resentful daughter and Tomei's indifferent dancer character. The sacrifices required by the relationships he hungers after are simply more than he's capable of making. In the end, the only interaction he can both nourish and be nourished by is the one between him and a roomful of strangers eager to see him execute one last Ram Jam or mutilate himself with a staple gun.

It certainly feels right for Randy "The Ram" Robinson to relate more to "Girls Girls Girls" than to "Smells Like Teen Spirit," but the question persists: Does the emotionally vacuous music he loves appeal to him because he's incapable of dealing with emotions, or did the music instruct him in the ways of emotional vacuousness—such that he can't understand a woman unless she's a stripper, such that he can summon genuine tears in asking for his daughter's forgiveness but can't be bothered to remember their dinner date less than a week later because he's having sex with a random groupie, such that he is desperate for sympathy but incapable of empathy? I'm not saying these are mortal sins (we've all done worse things to better people), nor am I trying to assert a moral argument about the film or the character, or even about Mötley Crüe. I'm merely suggesting that the music we love offers us certain lessons about life and how to live it (to cite another band The Ram probably isn't massively enamored of) and that it might be worth considering what happens when those lessons rub up against (which is not to say "pamper") life's complexities.

Of course, it would be absurd to suggest that just because a real person likes these bands (or any bands, or any *thing*) that he's incapable of experiencing meaningful emotions, or that all the people who like this or that strain of music represent some kind of hive mind. Still, for those who are attuned to it, pop music is more than just the background noise of our development. In an indirect but essential way, it teaches us how to live, by offering codes that we're free to decipher as we choose. Sometimes we agree. "The Times They Are a Changin'." Sometimes we differ. "Gotta Serve Somebody." But the "we" in question tend to gather around fixed points, and those points have a way of marking the attitudes and behavior of the gatherers. And by "attitudes and behavior," I obviously mean sex. Specifically as it relates to rock music, even more specifically to the strain of rock music known variously as punk, alternative, and indie rock.

(I'm just going to go ahead and say "indie rock," with a free-floating asterisk to indicate that I recognize and value the several important microfibers of distinction that will be lost in the assumption that, say, Hüsker Dü and Sugar might be part of the same stratosphere . . . I hereby stipulate that I understand, if anyone still cares, that punk is not the same as alternative is not the same as indie—to say nothing of good-old college rock. But they are all more like one another than they are like Poison. Plus "punk" is too specific and "indie" *sounds* better than "alternative," which, because of the age I was at the time of its ascendance, I always refused to say aloud anyway, like "Generation X" or "*Friends.*")

Indie rock never achieved the widespread cultural dominance that was reported or predicted at the time. For every *Exile in Guyville* there were far more *Tuesday Night Music Club*s or *Butterfly*s or whatever. And, asterisks aside, it's far more prominent in today's pop culture than it was in 1994, though the indie rock of today—found at the top of the Billboard charts, in movie trailers, TV shows, and beer ads—bears little relation to '90s indie, in sound, spirit, or psychological profile. In 1994, rock itself still had the distinction of at least *seeming* like the dominant voice of youth culture, and indie was at least a strong influence on its idea of cool. This was a time when the concept of "selling out" still existed, which it really doesn't today except as a voice from the fringe, a vote for Ralph Nader, a vegan Thanksgiving. Indie then was rock that was un- or possibly just pre-sold-out, and as it advanced toward and retreated from the musical mainstream throughout the '90s, rock music itself was busy lapsing out of relevance. It didn't die. It just mattered to fewer people. Possibly because fewer people were being addressed by the best of it.

The important indie bands of the day had about them an air of conscience (though not one of them would have made such a claim for themselves), offering proof that rock could thrive without the hoary clichés of *Wrestler* rock, which was still regnant at the turn of the decade that sucked. As a result of that air of conscience, the indie music of that period, while rich in variety and blah blah blah, had a collective tendency to abandon, in sound, lyric, and image, the traditional rock 'n' roll mandate of sexual primacy, and that abandonment became more pronounced (or perhaps just seemed more significant) as the strain's cultural influence grew. And because the music we cherish teaches us how to live, it's reasonable to assume that the decreased sexual energy of this music may even have affected the sexual attitudes and behavior, even the desires, of its audience during that period.

And by "its audience," I obviously mean me.

Generalizations about rock moments become easier to make, and of course more general, the further back you go, but no matter how you look at it, there's no mistaking the fact that sex and rock 'n' roll are linked so inextricably that the very term "rock and roll" actually means "sex." I also realize that this line of inquiry is both well- and oft-traveled and fraught with peril to every imaginable kind of cultural sensitivity. So at the risk of even further disclaiming, when I say "sexual primacy," I'm not talking about the racialist argument about the music's "primitivism," or the musicological Bermuda Triangle of linking the beat with irresistible urges in the body, or any of the other problematic tropes of gender, race, and class that have traditionally suffused this subject. I'm instead interested in the way that the Doors' status as "missionaries of apocalyptic sex," who seemed to be saying that "love was sex and sex was death and therein lay salvation," was what made them interesting to Joan Didion. Or how Harry Nilsson's recording of Badfinger's "Without You" could be transformed in Lavinia Greenlaw's young consciousness as "not so much a song as a continuum, a booming tunnel of desire through which we flew like static."

Because by the time these sources made it to my eyes and ears, they read respectively as an embarrassingly brazen sexual self-advertisement enacted by one handsome man and the three jazz dorks who played music so he could dance around and sing bad poetry, and as a saccharine dose of quasi-sexual mawkishness—so far from what I recognized as acceptable or pleasing evocations of desire as to constitute actual parody. The distinction here isn't about vicissitudes of musical taste or vagaries of gender. Like everyone with a radio, I have also felt myself flying through that same tunnel of desire—no matter that I was propelled by different songs. This sensation transcends generation and genre, and is one of the great thrills of being alive.

But time changes some things irrevocably. The gulf between my perception of the Doors now and the one that pulled Didion into the torpor of their recording studio in 1968 has everything to do with time—not because the Doors were valid 40 years ago and are not valid now. It's because my understanding of Jim Morrison is necessarily filtered through the gestures of the pop stars who followed. Plenty of whom have embraced the naked torso of his legacy. But some, whether by way of aesthetic preference or simple discomfort, left the erotic politicking to the erotic politicians, and kept their shirts on. So to speak. Time, as Vladimir Nabokov reminds us (in *Ada*), "is a fluid medium for the culture of metaphors."

And speaking of metaphors, if popular music is a city, everyone who lives in any of its many neighborhoods has an equal right to claim it belongs to them (and they to it). Though I had visited this city all my life, I never felt like I truly belonged there until the brief commercial heyday of alternative rock in the early '90s, hastened by the success of Nirvana. (I realize that admitting this here is akin to outing yourself at the RNC, so I'll keep it brief, but you know how people in the music business and certain quadrants of the press used to talk about how the mainstream success of underground-oriented bands formed a bridge between the subculture and the mass culture? Well, that bridge was built for me, and I crossed it, and I apologize, though I am not sorry.)

Newly immersed in this city of indie rock—I am kind of sorry for that phrase—I took immense pleasure in seeking out the experiences that would allow me to claim it as my own. Like many people who discover something anew, I assumed not only that it had been placed there for me, but that now was the most important time a person could be discovering it. I don't know why it was that these sounds were the ones that drew me in. It's not as though I had never liked the Doors. I had. I had liked a lot of music. But I had never felt like it was made for me specifically, that it belonged to me and I to it, that we were contemporaneous, consanguineous, until the early '90s, with its explicit and implicit backward reach to the late-'70s and mid-'80s. Can it have been a coincidence that this was the moment I first noticed that the bands making the music I loved tended to be fully dressed?

Of course, there have always been shirted artists. And not just the Association or whatever. The "unlikely" rock star has been with us as long as the "born" kind. For every Elvis Presley a Buddy Holly. For every Bob Dylan a Leonard Cohen. For every Jim Morrison a Van Morrison. Okay, maybe not everyone. Still, it's not like it was ever a question of Mick Jagger or nothing. But rock's defining gesture—in primary and secondary source material alike—was always a sexual leer, a sexual urge, a sexual seduction, a sexual plaint, a sexual attack. Sexual primacy. The hormonal explosiveness that attended the birth of rock 'n' roll plainly went through many changes and refinements as the decades wore on and the form became institutionalized and classed up. By the time it trickled down to me, the idea that there might be something other than sex for rock stars to be peddling—*other than*, not necessarily *more than*, and frequently in addition to—felt completely new and alien to my conception of rock music expressly as an outlet for raging hedonism. This was no school, or movement, really. More like a group of musical artists who happened to have had in common the impulse to subvert, to question, to confront, and/or to ignore— rather than simply to embody—the relationship of rock and sex.

The mask worn by the iconic and subiconic makers of this music, from Johnny Rotten to Ari Up to Michael Stipe to Bob Mould to Morrissey to Kurt Cobain to Calvin Johnson to Liz Phair to Kathleen Hanna to Polly Jean Harvey to Stephen Malkmus, advertised disdain for the clichés of rock virility, offering in their place a short but potent list of abstractions and deconstructions—antisexuality, homosexuality, pansexuality, nonsexuality, in-quotes sexuality, *etcexuality*. But these alternate models also became masks: for embarrassment about, veiled and unveiled hostility toward, meretricious reliance on, and general discomfort with sex of any kind.

Nirvana's quest to derail the hair-spray element of heavy music ("Hard rock as the term was understood before metal moved in," from Robert Christgau's Consumer Guide review of *Nevermind*) remains well-documented but worth remembering, because they were a total inversion of what a band was supposed to do with its fame, and set the stage for the idea that indie music was in the on-deck circle, which wasn't really true. It was in the hole. They wore dresses. They kissed each other on TV. They made sex sound like putrescence. They gave interviews in which they used the word "feminist" in a positive way and sang about rape as if it were bad. They were, in short, unheard of. The first time I heard *Nevermind*, I was stoned on the floor of an NYU dorm room on Halloween with a girl and—I'm not bragging here—it just seemed so appropriate *not* to make out. That was just the beginning of my '90s. Of course, you could do it to Nirvana (well, *Nevermind* anyway—hard to imagine getting sexually aroused by *In Utero*), and I'm sure many, many people did. But it also seemed like a violation of something. Nirvana reignited a culture of refusal that extended to everything you might choose to extend it to.

Sonic Youth had totally gone pop, kind of, and without getting into that whole discussion, there was no shortage of sex confusion and confrontation for the casual listener on an album like *Dirty*: Kim Gordon's growl voice on "Swimsuit Issue" and "Drunken Butterfly" extends the creepy sexual-harassment/seduction-burlesque of "Kissability" from *Daydream Nation*, while lines like "I believe Anita Hill" and "I've been around the world a million times and all you men are slime" make no secret of where Thurston Moore's sympathies lie. Most disturbingly, Lee Ranaldo's "Wish Fulfillment" gets inside the mind and mouth of a stalker in an eerily convincing impersonation. Desire is a subject here, but also a scold.

There was Pavement, the definitive '90s band, a notoriously arch and intellectual group whose classic rock gestures were always at least 80 percent critique. When they talked about girls, they were figurative, always an abstraction of an idea of Girl distilled from other songs they were thinking of—Summer Babe, Loretta's Scars, the queen of the castle/Pasadena/California thrill. They elevated diffidence to the vaunted place normally reserved for longing in pop songs, not knowing what to feel instead of Sweet Emotion. Confessional moments, such as they were, consisted of lines like "there is no castration fear" and the far more revealing "I trust you will tell me if I am making a fool of myself." One of their most conventionally "soulful" vocals concerned the absence of room to grow in a leather terrarium. Sex was utterly beside the point.

Neutral Milk Hotel: Album one, side one, song one: "Song Against Sex":

So why should I lay here naked
When it's just too far away
From anything we could call loving
Any love worth living for
So I'll sleep out in the gutter
You can sleep here on the floor.

Even when Bikini Kill released a song with the unambiguous title "I Like Fucking" (flip side: "I Hate Danger"), on which they declare a belief "in the radical possibilities of pleasure, babe" and that there is "anything beyond troll guy reality," the lines sound like encouragement from the singer to a female friend, as if to say, "It's possible to feel this way, despite everything." It's desire as a statement of purpose, not as seduction. (Another key line: "Just 'cause my world, sweet sister, is so fucking goddamn full of rape, does that mean my body must always be a source of pain?") Not exactly "Touch Me." Not hardly "Rape Me," either.

Again, other than Nirvana, this was not the music on the radio. So we abandoned the radio. It wasn't playing our music. When we did turn on the radio, the rock stations were obviously unlistenable (stuff like Stone Temple Pilots and Pearl Jam sounded unbearably macho in this context, which says a lot), so we'd flip around to hear what the rest of the world was hearing, the squares. A song like "Doin' It" by LL Cool J (and LeShaun) was genuinely shocking. How could something like this be on the radio? Was this pornography? Was it sexist? Was it real? Did we like it? Were we allowed to like it? What had happened?! I wish I were exaggerating.

The gap between the music I had chosen to teach me how to live—which I of course thought of as the vanguard, music that was too good, too important to be too popular—and the music that was teaching everyone else had stretched further than I knew how to reckon. I remained staunch, however, as indie rock abandoned its biological impulses, to say nothing of the bass register, and I wrestled with mine. I just thought it was the way things were supposed to be now.

The idea, I thought, was not to deny your sexual urges—that would be folly—but to keep them to yourself, to mute them, to deplore the fact that any expression of them was bound to be either vulgar or predictable or, worst of all, male. Male (the adjective, not the noun, although maybe the noun also) was definitely something you didn't want to be in the early '90s, if you could help it. But let's say *hypothetically* these deplorable urges every so often managed to link up to someone else's; when it came time to enact the traditional hormonal imperatives of youth, making out on the sofa for example, finding the appropriate contemporary soundtrack was often high comedy. In 1989, my high-school friend Jonathan Scott, a black teenager from Baltimore, preparing for a weekend at home, let me hear his "fuck tape," a 90-minute mix of songs recorded on the fly from late-'80s D.C. radio (beginnings and ends cut off) including Keith Sweat, Guy, LeVert, Bobby Brown, and Troop, with half a Prince song at the end of one side. He had made this tape just in case he managed to score with a girl and they needed something to listen to. Something current. I may have blushed when he said "fuck tape." I'm sure I was embarrassed. I could never have made such a tape. Every tape I ever made went out of its way to scream, "This is not a fuck tape." The music I liked the most in my most-hormonal years would not have qualified.

Songs About Fucking is an amazing album that I heard in an extraordinarily high percentage of the houses and apartments I visited between 1990 and 1996. But who could concentrate on losing themselves in a passionate embrace while Big Black was shearing skulls? Do you really want "Bad Penny" to come on during an intimate moment? Or how about Sebadoh, a band I worshipped, whose unstintingly detailed relationship dissections (the same relationship, dissected from every conceivable angle) and masturbation confessions trade off with spastic-screaming noise songs? It would be like using tears for lubricant. Who then? Slint? Smog? Tortoise? Palace? Silver Jews? Beat Happening? Daniel Johnston? I would be lying if I said I didn't take them on test drives. Of course there were important exceptions. But even with a conspicuously virile, happily sex-drenched band, like Afghan Whigs, there was a wall of explicitly misogynist persona to scale—as if, in the throes of sexual congress you might stop and say, "It's important to keep in mind that what Greg Dulli is doing here is a kind of impersonation of the male aggressor in an attempt to reveal the dark corners of male-female. . . ." Sadly, I wouldn't have put it past myself.

The self-conscious nature of the music, its very refusal to be mindless even when it had no particular ax to grind vis-à-vis sexuality, rendered it inadequate to the task of providing a sound you could lose yourself in. Loosely framed by the end of the cold war and President Clinton's impeachment for lying about sex, the times were self-conscious, too. The obvious was always suspect. The natural answer—getting it on to "Let's Get It On," for example—would have been suspect for being too obvious. Not to say you couldn't love Marvin Gaye, of course. You could even love sex. But obviousness, that was not going to fly. Even when the obvious answer was obviously the right one.

The hater line against indie, which was amply aired long before *The Wrestler*, is that it took all the fun out of rock. It's not like there's a counter to it; that was pretty much the defiant pro-indie argument then, too—it took *their* kind of fun out of it. Alternative rock, wrote Eric Weisbard in 1995, "is antigenerationally dystopian, subculturally presuming fragmentation: It's built on a neurotic discomfort over mas- sified and commodified culture, takes as its archetype bohemia far more than youth, and never expects that its popular appeal, such as it is, will have much social impact." And, indeed, in the end, it didn't have much.

It's curious to reflect, 15 to 20 years hence, how little influence that period has on contemporary sounds or attitudes, even as the current wave of indie rock has begun reaching a broader audience. You look at that broader audience, at mega indie-rock-oriented events like Sas- quatch! or the Capitol Hill Block Party, and you see demonstrable sexual confidence, even peacockishness, both in terms of the dress- extra-in-a-DeBarge-video fashion reality—all those louche sideways baseball caps!—and general presence. Not much neurotic discomfort on view, unless you count the nerve damage caused by skinny jeans. Compared to the way similar gatherings would have looked 15 to 20 years ago (not that they could have even existed; an indie-rock festival filling the Gorge for three days in 1994 would have been a laughable prospect)—all uncomfortable-verging-on-apologetic slouches, body- deemphasizing garments, chewed cuticles, and autistic gazes—the cur- rent cultural idea of indie seems not to have even descended from the old one. And who can blame it?

When I originally started thinking about this topic, I was trying to get around to discussing the idea that through some alchemical reaction with its culture, pop music somehow has a way of magically finding you when you need it. It wasn't long before I realized that it actually works the other way around. It would be ludicrous to suggest that these few bands I mentioned were the only bands around, or that there was no music in the '90s indie scene that wasn't defined—not to say thwarted—by muted or awkward sexuality. I mean, *obviously*. But if that's what you were looking for, if, say, you were prone to being unbelievably uptight, to being scared of wanting what you wanted, to missing the point about absolutely everything, the '90s were a smorgasbord. In that respect, they didn't suck at all.

Lady Gaga in Hell

Mary Gaitskill

*"... I was walking among the fires of hell, delighted with
the enjoyments of Genius; which to Angels look like torment
and insanity...."*

—*Proverbs of Hell*, William Blake

Lady Gaga, "Poker Face" *(2008)*

This video is to me a picture of hell. It is so normal, yet so terrible. The
girl looks like a dream vision of normal, a hologram of herself—and
then she looks like a reanimated corpse.

She can't move right, or doesn't move right; in some clips, shots,
whatever they are called now, half her body moves with wild energy
and the other part just hangs there; she walks across the hellish pool
patio in her leather suit, one arm swings freely, the other hangs there.
It's not that she can't move that arm, she sometimes moves it vigorously
and charmingly; at one point she sticks it out so some invisible thing
can kiss her hand. But it does not usually move in tandem with the
rest of her body, like whoever put the thing together forgot people's
bodies move in tandem.

When I remarked on this to an acquaintance, she said but that's
how the youth are walking now, that in particular neighborhoods, each
youth has his or her own very elaborate way of walking which could
involve half the body just hanging there.

Okay. But that still doesn't explain how Lady Gaga looks while
posing on the floor on one knee, her back arched intensely and her
head thrown way back; this posture would normally be a supple stretch-

ing action, but she simultaneously has her shoulders hunched way up around her head in a stiff protecting gesture. She looks likes she's in pain. She looks like she's old. She does so many moves that are just back and forth, back and forth, her hands opening and closing around her face. For one moment her hips and that one often-slack arm, move in tandem with the hips, but not like a body, like a machine.

This affect works with the music: It's adorable when she punches at the air with her fist like a sexy child. But then her face is heavy as a meat puppet or a painted mask with a card stuck between its teeth, a thing made by crude animation to flick the card from its lips onto the table or raise its arm in a wide arc and bring the card down while other holograms dance around it in fevered jerking motions.

Between the puppets and masks, see a fresh 13-year-old girl bursting with energy, bluffin with her muffin; see a faded middle-aged woman numbed and thickened before her time. She yells like a carny, "I promise this, promise this." The lights flash, the eyes are hidden by electronic words, steam rises from hell. You can't see the look on anybody's face. This is normal. This is fun. This is hell.

This on the other hand is life on earth. It's also adorable, straight up:

LoveGamesAtHome:
Michelle, Lorena, Chris & Geraldo dancing to
Lady Gaga's "Love Games"

And this is a moment of heaven on earth, carrying the creative seed of hell—that is, 'hell' in the Blakeian sense:

PS22 Chorus singing Lady Gaga's "Let's Dance"

"Man has no Body distinct from his Soul for that called Body is a portion of Soul discern'd by the five Senses, the chief inlets of Soul in this age."
—William Blake

Phil Ochs Greatest Hits
Chris Estey

"ONE WAY TICKET HOME"

The older boy always tries to make the younger boy sad. To bring him into sadness. His sadness; the world's sadness. He is tall and lean and has straight, long, death-black hair; the boy is small and blonde and deathly thin. They tickle each other on the bunk bed while watching ZOOM and The Brady Bunch on the small B&W TV in their room in the trailer. The TV's switch is broken off and a pair of heavy pliers sits on top of it to change channels, which they do when the news comes on, because if they wanted to see that, their father is watching it out in the living room anyways. Always. With a cup of coffee and Lucky Strike or a glass of cheap Scotch. Sometimes when it gets too hot their father sprays the trailer with the garden hose; everything cools down inside their room, and the comics they collect occasionally get sort of damp. That could be their sister's cat pissing on them, though.

He touches a live battery on his little brother's tongue while they listen to the descending third side of Elton John's *Goodbye Yellow Brick Road. Everyone who lives in a trailer court loves to hear songs about paradise going rotten for the lucky few.* They plan a suicide pact in the woods behind the trailer court to John Denver songs about reincarnation in the mountains in a sad voice he had borrowed. The woods where their sister's black cat sits at the bracken-strewn mouth back into the trailer court, whenever the small boy is left alone after they all play and leave.

The little brother never was much into John Denver, though felt a sweet melancholy when he'd hear "Rocky Mountain High" on the radio.

The two boys often heard the song when the older brother would take his brother for a ride to the library to look at Teen Beat and 16 Magazine and books about newspaper and Golden Age comics, the transistor radio tied to the back of the three-speed, behind where the little boy sat. On sunny days like this, coming into the town, the little brother could never be happier. Music, sunshine, movement on a vehicle powered by someone else, free books to look at in the park. Cutting the Monkees' pictures out of fanzines; making stories with them.

Years later, after Denver died in the woods, it came out in a record review that his main inspiration was a barely-successful protest singer (but accused musical journalist/performance artist) named Phil Ochs, who can also be spot-heard in the work of Neil Young, and not just in topical songs—also the sad ones, the emotional tumbleweeds that spill out of his cleverly constructed albums about deserts and vampires.

I owned the *Phil Ochs Greatest Hits* LP because a friend of mine, Billy, had put his song "My Life" on a letter-cassette from his parents' house in New Jersey. Billy was home from Rutgers and catching up on his correspondence and the easiest way to do this was to do taped letters, which were as common in those days as zines are thought to be. Billy had a lot of correspondence as the fanzine he published was very well known in the comics, science fiction, and punk rock fanzine worlds. His fanzine was one of the very few that blended all those things together, critically and with a sense of outside-cultural importance. I had a mad crush on his writing persona, and was flattered he spent so much time talking at me from NJ, making fun of some of our mutual zine friends, maybe flirting a little bit, insulting the bad stuff neither of us liked such as recent Marvels and poseur bands like The Knack, telling jokes, and then ending the re-recorded cassette time with some of his favorite music. That music turned out to be my favorite music back then, and still today. It always had Billy's bitter black humor, also either sad or extreme-sounding. On one of the tapes, Billy put Leonard Cohen's "Dress Rehearsal Rag" (a relentless story-song about a suicidal man who once had fame and romance, but now stared at his veins with a razor in his fist on his long way down) and "Diamonds in the Mine" (an anti-abortion song, which sort of made sense, as both Billy and I were Catholics, but we hated organized religion, and he probably just liked the caustic sarcasm in its tone). Both can be found on the album *Songs of Love & Hate*. But I can't remember if he combined it with "My Life" then, and I can't remember if he added any more Ochs songs.

"My Life," which is mid-tempo piano soul-pop through the declining existence of a protest singer who is "lucky to fail" and is sick of his phone being tapped and may or may not have had a bad relationship or two with women of a different color, maybe the same color as the men who strangled the singer several years later in Africa, is not on the *Greatest Hits* album. It is definitely one of Ochs' "greatest (non) hits"— but whatever estate chops up his posthumous collections leaves the song out. Perhaps because it is probably the proudest declaration of paranoia and failure you'll ever hear in a pop song—it actually inspires one to drink and fight and tear others away from his life as the dam-aged-voice Ochs did, before he hung himself in his sister's house in his 30s. It's like a proud honky-tonk country boast about a poverty-stricken physical and spiritual death for failed writers and troubadours and ac-tivists. It is the sound of a man setting himself on fire, and daring you not to listen to his screams; but hoping that you will.

Phil Ochs Greatest Hits was an album I found in a used record store in the Pike Place Market when my mother and I visited Seattle on a beautiful late summer weekend. In my hometown I hadn't found any Ochs records at the incense-smoky "head shops" I bought my punk rock imports and New Wave major label budget releases at, and I was thrilled. I may have been disappointed "My Life" wasn't on the track listing on the back of the worn, slightly torn album cover, but not sur-prised, as Billy wouldn't have told me what album the song was from anyways if I'd asked, as it was my job to track down the magical stuff he casually tossed my way after talking at me for awhile about baking a cake or masturbating. And I would have bought anything by Ochs I could afford, so it didn't matter.

It was a gorgeous day, as we headed back to our motel room with our "peanuts" (which my mom called cooked shrimp in their shells) and baguettes and a six pack of Mickey's Big Mouth for me. As we ate and drank I read rock magazines and stared at the album cover while my mom watched TV for hours. Ochs was chubby, daring to wear an ill-fitting gold lamé suit to mock Elvis, and I found that cute. I compared my shoulders and thighs to his, and was happy he wasn't a skinny guy I couldn't physically relate to, as on the LP covers of so many of my favorite punk records. (Elvis Costello got away with being skinny because he made it seem like a deficiency, and all the more sexier for that.) I was skinny at this point because I hadn't eaten more than one meal a day for the past year, a fat kid trying to find his way out of his peers' categorization. So I guess Ochs' weight problem was a bad influence. But on the back of the album he wore a black leather jacket like greaser rockabilly guys he grew up listening to, and I knew this meant he was no hippie "sunshine on my shoulder" folk singer—and that was the first time I wanted a leather jacket myself (not from Ramones album covers, where I thought it was dumb tough guys in a gang I wouldn't be included in). In both either the gold lamé and leather jacket, Ochs was delighting in glamorous play, making a statement about how we don't fit into our clothes/roles. This was heightened I think by the "50 Phil Ochs Fans Can't Be Wrong" headline on the back of the album jacket. "I am a loser trying to look like a star; and I can mock my lack of success long before you can."

We drove back to Eastern Washington and before I unpacked I put the album on my stereo. "One Way Ticket Home" is the first song, and though it rattled nicely on timpani and horns I was disappointed to spot the John Denver vocal similarity. (To make it clear, I heard Denver in Ochs before I heard Phil in Denver, but knew well enough about music history at seventeen to think it was a coincidence; no one as cool as Ochs would copy Denver, who I imagined had never heard Phil and at this point just happened to resemble him in this particular song.)

Phil Ochs Greatest Hits was a wonderful concept, by the way . . . it wasn't a greatest hits at all (!—*come on*), but an album loosely sculpted to show an alternate career for Phil, where he may have been more successful and accepted than he was. It was like what they say about French science fiction: What if Ochs the performer had had this other career, with pop songs, wandering guy folk songs, C&W, rockabilly rousers, and weird art-pop experiments? Dreamed up by Ochs: The author of Ochs. Bear in mind this is a while before *Breakfast with Champions,* or other narcissistic, "author-within" works in the 70s. And Ochs was drunkenly quoted from the stage around this same year (1969) between songs as saying that "God is a computer," captured on a live album recorded in Vancouver; yes, this is a creator re-programming himself.

Lyrically, the most amazing elements of the record's story-line include the power pop "Basket In the Pool," in which Ochs sings from the point of view of someone who watched Phil Ochs ruin a wealthy person's dinner party by throwing a large assortment of gourmet foods and wines in the manse's pool. He harshly criticizes this loutish image of himself and his impetuous action, but the tone is either that Ochs is genuinely sorry for bumming everyone out or taking the piss out of the people there for giving a shit. Is he Rasputin as a court jester, among the rulers and subverting their spoils? Or is he a misguided drunken redneck that is proud of himself for fucking up some Hollywood pussy's party? The answer to all these questions can probably be easily imagined.

As you listen to it, the album does seem like a chronological collection of an alternate career, but it also seems like new material in various genres at the same time. Bob Dylan had recorded an album a year or two later titled *Self-Portrait* that covered songs by some of the people he probably thought were copying him—*badly*. Ochs, with his respect for the working-class dollar and no lofty commercial perch to pull that kind of shit off from, instead copied John Denver eventually copying Phil Ochs—before he had actually done it of course, because God is a computer and Ochs was his creation out of time.

Back to "One Way Ticket Home": It's about a heralded performer (I believe) who just wants to *"watch my television and talk on my telephone."* He has done it all, or at least experienced enough of it, that he wants to start wallowing in Fat Elvis world, alone, home, alone. This of course is about ten years before Elvis did that to death, which Ochs prophesied: *"Elvis Presley is the King, I was at his crowning . . . my life just flashed before my eyes, I must be drowning."*

Ochs always said that if Elvis embraced the Left (and vice versa I imagine) then progressive culture could really take over. (He says this too between tracks on a non-posthumous live album, *Gunfight at Carnegie Hall*, while wearing the Elvis suit and breaking into a loudly berated medley of the King's hits for a bunch of less than grateful hippies). As Lou Reed sang, *"You've got to stand up straight unless you're going to fall . . . then you're going to die"* ("Coney Island Baby"). It seemed like

Ochs wanted the left to stand up straight, stop taking LSD, and march the fuck into Washington and stop Vietnam and racism, etc. They say that as America withered, so did Ochs—but what's clear is, as the "revolution" became compromised, we killed Ochs. A long, slow painful isolation and self-immolation that emitted some beautiful death-fragrance fumes, such as the wallowing of "One Way Ticket Home." A slight song, but significant for the "drowning" imagery which ties into "Basket In the Pool" and back to his best album's song "Scorpion Departs But Never Returns" (about martyrs on a submarine that can't be rescued, placed in the sequence right after "My Life"). And *Pleasures of the Harbor.* Title song and album; Ochs in seafaring wear on the cover. And "the sailor from the sea" in the title song for *Tape from California*, "who looks a lot like me," and sends his friend (you, me) a cassette letter about how poorly he's doing in a small apartment in Hollywood.

I fell in love with a man in Hollywood, David, and he would send me taped letters and bootlegs of rare Phil Ochs material when I lived in Spokane. (Those songs all eventually came out, due to his small, rabid cult.) I would go down to live with him several times, leaving my home in Washington, to stay in his tiny, bathroom-less apartment. He financed my independent cassette, *Shit-Stirring Songs*, and when we had sex he would grind himself against me like a Doberman. His twin brother had committed suicide when they were teenagers, two alien-like boys with accents not quite right for being from Brooklyn. His family prized intelligence, and David converted them all to Scientology. Which he later left and now opposes. His brother committed suicide because he had dented the family car and he thought their father would *be so angry* about it. David said it was stupid, he shouldn't have taken the cyanide, there were other ways of handling their dad. You just don't have to die because authority is angry at you.

Home is drowning, but Ochs wants to go there. *"There's a billboard on a throne,"* he sings weirdly in "One Way." Maybe human billboards, dying on toilets.

When Diane kept me in a room next to hers in her apartment in West Los Angeles, demanding that I clean her house several hours a day, I cried all night. Watching TV preachers on a small set I borrowed from her and taking diet pills so I wouldn't have to eat her food. Praying, even when she forced me to wear her clothes.

My brother sent me a ticket to the Tri-Cities, where I spent the holidays. He was a born-again Christian, but we bonded over Pink Floyd's *The Wall* and the cross-tops (speed) I scored from the guy whose marriage I fucked up.

"JIM DEAN OF INDIANA"

I was walking by the Galway Arms near where I live at midnight after a show and a few tattoo'd guys who think they're Irish out front were smoking and laughing and I heard one of them put down John Denver; so I decided to call them "cheap cunts" over it. The Vicodin and vodka probably helped me arrive at that decision, but this was a losing kind of battle, the only kind I've ever been interested in.

"John Denver died for you, man!" I said, poking the tallest guy in the chest. "It was a government plot. *He was sending a certain message to pop fans. . . .*"

They laughed at me, for awhile, as I ranted. "Phil Ochs commissioned him!" Then I tried to explain Phil Ochs, but they'd gone back inside the bar. I went home, but not before going into the loud party next door to where I live and turning off the stereo.

Immediately surrounded by several angry young black men, one of them asked, "What do you have in that briefcase?"

River Phoenix looks a lot like James Dean in *My Own Private Idaho*, which brings me sadness, as one afternoon I tried to read the Bible when Phoenix was downstairs on 2nd Avenue, raving it up with his crew for the movie *Dogfight*. I went down and told him to shut the fuck up.

"I'm sorry, man!" he said. He was wearing a baseball cap. He seemed genuinely apologetic. "It's the middle of the afternoon, I didn't think anyone would mind."

"But it's a *Sunday*," I said. I was tired from lectoring at Mass that morning and was enjoying my reading of the Gospel of St. John.

James Dean liked to go around in bars and ask people to put their cigarettes out on his chest. He was a really good actor, and Ochs tells his story in this song, but it's not his story, it's a bunch of stuff that sounds like a really sad story about a movie star neglected by his foster parents and even beaten and leaves the farm. Leaves his foster parents, and ends up with starlets, which means he's going to be buried soon back on the farm. Ochs does a great job with the lie. James Dean looked like a character from David Cronenberg's *Crash*, a movie about people who are sexually turned on by automobile accidents. Dean is one of the saints in Ochs' liturgy, the counter-culture man of sorrow who has to die to keep the poor people happy with what they don't have.

"MY KINGDOM FOR A CAR"

"I go fast until I'm going faster . . . look how far we've come, look how far." The music of the third song on the first side of *Greatest Hits* is rollicking pop-boogie, kind of rockabilly, actually not well thought out enough to have a genre. Friends of mine in Hollywood actually gave Ochs rides, because he didn't like to drive. He feared dying in a car accident like James Dean. I've never listened to this song very closely. *"Brings babes to their knees . . . I am master of all that's flying past me. Look how far we've come, look how far."*

This song is mocking, but I don't know what it's making fun of. Ochs seems to be attacking the machismo of drivers, the ones who run the planet he protests, and verses describing *"smoke in the air"* and picking girls up seem like a parody of *Born to Run*. Before that song existed, of course.

Ochs often attacked the "masculine American man." As Ann Powers once noted in the *Village Voice*, Elvis Costello didn't hate women, he probably just hated heterosexuality. This song is like William Blake terrorizing us for allowing the future to happen. More and more, I realize this is a science fiction album, like one of those French ones, about alternate histories.

Cars scare me, like fire to a caveman, or all kinds of things the future has brought. I never learned to drive and probably never will. The ringer has been broken on my phone for weeks with no fixing it in sight, and I don't watch TV. How did Ochs get back into town again?

"BOY FROM OHIO"

One of Ochs' perfectly mellifluous melodies, mordant in nostalgia, an impotent and finally necrotic ode to childhood, sweet smelling like a ripe corpse. Covered by grunge-era rock guys picking up acoustic guitars, influencing kids who would sign to Sub Pop.

This acoustic guitar–led ballad-waltz twangs and flows Kentucky flavor around lyrics about hiding in movie theaters when you're supposed to go to school . . . *"and how the freeway paved over the fields, where I used to be so happy"* . . . and how the English teacher didn't care (for journalist-accused Ochs, this was probably a terrible Sin, the most dreadful hypocrisy), yet *"the Spanish teacher did, but she was far too pretty."*

He never found one of those *"easy girls"* (they said) he moans for, I mean really moons after, that hung out at the burger bar. So very abruptly it's time for him to leave town again. *The eternal return.* Just a theory here, but it's perfectly possible Ochs was *warning us about nostalgia.* Like salad days' Joe Strummer in The Clash fuming about dimming obsession with *"fucking Beatles and the Rolling Stones"* Ochs is probably saying that all the troubadours pining after the pines and against the war were all just not getting any back home. It's a haunting song for someone who was once a boy and has lost the plot, but women probably see men in it the way Dylan watched the audience at the '66 concert at the Royal Albert whatever.

"GAS STATION WOMEN"

"Everything is going wrong, everything is bad," is how Ochs opens this fake honky-tonk; in the SF story he's writing it follows the 50s of "My Kingdom for a Car" (*in* the 50s, natch) and "Boy from Ohio" (the dickless new folk movement). This is the best C&W song ever written, because it's *utterly* fake, its exaggerated depression totally crossing the dialectical line of rhinestone stars weeping in their whiskey. It's obvious Ochs is stomping the guts out of his sanity like western swing maestro Spade Cooley stomped on his wife's stomach till she died. *"I never should have left my home, never left the farm,"* Ochs sings. *"I cannot face another girl / I believe I'll turn to drink."*

I used to ride on the back of Kathy's Honda 160 through beautiful, depressing Spokane, both of us high on her weed and whiskey from a suede canteen, my arms wrapped tightly around her, singing this song at the top of our lungs as we would ride out to the abandoned mortuary. We'd climb the stairs outside the old tenement building to the roof, and crawl down inside, rarely going down to where the punks and hobos partied next to the tables for examining and working on corpses, but sitting on the floor in the guts of the top floor of the building, staring into each other's eyes by candlelight, holding hands, but never touching otherwise.

Ochs buried James Dean earlier on the side, and then wrote rock and roll off as picking up girls in cars, but saves the most brutal blow for the poor and their alcohol-fueled morbidity. Which, if you know about his personal life, is probably the most obvious statement of his own suicide before he actually accomplished it.

"CHORDS OF FAME"

Side two begins with another country song, but this one is less a parody, and more a warning against *"the troubadour who tries to be a star. Play the chords of love my friend, play the chords of pain, but don't try to play the chords of fame."*

Yes, "50 PHIL OCHS FANS CAN'T BE WRONG!" the flip of the jacket proclaims. (I've probably met or slept with the other 49.) The back cover of this album has a silhouette of a big-breasted naked woman, and a couple rows of golden 45s, which Ochs never received, and which represent the songs on this LP. Ochs is *John Train* above them, between the naked girl and a big gauche musical note. His persona he adopted before his suicide. "John Wayne" mixed with "Trains" because trains are so American. Neil Young, Phil Ochs lover, loves model trains. Phil's photo: A rebel, like Elvis, with slicked up rockabilly hair and buried in a tough guy leather jacket, eyes probably tearing up about the old ladies beaten by enraged policemen at the Democratic National Convention, his sad eyes hidden behind the big black shades, cigarette burning from his lower lip.

"I've seen my share of hustlers as they've tried to take the world; when they find their melodies they're surrounded by the girls," he sings, warns, seduces.

"TEN CENTS A COUP"

Weakest song on here, in most people's opinion. "It's all a Madison Avenue nightmare," he explains about the recent elections in the longwinded introduction to the spare, plain protest song. It's a topical satire about our government overthrowing the governments of other countries. It's recorded "live" with fans laughing at slick, calculated-for-approval jabs at Nixon and Agnew. This is like when you hit yourself in the face before a bully can, out of anxiety, maybe to freak him out too. *"I've laughed so hard I've screamed,"* he sing-taunts the politicians who just get uglier and uglier; these dictators—these clowns. Then Ochs laughs, but the people laughing with him don't know why. He's laughing *at* them, the way Albert Brooks is laughing at us when we watch his wretched ventriloquist act in *Looking for a Comedy In the Middle East.* It's the bullied Jew who survives by giving just a little, who is smart enough to entertain just enough to keep from getting killed. But by who? Did the U.S. government put Ochs up to this? Did they force him to make fun of his own work in this song, were they the ones urging him to fail, so that he would see himself on the other side of fame? Key lyric, about Vice President Spiro Agnew: *"At his swearing in, he fell on his chin, he assassinated himself."*

The Canadian edition of this LP omits this song, possibly because it was about American politics. It was put out by the same record company, in fact, overseen by the label executive, it took years to get licensing agreements for several Light In the Attic reissues. That is what my ex-boss, co-owner of the label, does all the time—beg rich guys at companies who own music like this to let him release it so the artist or the artist's family can get a little money. But they love to sit on all this great old music, thinking someone with more money will come along and use it in a commercial or something. So much music from LPs that could change your life, like this one changed mine, are sitting in vaults somewhere, waiting for a deal that's probably never going to come. Call it the *Pink Moon Syndrome* of the music biz, I guess.

"BACH, BEETHOVEN, MOZART & ME"

"Ten Cents a Coup" is the dead Phil, finally, and this is the ghostly retirement with friends out in Hollywood or someplace like that. It is the death hallucination on the cross at the end of *Last Testament of Christ.* The wish of community that never came true, of artists and writers unable to make paradise work. *"I talk, I talk, they live by the sea, surrounded by a cemetery."*

A gorgeous art-song, and a shivery ode to exiles who *"can't get along."* But on Sundays they have a barbeque, and play the volleyball. These are the people left over from "The Party," a song on a previous album where Ochs made it quite clear he had nothing in common with anyone else, caustically picking on romantics, wallflowers, bullies, revolutionaries, and even the charitable, for all being fakes. *Fakes!*

As the day fades and the embers of the bonfire slowly turn to ash, his estranged collection of friends are knitting and doing crossword puzzles, lying on their backs. Ochs sings, *"I dream of the past."* The album should end here, and strangely enough it does on its somewhat inferior (less songs, inferior cover art) Canadian doppleganger. Before then on that version and after it in this one though is "Basket In the Pool" (see above) and then:

"No More Songs," arguably one of Ochs' very best songs, a trumpet-led death march into a euphoria of writer's block gone berserk, with his mentors and maidens and rebels all dying and leaving *"a white bone in the sand."*

A man who used to send me tapes from California, and who loved Ochs maybe even fiercer than I, as we played him in his single room occupancy in Hollywood near the big blue cult compound, who's heart I broke and who broke mine, insisted that *Phil Ochs Greatest Hits* should end with "No More Songs." I guess that makes sense. But whoever changed it on the Canadian version *heard* what Ochs was singing in *"Bach, Beethoven, Mozart & Me"—that they're all dead. Bach, Beethoven, Mozart & Ochs—all dead.* Surrounded by a cemetery.

That's the joke from beyond the grave then: Ochs knew a bureaucrat would fuck up the song order of the last available issue of his record, and had the song where he was a ghost come before "No More Songs," so that it could be moved back, in defiance of the artist's wishes. Ochs knew how to fuck up the bureaucracy from beyond the grave.

Adam's Return

By Tavia Nyong'o

Adam Lambert talks a hot fuck. When he boasts on "For Your Entertainment," the first single from his debut album of the same name,
that "I'm a work ya till your totally blown," he's not talking about your
mind. And even if *For Your Entertainment* (RCA/Jive 2009) doesn't
fully deliver on either score, "For Your Entertainment" gets things off
to a suitably subversive start. An ode to the joys of the power bottom
(even if Mr. Lambert is purportedly a top), "For Your Entertainment"
flips the script on a seducer who thinks he or she is getting someone
"soft and sweet," only to discover, too late, the whiplash intensity of
erotic passivity. The song might presage a future role for the out gay
entertainer in American culture. Lambert's promise "I'm about to
make it rough for you" drives another nail in the coffin of the sexless,
minstrelized images of Nineties "gay visibility." The insatiable, omni-
sexual persona he inhabits onstage—from *American Idol* to the American Music Awards—is a bitch slap at the era of the "limp wrist and a
shopping list" satirized by queer punk Ste McCabe on *Hate Mail*
(Cherryade Records, 2008). Of course, Lambert the L.A. fashion victim
and McCabe the "too poor to be gay" Mancunian are polar opposites.
But they share a discontent with—really, a disbelief in—what passes
for queer culture these days. In their different ways, each are doing
something musical about it.

When Lambert covered Sam Cooke's 1964 anthem "A Change is
Gonna Come" during the *American Idol* finals last spring, everyone
understood the analogy between African American civil rights and

gay rights he was risking. He might have ended up there, another "white boy trying to sing tough and black, with gravel and spit in his voice." But when not overreaching for gravitas, Lambert has chutzpah enough of his own to burn. It's too early to know whether or how his particular change is gonna come, but the broad outlines of his unabashedly commercial, unapologetically oversexed approach are already visible—and audible.

While indie audiences have welcomed out performers like Rufus Wainwright, The Gossip, and Antony & the Johnsons, *For Your Entertainment* solicits a broader, younger, more female fan base. Yet, Lambert doesn't do so by playing up the appeal of the gender-bending heart-throb familiar to rock since Bowie. True, he has at times exaggerated his bisexual appeal: planting comments in the media about tongue kissing girls, posing with a naked female model in *Details*, and miming a strutting, preening cock rocker at his shows. At moments, he even seems to enroll in Prince's "If I was your girlfriend" school of male effeminacy, encouraging shared obsessions over makeup and clothes, and a readiness to share feelings. None of this sums up what feels truly new about the Glambert phenomena, which is the direct sexual connection he can make in spite of or maybe even because he is openly queer. Gayness in public discourse these days seems to be about anything but sex: its about discrimination, violence, marriage, or disease. Lambert promises to bring gaysexy back, and not just to the gays, but to everyone who wants a little more glitter in their lives.

In relation to conventions of rock masculinity, Lambert's approach is mainstream without being assimilationist. Instead, his rockist calculations—from holding out for the cover of *Rolling Stone* to showboating with Queen, Kiss and Slash—show he wants to compete with, rather than simply service, straight men. He hopes to redefine what counts as mainstream, not fit into it. And while he demurs from seeing his role as political (which, given the lamentable state of a marriage-obsessed LGBT politics, might be a good thing), Lambert is too canny to be unaware of the cultural politics of his celebrity. That these politics are overwhelmingly about image may explain why, legendary as Lambert's wail already is, *For Your Entertainment* seems to push the envelope visually as much as it does sonically.

When I first saw his U.S. album cover art, I literally couldn't believe it. And then I had to hand it to him, not for showing me something that was particularly edgy or radical, but for reminding me how intimidated a reactionary culture has made us. The Pete Burns homage drove home how we need to liberate ourselves, not from our own particular prudishness, but from the self-censoring positions we take in deference to society's hang-ups. The album (thankfully) omits a tearful confessional song about coming out or wistful ballad about gazing into another boy's eyes, but Lambert uses the allure of dress up to appeal to freaks, geeks and weirdos everywhere. On "Master Plan," a bonus track, he dusts off the "face of a new generation" anthem and gives it a few licks of polysexual, androgynous paint. "Your skin is burning at the sight of me," he boasts, fronting an imaginary brigade of glamorous weirdos storming the barricades of normality.

Lambert's poses improvise upon a gendered binary that sits with increasing uneasiness upon the purportedly biological given. Their politics reside less in any simple blurring of femme and macho than in the sharp cultural fault-line they reveal in American youth culture, one deeper and more relevant than the current overhyped battle between Team Edward and Team Jacob. While gendered, this split is not necessarily between boys and girls, but about those who embrace artifice and those who prize sincerity. Cowboy-booted Miley Cyrus, tsk-tsking at "everyone in stilettos; I guess I didn't get the memo" is on the wholesome, all-American camp of this divide. Lambert, who definitely got the memo, is on the other, primped, corseted and ready to roll. And if Team Cyrus is all about crypto-Christian earnestness (*American Idol* winner Kris Allen, obviously, plays on Team Cyrus), Team Lambert is for the godless, glamorous diva in all of us (the cast of *Glee* included). Artifice is ultimately subversive even of the liberal image of lesbians and gays as upstanding citizens. To middle America, even progressive middle America, there remains an uncharted territory of gender and sexuality to which *For Your Entertainment* is an audioguide: brave and bold, post-heteronormative, and young, sexy and messy enough to enjoy not having all the answers.

If the sound doesn't quite match up to the image, that may not be surprising. Much of *For Your Entertainment,* musically, is paint-by-numbers. Like Lady Gaga, Lambert excels at recycling sounds and images from another time or place for the home market. "Fever" would sound like a rip off of the Scissor Sisters, if anyone in the US had ever heard the Scissor Sisters. "Sure Fire Winners" is a brazen attempt to steal fire from the gods, directly emulating Queen's "We Are the Champions." Most disappointing is "Broken Open," surprisingly the album's single nod to the goth-musical theater continuum that Lambert rode to American Idol success. "Broken Open" cynically attempts to reconstruct the opening moments of his legendary *American Idol* cover of Tears of Fears' 1982 "Mad World" note for note, on the condescending assumption that its audience won't to notice or care. Such transparent pandering bodes ill for Lambert's larger promise.

Still, how many pop albums lack filler? At its high points, *For Your Entertainment* joyfully harkens back to an Eighties I never realized I was nostalgic for. Not the edgy New Wave sound that keeps Eighties Nights perpetually grooving to "Don't You Want Me Baby," but the mainstream pop of the era, from Heart to Bryan Adams, replete with guitar solos, power vocals, and bombastic lyrics. This big-hearted Eighties—whose last, transformative hurrah might have been *4 Non Blondes* "What's Up?" (Adam covered the song on his pre-American Idol lounge act, and he recruited former 4 Non Blondes frontwoman Linda Perry to write one of the best tracks on *FYE*) seems to be the musical address at which Adam currently lives.

Still primarily a vocalist, Lambert can't compete with more rounded comparable pop artist like Mika, who writes his own material, is a multi-instrumentalist, and exerts a strong creative vision over his stage shows and videos. At least out of the gate, Adam seems more like a big kid with a huge voice having a ball while trusting in other people to make the important decisions. It is indeed an ironic reversal that it should be the cosmopolitan Brit Mika that is the cagey one about his sexuality, while the American Adam, burdened by our puritanical sexual mores, who is nonetheless out. And yet, it is the Boy in Cartoon Motion who remains at the avant garde of queer pop while Glambert, for all his raunchiness, seems overly wary about hitting his mark.

Perhaps out of such self-consciousness, Lambert's debut on the American Music Awards proved a bit of a stumble. Before you can play up the inherently subversive effects of entertainment, you first have to be entertaining. Unfortunately, rather than getting our minds (or other body parts blown), we got a bit too much American Idol-esque amateurism: out-of-key singing, flubbed lyrics and dance moves, and even a literal tumble on-stage. In the post-show fracas, Lambert showed a good sense of proportion, as well as a fairly impregnable self-esteem that luckily included the capacity to laugh at himself, admit mistakes, and get over with it. This will serve him well. But if he is to have more than just another successful career, and actually be a catalytic agent in pop, I hope he quickly realizes that no army of stylists, managers, songwriters, and choreographers can patch together a rock star. You have to do more than talk a hot fuck: you have to seize the spotlight and make it your own.

Voice of the Century

Celebrating Marian Anderson

Alex Ross

On Easter Sunday, 1939, the contralto Marian Anderson sang on the steps of the Lincoln Memorial. The Daughters of the American Revolution had refused to let her appear at Constitution Hall, Washington's largest concert venue, because of the color of her skin. In response, Eleanor Roosevelt resigned from the D.A.R., and President Roosevelt gave permission for a concert on the Mall. Seventy-five thousand people gathered to watch Anderson perform. Harold Ickes, the Secretary of the Interior, introduced her with the words "In this great auditorium under the sky, all of us are free."

The impact was immediate and immense; one newsreel carried the legend "Nation's Capital Gets Lesson in Tolerance." But Anderson herself made no obvious statement. She presented, as she had done countless times before, a mixture of classical selections—"O mio Fernando," from Donizetti's "La Favorita," and Schubert's "Ave Maria"—and African-American spirituals. Perhaps there was a hint of defiance in her rendition of "My Country, 'Tis of Thee"; perhaps a message of solidarity when she changed the line "Of thee I sing" to "Of thee we sing." Principally, though, her protest came in the unfurling of her voice—that gently majestic instrument, vast in range and warm in tone. In her early years, Anderson was known as "the colored contralto," but, by the late thirties, she was *the* contralto, the supreme representative of her voice category. Arturo Toscanini said that she was the kind of singer who comes along once every hundred years; Jean Sibelius welcomed her to his home saying, "My roof is too low for you." There was no rational reason for a serious venue to refuse entry to such a phenomenon. No clearer demonstration of prejudice could be found.

One person who appreciated the significance of the occasion was the ten-year-old Martin Luther King, Jr. Five years later, King entered a speaking contest on the topic "The Negro and the Constitution," and he mentioned Anderson's performance in his oration: "She sang as never before, with tears in her eyes. When the words of 'America' and 'Nobody Knows de Trouble I Seen' rang out over that great gathering, there was a hush on the sea of uplifted faces, black and white, and a new baptism of liberty, equality, and fraternity. That was a touching tribute, but Miss Anderson may not as yet spend the night in any good hotel in America." When, two decades later, King stood on the Lincoln Memorial steps to deliver his "I Have a Dream" speech, he surely had Anderson in mind. In his improvised peroration, he recited the first verse of "My Country, 'Tis of Thee," then imagined freedom ringing from every mountainside in the land.

Ickes, in 1939, bestowed on Anderson a word that put her in the company of Bach and Beethoven: "Genius, like justice, is blind. . . . Genius draws no color line." With the massive stone image of Lincoln gazing out over her, with a host of powerful white men seated at her feet—senators, Cabinet members, Supreme Court Justices—and with a bank of microphones arrayed in front of her, Anderson attained something greater than fame: for an instant, she became a figure of quasi-political power. In Richard Powers's novel "The Time of Our Singing" (2003), a magisterial fantasia on race and music, the concert becomes nothing less than the evocation of a new America—"a nation that, for a few measures, in song at least, is everything it claims to be." Fittingly, when Barack Obama became President, "My Country, 'Tis of Thee" floated out over the Mall once more, from the mouth of Aretha Franklin to a crowd of two million.

The seventieth anniversary of the Easter Sunday concert arrives on April 9th, and various commemorations are under way. The mezzo-soprano Denyce Graves will lead a tribute concert at the Lincoln Memorial on the twelfth, and the historian Raymond Arsenault has published a book entitled "The Sound of Freedom: Marian Anderson, the Lincoln Memorial, and the Concert That Awakened America" (Bloomsbury; $25). Last month, at Carnegie Hall and other venues, the soprano Jessye Norman curated a festival of African-American cultural achievement, entitled "Honor!," during which Anderson was often invoked. (In 1965, Norman saw Anderson sing at Constitution Hall, which had by then dropped its exclusionary policies.) Yet Anderson's legacy seems in some way incomplete. The Lincoln Memorial concert has lost much of its iconic status; many younger people don't know the singer's name. Within classical music, meanwhile, black faces remain scarce. No African-American singers were featured at the Metropolitan Opera's recent hundred-and-twenty-fifth-anniversary gala. A color line persists, more often politely ignored than confronted directly.

Anderson was born in 1897, in a poor section of Philadelphia. Her father died when she was young; her mother worked in a tobacco factory, did laundry, and, for some years, scrubbed floors at Wanamaker's department store. Her musical gifts were evident early, and new possibilities seemed open to her. Four years before she was born, the Czech composer Antonín Dvořák, the director of the National Conservatory, in New York, had declared that spirituals and Amerindian themes would form the basis of American music, and African-Americans were admitted to the school free of charge. Because of those encouraging signals, many black families saw classical music as a realm of opportunity. Yet, of thousands who pursued a hopeful regimen of piano lessons and vocal coaching, Anderson was one of very few who graduated into a real classical career. A core of self-confidence, rarely visible behind her reserved façade, allowed her to endure a series of potentially crushing disappointments. The sharpest setback is described in her autobiography, "My Lord, What a Morning": when she applied to a Philadelphia music school, in 1914, a young woman at the reception desk made her wait while everyone behind her in line was served. Finally, the woman said, "We don't take colored."

Anderson received enthusiastic notices throughout the nineteen-twenties—her first *Times* review, in 1925, described "a voice of unusual compass, color, and dramatic capacity"—but she needed time to master the finer points of style and diction in foreign-language songs. A notable aspect of her story, related in Arsenault's new book and at greater length in Allan Keiler's "Marian Anderson: A Singer's Journey," is that she found real recognition only when she began an extended European residency, in 1930, giving numerous recitals with piano accompaniment. German critics received her respectfully, and with little condescension. In Finland and the Soviet Union, there were near-riots of enthusiasm. In 1935, she sang in Salzburg, eliciting from Toscanini his voice-of-the-century plaudit, which the impresario Sol Hurok promptly spread through the press. During a series of American tours in the late thirties, she performed in sold-out halls night after night and found herself one of the better-paid entertainers of her time. (In 1938, she earned nearly a quarter of a million dollars, which, adjusted for inflation, comes to $3.7 million.) The American critics capitulated. Howard Taubman, of the *Times*, who later ghostwrote her memoir, called her the "mistress of all she surveyed."

What did she sound like in her prime? A slew of recordings made between 1936 and 1939 give an indication, although her voice plainly possessed the kind of incandescent glow that no machine can capture fully. The disks certainly demonstrate her legendary ability to produce a fine-grained, rich-hued timbre in all parts of her range, from the lowest tones of the female voice well up into the soprano zone. When she sings Schubert's "Erlkönig"—in which a child, his father, and the headless horseman speak in turn—you seem to be hearing three singers, yet there are no obvious vocal breaks between them. She is fastidious but seldom stiff; caressing little slides from note to note and a delicately trembling tone warm up what might have been an excessively studious approach. The incalculable element is the air of spiritual elevation that dwells behind the technique. Perhaps Anderson's most famous performance was of Brahms's "Alto Rhapsody," which she first recorded in 1939, with Eugene Ormandy conducting the Philadelphia Orchestra. (It can be heard on a Pearl CD that collects some of her finest early recordings.) In the Goethe poem on which Brahms's work is based, an embittered soul wanders the desert, eliciting a prayer for his redemption: "If there is on your psaltery, O father of Love, one sound acceptable to his ear, refresh his heart with it." Anderson effortlessly embodies the healing tone, but, before that, she mobilizes the lowest register of her voice to evoke the dark night of the soul.

Anderson was a musician of a pure, inward kind, to whom grand gestures did not come naturally. The historical drama at the Lincoln

Memorial was not something she sought, and, in fact, she contemplated cancelling the concert at the last minute. Throughout her life, she preferred not to make a scene. As Arsenault writes, her negotiation of Jim Crow America displayed a "spirit of pragmatism" that could also be interpreted as "quiescence." Although she refused to sing in halls that employed "horizontal segregation"—that is, with whites in the orchestra and blacks in the galleries—for many years she did accept vertical segregation, with whites on one side of the aisle and blacks on the other. She usually took her meals in her hotel room, in order not to cause complications in restaurants. "I always bear in mind that my mission is to leave behind me the kind of impression that will make it easier for those who follow," she explained in her memoir. Sometimes she extracted a certain dignity from the ugliness of segregation: when the Nassau Inn, in Princeton, New Jersey, refused to give her a room, she spent the night at the home of Albert Einstein. But at other times the humiliation must have been intense. In Birmingham, Alabama, during the Second World War, she had to stand outside a train-station waiting room while her accompanist, the German pianist Franz Rupp, went to fetch a sandwich for her. Sitting inside was a group of German prisoners of war.

By the time Anderson's career entered its final phase, in the fifties and sixties, such obstacles had begun to disappear. Segregated halls were no longer on her schedule. She broke a momentous barrier in 1955, when she became the first black soloist to appear at the Metropolitan Opera, as Ulrica, in Verdi's "Un Ballo in Maschera." By then, her voice was past its prime, the pitch unstable and the vibrato distracting. She went on singing for ten more years, less because she couldn't leave the spotlight than because audiences wouldn't let her go. They cherished not only what she was but also what she had been. And she might have achieved even more if the world of opera had been open to her earlier. To hear her assume soprano arias such as "Casta diva" or "Pace, pace, mio Dio" (transposed down a step) is to realize that she was capable of singing almost anything. If, as Toscanini said, such a voice arrives once a century, no successor is in sight.

What has changed since Anderson made her lonely ascent, basking in ecstatic applause and then eating alone in second-class hotels?

Certainly, she made it easier for the black singers who came after her, especially the women. Leontyne Price attained the operatic triumphs that were denied to Anderson, and after Price came such female stars as Shirley Verrett, Grace Bumbry, Jessye Norman, and Kathleen Battle— although the rapid flameout of Battle's career might indicate the difficulties that await a black diva who doesn't go out of her way to avoid making a scene. Opportunities for black males have been markedly more limited, despite the pioneering work of Roland Hayes, Paul Robeson, Todd Duncan, and George Shirley, among others. African-American conductors are hard to find; the most prominent is James DePreist, who happens to be Marian Anderson's nephew. According to statistics compiled by the League of American Orchestras, only two percent of orchestral players are black. African-American composers are scattered across college faculties, but they seldom receive high-profile premières. The black contingent of the classical audience is, in most places, minuscule.

As part of Norman's "Honor!" festival at Carnegie, Charles Dutoit led the Philadelphia Orchestra in an impressive concert dedicated to Anderson's memory. The program consisted of Darius Milhaud's "La Création du Monde," the first great classical takeoff on jazz; "Lilacs," a tersely eloquent Whitman song cycle by the African-American composer George Walker; Mahler's "Lieder Eines Fahrenden Gesellen," which Anderson sang at Carnegie in 1946; and Dvořák's "New World" Symphony, in which intimations of spirituals can be heard. Two gifted black singers, Russell Thomas and Eric Owens, performed the Walker and Mahler songs. There weren't many other African-Americans in the building that night. A far more diverse crowd turned up when Norman headlined a performance of excerpts from Duke Ellington's "Sacred Concerts," at the Cathedral of St. John the Divine. For many black listeners, "classical music" means Ellington, Armstrong, and Sarah Vaughan; the European kind doesn't enter the picture.

To a great extent, this racial divide stems directly from racial prejudice. Racism hardly disappeared from classical institutions after Anderson reached the zenith of her fame. Nina Simone, for one, aspired to become a concert pianist, but when she failed to win a place at the Curtis Institute of Music—for what she surmised were racial reasons— she turned instead to playing and singing in clubs. In her autobiography,

"I Put a Spell on You," she wrote, "My music was dedicated to a purpose more important than classical music's pursuit of excellence; it was dedicated to the fight for freedom and the historical destiny of my people." Miles Davis used harsher language when he explained why he gave up studying trumpet at Juilliard: "No white symphony orchestra was going to hire a little black motherfucker like me." He went on to mock a teacher who stated that "the reason black people played the blues was because they were poor and had to pick cotton." Davis, the son of a successful dentist, lost confidence in the school soon afterward.

Yet there is another, less baleful explanation for the absence of African-Americans from classical music: beginning with jazz, black musicians invented their own forms of high art. The talent that might have dominated instrumental music and contemporary composition migrated elsewhere. Perhaps Simone would have made a fine concert pianist, and Davis surely would have been a sensational first trumpeter in a major orchestra, but it's difficult to imagine that they would have found as much creative fulfillment along those paths. Instead, they used their classical training to add new dimensions to jazz and pop. Davis, an admirer of Stockhausen, made a point of criticizing the "ghetto mentality" that prevented some black musicians from investigating classical music. Several of Simone's songs are shot through with Bachian figuration, and her terrifying version of "Strange Fruit" rests on Baroque harmonies of lament.

Sadly, African-American classical musicians today seem almost as lonely as ever. They are accustomed to being viewed as walking paradoxes. The conductor William Eddins, who is the music director of the Edmonton Symphony, recently addressed the situation on his blog, Sticks and Drones. In the black community, Eddins writes, classical music is "looked on with intense suspicion," as "one of the last true bastions of segregation in America." Eddins sees it differently: "If you sat me down and asked me to describe one truly racist incident that has happened to me in this business, I'd most likely stare at you blankly. I can't think of a one." The problem is one of perception; African-Americans think that classical music is for other people, he says, and the almost total absence of music education in public schools prevents a different story from being told. "People tend to support and listen to the music that they hear from a young age," Eddins writes.

The irony is that classical music has become a far more heterogeneous culture than it was when Anderson sang on the Mall. The most talked-about conductor of the moment is Gustavo Dudamel; the superstar pianist is Lang Lang; the most famous of all classical musicians is Yo-Yo Ma. (When people talk about the "whiteness" of this world, they tend to count Asians as white.) No longer a European patrimony, classical music is a polyglot business with a global audience. Why does it still somehow seem inherently unlikely that a black person should compose an opera for the Met, or become the music director of the Philadelphia Orchestra? Unlikelier things have happened, such as the election of a half-Kansan, half-Kenyan as President of the United States. Incidentally, President Obama apparently has a taste for classical music; several years ago, he narrated a performance of Aaron Copland's "Lincoln Portrait." The conductor was William Eddins, who noted afterward that his soloist was well prepared. A few carefully staged recitals at the White House could break the stalemate that Eddins describes.

Anderson died in 1993, at the age of ninety-six. The obituaries singled out the Lincoln Memorial concert as the supreme moment of her career, but her autobiography gives the impression that other experiences gave her a deeper satisfaction. For Anderson, Easter Sunday, 1939, may have been an ambiguous triumph—marking a great moment in civil-rights history but, on a private level, intruding on her dream of a purely musical life. An artist became a symbol. Her happiest memories, one gathers, were of those international tours in the thirties, when the European critics declared her a singer to watch, and the Finns went wild, and Toscanini blubbered his praise, and she became nothing less—and nothing more—than one of the great voices of her time.

Vanishing Act

In Search of Eva Tanguay, the First Rock Star

Jody Rosen

To begin, a few facts. The singer, actress, and vaudeville star Eva Tanguay was born in 1878 in Marbleton, a small town in Quebec, Canada; grew up in Holyoke, Mass.; and died on Jan. 11, 1947, in Los Angeles, where she lived her last years in a style that some suggest was the model for Norma Desmond in *Sunset Boulevard*—in a Hollywood bungalow festooned with yellowing newspaper clippings and memorabilia from her heyday.

Tanguay made just one recording, a version of her anthem, "I Don't Care," released on a 78 rpm disc in 1922 by the Los Angeles label Nordskog. By rights, this song should be as familiar as "Over the Rainbow" or "Like a Rolling Stone" or "Rapper's Delight." And here we arrive at the crucial fact: For roughly two decades, from 1904 until the early 1920s, Eva Tanguay was the biggest rock star in the United States.

To call Tanguay a "rock star" is anachronistic but appropriate. She was not just the pre-eminent song-and-dance woman of the vaudeville era. (One of her many nicknames was "The Girl Who Made Vaudeville Famous.") She was the first American popular musician to achieve massmedia celebrity, with a cadre of publicists trumpeting her on- and offstage successes and outrages, and an oeuvre best summed up by the slogan that appeared frequently on theatrical marquees: "Eva Tanguay, performing songs about herself." She was the first singer to mount nationwide solo headlining tours, drawing record-breaking crowds and shattering box-office tallies from Broadway to Butte. Newspaper accounts describe scenes of fan frenzy that foreshadowed Frank Sinatra at the Paramount Theatre and Beatlemania. At the height of her stardom, Tanguay commanded an unheard of salary, $3,500 per week, out-earning the likes of Al Jolson, Harry Houdini, and Enrico Caruso.

If you read the press and popular literature of the first quarter of the 20th century, Tanguay is inescapable. Edward Bernays, the celebrated "father of public relations," called Tanguay "our first symbol of emergence from the Victorian age." The journalist and playwright George Ade dubbed Theodore Roosevelt "the Eva Tanguay of politics." One of her hits was titled "They'll Remember Me a Hundred Years From Now." To Tanguay's contemporaries, it must have seemed less like a boast than a foregone conclusion.

A century later, though, Tanguay is forgotten—vanished from the pages of pop music history. No one has written an Eva Tanguay biography, although biographies exist for many of her vaudeville contemporaries, all of them lesser stars. Tanguay herself claimed at various points to be working on her memoirs—in 1910 she told a reporter that she was writing an autobiography entitled *A Hundred Loves*—but she left behind no manuscript. A clunky Hollywood biopic, *The I Don't Care Girl* (1953), erased more than it commemorated, presenting an unrecognizably toned-down version of Tanguay's radical stage act and ignoring the facts of her raucous love life, including her rumored romance with black vaudeville star George Walker. *The New Grove Dictionary of American Music* has a 288-word Tanguay entry, and she gets a passing mention in Russell and David Sanjeks' *American Popular Music and Its Business*. But in the standard pop music histories, Tanguay's name does not appear.

Just about the only person to find a place in the canon for Tanguay is Ralph Bakshi, who included "I Don't Care" in his 1981 animated film *American Pop*, alongside the likes of "Blue Suede Shoes" and "Pretty Vacant." It took the director of *Fritz the Cat* and other X-rated cartoons to draw a line across the decades connecting Eva Tanguay and Johnny Rotten. Indeed, the self-proclaimed "I Don't Care Girl" and the self-proclaimed antichrist have quite a bit in common—the main difference being that Tanguay was considerably more punk rock.

Little is known about Tanguay's childhood. Her family moved from Canada to Massachusetts in the 1880s, and by the age of eight, Eva was playing child leads in summer-stock theater companies. She arrived in New York at age 19 and found work on the variety stage. That same year, her name surfaced in the newspapers: She was appearing in a production called *Hoodoo*, and when a fellow chorus girl accused her of hot-dogging onstage, Tanguay turned and choked her cast mate until the girl's face turned blue and she passed out. It was Tanguay's first taste of notoriety and her first big backstage altercation. There would be more of both in her future.

Tanguay's breakthrough came in 1904, in the musical comedy *The Sambo Girl*. Playing the lead "brownface" role, she stole the show with a new song, a lurching mid-tempo ballad by songwriters Jean Lennox and Harry O. Sutton. The tune was not written expressly for Tanguay, but it may as well have been. For the rest of her career, she merely enlarged on the character-sketch in "I Don't Care": a madcap woman on the verge, trampling the conventions of demure femininity, polite society, and musical theater. "They say I'm crazy and got no sense / But I don't care," Tanguay sang. "They may or may not mean offense / I care less."

The song was broadly comic but shocking nonetheless in 1904, when Victorian notions of female propriety prevailed. Blasting out "I Don't Care," Tanguay gave voice to an anarchic feminism that claimed the old stigma of female "hysteria" as a badge of honor—the Victorian neurasthenic recast as a liberated, libidinous 20th-century wild-woman:

> *I don't care, I don't care*
> *What they may think of me*
> *I'm happy go lucky*
> *Men say that I'm plucky*
> *I'm happy and carefree*
> *I don't care, I don't care*
> *If I should get the mean and stony stare*
> *And no one can faze me*
> *By calling me crazy*
> *'Cause I don't care*

The effect was heightened by Tanguay's outré appearance and performance style. She had a pudgy face and reddish-blond hair that stretched upward in a snarled pile. (She sometimes dumped bottles of champagne over her head onstage.) She was of average height and a bit lumpy, but athletic; she squeezed herself into gaudy costumes that flaunted her buxom figure and powerfully muscled legs. She delivered her songs while executing dervishlike dances, complete with limb-flailing, leg kicks, breast-shaking, and violent tosses of the head; often, she seemed to be simulating orgasm. Tanguay suffered severe cramps from her performances—backstage, she instructed prop directors to unknot her calves by beating them with barrel staves. She told reporters that her goal was "to move so fast and whirl so madly that no one would be able to see my bare legs."

Then there was Tanguay's voice. She sang in a slurred screech punctuated by yaps and cackles, ricocheting seemingly at random between her upper and lower registers. Beneath the hiss of the 87-year-old "I Don't Care" recording, you can hear the maniac's grin that Tanguay wore when she sang.

"I Don't Care" was a sensation. Tanguay soon moved onto her first headlining stint, at Hammerstein's Victoria, a theater famous for featuring freak-show performers—a good fit for the singer's musical P.T. Barnum routine. She was a star now. Her act caught the imagination of fans from across the class spectrum and drew bombastic praise from critics, for whom she seemed to sum up the exuberance and vulgarity of the young century. (Her nicknames told the story: "The Evangelist of Joy," "The Electric Hoyden," "The Queen of Perpetual Motion," "The Modern Mystery," "Miss Tabasco.") Critics marveled at the brazenness of songs like "Go As Far As You Like, Kid" (1909) and "I Want Someone To Go Wild With Me" (1912). They raved about her "cyclonic" energy, her "animalistic" abandon, and her hair, which seemed "so charged with electric vigor that no amount of combing or brushing could alter its assertive unruliness." (One of her hits, "Tanguay Tangle," winked at the disorderly coiffure.) To Aleister Crowley, Tanguay was "exactly and scientifically . . . the Soul of America at its most desperate eagle-flight." "Tanguay," Crowley wrote in 1912,

> is like the hashish dream of a hermit who is possessed of the devil. She cannot sing, as others sing; or dance, as others dance. She simply keeps on vibrating, both limbs and vocal chords without rhythm, tone, melody, or purpose. . . . I feel

as if I were poisoned by strychnine, so far as my body goes; I jerk, I writhe, I twist, I find no ease. . . . She is perpetual irritation without possibility of satisfaction, an Avatar of sex-insomnia. Solitude of the Soul, the Worm that dieth not; ah, me! She is the Vulture of Prometheus, and she is the Music of Mitylene. . . . I could kill myself at this moment for the wild love of her.

The Vulture of Prometheus may have been pushing it—but Crowley was right about the singer's distinctive Americanness. In Tanguay, old-fashioned Yankee individualism joined hands with the nascent 20th-century religion of showbiz and star power. "Personality, personality," she sang in one of her signature numbers, "That's the thing that always makes a hit / Your nationality or your rationality / Doesn't help or hinder you one bit."

With the help of her publicists, Tanguay writ her personality large, and in boldface. She concocted publicity stunts ("Eva Tanguay, the Only Actress in the World Who Ever Made a Balloon Ascension"); threatened to retire before making splashy "comebacks"; contrived tell-all confessional interviews for magazines; and struck an ironic attitude toward these machinations, confessing her lust for attention in songs like "I'd Like To Be an Animal in the Zoo" (1911). Like Madonna a century later, Tanguay was businesswoman-provocateur—an indefatigable plotter of new looks and fresh *succès de scandales*. A 1910 editorial cartoon in the *New York Review*, titled "A Tanguay Resting," showed the star scribbling with a giant pencil, surrounded by a growing mountain of notes for new schemes: "Bright Thoughts," "Original Ideas," "New Song," "New Act," "Manuscripts," "Offer," "Contract."

She was a clothes horse, famous for her lavish wardrobe budget, whose details she leaked to the press. Her performances were fashion shows as much as concerts; in the course of a 30-minute vaudeville appearance, she would change outfits 10 times. The costumes, which Tanguay claimed to have designed herself, were avant-garde and architectural: hats that rose several feet above her head, constructed from ribbons, bells, leaves, ostrich plumes; gowns made of feathers, beads, dollar bills, seashells, coral. A particular *cause célèbre* was Tanguay's "$40 dress"—a garment fashioned from 4,000 pennies. (It weighed 45 pounds.) When "Salome-mania" swept vaudeville in 1908, Tanguay made sure that her Dance of the Seven Veils was the raciest, her dress the skimpiest. "I can fit the entire costume in my closed fist," she told reporters.

For diva notoriety, her only equal was Sarah Bernhardt, and like Bernhardt, she knew that her performance didn't end once she'd left the stage. She kept newspapers busy with tales of her marriages, divorces, and affairs. She brought lawsuits against vaudeville circuit bosses and astrologers. She turned up for theatrical engagements and refused to play when she discovered that rival performers were on the bill. In 1905, Tanguay was fined $100 by an Evansville, Ind., theater manager for sleeping through a matinee. That evening, Tanguay took her revenge, shredding the stage curtain with a dagger. A 1909 performance in Louisville, Ky., ended with a backstage melee when a young stagehand, Clarence Hess, mistakenly stepped in front of Tanguay as she hurried to her dressing room. Tanguay produced a hatpin, and stabbed the youth in his abdomen three times. The star was arrested and taken to the police station, where, according to the *New York Times*, "Miss Tanguay produced a roll of bills and cried: 'Take it all and let me go, for it is now my dinner time.'"

Even when Tanguay kept her hatpins sheathed, she thrived on "beef." She staged high-profile feuds with Ethel Barrymore and vaudeville star Gertrude Hoffman. In 1918, the drama critic for the *New York Tribune*, Heywood Broun, slammed Tanguay for performing "La Marseillese" in a skimpy dress made entirely from French *tricoleur* flags. She took out a full page ad in *Variety*, and responded in verse: "Now you who have slandered, you are dirt beneath my feet / For I have beaten you at your game, and it's a hard game to beat."

Tanguay had many imitators. Decades before the first Elvis impersonator slicked up his pompadour, vaudeville was chockablock with performers donning Tanguay's outfits and belting out her songs. She took on the copycats in "Give an Imitation of Me" (1910):

> *If you are broke without a sou*
> *And really don't know what to do*
> *Just take my tip, go on the stage*

And you can be the season's rage
Watch me while I'm on the bill
Then jump into vaudeville
And give an imitation of me
Rush around the stage and fuzzle up your hair
Get a pair of tights and holler "I don't care."

American audiences had never encountered such bluster. (As one journalist noted, Tanguay's "whole performance is of herself, for herself, and by herself. She is motive, cue, subject and sub-subject.") But Tanguay's shtick was based on self-deprecation as much as self-aggrandizement. In the press and in song, she belittled her talent, framing her act as an elaborate spoof of virtuosity and professionalism. Critics called her singing "unlistenable," "awful," "a hairshirt to the nerves"—and she professed to agree with them. "I can't sing, I don't know how to dance. I am not even graceful," she declared. She elaborated on the point in "I Don't Care":

My voice is what you'd call a freak
But I don't mind it . . .
If teachers rates I could afford
Or I had studied hard abroad
I'd now be working for my board
And that's why I don't care
I don't care, I don't care
If I'm not Queen of Song
And while I am shouting
You may all be doubting
And hoping it won't last long . . .
My voice may sound funny
But it's getting me the money
So I don't care

Tanguay's voice did sound funny. But does that mean she couldn't sing? On the contrary: She sang very well, in a style that burlesqued the practice of "normal" singing. Which is something Tanguay knew how to do. She had played straight roles in musicals, both as a child actor and in her early years on the New York stage; at the height of her fame, in 1915, she had a huge hit with an unironic tear-jerker, "M-O-T-H-E-R, a Word That Means the World to Me." What we hear in "I Don't Care" is not a Progressive Era William Hung but a vocal stylist in command of her instrument, deliberately deploying comic effects: drawling, squeaking, and mixing straight-ahead singing with a kind of proto-rap patter. In "I Don't Care," Tanguay bragged about this technique: "Some lines I sing, some lines I don't sing / I don't care."

It was a sound of and for its time. The public's fancy was turning from old-fashioned music—sentimental parlor ballads and Viennese light opera—to the buoyant melodies and jagged syncopations of ragtime. And now Tanguay was waging her own revolt against 19th-century musical values and hoity-toity high culture. In concert, she interspersed songs with poetic recitations that parodied flowery Victorian verse. (An example can be heard at the end of the "I Don't Care" record.) In 1911, when she appeared on the same vaudeville bill with the Danish ballet star Adeline Genée, Tanguay brought down the house with a slapstick sendup of prima-ballerina dance moves. She kept the bit in her act for years, belting out "When Pavlova Sees Me Put It Over" while staggering through pliés and arabesques.

Tanguay's vocal style, meanwhile, mocked the Europhile emphasis on formal training, clear diction, pure intonation, and squarely hit notes. Think of her boast in "I Don't Care": "If teacher's rates I could afford / Or I had studied hard abroad / I'd now be working for my board." In other words: *Roll over, Beethoven.* (Or maybe it was: Step aside, Victor Herbert.) Vernacular pop culture was winning the day, and paying handsomely. In a country being remade by modernity—by new machines and new immigrants, by rising skylines and rising hemlines—Tanguay's madcap screech was audibly, if not scientifically, the soul of America.

This is where the received history of popular music begins to crack open. The standard pop music narrative regards vaudeville and Tin Pan Alley as quaintly pre-historic—the sepia-tone showbiz that was swept aside by "gritty" roots music and the triumphal rise of jazz and rock 'n' roll. But how do we account for Eva Tanguay, whose spectacular performances anticipated so much 20th century pop, and predated nearly all of it? If Tanguay tells us anything, it's that turn-of-the-century variety stage, where popular song first was transformed into mass entertainment, was rowdy and transgressive—as "rock 'n' roll" as rock itself. How did such a big star, such a heady period, slip from our view, and slide out of the history books?

In part, it's an issue of semantics. In the first decades of the century, when Tin Pan Alley songwriters counted on vaudevillians to break their new tunes, theatrical comedy and popular music were one and the same. The term "pop singer" had not yet been coined, and the period's top hit makers, like Tanguay, were referred to as *actresses* and *comediennes*. To the extent that Tanguay has been studied, it's been by historians of the stage and investigators of "the theatrical roots of modern feminism." These theater specialists fail to connect Tanguay and her vaudeville fellow travelers to the broader story of American popular music; most music scholars, meanwhile, remain indifferent to the pop pioneers who lurk on variety theater bills and in sheet music cover photographs.

The methodological mess is exacerbated by a dearth of the usual primary sources. In Tanguay's glory days, the recording industry was in its infancy. The period's wax cylinders and 78 discs were primitive and rackety, and the musical aesthetics—the broad comedic gestures and booming voices, raised to reach the theater rafters—were ill-suited to a medium that would come into its own with the invention of the microphone and the rise of dulcet crooners. Some big name stars, like Al Jolson and Sophie Tucker, left behind a decent body of recordings, but many others made just a few records, or none at all. Why bother with the rinky-dink record business, when the big money and the big glory waited on the vaudeville proscenium? Tanguay didn't bother stepping into a recording studio until the very tail end of her run. We can be thankful that she did—imagine how doubly obscure she would be without that "I Don't Care" 78.

Once Tanguay does come into focus, you can't unsee her. Her impact is, in certain cases, a matter of historical record. Mae West began her career as a Tanguay impersonator. Sophie Tucker cited her as an influence; so, surprisingly, did Ethel Waters. It's difficult to hear much Eva in Ethel, the blues queen famous for her queenly diction. But perhaps Waters transmuted her lessons from Tanguay to her own most famous fan, Billie Holiday? Can we detect in "Billie's Blues," the song that Holiday swiped from Waters in 1936, a trace of the slurry sound pioneered three decades earlier by a vaudeville heroine? That may be a stretch, but consider some other names: Betty Boop, Lena Lovich, Cyndi Lauper, Gwen Stefani, Björk—a lineage of screwball songstresses that descends directly from Tanguay.

Today's pop feels more than ever like one big reiteration of Tanguay's career. The braggarts and battle-rhymers of hip-hop—who can doubt that Tanguay got there first in "Eva Tanguay's Love Song" (1904), "Tanguay Rag" (1910), "Egotistical Eva" (1910), "If I Only Had a Regiment of Tanguays" (1917), and other haughty "songs about herself"? The divas that dominate the pop charts and tabloids, with their shape-shifting makeovers, extravagant song-and-dance routines, and multiple costume changes? Lady Gaga's wild headgear? In 2009, Tanguay is nowhere and everywhere. She's forgotten, but not gone.

For a star of Tanguay's stature, though, forgotten is worse than gone. Her decline was precipitous. As late as 1922, the year she recorded "I Don't Care," Tanguay's weeklong stand at Loew's New York State Theater raked in record box-office grosses. But tastes were changing, along with technology; radio and Hollywood talkies dealt a deathblow to big-time vaudeville, and Tanguay's bookings dried up. She lost her fortune in the 1929 stock-market crash, a few years after she had definitively lost her stranglehold on the zeitgeist to the sirens of the jazz age. By the mid-1930s, she was living in Los Angeles, crippled by arthritis, half-blind with cataracts, and nearly destitute. In 1934, she wrote a letter to Henry Ford, begging him to give her an automobile.

This letter is from Eva Tanguay (of the stage):

> I hope you remember me, once you were in the audience when I played Detroit—and anyone who has seen me before the footlights is interested in me. . . . I was thinking in the generosity of your heart could give me a car. . . . I have always had a car having owned eleven, but now have nothing. I live off a sort of an alley in a small house which is set in back of a big one, there is no view other than the backyards of other houses. . . . It is very sad to have had so much and be cut down to poverty, but my illness prevents me from doing

any work. Although I could sing on radio if the programme was without the audience viewing the entertainer, I have earned thirty-five hundred a week, three thousand and most always twenty-five hundred, so you may know I'm no tramp, having lived the very best, my home consisted of gold glasses silver plates and everything that meant refinement, now I'm alone and cut off entirely from my world I so loved. If I had a car I could go out afternoons and might connect some way with managers, agents—and find something to do.

This sob story failed to move Ford, whose secretary wrote to Tanguay expressing regret that her request could not be met. In her final years, Tanguay scraped by on her meager savings, and by selling her old stage costumes out of a storefront on Hollywood Blvd. Her name would turn up in the press occasionally, when reporters pilgrimaged to her home for a "Where are they now?" interview. In a *Life* magazine profile published shortly before her death, she complained bitterly that her legacy and—her word—"artistry" had been ignored. It seems Eva Tanguay did care, after all.

OTHER NOTABLE
MUSIC WRITING OF 2009

Mixed among the many great pieces of music writing included on this 2009 Other Notables list is a large selection of work about the life and death of Michael Jackson. Michael Jackson's death at age 50 was a shock and, to many, a tragedy. But out of this loss came something beautiful: a reassessment of his legacy that helped undo the damage to it caused by his problematic personal life, and which, as the tributes tumbled forth on the Web, became something else: a testament to the power of music writing.

Anonymous, "To the Legion Down Friday Night (Liegion Downstairs)," Craigslist, Calgary, June 26, 2009

David Amsden, "Never Mind the Pity," *New York Magazine*, October 18, 2009

Jake Austen, "The Jackson Find," *Chicago Reader*, September 10, 2009

J. Bennett, "Gylve & Ted's Excellent Adventure," *Decibel*, February 2009

Kevin Berger, Jeff Chang, Sarah Hepola, Margo Jefferson, Alex Koppelman, Andrew Leonard, Michaelangelo Matos, Andrew O'Hehir, ZZ Packer, Joan Walsh, Mary Elizabeth Williams, "Don't Stop 'til You Get Enough," *Salon*, June 26, 2009

Mark Binelli, "The Lost Brother," *Rolling Stone*, July 9–23, 2009

Melissa Bradshaw, "How Big Is Paul White's Ego," *Decks and the City*, November 20, 2009

Billy Bragg, "Billy Bragg Remembers Steven Wells," *Philadelphia Weekly*, June 30, 2009

August Brown, "Low End Theory: High-concept Music," *Los Angeles Times*, October 4, 2009

Carrie Brownstein, "Beth Ditto, Eaten Alive," *Monitor Mix*, June 2, 2009

Carles, "Animal Collective Is a Band Created By/For/On the Internet," *Hipster Runoff*, January 13, 2009

Jeff Chang, "The Creativity Stimulus," *The Nation*, May 4, 2009

Nate Chinen, "One-Stop Hub for Avant-Garde Jazz," *The New York Times*, March 26, 2009

Ta-Nehisi Coates, "The Mask of Doom," *New Yorker*, September 21, 2009

Paul Collins, "Sobbing Children and Singing Shillings," *The Believer*, July/August 2009

Del F. Cowie, "The Beautiful Struggle," *Exclaim!*, February 2009

Anwyn Crawford, "The Monarch of Middlebrow," *Overland*, Summer 2009

Kandia Crazy Horse, "Janelle, Erykah, and Santogold Are the Afro-Techno Revolution," *Village Voice*, January 21, 2009

Alvin Curran, "In Memory of Maryanne Amacher," *The New York Times*, December 27, 2009

David Dark, "Experiments In Sincerity," *Killing The Buddha*, December 21, 2009

Justin Davidson, "Arise!," *New York Magazine*, October 25, 2009

Isabelle Davis, "That Really Was It: Michael Jackson's THIS IS IT," *Two Day Old Shit*, October 28, 2009

John Doran, "The XX: Between Les Paul's Pick Up And The Akai MPC2000," *The Quietus*, August 27, 2009

Tom Ewing, "Chartopia," *Pitchfork Media*, July 10, 2009

kris ex, "Wordplay," *XXL*, October 2009

Mark Fisher, " . . . and when the groove is dead and gone . . . ," *k-punk*, June 28, 2009

Paul Friswold, "An Open Letter to Metallica Regarding Death Magnetic Friday," *Riverfront Times*, September 12, 2009

Kyle Gann, "The Epistemology of Elitism," *PostClassic (Arts Journal weblog)*, August 2009

David Gendelman, "Alex Chilton: 1975–1981," *Crawdaddy!*, November 12, 2009

Holly George-Warren, "James Hand," *Texas Music Magazine*, Fall 2009

Gary Giddins, "A Passage to India," *New Yorker*, March 2, 2009

Anne Giselson, "Our Hearts of Glass," *Oxford American Southern Music Issue*, 2009

Jeffery Goldberg, "Eight Days of Hanukkah," *Tablet Magazine*, December 8, 2009

Thomas Golianopoulos, "The Cross-Over," *XXL*, August 2009

Michael A. Gonzales, "Gangster Boogie," *Wax Poetics*, November/December 2009

Duncan Greive, "Then A Hero Comes Along," *Real Groove*, June 2009

David Hadju, "Keys to the Kingdom,"*The New Republic*, March 18, 2009

Dan Hancox, "Generational Resentment," *FACT Magazine*, February 13, 2009

Ernest Hardy, "Michael Jackson: Bless His Soul," *Blood Beats*, June 26, 2009

Jess Harvell, "Why The Misfits Are the Most Mythic of All New Jersey Artists," *Idolator*, July 28, 2009

Eric Harvey, "The Social History of the MP3," *Pitchfork Media*, August 24, 2009

Rob Harvilla, "Give the Vivian Girls a Break," *Village Voice*, September 1, 2009

Amanda Hess, "Top 5 Pseudo-Feminist Anthems," *Washington City Paper*, December 9, 2009

Robert Hilburn "Michael Jackson: The Wounds, the Broken Heart," *Los Angeles Times*, June 27, 2009

Nick Hornby, "The Thrill of It All," *The Guardian*, September 6, 2009

Barney Hoskins, "Dark Angel: The Genius of Laura Nyro," *MOJO*, January 2010

Colin Irwin, "The Battle over British Folk Music," *The Guardian*, April 23, 2009

Margo Jefferson, "TV Time In Negroland," *Bookforum*, June/July/August 2009

Maura Johnston and Christopher Weingarten, "The 50 Worst Songs of the '00s, F2K No. 1: Counting Crows ft. Vanessa Carlton, 'Big Yellow Taxi,'" *Village Voice*, December 22, 2009

Rich Juzwiak, "Go Transform Yourself," *Four Four*, December 8, 2009

David Kushner, "Kid Rock," *Blender*, February 2009

Andrew Lau, "Oar After 40 Years: Brilliant or Mere Ramblings?" *Crawdaddy!*, November 24, 2009

David Lester, Jean Smith, and Carl Wilson, "Mecca Normal Anniversary Art Series 1–6," *Zoilus*, May 2009

Alan Licht, "Lou Reed Invisible Jukebox," *Wire*, October 2009

Alan Light, "Another Country," *The New York Times*, March 29, 2009

Jack Malvern, "*The Times* Traces Bob Marley's White, English Family to North Devon," *The Times*, May 20, 2009

David Marchese, "Oklahoma Death Trip," *Spin*, October 2009

Greil Marcus, "Songs Left Out of Nan Goldin's Ballad of Sexual Dependancy," *Aperture*, Winter 2009

Michelangelo Matos, "Larry Harris," *The Onion A/V Club*, December 8, 2009

Sarah McElaney, "The Led Zeppelin Saga?" *This Horrid Life*, March 13, 2009

Pat McGuire, "Capturing the Flags: Fleeting Moments with Bonnie 'Prince' Billy," *Filter's Good Music Guide*, March/April 2009

Drew McWeeney, "Some personal thoughts on Michael Jackson's Passing," *Hitfix*, June 25, 2009

Katherine Meizel, "Judge Dread," *Slate*, March 26, 2009

Stephen Metcalf, "Jacksonian America," *Slate*, June 26, 2009

Gail Mitchell and Melinda Newman, "How 'Thriller' Changed The Music Business," *Billboard*, July 11, 2009

Chris Molanphy, "Letting Her Finish: Taylor Swift Completes Country's Pop-Chart Comeback," *Idolator*, September 25, 2009

Rick Moody, "Some Questions About the Tradition," *The Rumpus*, December 17, 2009

Alex Moore, "Jay Reatard: The Ballad of Jimmy Lee Lindsey, Jr.," *Death + Taxes*, November 2009

David Morris, "Only What Is Dead Can Live Forever," *Signal to Noise*, Spring 2009

Joe Muggs, "Boom! at the Top," *Mix*, November 2009

Gregory Nicoll, "Messiah of Mondo: R.I.P. Lux Interior of The Cramps (1946–2009)," *Stomp and Stammer*, March 2009

Andrew Noz, "Bun B talks Soul Food," *Cocaine Blunts*, October 22, 2009

Chris O'Leary, "Space Oddity," *Pushing Ahead of the Dame*, November 11, 2009

Henry Owing, "Online Music Journalist Application," *Chunklet*, 2009

Jon Pareles, "U2 in the Round, Fun With a Mission," *The New York Times*, September 24, 2009

Whitney Pastorek, "Guilty Pleasures, Round One: Nickelback v. Phish," *Entertainment Weekly*, August 17, 2009

David Peisner, "Jailhouse Rock," *Spin*, May 2009

Sam Quinones, "Musica de Muerte," *Vibe*, April 2009

Daniel Radosh, "While My Guitar Gently Beeps," *The New York Times Magazine*, August 11, 2009

Brian Raftery, "Purple Rain—The Oral History," *Spin*, June 2009

Andrew Ramadge, "Tall Tales and True," *Mess + Noise*, March 20, 2009

Pete Relic, "Empire State of Mind," *XXL*, December/January 2010

Simon Reynolds "The Cult of J Dilla," *The Guardian*, June 16, 2009

David Ritz, "Ray Charles' Heavenly Trio: Leroy 'Hog' Cooper, David 'Fathead' Newman and Hank Crawford," *Los Angeles Times*, February 22, 2009

Mike Rubin, "This Band Was Punk Before Punk Was Punk," *The New York Times*, March 15, 2009

Greg Sandow, "Silent Listening," *Sandow* (ArtsJournal weblog), February 23, 2009

Kelefa Senneh, "Vegan Jihad: A Conversation with Sean Muttaqi," *Bidoun* #16, 2009

Rob Sheffield, "'Not Like Other Guys': Rob Sheffield Remembers Michael Jackson," *Rolling Stone*, June 26, 2009

Philip Sherburne, "JD Twitch, Optimo: MX6," *Pitchfork Media*, January 29, 2009

Ben Sisario, "Ticket Resellers Step Out of the Shadows," *The New York Times*, August 28, 2009

Danyel Smith, "Michael Jackson, the Greatest Star," CNN.com, June 26, 2009

Marc Spitz, "Checkered Past," *Spin*, October 2009

Joshua David Stein and Noah Michelson, "The Lady Is A Vamp," *Out,*
   September 2009
Alison Stewart, "Asher Roth's White 'Bread' Is Not All that Fresh,"
   Washington Post, April 21, 2009
Patrick Stickles, "The *VICE* Magazine Party Is Decadent and Depraved,"
   Titus Andronicus blog, November 1, 2009
Andrew Sullivan, "Yes, Actually," *Out,* June/July 2009
John Jeremiah Sullivan, "MJ Tribute," *GQ,* September 2009
John Swenson, "You Can Never Go Home Anymore," *OffBeat,* November 1,
   2009
Sabina Tang, "Comparative Gig Reports," *Petronia LiveJournal,* October 10,
   2009
Charles Taylor, "The Jackson Reaction," *Dissent Magazine,* July 10, 2009
Datwon Thomas, "Hard to Kill," *XXL,* June 2009
Tommy Tomlinson, "Concord's Avett Brothers On The Verge of
   Stardom,"*Charlotte Observer,* September 26, 2009
Touré, "The Next Moment," *Vibe,* June 2009
Wyndham Wallace, "Vic Chesnutt RIP—A Recent Quietus Interview," *The
   Quietus,* December 29, 2009
Oliver Wang, "'C.R.E.A.M.': The Story of A Sample," *NPR Music,* April 22,
   2009
Jeff Weiss, "We're Jerkin," *LA Weekly,* August 6, 2009
Jonah Weiner, "TMZ Came To Bury Jacko, Not To Praise Him," *Slate,* June
   26, 2009
Steven Wells, "Thom Yorke: My Autobiography," *The Quietus,* May 20, 2009
Armond White, "In MJ's Shadow," *New York Press,* June 30, 2009
Jon Wiederhorn, "Baptized In Blood," *Revolver,* January 2009
Maxwell Williams, "Celebrity Skins," *Heeb,* Spring 2009
Mark Winegardner, "A Harmonic Force Field," *Oxford American Southern
   Music Issue,* 2009
Douglas Wolk, "Portable Hairdryer," *Significant Objects,* December 10, 2009
Joann Wypijewski, "Return of the Fabulous," *The Nation,* May 27, 2009
V/A, "Let The Pavement Reunion Backlash Begin . . . ," *The Daily Swarm,*
   September 17, 2009
Gary Younge, "Michael Jackson: We Span, Shuffled and Combed Our Hair
   Up High—To Be Like the Boy on Bandstand," *The Guardian,* June 26,
   2009

LIST OF CONTRIBUTORS

Nitsuh Abebe lives in New York and writes fiction and criticism. He has a monthly column at Pitchfork.com, titled "Why We Fight."

Timmhotep Aku (or Timothy Cornwall like it says on his birth certificate) is a writer and editor born, raised, and currently residing in New York City. He likes rap music and sandwiches, a lot. A former editor at *Complex* magazine and writer/producer at MTV.com, he helped launch the young men's lifestyle site StreetLevel.com for AOL and is the lead editor on AOL's theBVX.com, a site that targeting young African-American adults. He has written for *XXL*, *The Source*, *VIBE*, *Mass Appeal*, *The New York Post*, AllHipHop.com, and other online and print publications. Under the pseudonym "Timm See" he co-hosted 89.9 WKCR's underground hip-hop show "Squeeze Radio" program at Columbia University for six years. If he could be any animal in the world he'd be Falcor, the fictional flying dog from the 1980s cult classic film "The Neverending Story."

Philip S. Bryant was born on Chicago's South Side in 1951 and is author of several volumes of poetry, including *Sermon on a Perfect Spring Day* (New Rivers) and *Stompin' at The Grand Terrace: A Jazz Memoir in Verse* (Blueroad Press), which is accompanied by an original piano score by Carolyn Wilkins of Berklee College of Music in Boston. An avid jazz collector, Bryant is professor of English at Gustavus Adolphus College in St. Peter, Minnesota.

Jon Caramanica writes about music and other things for *The New York Times*.

Raquel Cepeda is an award-winning editor, new-media journalist, and documentary filmmaker (*Bling: A Planet Rock*) born and bred in New York City. A former magazine editor, her writings have been anthologized, and her byline has appeared in *People*, *The Associated Press*, *Village Voice*, *CNN.com*, and many other media outlets over the last 14 years. She lives in Washington Heights with her husband and daughter. Visit her at djalirancher.com/blog.

Carl Chery is BET.com's current executive music editor. He previously served as *XXL* magazine's digital content director and senior correspondent for SOHH.com. The Queens-based scribe has also contributed to *Vibe* and *Scratch Magazine*—interviewing the likes of 50 Cent, Kanye West, Lil Wayne, Jay-Z, Diddy, Bruce Willis, Hulk Hogan, Jessica Alba, and Terrence Howard, among many others. He's Brooklyn College graduate with a bachelor's degree in journalism with a minor in Africana Studies.

Robert Christgau writes regularly for *Barnes & Noble Review* and msn.com. He is a contributing critic at NPR's *All Things Considered* and teaches music history and writing in NYU's Clive Davis Department of Recorded Music. He has published five books based on his music journalism.

Nikki Darling writes for the *LA Weekly* music department and Huffington Post as a cultural critic. She received her Master's in Critical Studies from the California Institute of the Arts this past May. Nikki is currently finishing her thesis, a novel about objectification and fame in Depression-era America. You can follow her musical, feminist, and nonsensical ramblings at http://imnikkidarlingandyourenot.blogspot.com/.

Chris Estey began editing *BANDOPPLER* when the *Best Music Writing* series started, using his energies from personal zines like *Hot Ass* and *Ghetto Chicken* to make a more community-oriented art and music narrative collaboration. (Chuck D asked to be on the cover of our last issue.) That's how he met one of his very best friends, Mairead Case, who wrote for *BANDOPPLER* about comics and Michelle Tea. She introduced him to Ann and Daphne—though years before, Estey had written for legendary rock tabloid *The Rocket*, around the time Ann was an editor there. Strange how souls loop around.

Jason Fine is the executive editor of *Rolling Stone* magazine. He's edited books on George Harrison, Johnny Cash, and Michael Jackson. Currently he's writing an authorized biography of Brian Wilson. He was born and raised in southern California and lives in Brooklyn and Woodstock, New York.

Sasha Frere-Jones is an American writer, music critic, and musician. He has been on the staff of *The New Yorker* since 2004. In 2008, Frere-Jones was named one of the top 30 critics in the world by *Intelligent Life*, the lifestyle publication from *The Economist*.

Mary Gaitskill is the author of the novels *Veronica* and *Two Girls, Fat and Thin*; she also wrote the story collections *Bad Behavior, Because They Wanted To* and *Don't Cry*. A collection of her essays will be published by Random House in 2011.

Geoffrey Himes has been a full-time freelance music critic for the *Washington Post, Nashville Scene, Baltimore City Paper, Paste, Jazz Times*, and many more for 33 years. His lyrics have been recorded by the Kinsey Report, Edge City, and others. His book on country music in the '80s will be published next year by the Country Music Hall of Fame.

Eugene Holley, Jr., is an arts and culture journalist and essayist. His work has appeared in *Down Beat, Jazz Times, The New York Times Book Review, Vibe*, the *Village Voice*, and *Wax Poetics*. He co-produced the NPR and PRI-distributed documentaries *Dizzy's Diamonds* and *The Duke Ellington Centennial Radio Project*, served as music/program director for WCLK-FM, Atlanta, and contributed to the book *Albert Murray and the Aesthetic Imagination of a Nation*. He lives in Wilmington, Delaware.

Clover Hope is a writer and editor based in New York City. Her work has appeared in publications such as *Billboard, ESPN The Magazine, VIBE, XXL, Essence, King, Giant, Village Voice*, and *Amsterdam News*. Born in Guyana, South America, Clover moved to New York as a toddler and grew up in Brooklyn and Queens. Graduating magna cum laude, she earned a B.A. in journalism at New York University while interning at *VIBE, New York Newsday*, and *Amsterdam News*. In 2005, she landed her first job out of college as an online associate editor for *Billboard*, followed by a three-year stint at *XXL*. She's currently a senior editor at *VIBE*.

Jessica Hopper is a music and cultural critic in Chicago. Her work regularly appears in *Chicago Reader, Chicago Tribune*, and *SPIN*. She is the author of *The Girls Guide to Rocking* and music consultant for *This American Life*. She co-hosts the public radio podcast, Hit it or Quit it.

Hua Hsu teaches in the English Department at Vassar College. His work has appeared in the *Atlantic* (for whom he blogs), *The New York Times, Bookforum, Slate*, the *Village Voice*, and *The Wire* (for whom he writes a bi-monthly column). He was on the editorial board for *A New Literary History of America*.

Maura Johnston has written about music and culture for The Awl, the *Village Voice*, the Daily Beast, and gawker. She is a commentator on NPR and was one of the founding editors of Idolator. She lives in New York.

Jason King is the artistic director of the Clive Davis Department of Recorded Music, a leadership institute for aspiring music entrepreneurs at New York University. A music critic for magazines like *Vibe* and *Blender* and a producer and artist manager, Jason is the author of *The Michael Jackson Treasures: Celebrating the King of Pop in Memorabilia and Photos*, and the forthcoming *Blue Magic*, on the role of energy in the music of artists like Jay Z and Roberta Flack.

Josh Kun is a professor in the Annenberg School for Communication and Journalism at the University of Southern California, where he also directs the Popular Music Project at the Norman Lear Center. He is the author of *Audiotopia: Music, Race, and America* and co-author with Roger Bennett of *And You Shall Know Us by the Trail of Our Vinyl: The Jewish Past as Told By The Records We've Loved and Lost*. A contributing writer with *The New York Times* and *Los Angeles Magazine*, he is co-editor with Ron Radano of the book series *Refiguring American Music* for Duke University Press, and a member of the Idelsohn Society for Musical Preservation.

Aaron Leitko is a freelance writer living in Washington, D.C. His work has appeared in *Washington City Paper*, *The Washington Post*, and Pitchfork. When time permits, he plays bass in the band SPRCSS. As required by law, he has a beard and glasses.

As a writer, **Rob Markman** has contributed to the *New York Post* and publications such as *Vibe*, *Complex*, and *The Source* magazines. Since joining the *XXL* in 2008, first as the magazine's associate music editor, Markman has worked his way up the masthead to music editor and now deputy editor.

Phillip Mlynar writes about rap music, listens to records by Ida, and drinks pints of Bluepoint at Buttermilk bar in South Slope, Brooklyn. His first book, *The Hip-Hop Guide To New York*, will be out in time for the cash-in Christmas season.

Evie Nagy is an associate editor at *Billboard Magazine* and writes about music, culture, and comic books for a variety of publications. A former university administrator and speechwriter, she also co-wrote the afterword for an upcoming anthology of the late Ellen Willis's rock writing. She lives in New York.

Sean Nelson is a writer/musician/filmmaker who lives in Seattle. His debut solo album, *Make Good Choices*, will likely be released by Absolutely Kosher sometime in 2010. The feature film *Treatment*, which he wrote and co-directed, will be in film festivals in Spring 2011. www.seannelson.net is a poor thing but his own.

Tavia Nyong'o writes and teaches about performance and popular music from his perch at New York University. He is working on a book about the intersection of punk and queer.

Lola Ogunnaike is one of the leading pop culture authorities in the country. In her decade-long journalism career, she's interviewed everyone from Oprah Winfrey to Sting. For two years, she served as an entertainment correspondent for CNN. Before joining CNN, Ogunnaike spent five years as a culture reporter for *The New York Times.* She has also been a reporter at the *New York Daily News* and a contributing writer for *Vibe* and *Rolling Stone* magazine. Her work has appeared in *Elle, New York Magazine, USA Today, Glamour,* and *Food & Wine.* In May 2007, she was named one of *Ebony* magazine's "150 Most Influential Blacks in America."

Greg Pratt is a freelance journalist who lives in Victoria, British Columbia, with his wife and daughter. When not asking bands like Il Divo and Metallica uncomfortable questions, he works as assistant editor at the student newspaper at the local college and writes for publications such as *Exclaim!, Revolver,* bravewords.com, *Snowboard Canada,* and *Metal Maniacs.*

Timothy Quirk was the front guy in Too Much Joy and now records with Wonderlick. His work has appeared in the *San Francisco Chronicle,* the *San Francisco Bay Guardian, Popular Music, Raygun* (remember *Raygun?* that was a fine publication), and *Sassy,* among others. He spent most of this century working for Rhapsody, an online music service.

Starrene Rhett is a New York City–based freelance journalist who is currently a resident blogger for BET.com, where she interviews actors and muses about TV and film, Roc4Life.com, the newly reincarnated *Honey* magazine (Honeymag.com), where she focuses on feminism in hip-hop, *XXL* magazine, and DrJays.com. Previously, she has worked as fashion editor for Hiphopdx.com where she edited feature stories and spotted trends for the latest in urban fashion. Following that, she was assistant editor at *XXL* magazine, where she interviewed artists, conceived feature stories, and co-edited articles for the magazine's newly incepted TV and Film section entitled "The Watcher." She created GangStarrGirl.com as an outlet to post her ideas without being filtered and as a means of controlling the content she wishes to see more of in the media by featuring memoirs, written interviews, reflections, and originally produced video news packages. Her site has been featured by Essence.com and won the popular vote in the 2009 Black Web Log Awards for Best Hip-Hop Blog and Best Music Blog.

Randall Roberts is the pop music editor of the *Los Angeles Times.* He chronicles his writing life and offers mixtapes at www.glorygloryglory.com.

Alex Ross has been the music critic of *The New Yorker* since 1996. His first book, *The Rest Is Noise: Listening to the Twentieth Century,* won a National Book Critics Circle Award and was a finalist for the Pulitzer Prize. His second book, *Listen To This,* appears in fall 2010. In 2008 he was named a MacArthur Fellow.

Anslem Samuel has been a music/entertainment journalist for over 10 years. After a four-year stint as culture editor at *The Source,* the New York native became the founding editor-in-chief of *The Ave,* an independent quarterly publication that combined entertainment, social issues and politics. From there, he served as the senior editor for *XXL* magazine for three years before moving to his current position as digital content director. In addition to his writing appearing in *Essence, Blender, Penthouse, Complex, Vibe, King,* and *Rides,* Anslem also has radio experience, working as a weekly news correspondent for "Phat Saturdays" on Bahamas' 100JAMZ for several years. In 2008, Anslem started penning his own personal tales about the pursuit of life, love, and understanding the opposite sex on his hilarious and insightful daily blog, NakedWithSocksOn.com.

Composer **Maria Scheider** has conducted over 80 different groups in over 20 countries. She's most widely known through the Maria Scheider Orchestra founded in 1992. She's written for Toots Thielemans, the Carnegie Hall Jazz Orchestra, Peter Sellars' New Crowned Hope Festival (Mozart Festival in Vienna), Jazz at Lincoln Center, Los Angeles Philharmonic Association, American Dance Festival, Dawn Upshaw and the Saint Paul Chamber Orchestra, and Kronos Quartet, receiving eight Grammy nominations and two Grammy awards.

Mark Swed has been chief classical music critic of the *Los Angeles Times* since 1996. He has also covered music for *The Wall Street Journal, Los Angeles Herald Examiner,* and *7 Days in New York* and has written for *The New York Times, The New Yorker, The Economist, Musical America, Opera News, BBC Music, Gramophone, Stagebill, Schwann-Opus,* and many other national and international publications. From 1992 to 2000, he was 20th-century music editor of *The Musical Quarterly* and is currently writing a biographical study of John Cage. Swed has received awards in criticism from the Los Angeles Music Center, ASCAP, the American Music Center, and the Los Angeles Press Club. He was a finalist for the Pulitzer Prize in criticism in 2007.

Greg Tate is a writer and musician who lives in Harlem. His books include *Flyboy in the Buttermilk* and *Midnight Lightning: Jimi Hendrix and the Black Experience.* He is now at work on a book about *The Godfather of Soul, James Brown,* for Riverhead Press. Since 1999 Tate has led the umpteen member-conducted improv band Burnt Sugar The Arkestra Chamber.

Michelle Tea is the author of four memoirs, including the illustrated *Rent Girl*; the novel *Rose of No Man's Land*; a poetry collection, *The Beautiful*; and, with Beth Ditto, the memoir *Coal to Diamonds*. She runs RADAR Productions, which produces literary events, the Sister Spit performance tour, and the Radar LAB writers' retreat. She is part of the Ironing Board Collective fashion blog at ironingboardcollective.blogspot.

Erika Villani has mostly written about things that aren't music for publications that aren't in business anymore, so this was a nice surprise.

Barry Walters is a senior critic at *Rolling Stone*, where he's written about music and film for over 20 years. He also regularly contributes to *Spin*, *Out*, eMusic, iTunes, and other publications from his home in San Francisco. He was the first critic to be awarded by the National Lesbian and Gay Journalists Association.

Christopher R. Weingarten is a freelance music critic living Brooklyn whose work regularly appears in The *Village Voice*, RollingStone.com, *Revolver*, *Spin* and more. He is the author of *It Takes A Nation Of Millions To Hold Us Back* (Continuum) and the upcoming *Hipster Puppies* (NAL/Penguin). His Twitter is @1000TimesYes.

Chris Willman is the author of *Rednecks and Bluenecks: The Politics of Country Music*. Formerly the lead music critic for *Entertainment Weekly*, he can now be found arguing the primacy of both Bob Dylan and Taylor Swift in *New York* magazine, *TV Guide*, Yahoo!, *Rolling Stone*, and other publications.

CREDITS

"The Decade in Indie" by Nitsuh Abebe. First published on Pitchfork on September 16, 2009. Coypright © 2009 Pitchfork Media.

"Still Ill" by Timmhotep Aku, Carl Chery, Clover Hope, Rob Markman, Starrene Rhett, and Anslem Samuel. First published in *XXL* April 2009. Copyright © 2009 Harris Publications.

"Stompin' at The Grand Terrace: Excerpts From A Jazz Memoir in Verse" by Philip S. Bryant. First published in *Utne Reader*, July–August 2009; reprinted with permission from the book, *Stompin' at The Grand Terrace: A Jazz Memoir in Verse* (Blueroad Press). Copyright © 2009 Philip S. Bryant.

"Help From His Friends: The Return of a Fallen Idol" by Jon Caramanica. Published in *The New York Times* Arts & Leisure Section October 29, 2009. Copyright © 2009 *The New York Times*. Reprinted with permission.

"Another Love TKO: Teens Grapple with Rihanna vs. Chris Brown" by Raquel Cepeda, First published in the *Village Voice*, March 31, 2009. Copyright 2009 Raquel Cepeda.

"Paisley's Progress" by Robert Christgau. First published in *Barnes & Noble Review* November 18, 2009. Copyright © 2009 Robert Christgau.

"Appropriate for Destruction" by Nikki Darling. First published in Live From the Penis Gallery, December 8, 2009. © 2009 Nikki Darling.

"Phil Ochs Greatest Hits" by Chris Estey. First Published in *Get Well* zine, summer 2009. © 2009 Chris Estey.